SCHOOL SOCIAL WORK

EVIDENCE-BASED PRACTICES

SERIES EDITORS:

David E. Biegel, Ph.D.
Elizabeth M. Tracy, Ph.D.
Jack, Joseph and Morton Mandel
School of Applied Social Sciences,
Case Western Reserve University

Family Psychoeducation for Serious Mental Illness
Harriet P. Lefley

School Social Work
An Evidence-Informed Framework for Practice
Michael S. Kelly, James C. Raines, Susan Stone, and Andy Frey

Mental Health Treatment for Children and Adolescents
Jacqueline Corcoran

Individual Placement and Support
An Evidence-Based Approach to Supported Employment
Robert E. Drake, Gary R. Bond, and Deborah R. Becker

Preventing Child and Adolescent Problem Behavior
Evidence-Based Strategies in Schools, Families, and Communities
Jeffrey M. Jenson and Kimberly A. Bender

The Evidence-Based Practices Series is published in collaboration with the Jack, Joseph and Morton Mandel School of Applied Social Sciences at Case Western Reserve University.

SCHOOL SOCIAL WORK

AN EVIDENCE-INFORMED FRAMEWORK
FOR PRACTICE

Michael S. Kelly
James C. Raines
Susan Stone
Andy Frey

OXFORD
UNIVERSITY PRESS

OXFORD
UNIVERSITY PRESS

Oxford University Press is a department of the University of Oxford. It furthers the University's objective
of excellence in research, scholarship, and education by publishing worldwide.

Oxford   New York

Auckland   Cape Town   Dar es Salaam   Hong Kong   Karachi
Kuala Lumpur   Madrid   Melbourne   Mexico City   Nairobi
New Delhi   Shanghai   Taipei   Toronto

With offices in

Argentina   Austria   Brazil   Chile   Czech Republic   France   Greece
Guatemala   Hungary   Italy   Japan   Poland   Portugal   Singapore
South Korea   Switzerland   Thailand   Turkey   Ukraine   Vietnam

Oxford is a registered trade mark of Oxford University Press in the
UK and certain other countries.

Published in the United States of America by
Oxford University Press
198 Madison Avenue, New York, NY 10016

© Oxford University Press 2010

First issued as an Oxford University Press paperback, 2014.

Library of Congress Cataloging-in-Publication Data
School social work : an evidence-informed framework for practice / Michael S. Kelly ... [et al.].
p.   cm. — (Evidence-based practices)
Includes bibliographical references and index.
ISBN 978-0-19-537390-5 (hardcover); 978-0-19-935756-7 (paperback)
1. School social work—United States.   I. Kelly, Michael S. (Michael Stokely), 1968–
LB3013.4.S355 2010
371.7—dc22
2009036932

PREFACE

SCHOOL SOCIAL WORK AND THE UTILITY OF AN
EVIDENCE-INFORMED PROCESS

This book represents our attempt to help school social workers use the best available evidence to address many of the critical problems they face in their schools. Four assumptions permeate this text: (1) A practical evidence-informed practice (EIP) process to collect, organize, and assess practice choices would improve school social workers' ability to address the myriad problems presented in schools. (2) School social work is a unique specialization that should align practice choices with contemporary education models known to and valued by educators. (3) While no information should be eliminated from consideration in an evidence-informed process, elevated status should be afforded scholarly, school-based practice and intervention research. (4) Although informative, the empirical evidence base is inadequate in and of itself to guide practice.

The first three chapters provide an important backdrop for the remaining chapters. In Chapter 1, we highlight the apparent gap that currently exists between the practice choices of school social workers and the school-based prevention and intervention research and contemporary education models. In Chapter 2, we hypothesize about why this gap exists and describe a general EIP process that has been promoted in social work and related disciplines to narrow similar knowledge-practice gaps. In Chapter 3 we propose an evidence-informed process that is specific to school social work practice and is responsive to the criticisms of previous EIP models. This process is aligned with the aforementioned assumptions, informed by our own practice experience in schools, and builds upon the work of other social work scholars in the area of EIP (Gambrill, 2006; Gibbs, 2003). The remaining chapters in the book are designed to apply the evidence-informed process described in Chapter 3 to common problems faced by school social workers and reflect on our experiences.

For this volume, we are defining evidence-informed school social work practice (hereafter referred to as EIP) as the systematic integration of professional judgment and client values with the best available empirical research evidence (Davies, 1999; Raines, 2008b). Some of the resources that evidence-informed school social workers consult are available online through Internet databases and clearinghouses for empirically supported treatments (ESTs). And as we'll see in this book, there are many great ESTs and EIP resources online for school social workers to use to make their practice more evidence informed.

But with apologies to the classic line from the movie *Field of Dreams*, what if they (the researchers) build it (the research) and nobody comes? While preparing this book, we got an e-mail from a social work practitioner who had read about our survey research outlining how few school social workers used evidence-informed practice resources in their day-to-day practice. The colleague (who is a practitioner in gerontology, not schools) expressed surprise that only 30% of respondents to our survey reported using the Internet and the EIP tools that are available there to help inform their approach to the persistent and routine problems their school clients face (Kelly, 2008). The e-mailer speculated that respondents' average response would have been dramatically higher had we asked them "Do you use the Internet to help you evaluate the evidence for major purchases (e.g., cars, household appliances)?"

What's going on here? Clearly, many Americans who have access to computers and online connections see the value and utility of using the vast resources of the Internet to help them assess and weigh all kinds of evidence they need to go about their business. Are school social workers any different? What we are likely witnessing is a bifurcation between the professional reasons that school social workers are using the Internet and their personal reasons. And while not much is known empirically about this potential distinction, we do know that school social workers aren't alone in their underutilization of the available knowledge base to help them inform practice. Studies have shown that social workers, psychologists, medical professionals, and educators have all been slow to find and utilize the best available evidence, whether it is presented online or in published journal formats (Duchnowski & Kutash, 2007; Kelly et al., in press). Additionally, the tendency to make decisions about practice interventions appears to be less based on appraisal of available evidence and, instead, based on intuition and tradition for many school social workers active in the field (Frey & Dupper, 2005; Kelly, 2008; Raines, 2008b; Stone & Gambrill, 2007).

School social workers face heterogeneity in presenting problems, potential outcomes sought, potential intervention points, and school organizational culture—complexity that demands both practice wisdom *and* an "evidence" orientation. We hope that this book begins to merge the best available evidence with our own practice wisdom of having worked in schools for a combined three decades ourselves before we became researchers.

This book offers an evidence-informed process for school social workers that will help school social workers deal with (1) their complex roles and responsibilities in a host setting, (2) their status as practitioners whose work is inherently interdisciplinary, and (3) their need to respond to the press for accountability in education. Ultimately, the development of this process may offer a promising step toward narrowing the knowledge-practice gap and improving outcomes for children, families, and communities served by school social workers.

CONTENTS

1 THE NEED FOR AN EVIDENCE-INFORMED PRACTICE APPROACH IN SCHOOLS *3*

2 UNDERSTANDING AND NARROWING THE RESEARCH–PRACTICE KNOWLEDGE GAP *23*

3 AN EVIDENCE-INFORMED PROCESS FOR SCHOOL SOCIAL WORKERS *42*

4 EMPIRICALLY SUPPORTED TIER 2 INTERVENTIONS *52*

5 PARENT INVOLVEMENT *66*

6 INCREASING STUDENT COMPLIANCE WITH CLASSROOM TASKS *76*

7 BEHAVIOR INTERVENTION PLANNING *90*

8 HELPING STUDENTS COPE WITH THEIR PARENTS' DIVORCE *107*

9 PREVENTING BULLYING IN SCHOOLS *118*

10 EMPIRICALLY SUPPORTED SOCIAL SKILLS INTERVENTIONS *127*

11 HELPING STUDENTS WITH ANXIETY IN SCHOOLS *141*

12 PROBLEMS WITH ADHD IN A SCHOOL SETTING *148*

13 IATROGENIC INTERVENTIONS IN SCHOOLS   *161*

14 LESSONS LEARNED FROM OUR EVIDENCE-INFORMED PRACTICE
PROCESS AND FINAL REFLECTIONS   *169*

*Appendix A: National School Social Work Survey Instrument
School Social Work Survey 2008   189*
Appendix B: How We Investigated the Evidence   199
Notes   221
References   223
Index   273

SCHOOL SOCIAL WORK

1

THE NEED FOR AN EVIDENCE-INFORMED PRACTICE APPROACH IN SCHOOLS

School social workers have a wide array of practice choices at their disposal. In this introductory chapter, we set the stage for the remainder of the text by demonstrating that a chasm exists between the practice choices of school social workers and the research on school-based prevention and intervention as well as contemporary education models developed to guide the organization and delivery of school social work and other support services (e.g., school psychology, behavior consultation, and school counseling). This gap will be hereon be referred to as the knowledge–practice gap.

HISTORY OF SCHOOL SOCIAL WORK

In 1906, *four* urban school districts in the northeast United States *and in Chicago* independently hired social workers to work with truant students and help their parents better understand how to access the resources of the school for their children (Dupper, 2003). The first school social workers were called "visiting teachers," and many of their practice innovations, such as conducting home visits and consulting with teachers and principals, are still practiced today in the field of school social work (School Social Work Association of America, 2005). These visiting teachers formed their own association in 1921, which later merged into the National Association of Social Workers (NASW) in 1955. The NASW was the main national voice for school social work until the formation of the School Social Work Association of America (SSWAA) in the 1990s. Today there are school social workers in schools across the country serving children in pre-kindergarten, elementary, junior and middle as well as secondary school settings.

3

In 2006 school social work marked its 100th year as a subspecialty within the profession of social work.

Although not extensive, surveys of school social worker roles have yielded fairly consistent results. Costin (1969) and Allen-Meares (1977) demonstrated that although there was an awareness of prevention and macrolevel practice, school social work services were highly individualistic, with few attempts to identify target groups of children experiencing similar difficulties, such as truancy or behavior problems. Nearly two decades later, Allen-Meares's (1994) national survey of school social workers found that they are largely focused on delivering individual and group mental health services to students, predominantly those who qualify for special education services. In this study, school social workers described their role as being highly autonomous but dominated by crisis intervention for severely impacted students. Additionally, Astor et al. (1998) found that school violence prevention programs took a back seat to crisis intervention and individual counseling of students in need. More recently, state-level data in Illinois found the overwhelming majority of school social workers report that their main job consists of providing counseling and other intervention work with individuals and small groups (Kelly, 2008).

Finally, recently released results from the most comprehensive examination of school social work services nationally in over a decade confirms that school social workers engage in activities that largely target individual risk factors, often not even within the context of the natural school setting (i.e., classroom), through counseling and other intervention work with individuals and small groups. These studies confirm the persistent focus of school social work services that address individual risk factors (i.e., anxiety, depression, attention, social skill deficits) rather than those at the classroom, school, home, or community level (Kelly et al., 2009). (See Box 1.2 for a summary of our survey project's methodology and sample.)

Criticism of these practice choices by scholars of school social work have also been fairly uniform. Early critics invoked social work's historic focus on social justice as well as the profession's commitment to ecological theory as rationales for change. For example, Allen-Meares's hope that school social workers would be engaged in macrolevel practice or prevention programming was something most survey respondents said they had no time for, a result she characterized as "disappointing" (Allen-Meares, 1994, p. 564). More recently, looking at social work's commitment to ecological theory, school-based prevention and intervention research, and contemporary education models guiding the organization and delivery of school-based support services, critics have seen current practice as further evidence of an individualistic orientation, which indicates that a knowledge–practice gap exists (Frey & Dupper, 2005; Kelly et al., 2009). This

BOX 1.1 U.S. DEPARTMENT OF EDUCATION AND AMERICAN PSYCHOLOGICAL ASSOCIATION (APA) DIVISION 12 DEFINITIONS

Department of Education

Scientifically-based research:

a. means research that involves the application of rigorous, systematic, and objective procedures to obtain reliable and valid knowledge relevant to education activities and programs; and

b. includes research that –

1. Employs systematic, empirical methods that draw on observation or experiment;

2. Involves rigorous data analyses that are adequate to test the stated hypotheses and justify the general conclusions drawn;

3. Relies on measurements or observational methods that provide reliable and valid data across evaluators and observers, across multiple measurements and observations, and across studies by the same or different investigators;

4. Is evaluated using experimental or quasi-experimental designs in which individuals, entities, programs, or activities are assigned to different conditions and with appropriate controls to evaluate the effects of the condition of interest, with a preference for random assignment experiments, or other designs to the extent that those designs contain within-condition or across-condition controls;

5. Ensures that experimental studies are presented in sufficient detail and clarity to allow for replication or, at a minimum, offer the opportunity to build systematically on their findings; and

6. Has been accepted by a peer-reviewed journal or approved by a panel of independent experts through a comparably rigorous, objective, and scientific review (U.S. Department of Education, August 14, 2006, § 300.35).

APA Division 12 (1993)

Empirically supported treatments: are "clearly specified psychological treatments shown to be efficacious in controlled research with a delineated population" (Chambless & Hollon, 1998, p. 7).

Well-established treatments possess:

1. At least two good group design studies, conducted by different investigators, demonstrating efficacy in one or more of the following ways:

a. Superior to pill or psychological placebo or to another treatment

b. Equivalent to an already established treatment in studies with adequate statistical power (about 30 per group)

OR

2. A large series of single case design studies demonstrating efficacy. These studies must have:

a. Used good experimental designs and

b. Compared the intervention to another treatment

Further criteria for both 1 & 2:

3. Studies must be conducted with treatment manuals.

4. Characteristics of the client samples must be clearly specified.

Probably Efficacious Treatments possess:

1. Two studies showing the treatment is more effective than a waiting list group.

OR

2. Two studies otherwise meeting the well-established treatment criteria 1, 3, & 4, but both are conducted by the same investigator. Or one good study demonstrating effectiveness by these same criteria.

OR

(Continued)

BOX 1.1 U.S. DEPARTMENT OF EDUCATION AND AMERICAN PSYCHOLOGICAL ASSOCIATION (APA) DIVISION 12 DEFINITIONS (CONT'D)

Three Categories:

1. Meets evidence standards

2. Meets with reservations

3. Does not meet evidence standards

3. At least two good studies demonstrating effectiveness but flawed by heterogeneity of the client samples.

OR

4. A small series of single case design studies otherwise meeting the well-established treatment criteria 2, 3, & 4.

Experimental treatments

---

knowledge–practice gap provides yet another compelling reason for the school social work community to concern itself with the status quo. The next two sections provide a context for this knowledge-practice gap, followed by a more detailed summary of a recent national survey highlighting this gap.

SCHOOL-BASED PREVENTION AND INTERVENTION RESEARCH

A large body of specific empirical findings has been amassed to guide the selection of interventions for school social workers and other support service providers over the past decade. This literature base has several themes that provide evidence of a knowledge–practice gap in school social work practice. These themes include (1) integrated, sustainable intervention efforts that emphasize primary prevention; (2) early screening and intervention; and (3) comprehensive approaches.

Integrated, Sustainable Intervention Efforts that Emphasize Primary Prevention

The first theme in the school-based prevention and intervention literature relates to the promise of integrated, sustainable approaches emphasizing prevention. One characteristic of this theme is that effective approaches foster service cohesion by addressing the need for multiple interventions within schools in an integrated fashion. Walker et al. (1996) suggest that there is generally a lack of coordination among prevention and intervention efforts because no comprehensive strategic plan for coordinating and linking behavioral supports exists at the school or district level. Implementation of systemic interventions may provide the best hope for reducing the intensity and number of children who require additional support. Not only must supports be integrated and coordinated but a continuum of supports representing primary, secondary, and tertiary levels of intervention are also essential (Dunlap et al., 2009).

Within this continuum, the promise of primary prevention is increasingly being emphasized. This emphasis on primary prevention is important not only because it is efficient and effective (Greenberg et al., 2003) but also because the presence of high-quality primary prevention is increasingly being recognized as a prerequisite for more intensive interventions (Scott et al., 2009). For example, interventions that promote participation in positive academic and social groups, enhance school bonding or connectedness, and create positive and safe learning environments appear to be most promising approaches for promoting behavioral and academic success; these approaches are typically implemented schoolwide over the course of several years (Gottfredson & Gottfredson, 1999).

Screening and Early Intervention

A second theme in the school-based prevention and intervention research involves a focus on early screening and intervention. Whether in preschool or early elementary school, the importance of early screening for risk factors that lead to poor educational outcomes cannot be overstated. Educators are able to predict with minimal effort and great accuracy which children will require extensive academic or behavioral supports. Systemwide screening, particularly for emotional and behavioral indicators leading to school failure, may be the single most promising and cost-effective strategy to improve educational outcomes. Many experts believe that enhancing school readiness skills should be the primary focus of policy reforms (Nelson et al., 2004).

One reason early screening has received significant attention is because of the robust outcomes associated with early intervention. Hawkins, Catalano, Kosterman, Abbott, and Hill (1999) reported results of an important intervention study with a 12-year longitudinal follow-up period that demonstrates this point. Their study involved 643 students attending Seattle elementary schools that served high-crime areas. A total of 598 (93%) of the participating students were followed up at age 18 and assessed on a number of quality-of-life and health-risk variables. The study randomly assigned participating students to one of three conditions: early intervention (delivered in grades 1–4), late intervention (delivered in grades 5 and 6), and no treatment control. The intervention consisted of three coordinated components. In each intervention year, teachers were given five days of in-service training in how to manage student behavior and create a positive classroom ecology to promote school readiness. Parents of participating students were offered developmentally appropriate parenting classes during the intervention period. Finally, participating students were provided with developmentally adjusted social competence training.

The purpose of the study was to examine the combined effects of these three intervention components on adolescent health-risk behaviors at age 18 and to determine whether earlier intervention was more effective than later

TABLE 1.1 RISK FACTORS FOR ACADEMIC FAILURE BY LEVEL OF INFLUENCE

Level of Influence	Risk Factors
Individual	Learning related social skills (listening, participating in groups, staying on task, organizational skills)
	Social behavior
	Limited intelligence
	Presence of a disability
	Minority status
	Special education status
	Students who fail to read by the fourth grade
Family	Early exposure to patterns of antisocial behavior
	Parent–child conflict
	Lack of connectedness with peers, family, school, and community
School	Large school size
	Limited resources
	High staff turnover
	Inconsistent classroom management
	Percentage of low SES students
	School and classroom climate
	School violence
	Overcrowding
	High student/teacher ratios
	Insufficient curricular and course relevance
	Weak, inconsistent adult leadership
	Overcrowding
	Poor building design
	Overreliance on physical security measures
Neighborhood	Poverty
	Low percentage of affluent neighbors

Source: Reprinted from Frey, A. J., & Walker, H. M. (2005). Education policy for children, youth, and families. In J. M. Jenson and M. W. Fraser (Eds.), *Social policy for children and families: A risk and resilience perspective.* Thousand Oaks, CA: Sage.

intervention. Results indicated that the late intervention (delivered in grades 5 and 6) did not affect the status of health-risk behaviors at age 18. However, the early intervention group, who received the intervention in grades 1–4 showed superior effects to untreated controls on the following outcomes: fewer violent delinquent acts, better academic achievement, less school maladaptive behavior, less heavy drinking, less teenage sex, fewer pregnancies, fewer sex partners, and more commitment/attachment to school.

As measured over the study's longitudinal follow-up period, this intervention produced very robust outcomes. This is especially noteworthy given that the intervention was universal in nature as opposed to a more intensive intervention focused on individual students (Hoagwood, 2000). Furthermore, the intervention improved school engagement, attachment, and bonding to school, which appeared to serve as a general protective factor against later health-risk behaviors of a serious nature. The study demonstrates the power of early school intervention when the key risk factors that contribute to school failure are targeted.

Comprehensive Approaches

The third theme in the school-based prevention and intervention research is the emphasis on comprehensive approaches. Reviews and syntheses of the school-based prevention and intervention literature clearly demonstrates that effective strategies employ a comprehensive approach that targets multiple intervention agents (e.g., teacher, parents, peers), intervenes at multiple levels (e.g., school, home, community), and addresses multiple risk factors (Dupper, 2002; Sloboda & David, 1997; Walker, 2001). Thus, interventions that assume multiple causes for a problem and conceptualize their clients as not only the student but also the teacher, the parents, and the school are more effective than those that assume a singular problem or client. Risk factors that have been empirically related to academic failure are provided in Table 1.1.

CONTEMPORARY EDUCATION MODELS

The school-based prevention and intervention research has influenced models to guide academic and behavior support services in schools. Two of these models, response to intervention (RTI) and the clinical quadrant, are particularly relevant to the knowledge–practice gap within school social work practice.

RESPONSE TO INTERVENTION

Response to intervention (RTI) is defined as the practice of providing effective instruction and interventions that match students' needs, monitoring progress regularly to inform decision making about changes in instruction or goals, and using child response data to guide these decisions (Batsche et al., 2006). This approach is becoming familiar to school support staff who are responsible for identifying students with a specific learning disability (SLD); the Individuals with Disabilities Education Improvement Act of 2004 (IDEA 2004) permits school districts to "use a process that determines if the child responds to scientific, research-based intervention as a part of the evaluation procedures," in lieu of establishing a discrepancy between ability and achievement, to identify students with learning difficulties (PL 108-446 § 614[b][6][A]; § 614[b][2 & 3]). RTI can provide a decision-making framework for identifying students who need more intensive levels of academic or behavioral support and is intended to create systems to increase the capacity of school personnel to adopt and implement effective practices with fidelity. The RTI framework is dramatically changing the way related service providers, including school social workers, are being asked to identify and respond to student needs (Frey, Lingo, & Nelson, in press). Three important features of RTI, which are also shared by schoolwide positive behavior support (SWPBS) (See Sugai & Horner, 2008 and Table 1.2 for more information), are (1) the multitiered system of support, (2) empirically supported interventions, and (3) data-based decision making.

Multitiered Systems of Support

The multitiered system is based on the U.S. Public Health conceptualization of prevention and intervention strategies. This model addresses primary (Tier 1), secondary (Tier 2), and tertiary (Tier 3) prevention strategies to assist specific populations. Tier 1 involves the application of primary prevention strategies, which are applied to an entire population and designed to prevent initial occurrences of problem behavior through proactive interventions. Tier 2 includes targeted interventions, which are implemented with high-risk populations to prevent development or maintenance of problems. Finally, Tier 3, the top of the prevention framework, represents tertiary prevention. Tier 3 interventions focus on individuals who have serious problems that constitute a chronic condition. The three-tiered model suggests when more intensive interventions should be considered for individual students based on their response (or lack thereof) to interventions at prior levels of prevention. As shown in Figure 1.1, when Tier 1 strategies are in place and are effective, it may be anticipated that approximately 80% of students will achieve desired outcomes. However, another 20% can be expected to need greater levels of support to meet desired outcomes. Tier 2 strategies, if properly implemented, will allow many of these students (perhaps another 15%) to achieve desired outcomes. Yet, even with primary and secondary prevention supports in place, as many as 5% of students will demonstrate a need for Tier 3 interventions,

TABLE 1.2 CHARACTERISTICS OF SCHOOLWIDE POSITIVE BEHAVIOR SUPPORT (SWPBS), TIER 1, 2, AND 3 INTERVENTIONS

Prevention

Tier	Goal	Core Elements	Features
Tier 1 Primary Prevention	Prevent initial occurrences of problem behavior	• Behavioral expectations defined • Behavioral expectations taught • Reward system for appropriate behavior • Continuum of consequences for problem behavior • Continuous collection and use of data for decision making	• Apply to all students • Apply to all settings • Consist of rules, routines, arrangements • Implemented by all staff
Tier 2 Secondary Prevention	Prevent recurrences of problem behavior	• Universal screening • Progress monitoring for at-risk students • System for increasing structure and predictability • System for increasing contingent adult feedback • System for linking academic and behavioral performance • System for increasing home/school communication Collection and use of data for decision making	• Minimal time needed to implement • Procedures are similar for groups of students • Typically provide extra doses of primary interventions • Implementation coordinated by a schoolwide team
Tier 3 Tertiary Prevention	Reduce impact of a condition on functioning	• Functional behavioral assessment • Team-based comprehensive assessment • Linking of academic and behavior supports • Individualized intervention • Collection and use of data for decision making	• Individualized planning and implementation • Function-based intervention plans • Wraparound planning • Implemented by teams established for individual students

Source: Modified with permission from Horner, Sugai, Todd & Lewis-Palmer (2005).

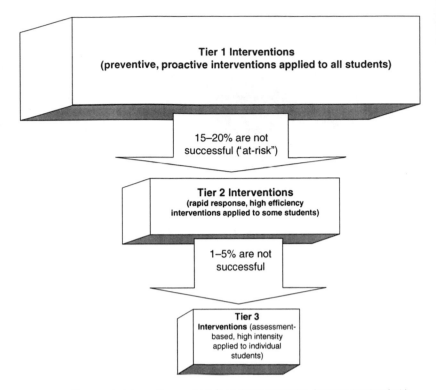

FIGURE 1.1 Response to intervention as a basis for making intervention decisions. Reprinted with permission from Frey, A., Lingo, A., & Nelson, C. M. (in press). Positive behavior support and response to intervention in elementary schools. In H. Walker & M. K. Shinn (Eds.), *Interventions for Achievement and Behavior Problems: Preventive and Remedial Approaches* (3rd Ed): National Association for School Psychologists.

the highest level of support. While these percentages began as heuristics (Walker et al., 1996), they are beginning to be validated empirically (Horner et al., 2005). It is also important to note that some schools may have relatively higher proportions of students requiring Tier 2 and Tier 3 supports. By monitoring specific outcomes across all students, school personnel can make data-based decisions regarding which students require more intensive levels of intervention.

Empirically Supported Interventions

In addition to the multitiered approach to service delivery, an important aspect of the RTI model is the notion that interventions should be *empirically supported*. This term is highly controversial and there are competing classification systems rating the extent of empirical support for intervention or intervention strategies These include the system devised by the Division 12 task force of the American Psychological Association (Chambless & Hollon, 1998). Similarly, the U.S.

Department of Education's (2006a) definition of the term *scientifically based research* is not universally accepted.[1] What constitutes "evidence" and which interventions meet this standard, is of course the main focus of this book and will be discussed in more detail in Chapter 3.

Data-based Decision Making

Another aspect of the RTI model is data-based decision making. This involves systematic screening and progress monitoring at individual and systems levels to guide implementation decisions and to determine which children are not responding to interventions and are therefore appropriate candidates for more intensive interventions.

RTI has been endorsed by national organizations such as the School Social Work Association of America (SSWAA), the National Association of Social Workers (NASW), the National Association of School Psychologists (NASP), the American School Counselor Association (ASCA), the American Counseling Association (ACA), the American School Health Association (ASHA), and the U.S. Department of Education.

CLINICAL QUADRANT

In an effort to better align school social work practice with the ecological perspective and the school-based prevention and intervention literature, Frey and Dupper (2005) offer a clinical quadrant framework, shown here in Figure 1.2.

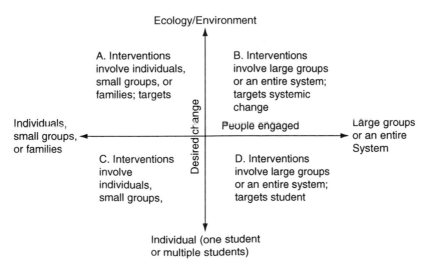

FIGURE 1.2 Clinical quadrant.

TABLE 1.3 ROLES OF SUPPORT SERVICE PERSONNEL TO SUPPORT SCHOOLWIDE POSITIVE BEHAVIOR SUPPORT (SWPBS) AND RESPONSE TO INTERVENTION (RTI) IMPLEMENTATION

Tier 1 Primary Prevention

- Create a vision for the school based on the principles and four key elements of SWPBS and logic of RTI
- Develop awareness and buy-in on the part of school administrative leaders
- Identify and assemble potential members for the leadership team
- Coordinate with and among all school staff, administrators, community agencies, and families
- Facilitate access to training, initially for the leadership team and eventually for all school personnel
- Identify potential Tier 1 interventions to meet the needs of school personnel and students
- Advocate for staff time and resources to improve and sustain effective supports
- Enter, summarize, and present data demonstrating that high-quality universal interventions have been implemented with fidelity and have been effective or ineffective

Requisite skills for fulfilling these roles include expertise in SWPBS and RTI frameworks; group facilitation and consensus-building skills; data entry, analysis, and presentation skills; collaboration and mediation skills; and knowledge of evidence-based Tier 1 interventions.

Tier 2 Secondary Prevention

- Identify potential Tier 2 interventions to meet the needs of school personnel and students
- Provide consultation to the general education teachers who serve on Tier 2 support teams (e.g., student assistance and student support teams) and who deliver targeted interventions
- Identify the training needs of leadership team members, student assistance or student support teams
- Establish a training program or long-range professional development plan to address training needs
- Advocate the reallocation of staff time and resources to improve and sustain effective supports provided by school and district administrators
- Provide coaching and feedback (e.g., praise, encouragement, and error correction) as a teacher implements the steps involved in an intervention practice or program
- Problem solve with teachers providing direct services as needed
- Coordinate with and among student assistance or student support teams, including family members
- Engage families to establish strong working relationships and develop trust
- Help the student assistance or student support team use data to determine when, and with whom, Tier 3 supports are needed

TABLE 1.3 ROLES OF SUPPORT SERVICE PERSONNEL TO SUPPORT SCHOOLWIDE POSITIVE BEHAVIOR SUPPORT (SWPBS) AND RESPONSE TO INTERVENTION (RTI) IMPLEMENTATION (CONT'D)

- Enter, summarize, and present data demonstrating high-quality Tier 2 interventions have been implemented with fidelity and have been effective or ineffective

Requisite skills for fulfilling these roles include group facilitation and consensus-building skills; data entry, analysis, and presentation skills; collaboration and mediation skills; and knowledge of evidence-based Tier 2 intervention practices.

Tier 3 Tertiary Prevention

- Identify potential Tier 3 interventions to meet the needs of school personnel and students
- Work with students individually (e.g., teaching replacement behaviors)
- Identify and engage participants in a collaborative, participatory process that values buy-in and motivation
- Manage the data that will identify appropriate candidates for this level of support and may be used to determine whether Tier 3 interventions are effective or ineffective
- Determine and address training needs; suggest reallocation of staff, time, or resources; and consider other systems changes that will improve and sustain the supports being implemented at this level
- Provide training and technical assistance regarding specific intervention procedures
- Facilitate wraparound planning, coordinating and brokering services that are needed but are beyond the ability of the school to provide
- Collect functional behavioral assessment (FBA) data; generate initial hypotheses regarding the function of the child's challenging behavior
- Oversee the initial writing, monitoring, and subsequent revisions of the individualized educational plan (IEP), behavior intervention plan (BIP), or wraparound plan
- Encourage the teachers who must implement these the FBA or IEP plan, and intervene when the plans are not being adequately implemented
- Facilitate meetings to review and revise the plans that are ineffective

Requisite skills for fulfilling these roles include group facilitation and consensus-building skills; data entry, analysis, and presentation skills; collaboration and mediation skills; knowledge of community services; and knowledge and expertise in Tier 3 interventions, particularly FBA and wraparound planning.

This framework can help practitioners consider how their clinical skills can be used to conceptualize multiple problems and leverage effectiveness by implementing interventions that seek to target multiple risk factors.

The clinical quadrant depicts two important dimensions. The horizontal axis divides tasks/interventions based upon whom the school social worker engages. Tasks/interventions on the left side of the quadrant engage individuals, families, and small groups; those on the right side engage large groups or an entire system. The vertical axis divides tasks/interventions based on whether they seek to promote change within the students' ecology (or environment) or the individual (one student or multiple students). Stated another way, interventions in quadrants A and B address risk factors in the classroom, school, or home domains by promoting change in the environment. Interventions in quadrants C and D address risk factors in the individual domain by seeking to change characteristics or skills within the child.

Frey and Dupper argue that school social workers should expand their idea of the "clients" they might serve beyond the traditional notions of students with acute presenting mental health problems, the ones most typically served in Tier 3. The clinical quadrant framework intends to show school social workers how prevention-oriented work and whole-school systemic practice are essential to school social work practice (Frey & Dupper, 2005).

Part of what makes the clinical quadrant framework attractive for many of the school social workers we've trained is that it acknowledges that many school social workers view their jobs through a clinical lens and are trying to ultimately use clinical skills (interviewing, active listening, showing empathy) to impact their school at both micro- and macrolevels. We believe that the challenge, as with all interventions in schools, involves knowing where best to start and how to bring the best available evidence to bear on the client's presenting issues. The school-based prevention and intervention research and RTI and clinical quadrant models are helpful tools to align the practice choices of school social workers and the prevention and intervention research. (For more details on different roles for school social workers related to different SWPBS/RTI tiers, see Table 1.3) Unfortunately, the evidence that does exist suggests that there may be a substantial gap between these knowledge bases and too many school social workers.

SCHOOL SOCIAL WORK PRACTICE CHOICES: THE KNOWLEDGE-PRACTICE GAP

Locating school social workers' practice choices within the school-based prevention and intervention research and the RTI framework and clinical quadrant model reveals the gap. The results of a recent national school social work survey, which represents the first representative data in over a decade, are highlighted in this section to demonstrate the chasm between these bodies of knowledge and self-reported school social work practice. In this study, investigators examined utilization patterns, characteristics, and practice choices of a national sample of 1,639 school social workers (Kelly et al., 2009; also see Box 1.2 for more details on the survey project).

Both the RTI framework and clinical quadrant model imply the need for school-based support service providers to maximize the reach of their services by improving the organization and delivery of related services, building the

BOX 1.2 DETAILS ON THE 2008 NATIONAL SCHOOL SOCIAL WORK SURVEY PROJECT

The survey was developed through an iterative process involving project researchers, School Social Work Association of America (SSWAA) staff, and an expert panel. Question construction was based on a review of school social work practice literature, and a modified version of the Illinois State School Social Work Survey (Kelly, 2008). The survey was revised with the input of a 23-person expert panel, consisting of academics, practitioners, and school social work leaders. Additionally, the survey was field tested by 11 Illinois school social workers for clarity, readability, and content.

The survey focused on three areas of inquiry: (1) practice modalities, (2) service population and utilization, and (3) respondent characteristics. Section one asked about how school social workers spend their time, what interventions they rely on, and how different modalities of practice are employed. Section two was designed to learn more about the service population, asking questions about referral sources, involvement in transition services, involvement in government programs, and engagement in nonschool-based interventions. Section three asked about demographics, school social work experience, licensure, and employment setting.

The sample was recruited from SSWAA and associations that represent school social workers (including state school work associations, state chapters of the National Association of Social Workers [NASW], and state school counseling associations that included both school social workers and school counselors) from 47 states, with Maine, Nevada, and West Virginia being the only states with no state organization participating. School social workers in these states were captured in the dataset if they responded through the SSWAA distribution. The survey was conducted online and all respondents were invited by e-mail to participate. Data collection for the survey started on February 28, 2008, and concluded on May 31, 2008.

Participation methods varied by association: 10 state associations provided a list to the study team for survey distribution; SSWAA and 36 state associations (including D.C.) distributed a link to the survey Web site themselves; and two associations provided the information in a newsletter or on their Web site without a direct e-mail about the survey.

Through direct distribution by the survey team, the survey was distributed to 1,790 participants. SSWAA distributed the survey through an Internet link to its 1,644 members (which represents 80% of their membership for whom valid e-mail addresses were available). By indirect distribution (through association

(Continued)

BOX 1.2 DETAILS ON THE 2008 NATIONAL SCHOOL SOCIAL WORK SURVEY PROJECT (CONT'D)

e-mails) the survey was distributed to 36 associations. Estimates from one-third of the associations suggest that the survey was sent indirectly to approximately 2,686 individuals. The other two-thirds of the associations were unable to provide numbers for their distribution lists. It is also possible that individuals who received the survey indirectly through the association also received the survey directly via SSWAA, impossible to calculate precisely.

Through all recruitment techniques, the process yielded 2,956 respondents. However, a significant portion of survey responses were incomplete. Respondents who did not complete the characteristics section of the survey were considered incomplete responders. Bivariate analysis was conducted to compare results for complete responders and incomplete responders. These results showed no significant differences between these groups for items for which they both responded. Given that data on the characteristics of school social workers enhances our understanding of school social work practice and the impact of context, incomplete responders were eliminated from further analysis. Removing incomplete responders from our analysis yielded a final sample of 1,639 respondents representing 48 states.

capacity of teachers to implement high-quality Tier 1 and Tier 2 interventions, and deliver high-quality Tier 3 supports directly within the context of the lower tier support (Frey, Boyce, & Tarullo, 2009). However, data from the national survey, like those studies that preceded it, indicate that school social workers are engaged in few activities likely to accomplish these goals. Specifically, they do not appear to target risk factors beyond the individual level; or operate in quadrants A, B, or D.

While a comprehensive summary of these findings is provided in Kelly et al. (2009), a few examples follow. First, while the primary vehicle for increasing the capacity of teachers to implement efficacious interventions with high fidelity is through professional development, less than 20% of survey respondents reported engaging in this activity *all or most of the time.*

Another finding suggestive of the knowledge–practice gap is that data suggest school social workers may not be organizing their services within a multitiered context in which high-quality primary and secondary prevention activities are implemented prior to delivering tertiary-level supports. For example, respondents report spending approximately 28% of their time on Tier 1 activities versus 59% of their time on Tier 2 and 3 activities. Additionally, given the historic emphasis on social skills instruction (Massat et al., 2009), it is interesting that such a small percentage (11%) of the sample reported delivering social skills curriculum within the context of the classroom or the entire school (i.e., social skills as primary prevention; quadrant D) *all or most of the time.*

Another finding relates to the use of empirically supported interventions. While the respondents were not asked which interventions they use specifically, there are some aspects of this data that raise concerns about the general intervention approaches being used *all or most of the time* by a large percentage of school social workers nationally. For example, despite a clear trend in the intervention research that demonstrates effective intervention strategies employ a comprehensive approach that targets multiple intervention agents (e.g., teacher, parents, peers) and intervenes at multiple levels (e.g., school, home, community) (Dupper, 2002; Greenberg, 2003; Sloboda & David, 1997; Walker, 2001), practice choices of our sample suggest that individually oriented interventions that are delivered in isolation from the context of regular school routines such as individual and group counseling are employed far more frequently, particularly at Tiers 2 and 3, than interventions that are far more integrated into the school culture, such as classroom management-based interventions, or improving the relationship between teachers and children. Additionally, less than 10% of respondents reported conducting sessions with children and their teachers—the activity that could potentially bridge counseling services with the child's daily educational experiences—*all or most of the time.*

While the emphasis on individually oriented interventions is not consistent with the RTI framework or clinical quadrant model, it did appear to match the respondents' causal attributions of the problems experienced by the children they work with at Tiers 2 and 3: a large percentage of school social workers participating in this survey attributed the problems experienced by children in their schools to individual risk factors such as weak social skills or behavior problems *all or most of the time.* This finding is perplexing given the historical commitment to the person-in-environment focus in social work education and the evidence base in the education literature highlighting the importance of systemic risk factors in the development of school-based behavior problems

Using the language from the RTI framework, one might say school social workers appear to teach social skills predominantly at Tiers 2 or 3. Using the language of the clinical quadrant model, one might say school social workers appear to spend a disproportionate amount of time in quadrant C. It is important to note that these services are not indicated in the absence of high-quality Tier 1 interventions, and the evidence base for social skills training for severely impacted children is scant, particularly if it is not offered in the context of high-quality interventions that address environmental (i.e., school or family) risk factors (Frey, Boyce, & Tarullo, 2009).

BOX 1.3 SCHOOL SOCIAL WORK SURVEY 2008: SUMMARY FINDINGS

School Social Worker Characteristics

- The population of school social workers remains largely unchanged since previous studies, with practice dominated by women who are Caucasian, hold a master's degree in social work, and have been practicing for more than 5 years (Allen-Meares, 1994).

Practice Context

- School social workers practice predominantly in public school settings, with a higher percentage practicing in elementary schools than other grade levels.
- School social work practice exists across districts of varying community sizes.
- School social workers often practice at multiple schools, with almost one-third serving four or more schools.

Population Served

- Respondents report that their caseload is referred primarily from teachers and rank behavioral and emotional problems as the most common reasons for referral.
- One-third of the respondents reported more than half of their caseload is served as part of an individualized education plan (IEP).
- Fewer than 10% of school social workers reported that the majority of their caseload received counseling or therapeutic services from an outside agency or professional.

Practice Choices

- School social workers do not appear to have embraced national trends related to school-based research, contemporary education frameworks, or evidence-based practice (EBP). They report spending more time on secondary and tertiary prevention activities (typically known as "micro" or "Tier 3" interventions) than on primary prevention ("Tier 1" or "Tier 2" interventions).
- Encouragingly, respondents would like to engage more in primary prevention and do use family engagement as a prevention strategy.
- Individual and group counseling remain the primary practice activities of school social workers with fewer engaged in teacher consultation and family-based practice.

(Continued)

- Respondents report high administrative demands and low involvement in schoolwide leadership or activities.
- EBP is not evident in the reports on what practitioners use to inform service delivery. They remain reliant on workshops and peer consultation rather than online research or journals.

Source: Kelly, M. S., Berzin, S. C., Frey, A., Alvarez, M., Shaffer, G., & O'Brien, K. (2009). The state of school social work: Findings from the National School Social Work Survey. Manuscript submitted for publication.

Another example demonstrating the knowledge-practice gap between the use of empirically supported practices and school social work interventions relates to how respondents in this study choose intervention strategies. Specifically, the resources respondents identified using most often may also help explain reliance on Tier 2 and 3 activities or activities that target individual change/risk factors. Even though students' complex needs require the profession to move toward more evidence-informed practice (Allen-Meares, 2007; Kelly, 2008; Raines, 2008b), few practitioners in this study report using online research, journals, or books to inform their practice. It is not surprising that the practice choices of many school social workers target individual risk factors if these practitioners implicate individual risk factors as the cause of the struggles being experienced by the children in their schools and if they are accessing each other rather than resources that would challenge the status quo.

Data-based decision making is another important feature of RTI. Results indicated that a relatively low percentage of school social workers engage in data analysis *all or most of the time* (14%), suggesting that they have not yet embraced this aspect of the RTI framework.

This study provides important data about the basic characteristics and practices of school social workers and provides confirmatory evidence of a knowledge-practice gap. However, it provides much less insight into why this gap exists. We suspect a complex mix of practitioner and contextual (e.g., school, region) factors, which we discuss in Chapter 2), may contribute to this (Frey & Dupper, 2005; Kelly & Stone, 2009). We believe that these data provide a useful starting point for dialogue about how the profession will shape and be shaped by the changing landscape of school-based support services. It is thus our intent in this text to move beyond a vague critique of practitioners to begin to arm them with skills to digest and apply research findings to their work in schools. (For more details on the national school social work survey findings, see Box 1.3.)

CONCLUSION

School social workers have tremendous latitude to determine which practices they select to support the children they serve, and evidence related to these choices suggests they typically engage in activities that target individual risk factors through counseling and other intervention work with individuals and small groups. These practices have been questioned by many school social work scholars over the years, who cite a misfit between this practice emphasis and social work's commitment to ecological theory, school-based prevention and intervention research, and contemporary education models guiding the organization and delivery of school-based support services.

We hope this book engages school social work scholars and practitioners in a dialogue about using evidence as part of this process to help practitioners align their historical commitments to the person-in-environment focus in social work education, with findings from the evidence base in the education literature highlighting the importance of systemic risk factors in the development of school-based behavior problems and actual practice strategies.

In this respect, we hope to help bridge the gap between an individualistic practice orientation and the empirical knowledge base. A vehicle for doing so is through use of both RTI and clinical quadrant frameworks. Both the RTI framework and clinical quadrant model imply the need for school-based support service providers to maximize the reach of their services by improving the organization and delivery of related services, building the capacity of teachers to implement high quality interventions Tier 1 and Tier 2 interventions, and deliver high quality Tier 3 supports directly within the context of the other tiers (Frey, Lingo, & Nelson, in press). In the next chapter we attempt to understand why this divide exists, and detail a process that has been proposed to reduce similar gaps in social work as well as other disciplines.

2

UNDERSTANDING AND NARROWING THE RESEARCH–PRACTICE KNOWLEDGE GAP

In this chapter, we consider several reasons for the existence of the knowledge-practice gap—a gap between the practice choices of school social workers and research on school-based prevention and intervention as well as readily available contemporary education models. We also introduce the EIP (evidence-informed practice) process as a potential vehicle to reduce the knowledge-practice gap and empower school social workers to make their practices more evidence-informed.

UNDERSTANDING THE KNOWLEDGE-PRACTICE GAP

In the absence of conclusive empirical data to explain the knowledge–practice gap, speculation is required. We believe there are at least three plausible explanations: (1) lack of familiarity by practitioners of current findings in the school-based intervention literature, (2) difficulty in implementing principles emerging from the knowledge base, and (3) rejection of knowledge.

LACK OF KNOWLEDGE

Being exposed to and understanding the school-based prevention and intervention literature and the contemporary education frameworks discussed in the previous chapter are prerequisites for implementing practice choices consistent with the key findings emerging from the knowledge base. These conceptual guides for organizing student support systems are increasingly being used by legislators and policy makers to form the conditions that influence school social work practice (Franklin & Kelly, 2009; Kelly, 2008; Raines, 2004). School social work preparation programs, workshops, and peer supervision are the most likely resources to influence practice choices. However, what little evidence there is suggests that this information may not be communicated in these forums. Although most school social work students feel that their training is enough to prepare them for the multiple roles and challenges they will face (Constable & Alvarez, 2006; Kelly, 2008), we are not sure that they acquire this content knowledge in the standard master's level social work curriculum, according to a recent analysis of school social work syllabi. Additionally, while school social workers report relying on workshops and peer supervision more than any other resource (see Kelly et al., 2009), knowledge of the prevention and intervention research and contemporary education models seems unlikely to be communicated by practitioners if few are practicing based on this knowledge base and its guiding frameworks.

BARRIERS TO IMPLEMENTING RESEARCH FINDINGS IN PRACTICE SETTINGS

Frey and Dupper (2005) note, and we concur, that no discipline is better qualified or prepared than school social work to deliver the services consistent with the prevention and intervention research and contemporary education models discussed previously. It is possible that school social workers would like to implement practices consistent with the knowledge base but are unable to do so due to factors beyond their control, particularly the influence of the professional landscape and the structure of educational institutions.

Professional Landscape

The models and interventions that school social workers draw from appear to be at least partially determined by professional roles that the profession has created for itself over the past century. That is certainly the case for school social workers in some midwestern states, such as Illinois, where many school social workers are employed. In the case of states that heavily emphasize providing individual services to students with individualized education plans (IEPs) and billing Medicaid for work with students from low-income families, focusing their time and energy on a full caseload of students with IEPs might be less of a personal practice choice than an expectation inherent to the system they practice within (Frey & Dupper, 2005; Kelly, 2008).

Structure of Educational Institution

Others note that school social workers' practice choices may relate to a lack of understanding, on the part of educators and schools, about their specific role, causing confusion about what school social workers "should" and "shouldn't" do with their time. Some school environments and states have more clearly defined rules about school social workers' role and responsibilities than others. The mission, goals, and functions of the American educational system represent another related factor (Gitterman & Miller, 1989). Dane and Simon (1991) contend that "predictable" organization-related dynamics often emerge for social workers in host settings. These include explicit or implicit discrepancies in missions and values, marginalization and isolation, and role ambiguity. Understanding such factors is central, given that trans-disciplinary knowledge, collaboration, and intervention strategies characterize evidence-informed processes and practices (Franklin & Hopson, 2007), and Duchnowski and Kutash (2007) attribute the slow adoption of evidence-based practices in schools largely to the discrepant perspectives of the education and mental health systems. Public health–derived models are increasingly utilized to frame prevention and intervention efforts (Duchnowski & Kutash, 2007). Such perspectives explicitly acknowledge important distinctions between the orientations of mental health and other child-serving systems and education systems in terms of different overarching influences, conceptual frameworks, theoretical influences, and foci of interventions.

Another important factor related to the educational institution is the expectations and immediate needs of educators. It is estimated that three-fourths of children who need mental health services are not getting them (Katoaka et al., 2002). School social workers who practice in contexts with high student-to-worker ratios understandably have increased expectations to engage in practice choices that are (or at least appear) responsive to current crises. In a recent national school social work survey, 65% of respondents indicated that large caseloads accounted for *all or most* of the discrepancy between actual and ideal time spent on primary prevention activities (Kelly et al., 2009). There is little available evidence to understand influences on practice choices. However, a recent analysis of a survey of school social workers finds that caseload size, grade level of pupils served, and district size were inversely related to frequent use of individual counseling but positively related to group counseling. In other words, while these results are difficult to interpret, they suggest that caseload and district-level factors may be important in shaping practice (Kelly & Stone, 2009). They also dovetail neatly with accumulating evidence that school contextual features (e.g., demographic composition, principal support) shape the implementation of school-based prevention and intervention strategies (Payne, 2008).

REJECTION OF EMPIRICAL KNOWLEDGE

Historically, social work has struggled with defining its professional identity. While much of the attention in the social work literature has focused on social workers as advocates for professional respect and recognition of their skills as helping professionals, an important critical literature characterizes social work as a profession that willfully ignores evidence, clients' real needs, and the societal structures that keep social work clients in need (Gambrill, 2006; Specht & Courtney, 1994) Although this has been forwarded as an explanation to characterize the social work profession, that view is not being endorsed in this text. We have worked too long ourselves as school social workers to support the idea that the profession of school social work is encouraging this willful ignorance, particularly given this new era of data-driven decision making and research-based interventions. If anything, we have written this book to try to identify and model an evidence-informed practice approach that captures the dynamism of school social work practice and that empowers practitioners to better understand and utilize the best available evidence to help their school clients. Consistent with the clinical quadrant model, we would suggest the "cause" is a combination of environmental and individual factors, and any strategy to remedy the problem must address both the systems in which practitioners are embedded and their specific clinical skills.

A system for utilizing evidence that is feasible and socially valid to school social workers is also essential. In the next section we define the EIP process that is generally promoted in social work and related disciplines to narrow knowledge-practice gaps such as those detailed in the first chapter.

THE ROOTS OF EVIDENCE-INFORMED PRACTICE

The originators of evidence-based practice (EBP) defined it as the "conscious, explicit, and judicious use of current best evidence in making decisions about the care of individual patients" (Sackett et al., 1996, p. 71). It involves a process of integrating the "best research evidence with clinical expertise and patient values" (Sackett et al., 2000, p. 1). Recently, the American Psychological Association (APA) agreed on a similar definition: "Evidence-based practice in psychology is the integration of the best available research with clinical expertise in the context of patient characteristics, culture, and preferences" (APA, 2005, p. 7) There are five basic stages in the process; Please see Figure 2.1 for more details: (1) formulation of answerable questions, (2) investigation of the evidence, (3) critical appraisal, (4) adaptation and application, and (5) outcome evaluation (Ollendick & Davis, 2004; Sackett et al., 2000).

ANSWERABLE QUESTIONS

First, practitioners must convert their need for information into answerable questions. An important caveat, however, is that not all questions are answerable

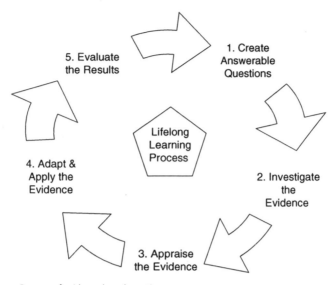

FIGURE 2.1 Process of evidence-based practice.

by science. There are two types of questions that science cannot answer. First, it cannot answer ethical or moral issues. Professional associations offer Codes of Ethics to guide clinicians' decision making about these questions. Second, it cannot answer client-specific questions, either at an individual client level or school level. The research can tell us what works for most people, not necessarily the one sitting across from us or the exact school we serve. This stage is similar to the assessment step mentioned above—it requires practitioners to identify the crux of the problem by formulating intelligent questions that need to be answered before treatment planning begins.

There are generally five kinds of questions that practitioners can ask (Gibbs, 2003), but there is no reason to ask all five about every case. Assessment questions can be phrased, "What is the best measure to screen/diagnose/monitor progress of a student with [psychosocial problem]?" Such measures should possess both reliability and validity. Reliability refers to the consistency of the measure while validity refers to the accuracy of the measure (Engels & Schutt, 2008). Reliability is always a prerequisite to validity. Descriptive questions may be framed, "What are the characteristics/symptoms of a student with [psycho-social problem]?" Such questions help practitioners ensure that they are meeting the needs of the whole child, not just the most obvious or disruptive attributes. It may also help us identify co-occurring problems that need to be addressed. Risk questions can be phrased, "Which students with [psychosocial problem] are most likely to commit [severe behavior]? While multiple-victim school shootings

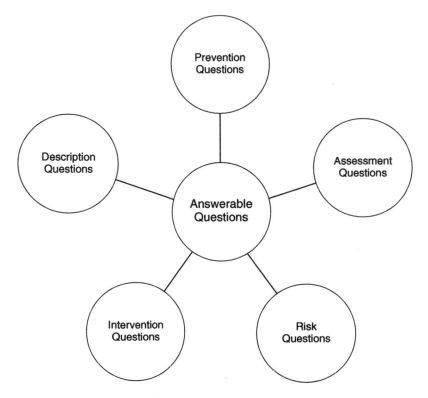

FIGURE 2.2 Five types of answerable questions.

have had the highest profile, other risks include drunken driving, drug overdoses, and suicides. As the FBI report issued after the Columbine shootings indicated (O'Toole, 1999), these risks can be extraordinarily hard to predict with precision (for an example, see Box 2.1—The Social Work Shooter). Prevention questions are usually worded, "What is the best way to prevent [social problem]?" Finally, intervention questions are usually framed, "What are the empirically-supported interventions for [psychosocial problem]?" For more examples of different types of EBP questions, please see Figure 2.2

INVESTIGATION OF THE EVIDENCE

Second, practitioners must be able to effectively and efficiently investigate the best evidence. Although these terms are often used in tandem – they do not mean the same thing. *Efficiency* means being able to do something with a minimum of time and effort. It requires specific skills in using electronic databases. Some

---

BOX 2.1 THE SOCIAL WORK SHOOTER

It happened on Valentine's Day, 2008. Steven Kazmierczak calmly walked into a large geology lecture hall at Northern Illinois University (NIU) with a shotgun and three handguns and injured 16 innocent people, eventually killing five plus himself. The next morning as I was preparing to teach my MSW class, I heard a rumor from a colleague that the gunman was an MSW student from the University of Illinois at Urbana/Champaign (UIUC) just 45 minutes down the road. I immediately shelved my plans for class and decided on a contingency plan.

When I arrived in class, I asked the students if they had heard what had happened at NIU. They had all heard some stories on the radio or TV. They expressed a range of feelings about the incident—some were angry, some were scared, some cried. Some looked around our seminar room and noticed that there was only one exit and only one window. They also observed that there was no lock on the door and no way to keep an intruder out. They felt vulnerable and confused about why our university seemed to have done nothing to increase their safety in the wake of the Virginia Tech shooting in April 2007.

Later that day I received confirmation that Steve Kazmierczak was an MSW student when I received a forwarded e-mail from a graduate of UIUC's social work program. That program released the following statement:

> The School of Social Work at the University of Illinois at Urbana-Champaign would like to express its deepest sympathies to victims' families and to the entire Northern Illinois University community in the wake of Thursday's tragic shootings on the DeKalb campus. Steven Kazmierczak, who has been identified as the person responsible for the shootings, was a student in the master's program in the U. of I. School of Social Work. For the social work community, the situation has been especially difficult to comprehend, as the person responsible for this tragedy was one of our own. As we provide support to our students, faculty/staff, and community, we remain mindful that such serious actions are not always predictable or understood. We intend to work together with everyone involved to bring an end to personal pain and senseless violence. (University of Illinois School of Social Work, 2008)

The phrase "one of our own" stood out to me. The UIUC School of Social Work had not disowned Steve Kazmierczak the way they might have been tempted to do. A week later, I saw two of my faculty colleagues from UIUC and one of them expressed it best when she admitted that she never saw it coming since he didn't seem to fit any "profile" of a killer.

(continued)

BOX 2.1 THE SOCIAL WORK SHOOTER (CONT'D)

Like many social work students, Steve was a complex character. He was born and raised in Elk Grove Village, a suburb of Chicago. At age 11, he sought help from his school social worker to adjust to the social pressures of middle school (Cohen & St. Clair, 2008). He played saxophone in his high school band and was a member of the Chess club. After graduation, he spent a year at Thresholds-Mary Hill House in Chicago because of cutting behavior and a bipolar disorder. His mother was diagnosed with Lou Gehrig's (ALS) disease around the same time. Again, it was a social worker at Thresholds who gave him new hope and direction. In 2001, he joined the army, but was given an administrative discharge six months later due to his previous psychiatric history. He enrolled at NIU where he earned academic honors with a double major in political science and sociology. He was elected vice president of the Academic Criminal Justice Association. He even co-authored academic papers with one of his sociology professors, who described him as "just a normal guy." He received a Dean's Award from the sociology department when he graduated in 2006. His mother finally succumbed to ALS three months later. When he applied to the University of Illinois' School of Social Work, he wrote in his admissions essay:

> I truly do feel as though I would be an altruistic social worker, mainly due to my past experiences, because I view myself as being able to relate to those segments of society that are in need of direction. (Cohen & St. Clair, 2008, p. 14)

In short, he simply wanted to "make a difference" in the lives of others and "give back" to society. In the summer and fall semesters of 2007, he earned straight A's in his social work classes. In September 2007, Steve got a job as a corrections officer at the Rockville County Correctional Facility on the Indiana-Illinois border, but never returned after working there for less than a month (Friedman, 2008). His academic adviser at UIUC described him as "engaging, respectful, conscientious, and gentle" (Zorn, 2008). His live-in girlfriend had broken up with him, but they continued to share a two-bedroom apartment (Esposito et al., 2008). In the last six months, he had added some disturbing tattoos (e.g., a clown from the movie *Saw*) and had recently stopped taking his psychotropic medication.

Should the social work faculty at UIUC have known that Steve was at risk for mass violence? Most pictures of him, appearing on the Internet shortly after the shooting, show a smiling clean-cut young man. His academic record was excellent. By all accounts, he was a popular student committed to social justice. This does not mean that he was unblemished; most social worker students have complex histories.

(continued)

QUESTIONS FOR DISCUSSION

We strongly recommend reading the FBI report created in the wake of the Columbine shootings (O'Toole, 1999). It recommends a four-pronged risk assessment that includes personality factors, family dynamics, school dynamics, and social dynamics.

1. What personality traits seem to offer clues that Steve was at risk?
2. What family dynamics might have increased his stress?
3. Why do you think he chose NIU as the place to commit violence?
4. What social dynamics in our society might have contributed to this episode?
5. If you did not know Steve's final act, would you have considered him at risk and notified authorities?

Final note: Steve Kazmierczak never wanted his motives to be known. He removed the hard drive from his laptop, destroyed his cell phone's memory card, and left no messages behind.

---

computer savvy investigators are efficient, but not effective. They can locate sources quickly, but the results are often irrelevant, weak, or inconsistent. *Effectiveness*, however, requires that users actually find the evidence that they are looking for. Typically, this requires that they learn to triangulate their search, using a variety of sources including clearinghouses, journal databases, and other scholarly texts (e.g., books).

The best investigators are both effective and efficient. They know how to search multiple databases and allow the computer to sift through mountains of data in a matter of minutes. This stage is similar to the treatment planning step—it requires social workers to go beyond mere brainstorming and investigate what interventions are most likely to help the client. This step will require access to professional books, university databases, and Internet clearinghouses. We offer a visual of how skilled EBP students can arrive at the "best evidence" in Figure 2.3.

We distinguish professional books from popular books by their level of rigor (Abel & Lyman, 2002). Typically, professional books are aimed at practicing professionals and will have textual citations and references for nearly every paragraph. Popular books are aimed at a general audience and rely almost exclusively on the author's authority for evidence with limited citations and references (McRae, 1993). The key difference, however, is the degree of peer review (Weller, 2001). University press books such as this one, undergo peer review twice—first at the proposal stage and again after the first draft.

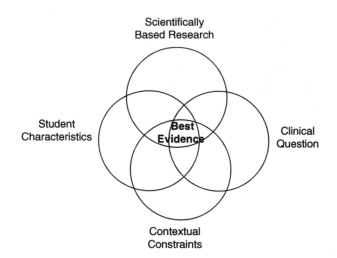

FIGURE 2.3 Four components of best evidence.

University databases are proprietary searchable databases that provide abstracts of scholarly journal articles. They require skills in the use of Boolean operators and search sets (see Box 2.2). Internet-based clearinghouses are edited for content by the organization or agency that supports them. Often, clearinghouses use a set of criteria for evaluating the extent of research support for a given set of interventions, including systematic reviews of prevention and/or intervention programs. Some well-known clearinghouses that contain relevant information for school practitioners include the following:

The Cochrane Collaboration (http://www.cochrane.org/)

The Campbell Collaboration (http://www.campbellcollaboration.org/)

The National Registry of Evidence-Based Programs and Practices compiled by the Substance Abuse and Mental Health Services Administration (www.nrepp.samhsa.gov)

The What Works Clearinghouse compiled by the Department of Education/ Institute of Education Sciences (http://ies.ed.gov/ncee/wwc/)

CRITICAL APPRAISAL

Third, once practitioners compile their sources, they should critically appraise the evidence for its validity and applicability to the practice problem that motivated the initial investigation. This is one of the ways that evidence-informed practice differs from treatment as usual: it requires critical thinking to determine what is the "best evidence." Practitioners need to keep their heads on and think critically about the "facts" that they uncover (Gambrill, 2006).

BOX 2.2 BOOLEAN OPERATORS AND SEARCH SETS

Boolean Operator AND	Boolean Operator NOT		Boolean Operator OR
Child & Adolescent Terms	Scientifically Based Terms	School-Based Terms	Intervention Terms
adolescen*	clinical trial	classroom	Counseling
boys	comparison group	school*	Intervention
child*	control group	teachers	Psychotherapy
girls	effectiveness		Treatment
teen*	efficacy		
youth	evaluation		
	multiple baseline		
	quasi-experimental		
	random*		

Combine similar terms with OR and dissimilar terms with AND.

Note: * is a wildcard character that enables databases to return any prefix or suffix, such as adolescence, adolescent, or adolescents.

Karl Popper (1992) discusses three important principles for critical thinking. The first principle is *fallibility*: the willingness to admit that we may be mistaken and the other person may be correct or the courage to admit that we could both be wrong! The second principle is *rationality*: the attempt to weigh our reasons, as impersonally as humanly possible, for or against a specific theory or practice. The final principle is *approximation to the truth*: the constant endeavor to converge multiple perspectives in order to obtain a complex and complete view of the situation.

For this book, we are especially interested in studies of the effects of both prevention and intervention strategies. There are two major types of studies.

First, systematic reviews aim to systematically collect, cull, and compare all of the scientifically based research on a particular topic. These reviews should be rigorous, transparent, and auditable. *Rigor* refers to the most meticulous standards for inclusion in the review. Typically, this means that reviewers accept only randomized controlled trials and quasi-experimental designs. *Transparency* refers to the clearness of the reviewers' explanation for how the studies were located, the criteria by which they are judged, and how the conclusions were reached. *Auditability* refers to sufficiency of specific details to enable another researcher to replicate the findings (Raines, 2008a).

Second, other studies consist of both randomized controlled trials and quasi-experimental designs. The U.S. Department of Education (What Works Clearinghouse, 2008b), for example, uses three criteria to judge the quality of these studies. First, *relevance* is determined by the study's topic, the adequacy of the outcome measures, and the adequacy of reported data. Relevance of the topic includes a relevant timeframe (e.g., 20 years), relevant intervention (e.g., cognitive-behavioral therapy), relevant sample (e.g., school-age children), and relevant outcome (e.g., improved behavior). Adequacy of the outcome measures means that the measure is both reliable (consistent) and valid (accurate). Adequacy of the reported data means that the researchers have provided means and standard deviations for both the treatment group and the comparison group before and after the intervention. Second, *strength* is determined by whether the researchers conducted a randomized controlled trial (RCT) or quasi-experimental design (QED). While RCTs contrast a treatment group to a control (no-treatment) group and QEDs contrast a treatment group to a comparison (different-treatment) group, the essential difference is that RCTs always randomly assigned subjects while QEDs do not. Third, *consistency* is determined by looking at the evenness of the intervention across different researchers, participants, settings, and outcomes. Ideally, the same intervention is tested by more than one research group, using diverse samples (races, genders, and socio-economic groups), different settings (urban, suburban, and rural schools), and different measures (observation, self-reports, or third-party rating scales). The U.S. Department of Education implicitly uses a hierarchy of evidence (ranging from mere clinical wisdom at the bottom to systematic reviews at the top; see Figure 2.4).

ADAPTATION AND APPLICATION

Fourth, practitioners should apply and adapt the results to their own clients. This step requires both cultural sensitivity and clinical practice wisdom. Seldom will a research study's participants be very similar to the actual clients we are trying to help so we must custom-tailor the intervention to fit the situation. This will involve a step that many browsers of research are likely to skip: reading the method section of the research. Good method sections have a paragraph on the population,

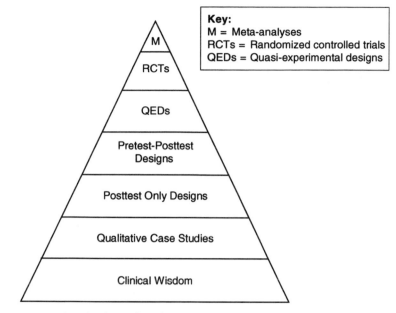

FIGURE 2.4 Hierarchy of scientific evidence.

sampling plan, and response rate. First, the population should be similar to the population of interest. Second, the study should have used a probability sample that makes the results generalizable to the population of interest. Third, the response rate should be high enough (50% or better) that we can be confident that respondents did not unwittingly bias the sampling plan. Adaptation has been a part of evidence-informed practice in medicine since the beginning. Sackett et al. (1996) explain the need for adaptation and application as follows:

> Good doctors use both individual clinical expertise and the best available external evidence, and neither alone is enough. Without clinical expertise, practice risks becoming tyrannized by evidence, for even excellent external evidence may be inapplicable to or inappropriate for an individual patient. Without best current evidence, practice risks become rapidly out of date, to the detriment of patients. (p. 72)

This stage is similar to the intervention implementation step: social workers must put what they have learned into action to initiate the change process.

OUTCOME EVALUATION

Finally, since adapting interventions automatically changes them, practitioners must begin to track and evaluate progress. It is this step that completes the circle and turns evidence-informed practice into practice-based evidence (Barkham & Mellor-Clark, 2003; Evans et al., 2003). One of the major weaknesses of research by related services personnel has been the failure to link mental health interventions with improved academic outcomes.

Outcome evaluation can be accomplished using either case-level or group-level designs. Case-level designs enable social workers to track the progress of individual students over time. Group-level designs enable professionals to track and compare groups of students over time.

WHAT EIP IS NOT

It is important not to confuse EIP with empirically supported treatments (ESTs) (Westen et al., 2005). A treatment is defined as the application of remedies to help a person recover from an illness or injury. Treatment sometimes assumes a medical model and usually presumes that the problem lies with the person, not the environment (Fonagy et al., 2002). In our view, the reason that ESTs do not qualify as evidence-informed practice is that they cover only the first two steps of integrating research and practice and leave out the final three steps (Ruben & Parrish, 2007; Walker et al., 2007). Ultimately, we believe it is more important for clinicians to know how to find the latest ESTs and then apply those ESTs to their specific school contexts than to know about a stand-alone list of ESTs. It is also important not to confuse evidence-informed practice with outcome evaluation (Constable & Massat, 2008). Outcome evaluation is concerned with carefully measuring the results of one's interventions (Bloom et al., 2005). Outcome evaluation is a critical component of EIP, but it is not synonymous with the evidence-informed practice we're articulating in this volume. The reason that outcome evaluation does not qualify as EIP is that it does not require social workers ever to use the professional literature. It simply jumps to the fourth step in the integrated process and leaves out the first three steps.

As Raines (2008b) states, the problem with both of the positions above is that they commit a philosophical error called a "category mistake" (Meiland, 1999). Both the EST = EIP and the Outcome Evaluation = EIP folks mistake a part of the process for the whole. EIP takes both into account. The EIP process definition outlined by Gibbs (2003) where "evidence-informed practice (EIP) is a process that can aid decision making critical to one's care, based on the best scientific evidence" (Gibbs, 2003, p. 2).

Gibbs (2003) offers this definition of evidence-informed practitioners:

> Placing the client's benefits first, evidence-informed practitioners adopt a process of lifelong learning that involves continually posing specific questions of direct

practical importance to clients, searching objectively and efficiently for the current best evidence relative to each question, and taking appropriate action guided by evidence. (p. 6)

Two parts of this definition are worth noting. First, good clinical practice requires that all professional helpers become "lifelong learners" (Howard et al., 2003; Murphy, 2005; Slawson & Shaughnessy, 2005). Second, evidence-informed practitioners seek "good-enough" evidence about current practice questions. There is seldom unequivocal evidence that lets clinicians know they are making exactly the right choices, so we must live with ambiguity.

CRITICISMS OF EVIDENCE-BASED PRACTICE AND EVIDENCE-INFORMED PRACTICE

Evidence-informed practice has received as much criticism from opponents in the practice and scholarship communities as it has garnered acclaim from proponents. Evidence-informed practice has intuitive appeal—who admits their work is not based upon evidence, or that they support practices known to be ineffective? As Hall (2008) states, "the word 'evidence' holds power and weight, and inspires confidence" (p. 385). Even those who oppose EIP generally support the values it embraces—seeking the best possible way to help clients. Despite the allure of EIP, some critics (e.g., Webb, 2001; Wendt & Slife, 2007; Witkin & Harrison, 2001) suggest it is problematic because (*a*) problems are not easily categorized and generalized; (*b*) EIP relies too heavily on linear-positivist mind-sets; and (*c*) this method uses deficit-oriented assessments that dismiss the contextual and political nature of problems (Hall, 2008). In the next section, we review these criticisms, in general and in the context of school-based practice. The criticisms, in part, provide a rationale for our decision to modify the five stages proposed above and to add three additional stages to the evidence-informed process we use in Chapters 4–12 and recommend to practitioners. In this section, it is not our intention to endorse or reject these criticisms. In fact, as a team of authors, we couldn't agree upon language that would acceptably communicate our various perspectives on the merits of these criticisms. What we do agree on, however, is that any model that has hope for reaching beyond the ivory tower—which is our goal—needs to address these issues.

EIP as Authority-Based Practice

The first major criticism of EIP is that it is simply authority-based practice in disguise (Gambrill, 2003). According to this viewpoint, EIP has been around for decades (e.g., Jayaratne & Levy, 1979; Marks, 1974; Mullen & Dumpson, 1972).

The "evidence" includes not only randomized controlled trials but also "opinions of respected authorities, based on clinical experiences, descriptive studies, or reports of expert consensus ... anecdotal case reports, unsystematic clinical observation, descriptive reports, [and] case studies" (Roberts & Yeager, 2004, p. 6). In other words, it is "business-as-usual" in the world of psychotherapy. As we hope this book will show, we believe that school social workers bringing an EIP lens to their work will be doing something that is both practical and highly responsive to their school's needs, the opposite of a lens that simply tells school social workers to do what they've always done.

Cookbook Practice

The second major criticism of EIP is that it is simply a rigidly controlled treatment that allows for no clinical creativity or flexibility, a phenomenon referred to as the clinical cookbook approach (Howard et al., 2003; Shlonsky & Gibbs, 2006). According to this perspective, if social workers will follow each carefully measured step with clients, then the results will turn out the same for all school social workers and their clients. This perspective presumes that EIP requires only the use of treatment manuals and ignores the unique personal characteristics of both the client and the social worker. As will be clear from the chapters that follow, there are many treatments or programs that have detailed treatment/intervention manuals that we found to deal with the most pressing problems reported by school social workers in our recent survey work (Kelly et al., 2009; Kelly, 2008). Where possible, we highlight these manuals and the intervention strategies they use to make changes for school clients.

While manuals alone won't make a school social worker more effective (we've seen too many of those manuals gathering dust in classrooms and colleagues' offices to say that), we do believe that manualized treatments have a crucial role to play in enhancing the effectiveness of school social work practice by increasing treatment fidelity and giving much-needed guidance to practitioners who are dealing with a wide range of complicated client problems in their schools. That said, based on our research for this book, we are concerned that many pressing school-based problems haven't been studied enough to settle on one or two manualized treatments. Based on the framework and information we share in this book, we encourage practitioners to seek out manualized treatments in the literature where they exist and where they can be applied to their schools, but also not to become discouraged if such a treatment doesn't exist yet for their specific client concern. The field of school-based intervention and treatment research has come a long way in the past few decades, but it is still in an early stage of development compared to other related fields of mental health (Hoagwood et al., 2007).

THE COMPLEX (AND EVER-CHANGING) NATURE OF SCHOOL SOCIAL WORKER CONTEXTS

School social workers face some unique challenges when trying to decide how to select their interventions. The first is in some ways the most basic: deciding who their "client" is. Hall (2008) articulates several issues related to the characterization of EIP as the application of ESTs to a specific client problem or disorder. The first is the operationalization of the client. Operationalization of a single client, particularly in the context of schools, is difficult. To effectively address many, if not most, problems in schools it is often helpful to conceptualize the client as a combination of the student, teacher, school (e.g., administration), and parents as the client.

Operationalization of the problem is no less difficult. Take a child who is exhibiting externalizing behavior problems in class. The problem could easily be conceptualized as a problem of self-control, classroom management, parenting, or lack of a safe and orderly school environment. As Hall (2008) suggests, the interpretation of the problem will likely have as many definitions as it does people who have an opinion, and conflict about the problem definition is usually a contributing factor to the struggles being experienced.

These challenges don't in any way preclude a school social worker's choosing a manualized treatment to address the client's presenting problem; rather, we raise these challenges to show how school social work practice can at times differ dramatically from social work practice with children in community mental health or private practice settings In the above scenario, a school social worker could operationalize the student problem as self-control, ADHD, or a conduct problem—all which locate the problem within the child. Fortunately, there are some treatment manuals that exist for students who have externalizing problems and the school social worker could choose to implement those individual or small group treatments in her office. However, the same school social worker could also choose to intervene primarily with the teacher to help him or her implement new classroom management strategies, or to work with the student's parents on ways they can handle the student differently at home. Again, the school social worker could consult the treatment literature for empirically supported treatments on improving classroom management and parent training for students with behavior problems.

In all the above hypothetical scenarios, the school social worker could then engage in a rigorous EIP process for all of these potential intervention scenarios and still implement interventions that are "evidence-informed" but inconsistent with the public health and education-specific frameworks and school-based literature. Perhaps most important for the individual context, the school leadership itself (principal, superintendent, school board) may be more concerned about improving that student's attendance or performance on standardized tests, and may prefer that the school social worker operate using more Tier 1 and Tier 2 interventions. Finally, Hall (2008) also questions what happens when the problem changes, as it inevitably does in most school social worker–student situations, particularly if the student is being served through an individualized education plan (IEP) over the course of several years.

Additionally, what about the contextual concerns beyond school social workers' control mentioned earlier? Most schools do not meet No Child Left Behind's recommendation of one school counselor per 250 students, one school social worker per 800 students; and one school psychologist per 1,000 students (Title V, P.L. 107-110). Low pay, high turnover, too many clients, too little supervision, and low morale negatively affect the quality of services that are provided (Dishion & Stormshak, 2007). Many school social workers often feel forced to choose short-term individual or group interventions simply due to the constraints of time and resources (Kelly & Stone, 2009; Lomonaco et al., 2000).

STATE AND ACCESSIBILITY OF THE EVIDENCE

Finally, although there may be a time in the future when access to the necessary databases are not restricted to personal or institutional subscriptions, that is not currently the case. With the search tools and strategies we will begin describing in Chapter 3 and modeling in all the chapters that follow, we are concerned that some of the databases (PsycInfo, Academic Search Premier) we consulted are not uniformly available to the average practitioner. Whenever possible, we have incorporated databases in our searches (such as ERIC and PubMed) that are accessible to anyone with an Internet connection. We empathize with the problems school social workers often encounter when they try to become more evidence-informed, and though it is entirely possible that school districts themselves could subscribe to the same databases that universities do, our anecdotal experience tells us that most school districts have not yet seen the benefit in making such an investment to help their faculty. Until practitioners with no ties to universities and typical workloads for the field see the process as socially valid and engage in it freely, it will be hard for EIP to become a regular part of social work practice and training, as is the case in parts of Western Europe that have built the EIP infrastructure to make evidence clear and accessible (Greenhalgh, 2006).

CONCLUSION

This chapter examines several reasons for the existence of the knowledge–practice gap—a gap between the practice choices of school social workers and research on school-based prevention and intervention as well as contemporary education models. Three plausible explanations for the knowledge–practice gap are forwarded, including (1) lack of practitioner familiarity with the knowledge base; (2) barriers to implementing principles and specific ESTs emerging from the knowledge base, and (3) a privileging of practice wisdom over empirical research, resulting in a rejection of current school-based research. We introduce the EIP process that has been proposed in social work and other disciplines to address the research–practice gap. While EIP has intuitive appeal, it has also received much criticism from the practice community. These criticisms, many of which are legitimate, have undoubtedly contributed to the slow embracing of EIP in practice. In the next chapter we forward an evidence-informed process that takes into consideration these criticisms, and privileges school-based prevention and intervention research. This process also examines the contemporary education models discussed earlier.

3

AN EVIDENCE-INFORMED PROCESS
FOR SCHOOL SOCIAL WORKERS

Rather than advocating that school social workers learn only a few evidence-informed practices (EIP) or engage in the EIP process described in Chapter 2, we argue that the process of becoming an evidence-informed practitioner is closer to our notion of what EIP looks like when it is delivered in actual school settings. In our view, evidence-informed school social work practitioners adopt a process of lifelong learning that involves regularly posing questions of direct practical importance to clients and engaging in a search for the best available evidence. Because there is accumulating evidence that school contextual features relate to the quality of both prevention and intervention programming (Gottfredson et al., 2002; Payne, 2008; Payne et al., 2006), we place emphasis on research generated on school-based prevention and intervention that is grounded in contemporary education frameworks and considers the multiple players in school settings as well as their goals and preferences. Many times, this will involve deciding with them to implement the most empirically validated treatment available, but only after the school social worker and child, teacher, or parent have joined in the EIP process outlined in this chapter.

EVIDENCE-INFORMED SCHOOL SOCIAL WORK PRACTITIONER STEPS

The EIP process that will be used in Chapters 4–14 employs the following steps: (1) defining the issue conceptually, (2) developing an answerable question, (3) investigating the evidence privileging school-based prevention and intervention research, (4) appraising the evidence, (5) examining the evidence within the context of contemporary education models, (6) adapting and applying the evidence within the context of school settings, (7) considering evaluation approaches, and (8) reflecting on the whole EIP process described above.

DEFINING THE ISSUE CONCEPTUALLY

Prior to identifying an answerable question, the issue under investigation is defined. Box 3.1 lists a "Top 9" of clinical and practice problems that were reported by a significant percentage of respondents in two recent surveys of school social workers (Kelly, 2008; Kelly et al., 2009). As can be seen from the box, these nine topics (check out "Lessons Learned," Chapter 14, for what happened to our 10th topic, effective interventions to help with the transition to adulthood) are really a composite of two sets of survey data, one of Illinois school social workers (n = 821) and the other of a national census sample of school social workers (n = 1,639). In these surveys, we asked these questions of school social workers: *"Which of the following problems do your students most often seek school social work services for?" "Which of the following are major psychosocial stressors that affect the families you work with most often at your school(s)?" "When working to support children prior to having them referred for your services, to what extent do you rely on the following approaches?"*

The topics we've chosen are by no means exhaustive, and it was not our intention in this book to claim to be the sole resource for school social workers wishing to be evidence-informed. These topics were, however, consistently rated by a significant portion of our school social work survey respondents as crucial clinical problems they struggled to address effectively. Rather than representing

---

BOX 3.1 THE TOP 10 SCHOOL-BASED TOPICS FOR *SCHOOL SOCIAL WORK: AN EVIDENCE-INFORMED FRAMEWORK FOR PRACTICE*

1. Tier 2 interventions for at-risk students
2. Increasing parental engagement with schools
3. Effective consultation with teachers and implementation of behavior intervention plans for students
4. Helping students cope with their parents divorce
5. Preventing bullying behaviors in school settings
6. Social skills training for children in schools
7. Assisting students in managing anxiety disorders at school
8. Creating effective interventions to help students with Attention-Deficit Hyperactivity Disorder (ADHD)
9. Increasing student compliance with classroom rules
10. Helping students plan for a successful post-high school transition

Sources for these 10 topics: 2008 National School Social Work Survey (Kelly, Berzin, Frey, Alvarez, Shaffer, & O'Brien, 2008); 2006 Illinois School Social Work Survey (Kelly, 2008).

an exhaustive list, the survey data we've collected in the past three years indicate to us at least some common themes in school social work practice that can serve as a starting point for modeling the evidence-informed approach in this book. This process accounts for the fact that some chapters focus on behaviors (e.g., noncompliance), intervention approaches (e.g., social skills groups), processes (e.g., behavior intervention planning), and diagnoses (e.g., attention deficit hyperactivity disorder, or ADHD). In addition to giving readers access to the actual resources and ideas contained in the following 10 chapters, it is our hope that they become engaged and even inspired by our EIP process and can them begin to use it to inform their own work immediately, whatever the presenting issues are that they face in their schools.

ANSWERABLE QUESTION

Because so many different kinds of questions can be asked in an evidence-informed process, we suggest that this first step be heavily informed by the school client's input into what the individual sees as the major problem, as well as what the school social worker is assessing based on the referral he or she was given for the school client. For a further discussion of developing answerable questions, see the previous chapter.

INVESTIGATING THE EVIDENCE

Clearinghouses, databases, and professional books were used in each search. In terms of clearinghouses, three of them are essential for school social workers. These include the Campbell Collaboration (www.campbellcollaboration.org), SAMHSA's Registry of Evidence-Informed Programs and Practices (www.nrepp.samhsa.gov), and the Cochrane Collaboration (www.cochrane.org). All of these databases are free and open to any practitioner, client, or researcher. For a comparison of the rigor used by these clearinghouses, see Box 3.2. With regard to databases, ERIC (www.eric.ed.gov), PubMed (www.pubmed.gov), PsycINFO, and Social Work Abstracts are often the most relevant databases for school social workers to search for EIP questions. Social Work Abstracts and PsycINFO, however, can be accessed only by academic users since they are proprietary databases that are typically subscribed to only by university library systems. Individual users can subscribe, but most would find the databases prohibitively expensive. (In Illinois, where several of us live, our state has a statewide library catalog that provides free access to journal articles and journal databases via local public libraries for residents with a library card. We suggest checking into your community and state's library system.)

Finally, professional books that specialize in school-based prevention and intervention were consulted. They include books that were readily available and relevant, and typically represented a combination of school social work books and those from other disciplines.

Before conducting the searches for this book, we discussed the extent to which we should standardize the specific sources from which we searched (e.g., specify that all authors utilize a particular set of proprietary sources). We discussed whether we should conduct our own formal systematic reviews (see Littell et al., 2008). And we wondered whether we should perhaps avoid "reinventing the wheel" and rely heavily on clearinghouses that have already classified the state of evidence undergirding particular prevention and intervention strategies. We decided against each of these approaches and opted instead to standardize only the type of source (e.g., clearinghouses, proprietary databases, professional texts) and allow each chapter's lead author discretion in the specific materials extracted, with the proviso that the search process be fully described.

We think there are several advantages to this approach. First, we believe that it better approximates the potential resources available to and time constraints on school practitioners; that is, we believe this approach has ecological validity. We make the assumption that practitioners do not likely have the training or time to conduct formal systematic reviews. We are also aware that some topic areas of interest to practitioners may not have been systematically reviewed. A second advantage of this approach is that it models the importance of utilizing both primary and secondary sources to compile information about school-based prevention and intervention strategies. This is perhaps most germane to the use of clearinghouses, which have come under attack recently on the grounds that they may overstate the benefits of particular intervention strategies—especially in areas of school-based prevention and intervention—and may contain important biases (for a discussion of these issues; Gorman, 2005). Third, we believe this approach—and our stance that our approach is a process—better reflects the inherent messiness in implementation in school settings (Franklin & Kelly, 2009). Finally, we believe that an abiding understanding of the uncertainty of and evolving nature of evidence is especially critical in the context of the emerging nature of the school-based practice knowledge base as well as the rapid proliferation of literature, where new evidence will be emerging in real time. In this sense, this approach is akin to developing a set of hypotheses about what may help and continually gathering evidence that addresses the extent of support for these hypotheses (see Gorman, 2005).

We believe these advantages outweigh the obvious limitations in this process—our reviews will, by definition, be selective and filtered through the unique experiences of each chapter author.

BOX 3.2 DIFFERENCES IN RIGOR AMONG MAJOR CLEARINGHOUSES

Campbell Collaboration (C2)	*NREPP*	*What Works*
Focus: Education, criminal justice, & social welfare.	Focus: Mental disorders & Substance use disorders	Focus: Academics, Character education, & Dropout prevention
C2 contains both randomized and nonrandomized experiments in separate databases.	Research quality is evaluated and rated by six criteria: 1. Reliability of measures	Research is evaluated and rated by six criteria: 1. Study design (RCTs or QEDs)
Searchable fields allow users to determine the level of rigor.	2. Validity of measures (e.g., criterion validity)	2. Attrition problems
Quantitative syntheses must contain some randomized experiments, but the estimate of intervention effects must separate the two types of experiments.	3. Intervention fidelity (e.g., use of a reliable & valid fidelity measure)	3. Baseline equivalence of control/comparison groups vs. treatment groups
	4. Missing data & attrition	4. Potential confounding factors (i.e., level of experimental control)
Aspects of study validity are never summarized into a total quality score.	5. Potential confounding variables (i.e., level of experimental control)	5. Reasons for not meeting standards (e.g., outcome measures)
	6. Appropriateness of analysis (i.e., sample size and statistical power)	6. Corrections and adjustments to effect size.
Source: Shadish & Myers (2004)	*Source:* U.S. Dept. of Health & Human Services (2008c)	*Source:* U.S. Dept. of Education IES (2008b)

CATEGORIZING AND INTERPRETING THE EVIDENCE

Each author categorized and interpreted the evidence that was generated through the search process. As we noted in Chapter 1, there are many rubrics by which evidence supporting interventions can be classified; the parameters outlining what constitutes "well-established" treatments outlined by Division 12 of the American Psychological Association as well as the Institute for Education Science/Department of Education guidelines are two such exemplars. Although these systems are not identical and may privilege efficacy (i.e., lab-based) versus effectiveness (i.e., real world) studies (Chambless & Hollon, 1998), both implicitly utilize evidence hierarchies and value the independent replication of studies (see Sackett et al., 2000). We thus elected to organize our evidence using (1) an explicit hierarchy (descending from systematic reviews/meta-analyses to experimental designs to nonexperimental designs), (2) emphasis on the extent of independent replication, and (3) criteria related to effectiveness—that is, the potential transportability into real-world school settings. Throughout, we provide details on the number of studies, whether replications were independent, and whether interventions were manualized so that the interested reader can readily compare these to APA and DOE (as well as other) frameworks.

For this book, each chapter had a lead author, and the selection of clearinghouses, databases, and books was left to the discretion of that researcher. This was done to increase the relevancy of the search process. For example, health-related problems that involve medication as a primary intervention modality, such attention-deficit disorders, are more likely to be covered in health-related databases such as PubMed (aka Medline).

We believe that practitioners will find the clearinghouses easiest to use when investigating the evidence. The information contained therein is free and already appraised by experts in the field. The databases will be the most difficult because it takes time and practice to learn effective search strategies that narrow the abstracts down to the most relevant and most research-based. Even with this skill, however, most full-text articles are not available outside of an academic setting. We strongly recommend that social workers form researcher–practitioner partnerships to overcome this problem (Barlow et al., 1993; Franklin & McNeil, 1992; Hess & Mullen, 1995). Finally, professional books occupy the middle ground. The danger here is that publishers have caught on to the idea that "evidence-based" is a hot topic and so titles may be deceiving when it comes to the actual strength of the evidence behind the interventions. A recent search of Amazon.com returned over 78,000 books with this phrase! We therefore issue a "caveat emptor" or "buyer beware" warning about professional books claiming to be empirically supported (Rubin & Parrish, 2007).

In the end, we combined both the APA criteria and the U.S. Department of Education criteria to create three categories by which to classify the quality of the evidence obtained. Interventions that earned the most rigorous classification— *Highly Recommend*—met the following criteria: (1) tested using a randomized controlled trial or quasi-experimental design, (2) tested with diverse child and/or adolescent populations, (3) tested in a school setting, (4) tested by independent researchers, (5) demonstrated to maintain progress six months after treatment, (6) submitted to a double-blind peer review, and (g) practical in terms of time and cost. (Time considerations are crucial when schools are understaffed, thus we were looking for interventions that could be conducted within one semester (18 weeks) of the school year. Most school social workers also have limited budgets, thus we were searching for interventions that cost less than $500/year. These criterion also dramatically cut down the number of feasible interventions.)

The second category—*Recommended (with caution)*—was assigned to interventions that have been (1) tested using a randomized controlled trial or

quasi-experimental design, (2) tested with different child and/or adolescent populations, (3) tested in a community setting, (4) tested by researchers at least twice,
(5) demonstrated to maintain progress at least three months after treatment, (6)
submitted to a double-blind peer review, and (7) feasible in terms of time and cost.

The third category—*Emerging*—was assigned to interventions that have been
(1) tested with a pretest/posttest design, (2) tested with child and/or adolescent
populations, (3) tested in a university setting, (4) tested by a team of researchers,
(5) demonstrated to maintain progress at least three months after treatment, (6)
submitted to peer and/or editorial review, and (7) feasible in terms of time and cost.

There is a fourth group of interventions that we might label *iatrogenic* because
they have been demonstrated to hurt some children or haven't been sufficiently
evaluated on the types of clients we encounter in a school setting. Some of these
harmful practices are unfortunately commonly employed in schools and we
outline some of them using an EIP process in Chapter 13.

An additional component in this text is to reflect upon the process. Chapters
4–12 attempt to promote transparency and facilitate discussion with regard to
the advantages and imperfections of engaging in the evidence-informed process
described here. We're also concerned that from the outset of this second section
we express our humility at trying to capture something approaching the key
issues for school social workers practicing all over this country. What follows is
our effort to be transparent about what we know (and still don't, or perhaps
worse, are still unsure about) even after pursuing the best available evidence
describing the fundamental practice issues school social workers face and what
we believe to be some of the potentially best interventions for them to pursue in
addressing those key practice issues.

EXAMINING THE EVIDENCE WITHIN THE CONTEXT OF CONTEMPORARY EDUCATION MODELS

The volume and quality of the interventions identified after we examined and
appraised the evidence are then discussed in relation to response to intervention
(RTI) models. In the final chapter, we discuss the findings in terms of how they
map onto the clinical quadrants. In situations where there is inadequate evidence
to guide practice, these models will be used to make recommendations regarding
the types of interventions that appear the most promising.

ADAPTING AND APPLYING THE EVIDENCE IN THE CONTEXT OF SCHOOL SETTINGS

Raines (2008a) argues that school social workers should take three primary
factors into account when adapting scientifically based interventions. These

include developmental considerations, cultural sensitivity, and contextual constraints of working in schools. These are considered in the context of practice with children in educational settings.

Developmental Adaptations

We should always be aware of the developmental level of the child. This includes adjusting the intervention to allow for more therapeutic engagement (especially for involuntary clients), affective vocabulary, cognitive abilities, "homework" tasks, and parental involvement. First, since students seldom self-refer, most pupils should be regarded as nonvoluntary. This means that prior to launching an empirically supported intervention, group leaders should slow down and enable the group to engage with the worker and the other members (McKay et al., 1996). Second, some students may not have an affective vocabulary beyond obscenities. Practitioners may need to temporarily suspend ordinary school prohibitions about vulgar language while simultaneously educating students about categories and intensities of feelings (Ribordy et al., 1988). For example, "angry" can be nuanced for intensity by brainstorming other forms, such as "ticked off" or "enraged." Third, many cognitive therapy techniques require metacognitive skills that younger students will not have mastered (Kingery et al., 2006). A developmentally appropriate approach requires that these be modified to fit their level of self-understanding. For example, the concept of cognitive distortions can be translated "thinking traps" and cognitive restructuring can be called "coping clues." Fourth, many behavioral therapy techniques refer to "homework." This is a loaded word for many children and can be neutralized by using terms such as "project" or "experiment" (Cooper, 2001). Finally, since externalizing children often require consistent structure and internalizing children often engage in referencing their parents' reactions to events, it is important to educate parents about these children's respective needs (McCart et al., 2006; Nock et al., 2004).

Cultural Variations

We should always address the issue of cultural sensitivity. This is especially important in schools that have the fewest minority students because they generally have a disproportional representation of minority students in special education (National Research Council, 2002). Turner (2000) posits that practitioners should attend to seven important factors when adapting programs for minority families. First, social workers should recognize that certain protective factors have greater salience among certain groups (e.g., church attendance among African Americans). Second, we should recognize that different families have varying degrees of cultural assimilation and comfort levels with majority traditions. Third, we should recognize intrafamily differences in acculturation so that children often adapt more quickly than their parents. Fourth, we should note that there are considerable differences in the reasons for migration. Families that emigrate from their homelands voluntarily have a much easier time adjusting than those who are forced to emigrate. Fifth, clinicians should be alert to the possibility of trauma for families that have left their home countries because of political oppression. Sixth, we should pay attention to the family's work status and economic stressors. Many former professionals lack credentials to practice in this country and are forced to assume low-paying jobs. Seventh, schools should not assume that families are automatically literate in their native language (Jensen, 2001).

Contextual Adaptations

Finally, we should consider the contextual constraints of delivering interventions within a public school. While schools have become the default providers of mental health interventions for children (Rones & Hoagwood, 2000), this does not mean that they are ideally suited to this purpose.

EVALUATION

Next, recommendations are provided for how interventions related to each chapter can be evaluated. Within this section, process and outcome evaluation strategies are addressed including instruments known to measure variables relevant to the behaviors likely to be addressed that are known to have established psychometric properties.

LESSONS LEARNED

An additional component in this text is to reflect upon the process. Chapters 4–12 end with a Lessons Learned section in an attempt to promote transparency and facilitate discussion with regard to the advantages and imperfections of engaging in the evidence-informed process.

CONCLUSION

We believe evidence-informed school social work practitioners adopt a process of lifelong learning that involves regularly posing questions of direct practical importance to clients; engaging in a search for the best available evidence privileging the school-based prevention and intervention research and contemporary education frameworks; and taking appropriate action in a transparent collaboration that is in concert with children's, teachers', and parents' goals and preferences. Many times, this will involve deciding with them to implement the most empirically validated treatment available, but only after the school social worker and child, teacher, or parent have joined in the EIP process outlined in this chapter. In the next several chapters, we apply the evidence-informed process to common problems faced by school social workers and reflect on our experiences.

4

EMPIRICALLY SUPPORTED TIER 2
INTERVENTIONS

This chapter discusses how to locate, appraise, adapt, and apply empirically supported Tier 2 interventions as an essential component of response to intervention (RTI). These ideas come from our national survey data, in which a significant number of respondents (70%) said that they regularly try to "lead effective small groups with students as a prevention activity." This chapter also demonstrates how to monitor the progress of students receiving Tier 2 interventions and evaluates the effectiveness of interventions employed using an evidence-informed practice (EBP) perspective.

Practitioners in some schools believe that their schools already offer Tier 2 interventions. First, many schools offer Title I reading programs for low-income youth who come from impoverished literacy environments both at home and in their communities. In these schools, reading specialists (or supervised paraprofessionals) design and lead reading groups for low-achieving students (Brown et al., 2005). Second, programs such as social skills groups, divorce groups, and problem-solving groups are often delivered by school-based mental health professionals (Openshaw, 2008). These offerings, however, too often depend on the inclination and competence of the individual educators or school social workers rather than on any systemic effort to ameliorate the psychosocial difficulties of students.

The problem-solving steps in RTI are described in Figure 4.1. These five steps offer a natural place to integrate EBP and RTI. First, *problem identification* requires social workers to determine whether there is a discrepancy between what is expected and what is actually happening. This means that social workers should be familiar with both academic and behavioral standards and know how

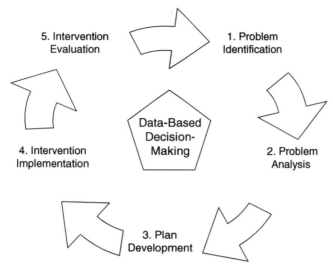

FIGURE 4.1 Problem-solving process in RTI.

to assess which students are not measuring up to expectations. Second, *problem analysis* demands that practitioners understand why the problem is occurring and use a student-in-environment perspective to do so. Fortunately, RTI is ideally suited for the ecological approach. Third, *plan development* compels school social workers to know which interventions are research-based and how to appropriately adapt them to fit the characteristics of students at their schools. Fourth, *intervention implementation* requires practitioners to be mindful of how the intervention will be carried out faithfully by teachers or other school personnel. Finally, *intervention evaluation* obliges social workers to know how to collect and analyze their own data to determine whether students are responding to the intervention.

EMPIRICALLY SUPPORTED INTERVENTIONS

This section follows the general outline for evidence-based practice discussed in Chapter 3. Accordingly, it addresses asking an answerable question, investigating the evidence, appraising the evidence, using clinical lenses, adapting and applying the evidence, and evaluating the outcome.

ANSWERABLE QUESTION

Gibbs (2003) recommends that practitioners formulate an answerable question before exploring the current research. For the following search, we used this question: "What are the empirically supported interventions for groups of students with social or emotional problems?"

APPRAISING THE EVIDENCE

The most surprising part of these multiple searches was the diversity of interventions found. In fact, only five common references occurred across the three searches: DeRosier (2004); Glodich et al. (2001); Masia et al. (2001); Reeker et al. (1997); and Saltzman et al. (2001). How do we account for the wide number of supposedly "empirically supported" interventions? Very simply, different researchers use different standards for evidence. This is why the U.S. Department of Education's definition of scientifically based research in Chapter 1 is so important. Readers may remember that the authors of this book added two extra factors to the Department of Education's criteria. First, the criterion that most studies failed to consider is follow-up. Only about 20% of the research studies conducted any follow-up measurement at all—whether we examined this by one month, three months, six months, or twelve months. Second, we were looking for interventions that were not only effective, but also efficient in terms of time and money spent. This criterion also dramatically cut down the number of feasible interventions.

HIGHLY RECOMMENDED

Among the group interventions that meet the criteria for *Highly Recommended*, we found three interventions. *Coping Cat* (www.childanxiety.org) is a manualized cognitive-behavioral intervention ("manualized" interventions are hereon defined as interventions for which a specific step-by-step treatment manual exists for use by practitioners) for anxiety disorders in youth, ages 6-17. There is also an accompanying workbook for children. The goal of the treatment is not to rid the child of anxiety but to teach a cognitive approach for coping with it. In addition to this cognitive component, there are behavioral skill rehearsals. These skill rehearsals include in-session role-plays and imaginary tasks as well as out-of-session homework to perform in real life. Generally, the program lasts 16 weeks with two interspersed sessions for parents. The first half of the program builds the FEAR plan, an acronym for Feeling frightened? (teaching relaxation techniques); Expecting bad things to happen? (challenging negative self-talk); Attitudess and Actions that might help (taking assertive steps); and Results and Rewards (with self-monitoring and contingent reinforcement). The second half of the program addresses exposure (both imaginal and in vivo) and practice (outside the office). Parent sessions are important because children often take their cues from adults (Kendall, Aschenbrand, & Hudson, 2003). *The Coping with Depression Course for*

Adolescents (http://www.kpchr.org/public/acwd/acwd.html) is a manualized cognitive-behavioral intervention for adolescents with depression. The main goal is to help teens become aware of unconscious negative attributions that blame the self for failures but do not give credit for successes. The program lasts 16 sessions and focuses on eight skills: mood monitoring, social skills, pleasant activities, relaxation, constructive thinking, communication, negotiation and problem solving, and maintenance of gains. To avoid relapse, booster sessions are recommended at four-month interludes over a two-year span (Rohde et al., 2005). *Social Information Processing* is based on Crick and Dodge's (1994) observation that cognitive distortions (e.g., hostile attributions) lead to socially inappropriate behaviors. This leads to interventions that target one of five social information processing stages: (1) encoding of situational cues, (2) interpretation of social cues, (3) selection of instrumental goals, (4) generation of possible responses, and (5) selection of a response (Lansford et al., 2006). Making Choices is a prevention program based on *social information processing* theory (Conner, 2006; Fraser et al., 2004; Smokowski et al., 2004; Terzian, 2007). The curriculum has seven units with 29 lessons. The units include the following topics: (1) Learning about emotions and feelings; (2) Encoding: Identifying social cues; (3) Interpretation: Making sense of social cues; (4) Goal formulation and refinement: Setting social goals; (5) Response search and formulation: Inventing options; (6) Response decision: Making a choice; and (7) Enactment: Acting on choices (Fraser et al., 2000). Unfortunately, each of the program evaluations have been conducted by the same team of researchers or their students that developed the intervention itself with no independent evaluations being conducted by researchers without any stake in the intervention's success. For another *social information processing program*, see Chapter 10.

RECOMMENDED (WITH CAUTION)

Among the group interventions that meet the criteria for *Recommended*, we find the following four interventions. *Accelerated Middle Schools* (www.whatworks.ed.gov) are self-contained programs for middle-school students who are behind at least one grade level that aim to help them catch up with their same-age peers. This program can be a stand-alone middle-school intervention or a program within a regular school. *Accelerated Middle Schools* were successful in helping students stay in school as well as progress in school. Unfortunately, there were no long-term data to demonstrate that it helped students complete school. *Check & Connect* (http://ici.umn.edu/checkandconnect) is a manualized mentoring program for elementary and middle-school children aimed at increasing student engagement. Mentors routinely "check" school functioning indicators (e.g., attendance, grades, suspensions, and tardiness), "connect" with students, and keep parents apprised of their progress. Teachers are asked to rate indicators of academic engagement such

TABLE 4.1

Group Intervention	Research Design	Participants (Child/ Adolescent)	Test Site	Researcher Teams	Follow-Up Period	Review Process	Feasibility (Cost & Time)
Accelerated Middle Schools	RCTs	6th–8th grade	Schools	2	1 year	Blind peer review	$11,000/child 2 years
ACTION Program for Depression	RCTs	Ages 9–14	Schools	1	3 months	Blind peer review	$24/Leader's manual $26.95/workbook 20 group sessions + 2 individual sessions
Behavior Education Program	QED	K–9th grade	Schools	1	None	Blind peer review	N/A20–30 min/day
Check & Connect	RCTs	4th–12th grade	Schools	2	1 year	Blind peer review	$1400/child2–4 years
Cognitive-Behavioral Social Skills	RCT	Ages 14–21	School	1	None	Dissertation committee	N/A 6 group sessions
Cognitive Therapy for Adolescent Stress	RCT	7–12th grade	Schools	1	None	Dissertation committee	N/A 5 45-min group sessions + 5 20-min individual sessions
Coping Cat	RCTs	Ages 6–17	Community & School	3	1–3.5 years	Blind peer review	$46/child 16 weeks
Coping Koala/FRIENDS	RCTs	Ages 7–14	Schools	1	6 months	Blind peer review	$49.50/Leader's manual $17.60/workbook 10 group sessions
Coping with Depression Course—Adolescents	RCTs	Ages 14–18	Community & School	3+	2 years	Blind peer review	N/A 16 2-hour group sessions
Cultivating Hardiness	RCT	9th grade girls	Schools	1	None		N/A 8 weeks

						Dissertation committee	
Early Risers Skills for Success	RCT	K–4th grade	Community & School	1	2 years	Blind peer review	$1710/child ff day 6-week summer day camp + 32-week school group + 5 family nights
Incredible Years	RCTs	Ages 2–12	School	3+	6–18 months	Blind peer-review	$775/child 14 weeks
Social Information Processing	Meta-analysis	Ages 6–16	School	3+	2–52 weeks	Blind peer-review	$50/group session 8-16 weeks
Trauma/Grief-Focused	RCTs	Ages 12–18	Community & School	1	4 months	Blind peer-review	N/A 15–30 weeks

Note: N/A = Not available or varies widely; RCT = randomized control trial; QED = quasi-experimental design.

as preparation for class, work completion, and persistence (Anderson et al., 2004). Students remain in the program for at least two years (Lehr et al., 2004). Regrettably, all evaluations of the program have been done by the same research team or their students. *Early Risers* (http://www.psychiatry.umn.edu/psychiatry/ research/earlyrisers/home.html) is a multimodal program for elementary and middle-school youth that aims to prevent juvenile delinquency and substance abuse. The five components include (1) an academic and social development summer program; (2) a two-hour per week after-school program; (3) child support through monitoring and mentoring as well as teacher consultation and parent support; (4) parenting skills programs five times per year; and (5) family support such as motivational counseling, assistance with basic living needs, and crisis intervention. Benefits of participation for students included academic achievement, greater self-regulation of behavior, and improved social skills. Benefits of participation for parents included stronger investment in their children and decreased personal distress. Unfortunately, the only program evaluations have been carried out by the research team that designed the intervention, and the intervention, like most multicomponent programs, is expensive. The Incredible Years program (www.incredibleyears.com) is discussed in more detail in Chapters 5 and 10.

EMERGING

Among the group interventions that meet the criteria for *Emerging*, we find the following: the ACTION program for depressed children (Stark et al., 2004a, 2004b); the Behavior Education Program (Crone et al., 2004); the Coping Koala/FRIENDS program for anxious children (Barrett et al., 1999a, 1999b, 1999c); and the Trauma/Grief-Focused Group Psychotherapy (Saltzman et al., 2006). Most of the other interventions failed to qualify due to a lack of three-month follow-up results. For a complete summary of the seven criteria applied to each of these programs, see Table 4.1.

CLINICAL LENSES

Subsequent chapters will address where the interventions fit in terms of both the clinical quadrants and response to intervention. This chapter discusses primarily the RTI framework is the basis for the Tier 2 interventions being discussed in his chapter.

CLINICAL QUADRANTS

Not surprisingly, the majority of the interventions would fall under quadrant C—Interventions that involve and target individuals, small groups, and families.

One of the interventions would fall under quadrants B and D since it involves large groups and targets both systemic and student change. This is the *Check & Connect* program that identifies student, family, peers, school, and community contributions to students dropping out. For example, some of the school policy barriers include out-of-school suspensions, administrative transfers, and limited parent outreach (Evelo et al., 1996). Three of the interventions, however, would fall under quadrant D. These are Accelerated Middle Schools, the Behavior Education Program, and *Early Risers*. Accelerated Middle Schools is a schoolwide intervention that enables students who are struggling academically to catch up with their grade-level peers. The Behavior Education Program involves ALL teachers in monitoring the behavior of at-risk students and reporting to the students' monitors. The *Early Risers* program is a multicomponent program that offers a community-based six-week summer component to help students maintain academic and behavioral skills over the summer break.

ADAPTING AND APPLYING THE INTERVENTION

The first three steps in the problem-solving process were to identify which children were not responding to general education/prevention; analyze the problem; and develop a plan using scientifically based interventions. The fourth step is to implement the intervention, but we must first ask the important question, "Should I apply the intervention exactly as it has been tested?" The answer in most situations is "No." There are two compelling reasons for this negative reply. First, Pollio (2006) offers this explanation: "Clinicians need to be willing to combine the existing evidence from the literature with their own analysis of the dynamics of the situation to guide specific responses and strategies to situations" (p. 228). Second, evidence-informed practice is meant to be a collaborative endeavor (Kelly, 2008). Clinicians are supposed to take client values and preferences into account when making decisions about what intervention to employ (Haynes et al., 2002). A personal anecdote illustrates this:

> Leonard was diagnosed with ADHD and managed to obtain the highest score possible on the Conner's Teacher Rating Scale. If ever there was a candidate for Ritalin, it was Leonard. There was one problem, actually two problems. His father was a recovering alcoholic and his mother was a devout Jehovah's Witness. There was no way they were ever going to give Leonard "drugs" to help him behave. Given this situation, we opted for a behavior management plan that aimed for consistent rules and reinforcement at school and home. Such a plan would have been an excellent complement to psychotropic medication for Leonard, but given the situation we had to implement a less than optimal intervention for him and this definitely slowed down his progress.

CULTURAL ADAPTATIONS

Three different examples of culturally sensitive school-based group interventions follow. White and Rayle (2007) adapted the Strong Teens curriculum for African American male adolescents as part of a 12-session group. They used famous African American historical figures as role models to illustrate the theoretical concepts. Constantino, Malgady, and Rogler (1984) adapted Puerto Rican folktales and used them over 20 sessions to help children in kindergarten through third grade to cope with their anxieties. Kim and colleagues (2006) used popular Korean music to help Korean adolescent schoolgirls to improve relationships and self-control. The groups met for 90 minutes over six sessions. These illustrations demonstrate that culturally sensitive practitioners can use heroes, stories, and songs to increase the relevance of group interventions for their specific student populations.

CONTEXTUAL ADAPTATIONS

Context has a direct influence on two essential aspects of Tier 2 interventions: time and location. Time considerations include the frequency, duration, and scheduling of Tier 2 interventions. The frequency of Tier 2 interventions can range from one to three times per week, but most psychosocial interventions will probably occur weekly. The duration of Tier 2 interventions will depend somewhat on the frequency, but most will last for at least one marking period or typically nine weeks (Mellard & Johnson, 2008). The scheduling of Tier 2 interventions can be done three ways, each with its own advantages and disadvantages (Burns & Gibbons, 2008).

Many schools see Tier 2 interventions as strictly supplemental services. Tier 2 services must generally be scheduled during regular class times. Since No Child Left Behind measures school performance on reading, math, and science, most schools would frown on using these class times. This restriction leaves other classes, such as technology, social studies, physical education, music, and art, as the only possible time to schedule the services. The strength of this approach is that students do not miss any of their core classes, but the weakness is that students often enjoy and excel at the other classes and would be reluctant to miss them. Practitioners would be wise to avoid always picking the same class from which to pull students on a regular basis and will probably want to choose those classes where the student is not struggling to meet grade-level expectations.

Other schools have appropriately adopted a schoolwide approach to RTI and this produces two other possibilities. Some of these schools have adopted a schoolwide RTI time or a regular period in which all students either receive supplemental (e.g., gifted) services or targeted (Tier 2) services. The strength of this approach is that practitioners have a standard time for intervention; the weakness is that even if school social workers conducted a different group every day of the week, they couldn't cover the entire school during this period alone and would have to compete with other specialized support personnel if a particular child needed more than one related service. The final and perhaps best solution is to have a floating RTI time. This requires substantial centralized planning. In this model, each grade level would have its own unique RTI period during which supplemental or targeted services can be delivered. For example, the time for kindergarten may be 9–9:40 A.M., the time for first grade may be 9:40–10:20 A.M., and the time for second grade may be 10:20–11:00 A.M. The strength is that different support personnel can rotate the days of the week and still have time to reach every grade level; the weakness is that it assumes the school social worker is at the school five days per week.

The location of Tier 2 interventions has two main options. First, some school systems (e.g., Chicago Public Schools) are increasingly requiring that most services occur within the classroom. This requires practitioners to "push-in" rather than "pull-out." If 15% to 20% of children are to be served with Tier 2 interventions, then the average classroom ($\sim$ 25 students) would have five students served in this tier. The strength of this approach is that school social work services gain transparency; teachers can observe effective group management strategies and emulate them. The weakness is that there is no expectation of confidentiality regarding student disclosures (Raines, 2008a) and there is no room for differentiated intervention; every group would need to be cross-categorical (e.g., a problem-solving group). Second, school social workers can meet in a separate location, such as the social worker's office or other vacant space. The strength of this approach is that students can express confidential concerns and social workers can gather students from several classrooms for a targeted intervention. The weakness is that it assumes the school building actually has sufficient space to meet in small groups and this may not be true in overcrowded schools.

EVALUATION

Evaluation should be done on two levels. First, practitioners should conduct a process evaluation to determine whether the interventions were employed as intended. Second, practitioners should conduct an outcome evaluation to determine whether the students responded as hoped.

PROCESS EVALUATION

While we have suggested that practitioners adapt the scientifically based intervention before implementing the intervention, this should not be interpreted to mean that "anything goes." Burns and Gibbons (2008) recommend eight questions regarding Tier 2 reading instruction that can be adapted for social-emotional interventions.

1. Was the intervention implemented by a qualified teacher/trainer? (e.g., Did the instructor receive specialized training, continuing education, or supervision on the intervention?)
2. Was the intervention delivered to a group of six or fewer children?
3. Was the intervention delivered as frequently as the research suggested? (e.g., twice weekly).
4. Was the intervention provided in addition to (not a substitute for) a Tier 1 intervention?
5. Was the intervention delivered for as long as the research suggested? (e.g., nine weeks).
6. Was progress regularly monitored throughout the intervention?
7. Did the intervention include the core components necessary for effectiveness?
8. Was the intervention employed with empirically supported generic factors (i.e., strengths-focus, empathic relationships, and positive expectations)?

EVALUATING PROGRESS

An astute question about employing empirically based interventions is that once we have adapted and applied them, "How do we know they're effective?" The short answer is, "We don't!" In fact, even if we did not adapt them, we would not necessarily know whether they were effective for our group of students.

DATA COLLECTION

To determine effectiveness we must routinely collect and analyze relevant data. Malecki and Demaray (2007) use the RIOT acronym to summarize the various ways to collect data in RTI.

R is for Review records. Schools regularly collect an enormous amount of data about students but they seldom analyze it to monitor student progress. Some of the best archival data that school social workers can use includes school attendance, tardiness, office disciplinary referrals, nurse visits, and in-school work completion ratios. Let's discuss each in turn. Attendance is vitally important for two reasons: students who don't attend can't learn, and a school's funding often depends on its attendance rate (Dibble, 2004). Tardiness is especially important because many schools deliver their core instruction first thing in the morning, so that students who arrive late miss vital teaching. Office disciplinary referrals are a global indicator of a student's deportment in school (Irvin et al., 2006). Smart monitors of office disciplinary referrals also analyze which teachers refer most often, where the infraction occurs, and the time of the outburst. Nurse visits are an easy way to track internalizing children who present with somatic complaints like headaches or stomachaches. A work completion ratio is the number of assignments completed divided by the number assigned. While homework completion is notoriously unreliable due to the number of unknown variables (including who actually did the homework), in-school work completion tells us more about the ability and willingness of the student to manage the workload.

I is for Interview informants. Gerber (2003) notes that teacher performance is still the largest factor in student achievement. Interviewing teachers about students' progress enables us to obtain an in-depth perspective. Raines (2008b) has developed a set of rubrics for teachers that enables them to rate how well a student is performing in the areas of emotional expression, on-task behavior, and social cooperation. Since teachers are accustomed to rubrics, they represent a user-friendly and efficient approach to collecting these data (Montgomery, 2000; Ross-Fisher, 2005). Another easy way to monitor progress is to interview students and ask them a scaled question. Scaled questions for pain are now one of the vital signs that nurses use by asking, "On a scale from 1 to 10, how would you rate your pain?" (Joint Commission on Accreditation of Healthcare Organizations, 2004). Raines (2008b) points out that the last word in this question can address any feeling state, such as sadness, anxiety, or anger.

O is for Observation. Volpe et al. (2005) compared seven widely used observational coding systems. Most of these recommend that observers use an index peer (of the same age and gender) to obtain normative data. Two of the systems could be used with a personal digital assistant (or Palm): Behavioral Observation of Students in Schools (Shapiro, 2004) and the Student Observation System of the BASC (Reynolds & Kamphaus, 2004). Volpe and colleagues concluded that most observational systems were treatment sensitive and appropriate for progress monitoring.

T is for Testing. The problem with most of the generic behavioral rating scales used in schools is that they seldom match the reason for referral. Aside from the diagnostic measures mentioned above, practitioners should become familiar with rapid assessment instruments (RAIs). Fischer and Corcoran (2007) have compiled almost 60 RAI measures for children and adolescents that enable practitioners to quickly determine students' responsiveness to intervention, but new ones can be found by searching PsycINFO as well. For example, a group of school social workers recently approached me about how to measure the effectiveness of a social skills group for adolescents with autism. Working collaboratively, we found the Autism Social Skills Profile (Bellini & Hopf, 2007), a strengths-based RAI designed for children 6–17 with autism spectrum disorder to monitor their progress toward IEP goals.

LESSONS LEARNED

STRENGTHS

The answerable question led to a wealth of group interventions for children and adolescents. There are few common problems that students face that cannot be addressed in a group format. That said, clearly practitioners should be wary of a "one-size-fits-all" approach and screen students accordingly. There may be some children who are contraindicated for group work. Such children would include those with no desire to help their peers or those who would want to manipulate their peers for their own ends. If, however, students are willing and able to engage in mutual support, group interventions are a great opportunity to do so.

Many of the group programs have a treatment manual or similar guide that novice practitioners will appreciate and gradually adapt as they become more familiar with the material. Wiggins (2005), in a book review of Waterman and Walker's (2001) group program, appreciates that the manual offers seven different modules and a host of forms in the appendices. Other practitioners will find similar characteristics in other group programs.

WEAKNESSES

First, it was disappointing that so few of the group programs had been followed for their long-term effectiveness. Less than 20% of the interventions provided any follow-up data that tracked participants' progress for three months after the program was over. To be fair, the U.S. Department of Education does not require this as one of its appraisal criteria, but we think it should. If schools are going to invest large sums of money in secondary prevention programs, they ought to have some inkling about whether these programs deliver results that will stand the test of time. Second, it was disappointing that so many programs had not been tested by independent teams of researchers. It should be noted that this was not easily determined. On many occasions a dissertation seemed to offer an independent evaluation; only later did the reader discover that the program developers had served as the dissertation advisers.

CONCLUSION

This review allows us to conclude that there are empirically supported interventions for school social workers to use at Tier 2. Most of these fall squarely into quadrant C, but a few involve systemic interventions that should be one of the strengths of school social workers (Raines, 2006). These interventions should not be employed woodenly, but they should be filtered through practitioners' clinical expertise and experience with students in their school. This means that the interventions will need to be adapted for a good fit. These adaptations include developmental, cultural, and contextual modifications to the strategies or programs used. There is no empirically supported intervention that will work for all students. This is the reason for continual progress monitoring throughout the process of intervention. Progress monitoring involves the regular and timely collection of data. In RTI, there are four approaches to data collection: Reviewing records, Interview, Observation, and Testing. Armed with this practice-based evidence, the school-based team can make data-based decisions about how students are responding to intervention.

5

PARENT INVOLVEMENT

There is widespread consensus that parent involvement in their children's schooling plays an important role in both positive student- and school-related outcomes. Since 1975, federal legislation and directives have placed an explicit value upon and have encouraged efforts related to the promotion of parent involvement in schooling (for a brief review of this history, see Broussard, 2003). Key examples include federal directives for schools and districts to enhance parent involvement specified in the Goals 2000 Act; the stated and inherent values of active collaboration, information sharing, and problem solving among parents and educators to meet the educational needs of students with disabilities, provided for in federal special education legislation; and current emphases on increased accountability to parents and communities through transparent state achievement standards and measured progress toward those standards and school choice embodied in No Child Left Behind. Second, there is recognition that basic premises of family-driven care philosophically unify all child-serving systems including mental health, education, and child welfare services (Duchnowski & Kutash, 2007). Finally, and perhaps of most salience to school social work practitioners, brokering home-school communication patterns and processes represents what is historically generally agreed to constitute a central professional role (Bowen, 1999; Broussard, 2003; Shaffer, 2006), and national survey data suggest that many schools and districts still engage in limited forms of parent involvement efforts (Michael et al., 2007).

CONCEPTUAL DEFINITION OF THE ISSUE

Parents may be involved in their children's schooling in multiple ways (Epstein & Sanders, 2002; Grolnick & Slowiaczek, 1994). Rosenzweig (2000) proposes a tripartite classification system including parenting practices covering fundamental (e.g., basic child rearing practices), academic-oriented (monitoring school progress, school-related communication, assistance with academic skill development), and school participation domains (see also Nettles et al., 2008). Hoover-Dempsey and her colleagues (2005) argue that how parents become involved in school depends on a complex mix of their own beliefs and attitudes toward involvement, characteristics of their child, family background characteristics, and school and school staff factors. Given this multiplicity of factors and depending on the nature of the involvement—as well as school support for involvement—we would expect that a given form of parent involvement could variably relate to a multiple set of outcomes at child, parent, and/or school levels.

ORGANIZING AND INTERPRETING THE EVIDENCE

With the broad definition of parent involvement and the potentially wide range of outcomes possible, the guiding question was purposefully posed narrowly: How can school staff intervene to directly involve parents in school or their children's academic lives, especially as it results in school participation and engagement? Relevant clearinghouses, databases, and academic texts were examined to investigate the answerable question. Table 5.1, Investigating the Evidence: Parent Involvement, summarizes the search strategies and results. In this section, the evidence related to the content, effectiveness, and fidelity of parent involvement approaches was examined. The section on effectiveness follows a hierarchy of evidence approach.

As shown in Table 5.1, both meta-analyses and peer reviewed studies were identified through our search. Before discussing findings generated from these meta-analytic reviews, note two important issues that have direct relevance to interpreting the evidence in this area. First, evidence hierarchies often make a distinction between meta-analyses that synthesize experimental versus observational findings, privileging the experimental over the observational. A group of meta-analytic reviews in this area are meta-analyses of observational studies (e.g., comparing children who did or did not possess or receive a particular form of parent involvement). Second, most research studies synthesized in prior meta-analytic reviews focus on fundamental and academic-oriented forms of involvement and results are weighted toward academic-oriented forms of involvement. Jeyne's meta-analysis of urban elementary ($n = 41$ studies) finds the following effects: expectations (ES = .58), reading (ES = .42), parenting style (ES = .35), global involvement (ES = .35), communication (ES = .24), and or attendance or participation at school (.21) and help with homework (ES = -.08). These are comparable to results obtained by Fan and Chen (1999; $n = 25$ studies) and (Rosenzweig, 2001; $n = 34$ studies) as well as other meta-analyses conducted on minority ($n = 21$ studies) and high school students ($n = 52$ studies), respectively (Jeynes, 2003, 2007).

TABLE 5.1 INTERVENTION APPRAISAL GRID: INTERVENTIONS FOR PARENT INVOLVEMENT

Intervention	Research Design	Participants (Child/Adolescent)	Test Site	Researcher Groups	Follow-Up Period	Review Process	Feasibility
Direct or indirect parent tutoring or training***	Four meta-analytic reviews; 1 systematic review; 8 recent randomized trials	Elementary through early middle schoolers	School; School-home	3+	Variable (mostly <4 weeks)	Blind peer review	NA
Nonspecific family support***	One meta-analytic review	Elementary schoolers	School and community settings	3+	Variable	Government sponsored review	NA
Project Fast**	RCTs	Elementary and middle schoolers	Schools	2	Variable	Blind peer review	$11,000 per cycle, plus training costs
Comer Model**	QED RCT	5th–8th graders	Schools	2	4 Years	Blind peer Review	Materials, training information, consultation materials available at http://www.med.yale.edu/comer/programs_services/index.html
Incredible Years Teacher Training Component**	RCT	Kindergarten and first graders	School	1	9 months (school year)	Blind peer review	Materials and training costs estimated at $510 per teacher, available at http://www.incredibleyears.com/program/teacher.asp

Note:
* indicates that the intervention was rated "highly recommended";
** indicates that the intervention was rated "recommended (with caution)";
*** indicates intervention was rated as "emerging." RCT randomized controlled trial; QED = quasi-experimental design.

Finally, specific programs of parent involvement (broadly defined) showed effect sizes ranging from .29 to .36; such effects are considered moderate (Cohen, 1988).

More recent individual studies not covered in prior meta-analytic reviews fell into three areas: parent tutoring/participation in literacy and informal learning activities (Cadieux & Boudrealt, 2005; Kim, 2006; Powell & Peet, 2008; Saint-Laurent & Giasson, 2005; Sylva et al., 2008; White & Kim, 2008); increasing teacher practices of parent involvement or school practices of parent support (Colvin et al., 2008; Kyriakides, 2005; Sirvani, 2007; Spoth et al., 2008; Wolraich, Bickman, et al., 2005); and an evaluation of the Comer Model (Cook et al., 1999).

In the following sections, we classify intervention studies into *highly recommended, recommended,* and *emerging* strategies. These programs and strategies are summarized in Table 5.1.

HIGHLY RECOMMENDED

Results from meta-analyic reviews and current intervention studies indicate that direct or indirect parent training or tutoring is likely an effective intervention for enhancing children's academic skills (Erion, 2006; Mol et al., 2008; Nye et al., 2006; Senechal, 2006), and evidence is continuing to accumulate substantiating the benefits of such strategies. Specifically, positive effects are seen on a variety of outcome domains including curriculum-based skills, measures of expressive vocabulary, and measures of reading, mathematics, and science achievement. There is wide variety in the extent to which such interventions are conducted with a treatment manual, i.e. manualized. However, recent refereed articles provide sufficient detail as to how these activities were planned and initiated (Cadieux & Boudrealt, 2005; Kim, 2006; Powell & Peet, 2008; Rasinki & Stevenson, 2005; Saint-Laurent & Giasson, 2005; Sylva et al., 2008; White & Kim, 2008). Many of these activities require high levels of teacher (or at least other relevant expert) input (e.g., in terms of identifying appropriate curricular activities). General programs of family support (delivered in either school or nonschool settings) appear to have positive, albeit weak, effects on child cognitive skills (Layzer et al., 2001).

An important theme related to parent training/tutoring—which is somewhat unique to this topic area—is that there are few specific, named "programs" that emerged. Rather, reviewed studies, in general, represent an amalgam of strategies whereby parents were coached or directly assisted in providing various forms of academic support to their children. Nye et al. (2006) categorize these strategies into four general types: facilitation of joint reading activities between parents and children, programs to support parents in acquiring specific skills, reading and math games, and parental rewards and incentives. Overall, a conclusion of the meta-analytic review, indicated that approaches that used rewards and incentives and those that provided education and training to parents showed relatively larger effects sizes, for older elementary and younger elementary students respectively. Programs reviewed varied significantly in length (from three weeks to two years). Of note, Nye et al. (2006) find no relationship between the length of intervention and treatment effects.

Given that the extent to which interventions contained in the Nye et al. meta-analytic review were manualized varied considerably, recent refereed articles provide additional and specific detail as to how such activities may be planned and initiated (Cadieux & Boudreault, 2005; Rasinki & Stevenson, 2005; Sylva, Scott, Totskia, Ereky-Stevens, Crook, 2008; Kim, 2006; Powell & Peet, 2008; Saint-Laurent & Giasson, 2005; White & Kim, 2008). While these studies are not necessarily replications of studies covered in the Nye et al., (2006) review, they are distinctive because they build on prior work and typically use large sample (n = 100 and above), randomized designs. Three of these studies utilized school level, randomized designs (Cadieux & Boudreault, 2005; Powell & Peet, 2008; Rasinki & Stevenson, 2005; Sylva, Scott, Totskia, Ereky-Stevens, Crook, 2008). Specifically, Cadieux and Boudreault, 2005 implemented a ten-month program utilizing two trained reading specialists. Specialists guided parents to engage in paired-reading activities with their first grade children for 5-15 minutes per day (5 days per week); specialists provided regular home visits to parents to monitor paired reading activities. A similar approach characterizes both the (1) Fast Start reading program (manual available), but parents received a single training (Rasinski & Stevenson, 2005) and (2) Saint-Laurent and Giasson's program which included nine, ninety minute parent workshops delivered bi-monthly over the school year.

The Supporting Parents on Kids Education in Schools (SPOKES; Sylva et al., 2008) targeted parents of five and six year olds. SPOKES draws upon both the *Incredible Years Training Program* (Webster-Stratton & Hancock, 1998) as well as the Pause Prompt Praise literacy strategy (PPP; McNaughton, Glynn, & Robinson, 1987). The program was delivered over a school year, whereby parents initially participated in 12 weekly 2.5 hour sessions modeled on the Incredible Years. Then, parents attended 10 weekly groups focused on the PPP intervention. Finally, parents participated in a six-week "top-off" reviewing both programs. Home visits occurred throughout the school year.

The Links to Learning (Powell & Peet, 2008) program targets parents of children in kindergarten through fourth grades and is delivered over 10, ninety minute group sessions. Topics include: "(1) children's futures, (2) how learning happens, (3) learning in family routines, (4) conversations as learning, (5) asking questions, (6, 7: two sessions) family–school relations, (8) extracurricular activities, (9) libraries, and (10) parental expectations of children." (p. 265).

Other interventions target voluntary summer reading (Kim, 2006; White and Kim, 2008) among third through fifth graders. These programs included teacher and parent "scaffolding," whereby parents received a letter asking them to encourage their child to read aloud, discuss their improvement, and included comprehension questions.

Finally, general programs of family support (delivered in either school or non-school settings) appear to have positive, albeit weak, effects on child cognitive skills (Layzer, Goodson, Bernstein, & Price, 2001).

RECOMMENDED

Four programs and two strategies would meet criteria to be placed in this category. Families and Schools Together (FAST) (see Soydan et al., 2005) shows mixed evidence related to long-term benefits (up to two years) on some child behavioral, academic competence, and, in one case, direct parent involvement domains. In this intervention, families are either universally or selectively recruited into one or more eight-week cycles of multifamily groups focused on building social capital among parents, increasing family functioning through family therapy techniques, and building parenting skills. Parents "graduating" from the program then aid in facilitating subsequent groups. Of note, weaker effects were obtained from an independent evaluation of the project.

The Comer School Development Program (Comer SDM; Cook et al., 1999, 2000; Millsap et al., 2000) shows modest effects on a wide range of student and school outcome domains, including school achievement in randomized and well-controlled quasi-experimental studies. In these models, parent involvement (through direct participation in school governance) is one component of a larger schoolwide effort at reform.

Using the teacher training component of the Incredible Years Program, Webster-Stratton et al. (2008) found that kindergarten and first grade teachers trained to use the program reported greater levels of efforts to involve parents than did peers who did not receive the intervention.

A fourth program, the Iowa Strengthening Families Program (ISFP), provides general parenting skills and family competency training over seven weekday evenings to parents and their sixth grade children in schools with high proportions of children receiving free or reduced-price lunch. It showed favorable effects on parenting competencies as well as reducing child substance abuse risk and increasing school engagement and academic success (Spoth et al., 2008).

Finally, two additional recommended strategies include teacher communication with parents via written notes regarding math curriculum, homework, and student performance; this was associated with higher student mathematics grades relative to those who did not receive such communications (Sirvani,

2007). Weak but positive increases in parent–school communication were achieved for an intervention that educated teachers and parents of children with attention deficit/hyperactivity disorder about the importance of home–school communication, suggesting that a more intensive intervention may be warranted in this case. A second strategy showing positive effects on child school performance includes directly inviting parents to elementary school classrooms (Kyriakides, 2005).

EMERGING

One emerging strategy was a prevention-oriented school social work counseling model based on a task-centered model, which focused on increased communications with parents. It also showed favorable effects on student school performance, based on a quasi-experimental design (Colvin et al., 2008).

REFLECTIONS

In this section, we offer reflections related to the search process, the content revealed, and the extent to which the evidence is located within the RTI framework.

PROCESS REFLECTIONS

Reflecting on the process, several points are noteworthy. There were many recent, relevant meta-analyses that made the search process relatively easy. Thus, it is likely that a practitioner could easily locate the relevant meta-analyses and the studies they used for their analysis.

CONTENT REFLECTIONS

Note that most interventions found in the search deal mostly with parent skills training and, as in the case of FAST, those that have in most cases, been weighted toward child outcomes. There was little evidence of wider programs of parent involvement. To be sure, the search did yield a few examples of such efforts; however, virtually no evaluation data were generated for any of these practices.

Overall, two main findings can be gleaned from this review. First, the efficacy and flexibility of various forms of parent-directed learning activities are strengths of this literature. A safe conclusion based on this review would be to strongly encourage practitioners to familiarize themselves with the many ways these kinds of activities can be used to support student learning as well as engage students and parents in school work together. It is encouraging that these strategies do not appear to vary in their effects between low-performing and higher performing students. It is also encouraging that the current evidence suggests that the Incredible Years Program may positively relate to teacher-directed efforts of parent involvement.

On the other hand, the strategy of direct parent training of academic skills, in many ways, does not address the broader question of how schools can enhance their relationships with parents and communities—that is, moving toward family-driven care, where families and schools collaborate to meet the needs of children across developmental domains (Duchnowski & Kutash, 2007). This search did not locate intervention studies that directly assessed these issues. This is of grave concern as many schools and districts still do not routinely make fundamental efforts to engage and involve parents (Michael et al., 2007) and a large body of scholarship addresses the importance of school staff–parent–student trust and subsequent, consistent efforts that must under-gird authentically collaborative activities (Hiatt-Michael, 2006; Raffaele & Knoff, 1999; Schutz, 2006.)

On a final note, as the findings from meta-analytic reviews suggest that parent expectations show the largest effect on school performance and achievement, it was surprising to see little evidence that interventions addressed this seemingly important factor.

RESPONSE-TO-INTERVENTION

Intervention programs and strategies reviewed represent the full continuum of Tier 1 to Tier 3. The Incredible Years, ISFP, and the Comer SDM represent Tier 1 interventions. FAST, if delivered universally, would also fall into this tier. Tier 1 strategies include encouragement of visitation. FAST, however, in literature searched, is usually applied as a Tier 2 intervention (that is, targeting children at risk of behavioral difficulty in school). The only strategy specific to school social work is a Tier 3 intervention. Of note, direct parent training of academic skills can be flexibly used and has been evaluated across all intervention tiers.

ADAPTING AND APPLYING THE EVIDENCE

DEVELOPMENTAL ADAPTATIONS

Most direct parent training strategies—those with the most empirical evidence supporting their effectiveness—have been tested in early elementary contexts, although some have extended through middle school. Only one recommended program (IFSP) and one emerging strategy (prevention-focused, task-centered school social work) focus on middle to high school students.

Cultural Variations

A distinct advantage of programs and strategies extracted from this search is that they have been tested on both racially/ethnically and sociodemograpically diverse student populations. Beyond the generalizability of these strategies and interventions overall, the Incredible Years Program, FAST, and parent-directed tutoring and training activities encourage adaptation to be compatible across diverse cultural groups.

Contextual Adaptations

While virtually all interventions and strategies reviewed were implemented within schools or in close collaboration with teachers and other school per-sonnel, we located little information that addressed how much school contextual features might shape the features or outcomes of these interventions.

EVALUATION

PROCESS EVALUATION

As would be expected, there was a strong divide in the extent to which literature searched addressed implementation issues. Formal programs (Incredible Years. IFSP, FAST, Comer SDM) require either formal training components or include fidelity measures. In all of these cases, developers of these programs argue that strong fidelity to program materials and processes is essential. For the Comer SDM, evaluators empirically link strength of adherence to the program to school achievement outcomes (Cook et al., 1999, 2000; Millsap et al., 2000).

OUTCOME EVALUATION

The evidence yielded by this search would likely focus a practitioner on group, single-subject, or within-subject methodologies. Within-subject methodologies may be particularly germane—at both student and school level—when evaluating more universally oriented programs or strategies (Incredible Years, IFSP, and school-directed parent-delivered literacy activities). Results of parent-directed academic skills training could easily be evaluated using single-subject designs given availability of directly accessible and observable measures (e.g., homework completion, assignment grades).

RELIABLE AND VALID MEASURES

Interventions reviewed herein implicate two sets of outcome measures: school performance records (assignment grades, test scores), direct measures of parent involvement, measured from student, parent, and teacher perspectives. Such measures—they cover the range of parent involvement types across primary and secondary grades—are available from the National Network of Partnership Schools at Johns Hopkins University (http://www.csos.jhu.edu/p2000/survey.htm). These measures are widely used and appear reliable, but information on other psychometric properties (e.g., assessments of multiple forms of validity) is unknown.

CONCLUSION

Results of several meta-analyses confirm a positive association between parent involvement, broadly defined, and various academic outcome domains (e.g., grades, achievement); and these positive associations hold across key subgroups of children, including students in general and gifted education, minority and nonminority students, elementary and high school students, and children in living in urban, rural, and suburban regions (Fan & Chen, 1999; Jeynes, 2003, 2005, 2007; Kim & Choi, 2002; Rosenzweig, 2000). Thus, the research literature certainly implies that investments in parent involvement in schooling may have important educational benefits for children and youth. Whether such involvement can be induced, however, is more equivocal. Overall, there is one highly recommended strategy identified in our review most relevant to enhancing parent involvement to promote student success—parent-directed academic skills training. Programs such as the Incredible Years and FAST, which are recommended, have shown effects on teacher- and parent-initiated involvement, but these programs are largely targeted to prevention and intervention for children at risk for behavioral difficulties. That is, they are not stand-alone programs of parent involvement. This search suggests that furthering efforts to develop such programming would be of great importance to the field in general and school social work practitioners in particular.

6

INCREASING STUDENT COMPLIANCE WITH CLASSROOM TASKS

Following directions and listening to teachers have been defined as "academic enablers" (DiPerna & Elliot, 2002) and are fundamental to the development of social competence and effective learning (Gresham et al., 2004). To a large extent, behaviors related to lack of compliance provide the behavioral content and clinical foundation for oppositional defiant disorder, which often precedes and co-occurs with conduct disorder. Eddy, Reid, and Curry (2002) suggest that between 2% and 16% of youth in the United States can be characterized as having oppositional defiant disorder combined with conduct disorder, and Stoep, Weiss, Kuo, Cheney, and Cohen (2003) argue that over half of U.S. adolescents who fail to complete their high school experience have a diagnosable psychiatric disorder. Not surprisingly, the presence of young children in school settings who display challenging behavior patterns that severely stress the management skills of teachers is at an all-time high and is of significant concern to teachers (Rimm-Kaufman et al., 2000). Children who fail to negotiate the demands of teachers, (the ones who control instructional settings), often do not get off to a good start in school and set in motion a downward spiral that can severely impair their school success. This failure can eventually lead to delinquency and school dropout in adolescence, and finally to a host of adult adjustment problems including welfare dependence, criminality, marital difficulties, employment problems, and hospitalization-mortality rates that are higher than the norm. Box 6.1 shares a vignette about how to help noncompliant students.

BOX 6.1 NOT FOLLOWING DIRECTIONS VIGNETTE

Ms. Davis has referred Joey (age 11) because he "never listens" and is "disrupting the entire class." Prior to meeting with Ms. Davis to set goals and develop a plan of action, I decided to observe the classroom in an attempt to determine if focusing my efforts on the risk factors at the individual (i.e., social behavior), school (i.e., classroom management, classroom climate, curricular relevance), or both were of central importance. During the observation I assessed the classroom management strategies and classroom climate. I also interviewed a few students in the class, which confirmed my initial belief that the current classroom management practices were ineffective and inconsistent, and that many children in the classroom had difficulty following directions. Specifically, there was little or no evidence that Ms. Davis had defined and actively taught behavioral expectations to all children, employed a system for acknowledging and rewarding appropriate behavior, and consistently delivered a continuum of consequences for behavior expectation or rule infractions. There was a general lack of respect for the teacher displayed by several members of the class, and in general the relationship between Ms. Davis and the children was poor. I also examined the communication between the teacher and parents/guardian via an interview with Ms. Davis. Finally, I examined office disciplinary referrals and learned Joey has not been referred to the office all year.

Next, I sat down with Ms. Davis and discussed my understanding of the evidence related to following directions. Specifically, I stated that while many teachers request that I work directly with the child, that is only effective if certain strategies are in place at the classroom level. I asked her permission to start there and expressed a sincere desire to work individually, teaching social skills if it seemed necessary after these strategies were in place. We had a single goal: to have Joey respond favorably to teacher requests 70% of the time. Ms. Davis estimated that Joey currently did so less than 20% of the time. I proposed a three-part process: (1) articulate, teach, and positively reinforce behavioral expectations; (2) provide opportunities for children to have input into problem solving and other decisions that affect them; and (3) consistently reinforce a hierarchy of consequences in response to rule infractions. I facilitated daily class meetings for 3 weeks. With Ms. Davis's assistance, I solicited the children's help in identifying expectations and consequences. The children proposed a warning for the first infraction during the day followed by a 2-minute delay for recess, a 5-minute delay for recess, a call home, and an office referral, respectively, for each subsequent violation. If a child's parents were called home more than 2 times in a week they agreed to have a parent-teacher conference. I crafted a letter explaining the new system that Ms. Davis polished and sent home. I also challenged her to increase the ratio of her positive to negative interactions with children to 4:1, with most positive comments relating specifically to the behavior expectations.

(Continued)

BOX 6.1 NOT FOLLOWING DIRECTIONS VIGNETTE (CONT'D)

I spent 1 hour in her room every day monitoring the ratio of her positive to negative interactions, and also monitored rule infractions that were ignored or not handled consistent with our new system. Ms. Davis was asked to make between 8 and 0 specific requests to Joey each day and log if it was followed with 5 seconds or not.

CONCEPTUAL DEFINITION OF THE ISSUE

Not following classroom rules is defined as noncompliance within the classroom setting. Noncompliance can include overt (e.g., refusal to follow rules, direct challenges to the teacher's authority) or covert (e.g., passively ignoring rules or requests) student responses. For the purpose of this chapter, intervention programs or strategies for which the *primary* outcome is to improve compliance in the classroom were investigated.

ORGANIZING AND INTERPRETING THE EVIDENCE

The evidence-informed practice (EIP) question guiding this search was framed broadly: What prevention or intervention programs or strategies are effective for improving compliance with teacher requests or classroom rules within the classroom setting? However, since noncompliance is a gateway behavior that can lead to more severe and potentially chronic behavior problems (Walker et al., 2004), it is common for noncompliance within the classroom to be addressed by intervention packages that are framed as substance abuse, violence, dropout, or bully prevention programs. To be sure, there would be substantial overlap in EIP searches framed from any of these perspectives. However, since the topic was framed narrowly within the referral (e.g., following rules in classroom settings), we did not include in our search interventions in which learning to get along with peers or developing social competence in general were the primary focus, even if they included components related to compliance. Additionally, interventions that were framed as substance abuse prevention, bullying prevention, or character education were excluded. Interventions that were considered violence prevention were included only if compliance in the classroom setting represented them as the main focus of the program or intervention strategy. Relevant clearinghouses, databases, and academic texts were examined in relation to the answerable question.

The section in Appendix B titled Investigating the Evidence: Increasing Student Compliance (Chapter 6) summarizes the search strategies and results. In this section, following a hierarchy of evidence approach, we first focus on interventions that have demonstrated effectiveness as shown in meta-analyses systematic reviews, or randomized controlled trials (see Table 6.1).

TABLE 6.1 INTERVENTION APPRAISAL GRID: COMPLIANCE

Intervention	Research Design	Participants (Child/ Adolescent)	Test Site	Researcher Groups	Follow-Up Period	Review Process	Feasibility
High probability requests/ behavioral momentum (praise enhanced effectiveness)	Meta analyses	Individuals with severe to profound mental retardation compared with adults	Schools	Lee, 2005	none	Blind Peer Review	$0
	Single subject	Children with autism	Schools	Banda & Kubina, 2006	none	Blind Peer Review	No cost
Positive behavior support	Case study	Adolescents	Schools	Leedy et al. 2004)	none	Blind Peer Review	No cost
	Synthesis	N/A	Schools	Sprague & Horner, 2006	none	Blind Peer Review	No cost
Early Risers "Skills or success"	Experimental	Elementary school students	Schools	August et al. 2006	3 years	SAMHSA	2- day training required $7,000. Also encouraged to use the PATHS curriculum (^29); $800-1,200 for school supplies; and staff alaries, $25,000-$30,000 per year. Cost per student is $1,500 to $2,500.

TABLE 6.1 INTERVENTION APPRAISAL GRID: COMPLIANCE (CONT'D)

Intervention	Research Design	Participants (Child/ Adolescent)	Test Site	Researcher Groups	Follow-Up Period	Review Process	Feasibility
Errorless compliance	Single subject	Two children with Down's syndrome	Schools	Ducharme & DiAdamo, 2005	None	Blind Peer Review	Unable to find
The Clocklight program (behaviorally based class-wide management strategy	Case study	Single classroom	Schools	Ritter et al, 1997	None	Blind Peer Review	Unable to find
Decision-making process-12-week program	Action research		Schools	Stout-Harris, et al, 1999	None	Blind Peer Review	

After the search process was complete, the evidence was weighed and cate-gorized using the *Highly Recommend*, *Recommend*, and *Emerging* distinctions discussed in Chapter 3.

HIGHLY RECOMMENDED

Early Risers: Skills for Success was recommended by SAMHSA's National Registry of Evidence-Informed Programs and Practices, which has a higher standard for review than our most rigorous criteria. In this review, a single, multiyear rando-mized control trial resulted in multiple peer-reviewed publications based on results after one, two, and three years. This intervention package is a multi-component enhancement program targeting 6- to 12-year-old elementary stu-dents at risk for conduct problems. The program uses integrated child-, school-, and family-focused interventions, which are implemented by a "family advocate." The intervention includes a summer day camp, a school year friend group, and a school support component to modify academic instruction and address chil-dren's challenging behavior. The school support component includes parental and teacher training and support. The program requires certification, obtained through a two- day training that costs $7,000. *Early Risers* was not identified in our database or book search procedures.

Incredible Years: Parents, Teachers, and Children Training Series also met our highest criteria and includes a comprehensive set of curricula designed to promote social competence and prevent and ameliorate aggression and related conduct problems for babies through school-age children. Three integrated interventions—parent training, teacher training, and child training programs—can be implemented in isolation or in combination (recommended). Develop-mentally appropriate parent training intervention materials are available for babies/toddlers, preschoolers, and school-age children; the cost of a single parent training program is approximately $2,000, and all three sets can be purchased for approximately $5,000. Small group (therapy) and prevention versions of the child training curriculum materials are approximately $1,200 each. The teacher training material costs $1,250. Incredible Years was not identi-fied in our database search but was named in one book review.

First Step to Success also warranted a highly recommend categorization, although this was done post hoc, a decision that is discussed in the Reflections section of this chapter. First Step is an early intervention program designed for at-risk primary level, elementary school children who show signs of emerging externalizing behavior patterns (e.g., aggression toward others, oppositional-defiant behavior, tantrums, rule infractions, escalating confrontations with peers and adults, etc.; Walker et al., 1997); it is a collaborative home and school early intervention whose purpose is to assist at-risk elementary school-age children in getting off to a good start in their school careers. First Step requires approximately two to three months for implementation from start to finish. It is coordinated by a coach, is implemented in regular K–3 classrooms, and is applied as part of the regular classroom routine. The intervention systematically teaches the following school success skills in both school and home settings: communication and sharing in school, cooperation, setting limits, solving problems, making friends, and developing confidence. The role of the target child is to learn and master the skills; the role of the parents is to teach and strengthen the skills; and the role of the teacher is to also teach the skills and to recognize, praise, and reward children when they display these skills at school. The startup kit costs approximately $150 (serves three children), and training is not required.

RECOMMENDED (WITH CAUTION)

Two practices were recommended with caution based on our search findings. As can be seen in Table 6.1, high probability requests were identified in a meta-analysis as an effective practice. Additionally, the search revealed a case study and a single case design study supporting the effectiveness of this practice. High probability requests/behavioral momentum refers to a sequencing strategy in which two to three requests associated with compliance precede a demand associated with noncompliance. The database search resulted in studies and a quantitative synthesis of high probability requests. Neither the clearinghouse search nor the book reviews identified high probability requests as a strategy.

EMERGING

The majority of strategies identified through this search process met the criteria for an emerging practice. Establishing a positive ecology/climate includes those strategies identified as part of schoolwide positive behavior support (SWPBS) and also is inclusive of democratic strategies such as involving students in the establishment of rules and consequences; discussing rules and behaviors in class; promoting cooperation and offering opportunities for students to voice needs and opinions. This strategy, or the strategies that constitute the broader construct, was identified in other related discipline texts and one of the five school social work texts. It was not identified through the database or clearinghouse searches.

Establishing and communicating high and clear expectations was also identified as an independent strategy in other related discipline texts and one of the five school social work texts.

Incentives and motivational strategies based on operant learning strategies, or classroom management strategies, were prevalent in the literature. These include individualized instruction, cues, prompts, debriefing, coaching, and positive incentives; sanctions for rule infractions; keeping teacher reactions as neutral as possible; group contingencies; and praise and encouragement for task completion and accuracy. Some combination of these incentive and motivational strategies was represented in each intervention package highlighted, was identified in the database search, and was identified in five of the six school social work texts and both related discipline texts.

A number of other strategies were identified by one or two of the texts. These include establishing clear and predictable routines; reducing transition time; using cooperative learning strategies (e.g., Good Behavior Game); matching academic programming with skill levels of low-performing students; home-school communication, behavioral consultation; assisting families to manage behavior in the home setting; and in-service training.

Systematically teaching social skills was identified by six of the eight texts as a strategy to improve compliance. Anger control and stress inoculation training and group assertiveness training were mentioned specifically in one text.

Pharmacological interventions for children diagnosed with oppositional defiant disorder were identified as ineffective by Linseisen (2006). Additionally, Walker et al. (2004) indicate that pharmacological interventions are effective for reducing overall rates of impulsive and disruptive behavior and increasing compliance but do not recommend them since they only suppress behavior. Cognitive-behavioral therapy and contracting were identified by a single text. Self-monitoring was recommended by two texts. Walker et al. (2004) specifically identify psychotherapy and counseling as ineffective.

REFLECTIONS

In this section, we offer reflections related to the search process, the content revealed, and the extent to which the evidence is located within the response to intervention framework.

PROCESS REFLECTION

While it is not clear if it is an error in the procedure or implementing the procedure, the information obtained misrepresents the actual evidence supporting practices relevant to following directions in the classroom to some extent. It is important to note that every effort was made to suspend prior knowledge of the evidence base during the search. However, having completed it, this limitation appears relevant. Specifically, First Step to Success was recognized by a single text and was categorized as an emerging practice using our search procedure. However, we were unable to suspend our knowledge of the evidence for this intervention. Specifically, First Step has been the focus of two randomized control trials and multiple well-controlled quasi and single subject design studies (Beard & Sugai, 2004; Golly et al., 2000; Golly et al., 1998; Overton et al., 2002; Walker, Kavanaugh, et al., 1998; Walker, Stiller, Severson, & Golly, 1998). In addition to the research base, the home component (homeBase) was developed in conjunction with social workers and is extremely consistent with the value base of the profession. Our point is not that First Step to Success received the short end of the stick but rather that in this situation the EIP process likely misrepresented other practices—for better or worse—as well.

Further, despite the clearly defined process, a number of subjective factors are likely to result in different outcomes with different users. In this search, many steps—from the selection of search words, to the book available for one to review, to the chapters one selects as relevant—of this search would be different with different practitioners, and each would affect the intervention strategy. In the end, the lead author of this chapter (AF) largely confirmed what he thought he already knew. Andy is predisposed to reject "therapy" and individual counseling by school social workers. However, if he passionately defended these services, he might well have justified them through the search process, although he would have had to rely exclusively on the school social work texts to do so. This is not to say there may not be a literature base validating the effectiveness of these practices. In fact there is. However, this literature base does not fit the reason for referral, which in this case was from the teacher and specific to following directions in the classroom. If the parent made the referral, and improving classroom behavior was not the main priority, the search process and recommendations would have been very different. We were able to suspend our prior knowledge when conducting the search; that proved impossible (and why would you want to?) when developing a course of action.

CONTENT REFLECTIONS

A couple of issues are worthy of reflection with regard to the content found. First, the volume of evidence available for practitioners with regard to this common reason for referral is encouraging. Additionally, there are a number of pre-packaged interventions that assemble the strategies creatively and provide resources to implement them effectively.

LOCATING THE CONTINENT WITHIN THE RTI FRAMEWORK

From an RTI perspective, the individual intervention strategies (e.g., high probability requests, high and clear expectations, incentives and motivational strategies, clear and predictable routines, etc.) can be implemented as Tier 1, 2, or 3 approaches. Specifically, many of these can be implemented across an entire classroom or school, in which case they are Tier 1 strategies. However, if they are implemented with small groups of children who are at elevated risk because they have already exhibited problems with following directions, the strategies would be considered Tier 2 strategies. Many of the strategies in this chapter also constitute the most effective strategies for children requiring Tier 3 support and would be appropriate to include in a Behavior Intervention Plan (BIP). However, at Tier 3, interventions are typically selected and modified based on individual assessment results (e.g., functional assessment), require a team to implement, and necessitate the assistance of service providers external to the school. Whether they are differentially effective when implemented on different tiers was not examined but is an important empirical question. While the teacher training programs associated with Incredible Years, First Step, and *Early Risers* can all be considered Tier 1 supports, the child and family components for each are clearly Tier 2 interventions. Within the RTI framework, it would be important to ensure that if these strategies are being used as Tier 2 supports, this is done only after children have been exposed to high-quality Tier 1 interventions and systematically identified as nonresponders to these Tier 1 supports thorough a databased decision-making process.

ADAPTING AND APPLYING THE EVIDENCE

In this section, developmental, cultural, and contextual adaptations identified in the literature are discussed. If no adaptations were identified, potential adaptations are recommended.

DEVELOPMENTAL ADAPTATIONS

While the literature did not address developmental adaptations to these strategies, a few appear relevant. First, the level of abstraction for behavior expectations and rules must be developmentally appropriate. Thus, the children learn well from routines and from environments that explicitly indicate the required expectations (e.g., where to hang coats, what to do with their hands when waiting in line for the restroom), from clear examples, and also from imitation of peers. Thus, while older children should be able to understand abstract expectations such as "be responsible," children in the primary grades and preschool will need more concrete language. Another developmental consideration is the use of external reinforcement such as stickers or candy like those typically seen in token economies. Young children whose behavior is not yet persistent and chronic may likely be responsive to nontangible reinforcers such as acknowledgment and praise (e.g., positive attention). These should be used only when necessary and are probably less necessary with younger children. Third, preschoolers and those in the primary grades have developmental characteristics relevant to teaching social skills which are important. For example, they tend to rely on information derived from their senses, so it is easier for them to understand new learning when they can see, touch, or hear it. They learn better from an experiential rather than a "sit still and listen" approach. Additionally, memory is often context specific, so they may not generalize rules or skills from one situation to another. Young children may also be less capable of building empathy skills and in general taking the perspective of others. Young children may be egocentric and have difficulty taking another person's point of view, but they can learn well when adults use teachable moments to help them understand. Thus, younger children will need more practice with these skills than older children. Additionally, older children are more likely to have the skills but choose not to use them because the alternative behavior is more effective at getting their needs met. This situation requires a very different approach. Finally, with regard to establishing democratic classroom climates, older children, whose development revolves around issues of independence and competency, may need classrooms in which they feel heard and in which their input and ideas are valued.

CULTURAL ADAPTATIONS

The literature offers no specific cultural techniques for improving classroom compliance for minority children. Nonetheless, the literature does suggest some commonsense approaches. First, given the collectivist culture of Asian families, family therapy or parental guidance treatment would be more appropriate for children with oppositional defiant disorders. Providing these services outside of the local school would allow these families to "save face" while correcting dysfunctional parenting patterns (Satake et al., 2004; Zhen & Xue-Rong, 2006). Second, a common assumption about African American youth is that oppositional children are disengaged from school and unmotivated to achieve. In fact, the research shows that these youth do believe that education is the route to success (Addo, 1997), but they are consistently overidentified by teachers for behavioral problems (Donovan & Cross, 2002; Nolan et al., 2001), a situation that could easily become a self-fulfilling prophecy. School social workers might be more effective helping teachers adapt their curriculum to black culture (Hunsberger, 2007) and improve their relationships with black students

(Hughes & Kwok, 2007; Rey et al., 2007). Third, it seems that Hispanic children's compliance is linked to positive family relations that often deteriorate when they emigrate to the United States (Bird et al., 2001). Similar to the approach used with Asian families, improving family ties might be an effective strategy for practitioners helping helping Latino students.

CONTEXTUAL ADAPTATIONS

One of the most important contextual issues is whether noncompliance is an issue that requires attention at the individual, classroom, or school level. If the school culture/ecology is not favorable, it would be wise to consult with administrators regarding the extent to which they perceive a need or potential benefit in addressing the issues raised through this referral schoolwide. Specifically, administrators should be canvassed with regard to the extent to which they believe building teachers are proficient in preventative classroom management practices; their perception of the quality of the relationships between teachers, students, and families; and their perception of the effectiveness of the school-wide discipline polices and preventative social skill instruction occurring across all classrooms. If there is administrative support for a schoolwide effort, the initiative would likely be a three- to five-year project to improve school climate and culture while simultaneously providing immediate support to the referring teacher. The key features and implementation guidelines promoted by the Technical Assistance Center on Positive Behavioral Interventions and Supports (see http://www.pbis.org/main.htm) would be a valuable resource at this point. This would involve a year of planning to recruit a school-based leadership team to guide the effort and collect data from teachers, students, administrators, and parents on school climate issues. In the second year one might initiate a series of venues both formal (e.g., workshops) and informal (e.g., brown bag opportunities for staff to share ideas and reflect on and shape new schoolwide procedures). After schoolwide procedures are in place, the focus of these professional development opportunities could shift to practices at the classroom level. Although this process would largely be guided by the leadership team, implementing the teacher training component (e.g., Incredible Years teacher component) in year two or three might be indicated. The teacher training would be best if systematically linked to schoolwide behavioral expectations and any new policies and procedures that were implemented in years one or two. In the fourth year, a parent component that builds on and reinforces schoolwide and classroom level practices, and the Incredible Years, *Early Risers*, or First Step to Success programs all offer options that could be considered. A schoolwide social problem-solving component would also be critical. If adopted, a specific search for this type of intervention could be completed and presented to the leadership team. Once these are in place, the leadership could adopt an evidence-informed, secondary or tertiary level intervention (e.g., First Step or the child component of the Incredible Years package), but should also conduct another search specific to this topic.

EVALUATION

In this section, process and outcome evaluations are discussed, followed by recommended measures that are both reliable and valid.

PROCESS EVALUATION

The fidelity of the intervention would need to be monitored irrespective of the practices chosen. If the program is implemented at the school level, the Technical Assistance Center on Positive Behavioral Interventions and Supports (see http://www.pbis.org/main.htm) has a number of resources available to monitor fidelity. Additionally, the Center for the Social and Emotional Foundations for Early Learning publishes a free Teaching Pyramid Observation Tool to monitor implementation fidelity in preschool classrooms (Hemmeter & Fox, 2009). When the focus is on the classroom environment, a checklist that contains the strategies the teacher agrees to focus on, along with a rating system for each indicating the extent to which it has been implemented, may be useful. Although intended for use at the school level, the School-wide Evaluation Tool (SET; Horner et al., 2004), a fidelity measure to assess the extent to which features are in place schoolwide, may be useful. If implemented with a single teacher, fidelity should be monitored by the school social worker through direct observation, the teachers (self-assessment), or both. We suggest that weekly consultation meetings be set up with the classroom teacher to monitor implementation fidelity and to troubleshoot. One advantage of manualized programs such as First Step and Incredible Years is that they often come with tools to measure implementation fidelity.

OUTCOME EVALUATION

A variety of data could be used whether the strategies in this chapter are implemented schoolwide or with a few teachers. The outcomes should be tied to the goals that have been established, and the use of Office Discipline Referral (ODR) data, when it is available, can prove useful. The systematic analysis and use of ODR data can serve as a basis for making decisions regarding whether primary prevention strategies are working, and when, where, and for whom adjustments should be made. A Web-based tool, the School-Wide Information

System (SWIS), is available to facilitate the use of ODR data (www.swis.org). If evidence-informed Tier 1 strategies are in place, ODR rates are a meaningful metric for identifying students whose lack of response to these supports establishes their eligibility for Tier 2 interventions. Another useful measure is the teacher perception of effectiveness; simply asking the teacher what has improved since the previous week provides school social workers with valuable information. In large-scale applications, focus groups can be facilitated. Finally, there are a number of valid and reliable measures to assess externalizing behavior problems that frequently include items related to following rules, such as the Social Skills Rating System (Gresham & Elliot, 1990), Child Behavior Checklist (Achenbach, 1991), and Systematic Screening for Behavior Disorders (Walker & Severson, 1990).

CONCLUSION

A recent national of survey of school social workers indicates that teachers frequently refer children for school social work services because "they don't follow classroom rules." Relevant clearinghouses, databases, and academic texts were examined. Three interventions—*Early Risers: Skills for Success*, Incredible Years, and First Step to Success—were *Highly Recommended*. High probablility requests and schoolwide positive behavior support were *Recommended with Caution*. A variety of strategies met the *Emerging* criteria.

Interestingly, each targets multiple intervention agents (child, parent, teacher) and multiple risk factors (e.g., social skills, parent-child conflict, connectedness with family and school, classroom management), and are therefore consistent with social work's emphasis on the environment. Again, these programs are essentially well packaged combinations of the individual intervention strategies presented in this chapter.

7

BEHAVIOR INTERVENTION PLANNING

Consultation is widely recognized as a major role of school social workers (Constable, 2007b; Franklin & Harris, 2007; Lee, 2007; Sabatino, 2009). Franklin and Harris (2007) explain that consultation is a method of intervention in which the school social worker provides information, education, and support to assist consultees to become interventionists and develop an action plan. Additionally, developing behavior intervention plans (BIPs) or behavior intervention planning (BIP) is recognized as an important aspect of consultation within school social work (Constable, 2007a; Frey et al., in press), school psychology (Frey, Lingo, & Nelson, 2009), and clinical child psychology (Scott et al., 2009). Amendments to the Individuals with Disabilities Education Act in 1997 required the use of functional behavioral assessment (FBA) and positive behavior supports and interventions, and undoubtedly account for the embracing of BIP across multiple disciplines within the context of school-based support services. Behavior intervention planning is consistent with the person-in-environment perspective. As noted by Horner, Sugai, and Horner (2005), many school personnel mistakenly believe the purpose of a BIP is to change a child's behavior, and while this is the ultimate outcome of a BIP, the plan should focus on changing environmental contexts (i.e., physical environment, daily schedule, the timing of interactions with certain individuals) or the behaviors of adults or peers.

CONCEPTUAL DEFINITION OF THE ISSUE

A BIP is a plan of action that comprises proactive and comprehensive interventions, generated through a process by which individual assessment results are used to better understand who, what, when, and where challenging behavior occurs (Scott et al., 2009). Functional assessments are organized around routines the team determines to be associated with high levels of problem behavior, and they conclude with a summary statement that describes the student's problem behavior; the settings, events, and conditions that typically preceded the behavior; and the team's best guess regarding the consequences that maintain the behavior (i.e., make it work for the child) (Horner et al., 2005). Although there is not one "correct" way to conduct an FBA, most intervention planning teams use a combination of direct and indirect tools and procedures to determine the function. Multiple direct observations use an antecedent-behavior-consequence (ABC) recording or scatter plot in the setting(s) in which challenging behaviors occur. Conducting structured teacher and parent interviews and gathering teacher rating scale data from multiple informants are examples of indirect procedures.

This assessment data, in turn, provide an understanding of why the behavior occurs and therefore allow interventions to be "individualized" to maximize the possibility of success. Behavior intervention plans typically contain the following components: (1) identification of a functionally equivalent, appropriate replacement behavior; (2) instruction necessary to teach this replacement behavior; (3) environmental modifications to occasion and reinforce the replacement behavior and discourage the maladaptive challenging behavior; and (4) a systematic plan to monitor and evaluate the effects of the intervention (Crone & Horner, 2003; Kerr & Nelson, 2006;).

Fairbanks et al. (2007) indicate that most function-based interventions include some combination of the following elements:

- Providing teacher attention
- Self-monitoring
- Teaching social skills
- Reducing task duration and breaking down task steps
- Interspersing instruction between preferred activities

The BIP is drafted by a designated team member after the meeting and distributed to all team members. This written plan clearly identifies which team members are responsible for which components of the plan. The team subsequently meets regularly to monitor data on targeted goals and behaviors, review progress, and make adjustments to the plan as needed. If the student has been identified as eligible for special education and related services, the BIP may be incorporated into his or her individualized education plan (IEP). While Knoster and McCurdy (2002) acknowledge similar content, they also address process. Specifically, they suggest that the related service provider facilitating the process (identified in this chapter as the school psychologist) (1) assess and effectively influence environmental barriers to team implementation efforts; (2) collaborate with staff, families, and the student (where appropriate) to design and implement interventions derived from the FBA hypotheses; (3) understand and guide implementation within the context of continuous progress monitoring; and (4) facilitate effective problem solving among team members.

The purpose of this chapter is to identify, appraise, adapt, and evaluate the evidence base when empirically supported strategies are implemented within the BIP process.

ORGANIZING AND INTERPRETING THE EVIDENCE

The guiding question for this search was the following: To what extent are BIPs effective? Relevant clearinghouses, databases, and academic texts were examined to investigate the answerable question. Our book's Appendix Investigating the Evidence: Behavior Intervention Planning summarizes the search strategies and results. In this section, the evidence related to the content, effectiveness, and fidelity of BIP was examined. The section on effectiveness follows a hierarchy of evidence approach.

Table 7.1 shows that 10 peer-reviewed studies were identified through the search. Of these, seven examined effectiveness and employed a single case design while the remaining three employed a posttest only design that examined the extent to which educators implemented BIPs with fidelity. Based on the effectiveness studies revealed in this search alone, BIP would be classified as an emerging practice. However, because behavior intervention planning is, by definition, individualized for each child, it is not possible to examine this practice within the context of a group design, and therefore will never fare well in the context of a hierarchy of evidence approach in which meta-analyses and randomized controlled trials (RCTs) are given elevated status. Given the inability to examine BIP within group design studies, clinical wisdom from experts in the field was believed to be particularly important. Scott et al. (2009) notes there is "a significant research-to-practice gap" (p. 429). Specifically, these authors observe that the literature provides little guidance that would inform practitioners which FBA methods are the most reliable and valid. Further, they suggest that the vast majority of studies evaluating the effectiveness of BIP based on FBA have been conducted by researchers or have included extensive training and coaching to support teachers. Walker et al. (2004) suggests that "research over the past 30 years in the field of applied behavior analysis indicates that FBA methods contribute to beneficial outcomes for children and youth" (p. 105). The authors of the remaining texts do not offer clear positions on the effectiveness of BIP or do not address the issue of effectiveness. When applied with adequate fidelity (i.e., as described above),

TABLE 7.1 INTERVENTION APPRAISAL GRID: BEHAVIOR INTERVENTION PLANNING

Intervention	Research Design	Participants (Child/Adolescent)	Test Site	Researcher Groups	Follow-Up Period	Review Process	Feasibility (Cost & Time)
Behavior intervention planning	Single case: ABAB withdrawal	One 8-year old male; bilingual	Urban elementary school	Christensen, Young, & Marchant (2007)	N/A	Peer reviewed	N/A
Behavior intervention planning	Single case: ABAB withdrawal (across years)	One 10-year-old, African American male with developmental disabilities	Elementary school	Kern, Gallagher, Starosta, Hickman, & George (2006)	N/A	Peer reviewed	N/A
Behavior intervention planning	Single case: Altering treatments	Third grade male with a learning disability	Suburban elementary school	Burke, Hagen-Burke, & Sugai (2003)	N/A	Peer reviewed	N/A
Behavior intervention planning	Single case: Concurrent AB designs	A 5-year-old male with characteristics of autism	University College, Dublin	Taylor, O-Reilly, & Lancioni (1996)	N/A	Peer reviewed	N/A
Behavior intervention planning	Single case: Multiple baseline, AB design across subject	Four elementary, African American students	Urban elementary school	Lo & Cartledge (2006)	N/A	Peer reviewed	N/A
Behavior intervention planning	Single case: Multiple baseline, AB design across subject	Three middle school students	Middle school	March & Horner (2002)	N/A	Peer reviewed	N/A
Behavior intervention planning	Posttest only	70 educators	University setting	Kroeger & Phillips (2007)	N/A	Peer reviewed	N/A

TABLE 7.1 INTERVENTION APPRAISAL (CPP): BEHAVIOR INTERVENTION PLANNING (CONT.)

Intervention	Research Design	Participants (Child/Adolescent)	Test Site	Researcher Groups	Follow-Up Period	Review Process	Feasibility (Cost & Time)
Behavior intervention planning	Posttest only	31 educators	University setting	Scott (2005)	N/A	Peer reviewed	N/A
Behavior intervention planning	Posttest only	58 school personnel and 12 behavior support teams	University setting	Benazzi, Horner, & Good (2006)	N/A	Peer reviewed	N/A

BOX 7.1 BEHAVIOR INTERVENTION PLAN (BIP)

Joey is a 5-year-old boy who was referred by his kindergarten teacher because he "hits other students and destroys property." The teacher reports having implemented a well-established primary prevention program (Second Step) to teach positive social skills within the classrooms and the assistant teacher has reinforced these lessons with Joey individually and in small groups for three months. Mrs. Swartz, the school social worker, suggested a BIP be created and implemented. Mrs. Swartz completed antecedent-behavior-consequence (ABC) recording forms during two or three direct observations and conducted structured teacher and parent interviews. These data were then brought to a weekly team meeting attended by Joey's parents, the kindergarten teacher, and the assistant teacher. During these meetings, a hypothesis was developed and then a BIP created. Mrs. Swartz typed the plan that was drafted during the meetings and distributed it to the team members. The consultant visited the classroom for approximately 30 hours per week over the next four weeks, supporting the teacher in a variety of ways, such as directly teaching the child new skills, creating resources necessary to implement the behavior plan, and modeling new responses to challenging behavior. A Likert-style checklist, modified by Mrs. Swartz, was completed to assess the extent to which behavior plans contained the needed components and the extent to which the plans were implemented consistently by Mrs. Swartz (See Appendix x.B). Both the components and implementation sections of this measure con-tained five statements, with response options ranging from 5 (*definitely*) to 1 (*not at all*). The school social worker also completed direct observations of Joey's behavior before the intervention, while she was supporting Mrs. Swartz directly, and after Mrs. Swartz took over implementation without support. Observations were completed using definitions and a coding system similar to that used by Golly, Sprague, Walker, Beard, and Gorham (2000). Socially Engaged Time, a measure used for the third stage of the Early Screening Project (ESP) assessment system (Walker, Severson, & Feil, 1998) was used. The figures in Box 7.4 demonstrate that the BIP was somewhat effective in increasing socially engaged time and decreasing challenging behaviors.

(*continued*)

BOX 7.1 BEHAVIOR INTERVENTION PLAN (BIP) (CONT'D)

BEHAVIOR INTERVENTION PLAN FOR JOEY

PURPOSE OF CHALLENGING BEHAVIOR

When Joey wants to escape something, and the situation calls for engaging in academic endeavors or sitting for long periods of time, he appears to have trouble beginning tasks and/or is inattentive. Based on a functional behavioral assessment, I hypothesize that Joey engages in these behaviors to escape structured, academic activities and sitting at circle time. When Joey engages in these behaviors and adults ignore him, his inattentive behaviors increase and he tends to do what he wants (e.g., continues engaging in the tasks he enjoys, rolling around on the floor, speaking when the teacher is speaking).

PREVENTIVE STRATEGIES

These strategies will prevent Joey from being inattentive and help him stay on task.

Teach Social Skills Interactions

Joey's instructional assistant has been given worksheets that will help him improve his social skills. These include teaching him how to make friends, suitable ways to get the teacher's attention, and the difference between appropriate and inappropriate peer interactions. Joey and his instructional assistant will complete one worksheet a week in the gym during nap time (after lunch).

Redirect

When Joey has been seated at circle time for approximately five minutes, his instructional assistant and he will take a walk or run laps in the gym. This will be at the teacher/assistant's discretion and will not necessarily happen every time circle time occurs. This will be one way to alleviate the pressure for Joey to remain seated for long periods of time.

Provide consistency with regard rules and schedules

Teacher/support staff will provide a visual classroom schedule and establish and teach classroom rules. Teachers will enforce classroom rules during circle

(continued)

time and during centers time. The Teacher's Aide assigned to Joey will also provide positive support and offer one-on-one assistance with transitions.

Positive Reinforcement

When an adult witnesses Joey doing something he is expected to do or has been told to do, he or she should immediately give one chip to Joey to place in the designated coin jar. After receiving six tokens, Joey will immediately visit the treasure box with his instructional assistant and choose one item. He may take as many trips to this box as his behavior allows. Joey can also lose chips for not doing something that is expected of him or that he has been asked to do. Only one chip can be removed for every 30 seconds he is disobeying the rules.

Self-Monitoring

Joey will continue to work toward receiving green marks on his daily schedule. If he receives three reds in one day, his mom has agreed to ground him from playing with his favorite toy or his video games for a number of minutes that she will choose.

Comfort Area

In order for Joey to rest more peacefully during nap time, he will be moved to a more secluded area, away from noisy distractions. In case he does not want to sleep, he will be given several books to read. This is intended to keep him from distracting others during nap time.

Engagement

Teacher and her assistants will work to engage Joey more during circle time. When he is sitting properly, teacher should call on him to answer questions, give him feedback, and basically make him feel more involved in circle time.

REPLACEMENT SKILLS TO BE TAUGHT

Learn to Follow Classroom and Circle Time Rules

Joey will be taught the classroom and circle time rules and have opportunities to practice them.

(*continued*)

BOX 7.1 BEHAVIOR INTERVENTION PLAN (BIP) (CONT'D)

Learn to Obtain Adult Attention

Specific attention will be given to teaching him to raise raising his hand and waiting to be called on when he wants to speak. Joey needs to learn how to get Ms. Steen's attention. He needs to understand that loud noises and calling her name will not work, but raising his hand or signaling in a quiet manner will.

LEARN THE CORRELATION BETWEEN GOOD BEHAVIOR AND RECEIVING TOKENS

Teachers must be thorough with instating the token system in order for the child to notice the direct correlation between receiving a certain number of chips and receiving a prize.

WHEN THE BEHAVIOR OCCURS

If Joey has trouble staying on task . . .

Give the child the choice of doing the right thing and receiving a token, or having a consequence and having a chip removed.

Ignore the Behavior

Used sparingly and when it is possible, planned ignoring of the negative behaviors should occur.

Use If/Then Statements

Remind Joey that he has the opportunity to earn a token or receive a green check on his mini-schedule. Calmly continue instructing other students and/or ask them to ignore what he is doing. For example, the adult might say, "Joey, if you sit quietly on your spot for five minutes during circle time, then you will earn a token."

---

duration, and intensity, a body of research exists, warranting a *recommend* (*with caution*) classification.

Additionally, many leaders in the field of behavior disorders have argued for the use of this process for children exhibiting challenging behavior in the school context. However, the usability and feasibility of BIP, addressed later in this

BOX 7.2 FIDELITY RATING SYSTEM

	Definitely		Somewhat		Not at all
Components of the plan (completed by independent rater)					
Plan is based on functional behavioral assessment	5	4	3	2	1
Plan lists realistic prevention strategies tied to triggers	5	4	3	2	1
Plan lists appropriate new skills to be taught (e.g., should be effective in meeting function)	5	4	3	2	1
Plan lists responses that can be expected to adequately reinforce new skills and discourage problematic behaviors	5	4	3	2	1
The overall plan appears to be adequate	5	4	3	2	1
Implementation of the plan (completed by Mental Health Consultant)					
The plan was disseminated to key stakeholders via individuals and team meetings	5	4	3	2	1
The prevention strategies listed in the plan were implemented consistently by all key stakeholders	5	4	3	2	1
The new skills were directly taught to the student	5	4	3	2	1
The new skills were practiced individually or in small group	5	4	3	2	1
New responses should reinforce new behaviors and discourage problematic ones	5	4	3	2	1

Components subtotal ___

Implementation subtotal ___

Total fidelity rating ___

chapter, has been questioned. Specifically, little evidence suggests that the BIP process can be implemented with fidelity when completed by school personnel without resources (i.e., time and expertise) that exceed those typically found in schools.

The issue of treatment fidelity is a limitation of BIP that was identified through the database search as well as the texts reviewed in this evidence-

BOX 7.3 CODING FORM AND DEFINITIONS FOR SOCIALLY ENGAGED TIME (SET) AND DISCRETE CLASSROOM BEHAVIORS

Observer: ___ Date: ___ Student: __

Time Start: ____ Time Stop: ____

General observations:

DURATION RECORDING

Socially Engaged Time	Socially engaged time is when a child is involved in positive social engagement, parallel play, and/or following established rules. Antisocial and nonsocial behavior are defined as (1) a negative reciprocal exchange, either verbal or physical; (2) disobeying established classroom rules; (3) tantruming; and (4) solitary play (being alone).

SET: 12 minute observation

3 minute SET observation periods 1 2 3 4

Seconds on stopwatch at end of observation: _____/720 seconds

(total observed time) × 100 = _____ (% SET)

EVENT RECORDING

3 minute event recording observation periods 1 2 3 4

Touch
Other

Touch
Prop.

    : : : : : 1:00 1:10 1:20 1:30 1:40 1:50 2:00 2:10 2:20 2:30 2:40 2:50 3:00 Total
    10 20 30 40 50

Behavior	Definition
Touching others	The student touches other with hands, feet, or objects or pulls other students. Also includes the student's pushing, grabbing, or exhibiting any other physical contact.
Touching others' property	The student touches others' property with hands, feet, or object (without permission). Also includes pushing, grabbing, or exhibiting any other negative physical contact.
Noncompliance	The student fails to do what he or she is told to do by the teacher within 5 seconds.

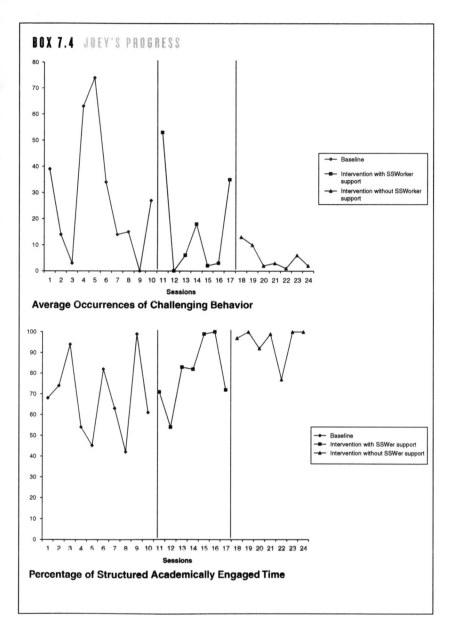

BOX 7.4 JOEY'S PROGRESS

Average Occurrences of Challenging Behavior

Percentage of Structured Academically Engaged Time

informed practice (EIP) process (Benazzi et al., 2006; Kroeger & Phillips, 2007; Scott et al., 2005). Referring to the BIP body of evidence, Scott et al. (2009) states that "even if a school has access to individuals with expertise in advanced methods of FBA, it is unlikely that teachers will be able or willing to participate in extensive and complex FBAs" (p. 429). Lack of training is identified as one of the main reasons for skepticism with regard to whether FBA procedures can be implemented in schools by typical school personnel (including school social workers and other related service providers). It is for this reason that they recommend a team-based method for conducting FBAs and developing BIPs in which a cadre of two to five people are trained to facilitate the BIP process. To help make the ideas in this chapter more concrete, we offer the case study of "Joey," a five-year old kindergartner who is referred to the school social worker for behavior problems in Box 7.1.

REFLECTIONS

In this section, we offer reflections on the search process, the content revealed, and the extent to which the evidence is located within the response to intervention (RTI) framework.

PROCESS REFLECTIONS

Reflecting on the process, we found several points to be noteworthy. First, while we consider ourselves quite well versed in the BIP literature, we were not aware that virtually all of the literature describes the same process, and that there is no such thing as a BIP that does not base the intervention strategies on FBA data. Second, we were surprised to find that the free online resources all appear useful. Additionally, we discovered that nearly all of the articles identified in the search were easily found. In this instance, the search strategy did not identify a very large volume of studies that I know exist. The quality of the articles that were not discovered in the search–and with which I am familiar–were similar to those that were, so finding them would not likely have changed the appraisal of the evidence.

CONTENT REFLECTIONS

Interestingly, school social work literature addresses BIP differently from the other related disciplines. While BIP appears central to school-based intervention books published by authors in related disciplines, it was not privileged in the school social work texts examined. For example, in one school social work text the author promotes a BIP process that is not based on individual assessment results. Other school social work texts address it in a paragraph or not at all despite the fact that BIP is arguably one of only two practices at the tertiary level with any type of evidence base (wrap-around planning being the other). Another school social work text has a chapter on individual work and BIP is not mentioned.

LOCATING THE EVIDENCE WITHIN AN RTI FRAMEWORK

Most of the recent literature on BIP discusses the process as being appropriate only within a multitiered framework such as Positive Behavior Supports (PBS) and RTI (Scott et al., 2009). Behavior intervention planning clearly represents support at Tier 3 since it takes extensive resources (time and expertise), because each plan is individually tailored to a child's FBA data, and because each intervention team is unique. As a Tier 3 support, this process should be reserved for children who have been exposed to high-quality universal and targeted interventions and have still been unresponsive.

The fourth component of BIPs, systematically monitoring and evaluating the effects of the plan, is consistent with the RTI emphasis on data-based decision making. Behavior intervention planning appears consistent with the RTI emphasis on high-quality interventions. Although the empirical support for BIP warrented only an *emerging* categorization based on our criteria, the interventions that are typically endorsed for BIPs are very similar to those that are *recommended* or *recommended with caution* in other chapters of this text, particularly Chapter 6 (Compliance).

ADAPTING AND APPLYING THE EVIDENCE

In this section, developmental, cultural, and contextual adaptations identified in the literature are discussed. If no adaptations were identified, potential adaptations are recommended.

DEVELOPMENTAL ADAPTATIONS

While no literature was identified in this search that addressed developmental adaptations to the BIP process, a few adaptations appear relevant. As discussed in Chapter 6, younger children are particularly responsive to consistent routines and schedules. The Center for the Social and Emotional Foundations for Early Learning (http://www.vanderbilt.edu/csefel/) has developed a variety of training materials (modules 3a and 3b) and other resources to modify the BIP for preschoolers, including teacher and parent interview forms, antecedent-behavior-consequence (ABC) observation cards, scatter plots, and BIP templates. These resources take into consideration the unique developmental stages associated with young children including their need for more concrete language and experiential opportunities that utilize their senses. Frequent practice in multiple settings to facilitate the generalization of new skills from one situation to another is also necessary for young children.

CULTURAL/CONTEXTUAL VARIATIONS AND ADAPTATIONS

While we found no evidence to suggest that the process should be different with diverse populations, it is in some sense culturally sensitive since it is based largely on interview data from the teacher and, ideally, the family. The empirical studies cited in this chapter included children from a variety of cultural backgrounds as well as children with diverse behavioral profiles. In this sense, teachers and families define the problems to be addressed. Additionally, Lo and Cartledge (2006) propose BIP as a strategy to prevent the overrepresentation of African American boys in disciplinary and special education referrals. Because it is based on behavioral principles and assumes the fit between the child and the environment is the problem, rather than individual risk factors, BIP is less likely to cause stigmatization than practices that are pathology oriented.

When assembling a school-based team that will conduct the FBA and facilitate the BIP process, the team should be a diverse group of professionals. Additionally, when working with families who may be reluctant to receive assistance from school professionals, whether it is because of their own poor experiences with school or for other reasons, teams may want to consider using fewer personnel.

EVALUATION

In this section, process and outcome evaluations are discussed, followed by recommended measures that are both reliable and valid.

PROCESS EVALUATION

The documented problems with fidelity account for the plethora of measures available to monitor implementation efforts. For example, Kroeger and Phillips (2007) and Gable et al. (2000) have developed a map that helps a team consider all relevant aspects of a support plan. Additionally, Powers (1985) and Schippers (2005) both provide a framework to identify target behavior, determine controlling variables, develop an intervention plan, and evaluate the effectiveness of the intervention.

Given the documented struggles with implementation fidelity, soliciting feedback from teachers about their satisfaction with the plan, the feasibility of the recommendations, and the perceived impact on student outcomes is critical.

OUTCOME EVALUATION

Evaluating behavior intervention plans is fairly straightforward because a sound plan should contain operational definitions for the behaviors to be reduced or eliminated, as well as the socially appropriate behaviors one would like to see more of. Because each plan is unique to the child, evaluations will likely use a single case design. We recommend that frequency data on problem and replacement behaviors be collected by the teacher and monitored by the team. The easiest way to monitor the effectiveness of a BIP is to directly observe, or request the teacher to track, the frequency of behaviors the plan is designed to increase and decrease. Boxes 7.1–7.3. provides an example of a single subject design evaluation for a BIP using replacement behaviors as the outcome variable. Office disciplinary referrals may also prove a useful outcome measure. Another practical measure is to record the frequency of socially engaged time (Feil, Severson, & Walker, 1998). Socially engaged time is when a child is involved in positive social engagement or parallel play, and/or is following established rules. Nonsocial behavior is defined as (1) being involved in a negative reciprocal exchange, either verbal or physical; (2) disobeying established classroom rules; (3) tantruming; and (4) engaging in solitary play (being alone).

RELIABLE AND VALID MEASURES

Finally, a number of valid and reliable measures are available for assessing behavior problems common to students requiring Tier 3 supports, such as the Social Skills Rating System (Gresham & Elliot, 1990), Child Behavior Checklist (Achenbach, 1991) Systematic Screening for Behavior Disorders (Walker & Severson, 1990).

CONCLUSIONS

Behavior intervention planning is rated as an extremely important aspect of school social workers' job description, and consultation in general is widely recognized as a major role of school social workers. The evidence related to the content of behavior intervention planning based on functional behavioral assessment is a very clearly articulated process with content representing very specific components. The effectiveness evidence is fairly thin. While numerous studies demonstrate its effectiveness, all of the studies employ a single case design. With regard to treatment fidelity, the evidence suggests that it is questionable whether teachers will be able or willing to participate in extensive and complex FBAs. The literature does not indicate whether school social workers have the skills necessary to complete the BIP process. Viewed within the RTI framework, BIP clearly represents support at Tier 3 because it takes extensive resources (time and expertise), because each plan is individually tailored to a child's FBA data, and because each intervention team is unique. As a Tier 3 support, this process should be reserved for children who have been exposed to high-quality universal and targeted interventions and have still been unresponsive. Behavior intervention planning is consistent with the RTI emphasis on databased decision making and high-quality interventions. Interestingly, school social work literature addresses BIP differently from the other related disciplines. While BIPs appears central to school-based intervention books published by authors in related disciplines, it was far less present in the school social work texts we reviewed.

8

HELPING STUDENTS COPE WITH THEIR PARENTS' DIVORCE

Based on our recent survey work, divorce and separation of parents were rated highest among the family-based stressors that school social workers reported seeing in their practice (Kelly, 2008). In this chapter, we show how to conduct an evidence-informed practice (EIP) process, grounded in the best available evidence, for group school-based interventions for children coping with divorce; we also pay close attention to how these interventions can be adapted and applied in a range of school contexts. Using the same basic EIP process approach outlined in previous chapters, we show how we located information about this important psychosocial stressor and how we suggest using the EIP research we obtained to adapt an intervention for students in school settings.

CONCEPTUAL DEFINITION OF THE ISSUE: DIVORCE/SEPARATION OF PARENTS

An average of 1.5 million children experience their parents' divorce in the United States each year (Haine et al., 2003; National Marriage Project, 2006). Roughly 45% of American marriages end in divorce each year, and these statistics don't count the students who live with single parents who never married; there are clearly many students in schools who are at risk for various negative life outcomes because they are living in single-parent or what social scientists call "fragile" family situations. (The phenomenon of single-parent families and the impact that it has on students' mental health and academic achievement might merit an EIP process all its own for students about whom school social workers are concerned.) Divorce affects all races and social classes in the United States,

TABLE 8.1 HELPING STUDENTS AND PARENTS COPE WITH DIVORCE: INTERVENTION APPRAISAL GRID

Intervention	Research Design	Participants (Child/ Adolescent)	Test Site	Researcher Groups	Follow-Up Period	Review Process	Feasibility
Children's Support Group (Stolberg & Mahler, 1994)*	Experimental design with random assignment	Children 8–12	Schools	See cites	One-year follow-up	Peer Review	Resources Available
Children of Divorce Intervention Project (Pedro-Carroll et al., 1999) *	Experimental design	K–8th Graders	Schools	2+	Two-year follow-up	Peer Review	Resources available
School-based children's divorce groups (Rich et al., 2007; Crespi et al., 2005; DeLucia-Waack & Gerrity, 2001)***	Case study and program description only	K–12th Graders	Schools	3+	None	Peer Review	Resources Available
Oregon Divorce Study-II (DeGarmo & Forgatch, 2005) **	Experimental design with random assignment	K–12th graders	Clinic	1	Longitudinal study; three-year follow-up noted here	Peer Review	Resources Available
New Beginnings Program (Wolchik et al., 2002) **	Experimental design, with random assignment	3rd–6th graders	Clinic	1	Six-year follow-up	Peer Review	Resources Available
Rainbows Program (Skitka & Frazier, 1995)***	Pre/posttest design	K–12th graders	Schools	1, Possibly another evaluator	None	Peer Review	Resources Available
Kids' Turn (Gilman et al., 2005) ***	Pre/posttest design	2nd–4th graders	Clinic	"	None	Peer Review	N/A
Dads for Life (Cookston et al., 2006) **	Experimental, with random assignment	Pre-K–6th graders	Clinic	"	2-year follow-up	Peer Review	N/A

Note:* indicates that the intervention was rated "highly recommended";

but it hits racial minorities hardest, with over 52% of African American children being raised by a single parent, compared to 18% of white children (National Marriage Project, 2006).

In this chapter, we define the issue of children and divorce to encompass students who are living within the context of a family with parents who have chosen to separate and/or divorce. As mentioned earlier, this excludes students who are living with never-married single parents, who, while likely to have their own challenges, are not dealing with the same grief and conflict issues experienced by children living through divorce and separation. We thought it would be useful to conduct an EIP process on students coping with divorce and/or separation because of the numbers of students we have seen in our experience as school social workers who are adversely affected by their parents' divorce.

For this EIP process, we posed the following question: What are effective school-based programs that can help children and families deal with the impacts of divorce and separation? The results of this search process are summarized in Table 8.1.

ORGANIZING AND INTERPRETING THE EVIDENCE

HIGHLY RECOMMENDED

The EIP process detailed here revealed two *highly recommended* interventions, described in the next section, that could be feasibly adapted immediately in many school contexts.

Children of Divorce Intervention Project (CODIP) is a 12-session intervention for kindergarten though eighth grade students designed to provide emotional support, instruction in identifying feelings related to the issues they are experiencing with their parents' divorce, and ideas in how to maintain positive perceptions of themselves and their families with the changes wrought by divorce (Winslow et al., 2004). It is delivered in the school and can be incorporated into regular classroom instructional time or in social work pull-out groups. Box 8.1 provides an overview of the curriculum of a sample CODIP program for second and third graders.

Children's Support Group (CSG) is also school based and is designed for children in later elementary grades. Like CODIP, which partially inspired it, CSG seeks to develop student self-awareness and provide emotional support while attempting to decrease externalizing and internalizing behaviors commonly associated with students who are experiencing a divorce in their family (Winslow et al., 2004). CSG also incorporates four parent workshops and materials for parents to use with their children at home. Both CODIP and Children's Support Group have been evaluated with clinical trials using

BOX 8.1 EXCERPT FROM THE CURRICULUM OVERVIEW OF THE *CHILDREN OF DIVORCE INTERVENTION PROJECT (CODIP) PROGRAM FOR SECOND AND THIRD GRADERS*

Developmentally relevant aspects of Wallerstein's (1983) concept of psychological tasks facing children of divorce are also reflected in the curriculum. Specifically, the six hierarchical, divorce-related coping tasks identified are the following:

1. Acknowledging the reality of the divorce and achieving a realistic cognitive understanding of it.
2. Disengaging from parental conflict and resuming the child's agenda.
3. Resolving the many losses that divorce imposes.
4. Resolving problems of anger and self-blame.
5. Accepting the permanence of divorce.
6. Achieving realistic hope about one's future relationships.

Mastering these sequenced tasks, starting at the time of the parental separation and continuing through late adolescence, enables the child to integrate the experience of parental divorce and to develop the capacity to trust and love in the future. To that end, the program emphasizes the importance of developing a supportive group environment in which these tasks are addressed and incorporated into intervention goals.

The program has four primary parts:

1. Feelings, families and family challenges.
2. Coping skills: learning how to handle feelings and problems.
3. Child-parent relationships.
4. Children's perceptions of themselves and their families.

Sources: Pedro-Carroll, Alpert-Gillis, & Sterling, 1997; Wallerstein, 1983

random assignment and have both been shown to decrease students' anxiety symptoms and adjustment problems in school at a year follow-up.

RECOMMENDED (WITH CAUTION)

Three interventions from the review met our criteria for recommending with caution. (The "caution" for all three was based almost entirely around issues of feasibility and their not being tested in a school setting, issues we deal with later in this chapter and in Lessons Learned from EIP in Chapter 14, later in this volume). The three recommended (with caution) interventions are discussed next.

The Oregon Divorce Study-II (ODS-II) is the second wave of a larger longitudinal study trying to understand the variables that adversely impact children and parents dealing with divorce. The ODS-II intervention uses a 14-session parent group held at the Oregon Social Learning Center clinic (OSLC) that primarily emphasizes developing effective parenting practices and learning how to use contingent positive reinforcement in handling conflicts and discipline with children. Children are not directly involved in the ODS-II intervention. The entire ODS-II intervention is fully contained in the treatment manual *Parenting through Change*. The Parenting through Change program is available by contacting the study authors directly, though it is unclear how much the manual costs or if there is additional training the authors believe is required to implement the program. Though the program could conceivably be offered as a parent group in schools, to date no independent evaluation of the program has been conducted in a school setting.

New Beginnings is a program developed at the Prevention Research Center at Arizona State University (Wolchik et al., 2002); it was originally conducted as two prevention programs, one solely with custodial mothers and the with mother and child together. It is targeted at children between 3 and 17 and consists of 10 group sessions and two individual sessions. It appears from the program description that the intervention is based largely on a lecture/discussion format with an emphasis on practicing specific skills and then augmenting those skills in the individual sessions. The National Registry of Evidence-based Programs and Practices (NREPP) estimates the cost of the program at about $8,800, excluding the $2,800 stipend for the two group leaders recommended for the group. New Beginnings has to date not been implemented in a school setting, but it has been replicated by several independent researchers (NREPP, 2007). The 2002 study cited here is based on a six-year follow-up of the program examining its impact on significant adolescent risk factors (substance abuse, rates of diagnosis of mental disorder, number of sexual partners) and found significant impacts on these factors in the experimental group versus the control group at a six-year follow-up. As the authors write, "To our knowledge, this is the only randomized controlled trial to document long-term benefits of preventive intervention for children whose parents have divorced" (Wolchik et al., 2002, pp. 1879–1880).

Dads for Life (DFL) is the most specific intervention we reviewed for this chapter, in that it targets noncustodial fathers and attempts to keep them involved in their children's lives and also decrease the divorce risk factors for their children (Cookston et al., 2007). It follows a 10-session parent group model and is in part built on the New Beginnings Program already being used with custodial parents by associates of the researchers (Wolchik et al., 2002). An additional short film entitled *Eight Short Films about Divorced Fathers* is also integrated into eight of the 10 sessions, in part to highlight ethnically diverse fathers and parenting styles (Cookston et al., 2007). Like the other programs noted in this section, this one has not been implemented in a school setting. Also unclear is how these materials can be accessed and what cost is involved, aside from a suggestion from the researchers that the Prevention Research Center faculty involved in the project should be consulted.

EMERGING INTERVENTIONS

We found three interventions based on the EIP process that had been described in the literature but had either mixed findings or lacked an experimental design and six-month follow-up. We describe two of the interventions here and devote a separate box to the Rainbows Program due to the interest in the program and debate over its effectiveness:

The first of the interventions is actually several articles that described individual counseling for children of divorce; the articles contained only case studies and intervention descriptions, with limited information on how to replicate the intervention strategies. One reason we include them despite their lack of methodological rigor and detail is that they were school-specific and might offer at least some ideas to school social workers looking for ways to provide individual counseling services to children struggling with divorce-related issues.

Kids' Turn is a six-week education program offered to children in second through fourth grades to help them develop coping skills and healthier attitudes related to their parents' divorce. The program was evaluated with only a pre- and posttest and was not evaluated in a school setting, though information available on the intervention's Web site (www.kidsturn.org) indicate ways that the program could be adapted to a school setting. In addition to the need for more research on its effectiveness, the program appears to be confined to parents who can get to the San Francisco area to take the six-week workshop. While there are a number of books that are described as being "based" on Kids' Turn, no training manual is available from the Web site nor any distance learning training opportunities.

RAINBOWS FOR ALL GODS' CHILDREN: A CAUTIONARY TALE FROM THE EIP PROCESS

Rainbows is a program that started in three schools in the Chicago area in 1983 and has expanded to 49 states and 15 countries (Rainbows, 2009). There are four additional related programs that offer a variety of supports to children, adolescents, and parents dealing with divorce and death of parents and other significant family members. The program is based around a small group skill-building/support framework that encourages children to share their experience of loss and to use activities, games, and personal journals to gain increased self-esteem and emotional well-being. Leaders of the Rainbows groups are required to be trained by certified trainers, and there are registered trainers and trainings for

Rainbows listed on the organization's Web site for the United States, Ireland, Canada, Great Britain, and Australia (Rainbows, 2009).

We are dealing with Rainbows separately for two reasons: (1) it is by far the most widely adopted and recognized school-based program for kids and families dealing with divorce, and (2) the only peer-reviewed evaluation study of Rainbows to date (Skitka & Frazier, 1996) has actually shown Rainbows to have no effect on these issues for children. There are two studies cited on the Rainbows Web site, one by Laumann and Kramer (2000) (cited on the Web site but not in any peer-reviewed journal) and another by Farber (2006). The Laumann and Kramer study was a wait-list control quasi-experimental design of fourth to sixth graders (total n = 224) claiming to show that Rainbows was "associated with self-perceived gains in personal well-being" such as "helping children better understand their feelings," "demonstrating rule-governed behaviors, especially in school," and using "effective coping strategies" (Rainbows, 2009). In addition to this study not being submitted for peer review, there is little information about how these gains were measured, making it impossible to replicate the authors' findings. Interestingly, the authors did publish a qualitative study done in the same schools where the program was conducted on how best to implement Rainbows and to understand what makes the program attractive to some schools and not for others; they acknowledged in their review of the Rainbows literature that this program "has never been formally evaluated" (Kramer et al., 2000, p. 41). (Of further interest, the study of fourth to sixth graders mentioned above was not available on the Rainbows site three months after our initial visit to the site, another detail we contacted Rainbows to inquire about.)

The second study, conducted by Farber (2006) is described on the Rainbows site as an "independent evaluation" even though the data appear to have been collected by the Rainbows organization itself (and then analyzed by Farber) and the report itself is not directly accessible from the Rainbows site. The claims made based on these data (which are characterized as pre/posttest data) appear to have been made by children but not their teachers or parents. Even though the data collection process is hazy at best, the site claims construct validity and reliability, statistically significant change in students' abilities to share their feelings, and change experienced across all ages, genders, and types of losses (Farber, 2006). The site asks for interested parties to contact the site administrators for more information on the Farber report, which as of August 2009 had not been published in a peer-reviewed journal.

There is no small irony that an intervention we've characterized as "emerging" in our review of our EIP process is by far the most widely disseminated, available, and practiced school-based group for children of divorce. While this may seem contrary to the dictates of EIP and the process that forms the basis of this book, we believe that Rainbows proves the necessity of school social workers having the research and appraisal skills of an evidence-informed process.

Consider these details about Rainbows, gleaned from their Web site and promotional materials:

- Rainbows is described by President Suzy Yehl Marta as "the largest international not- for-profit charity dedicated to helping children" that gives children "the skills to thrive" when confronted with divorce and other significant losses (with none of the evidence that is demonstrated by the five interventions in our "highly recommended" and "recommended with caution" categories).
- The "Endorsements" page on the site is full of testimonials from children, parents, and adults (with no explicit acknowledgment that the program's effectiveness is debatable at best, a very common feature of programs that are authority-based rather than evidence-informed).
- A "National Academic Advisory Board" page describes four members who are professors with stated expertise in "youth, loss, grief, depression, or trauma." Three of the four members are names we've already heard from (Farber, Kramer, and Laumann) and again, none of their independent peer-reviewed work appears to validate the claims of Rainbows as an effective school-based program. (A feature of many authority-based interventions is to surround the program or intervention with "experts" who can validate the intervention with their name without necessarily providing peer-reviewed evidence that the intervention works.)

As a program that claims to be effective at "guiding kids through life's storms," Rainbows has set a very high and possibly unrealistic bar to reach for all children who are dealing with divorce, death, and trauma. One problem that immediately occurred to us, which we can't verify with the data Rainbow claims to have, is whether the program adequately deals with the multiple losses they claim to address and the potential comorbidities that their students might be realistically expected to have (depression, PTSD, anxiety, phobias). While it's entirely possible that Rainbows has done all that it claims to do for children and adolescents in schools, for this to be so the intervention would have to be arguably more potent than many of the empirically supported interventions listed on the SAMHSA (Substance Abuse and Mental Health Services Administration) database that are trying to deal with highly challenging youth mental health problems like depression, anger, and trauma symptoms.

Finally, the one peer-reviewed study we could find on Rainbows' effectiveness (Skitka & Frazier, 1996) states flatly, "The results of this study indicated that the intervention was not effective in improving children's beliefs about divorce, decreasing their depression, or improving their behavioral academic self-esteem" (Skitka & Frazier, 1996, pp. 170-171). Whether this claim is true is not our point here; rather, it appears significant to us that the one peer-reviewed study our EIP process found is never disputed or refuted in any of the Rainbows materials provided on their site. Another feature of authority-based practice is to respond to disconfirming evidence by simply reasserting the belief that your program is effective (Gambrill, 2001).

Again while it's entirely possible that Rainbows may yet prove to become a practice that we can someday rate as recommended with caution or even highly recommended, what's striking about the Rainbows program is its seeming imperviousness to our evidence-informed process. It has its members, its 1.6 million people served, its franchises here and around the world, so why does it need to prove it works? Will the program leaders ever submit their findings to peer review? Will they ever attempt to join the ranks of interventions that we found on SAMHSA's NREPP or other evidence-informed databases? Will we (as school social workers, parents, and consumers of mental health) demand that they do so?

LOCATING THE CONTENT WITHIN AN RTI FRAMEWORK

All of the interventions we have profiled here fit well within Tier 2 and Tier 3 (prevention work with at-risk school populations and individual work with clients and their families), with the parent groups also having implications for Tier 2. It is easy for us to imagine that a school district that committed to using the CODIP or Children's Support Group interventions could be implementing them in classrooms building- or districtwide to teach children how to handle their feelings about divorce (and to arguably empower others to learn new ways to understand and empathize with what their peers are going through, in the event that their own parents aren't divorced or separated). It's also possible to imagine the other parent- or group-based interventions being included as a Tier 2 intervention strategy that all parents in a school district could participate in, possibly offered at the school site in partnership with a local community mental health agency. What stands out in our EIP process is how relatively little we can say we know about school-based individual and group interventions for individual students who are having acute symptoms as a result of their parents' divorce. It's possible that some of the interventions related to anxiety (see Chapter 11) as well as other effective interventions for children and adolescents dealing with depression might address some of the issues associated with divorce, but that would be a question for another review (we will deal with the idea of multiple EIP processes based on our first question in our Chapter 14, Lessons Learned).

ADAPTING AND APPLYING THE EVIDENCE

DEVELOPMENTAL, CONTEXTUAL, AND CULTURAL VARIATIONS AND ADAPTATIONS

We see that the evidence contained in these studies maps out some fairly feasible and practical intervention strategies for young children through eighth graders; however, with the possible exception of the ODS-II, none of the five interventions we rated as "highly recommended" or "recommended (with caution)" had been tested on a high school-age population. Given the many developmental issues that arise in adolescence (choice of dating partners, experimentation with alcohol and drugs, separation from parents), the need for more study on this age group and their needs as children of divorce is clear.

Even for those students in prekindergarten through eighth grade, the specific school context will be important in assessing the evidence collected in this chapter. Many school social workers do not run groups for parents or do family-based activities that might require them to stay late at night (Kelly, 2008). Additionally, though both Children's Support Group and CODIP could be delivered by teachers in the classroom with consultation from a school social worker, recent survey data indicate that school social workers infrequently deliver such services in their classrooms (Kelly et al., 2009). The article on implementing Rainbows raised another issue: who will be "in charge" of making sure this intervention is done, the materials are ordered, and the intervention is done with fidelity (Kramer et al., 2000)? Like all group and curricular interventions, the need for an "in-house" person to deliver and coordinate the interventions is a persistent problem in the field of school-based mental health (Frey, Lingo, & Nelson, 2008).

EVALUATION

PROCESS EVALUATION

Of the five interventions in our top two categories, only CODIP, Children's Support Group, and New Beginnings are easy to adhere to in terms of treatment fidelity: all three have a treatment manual, training process, and/or workbooks that are easily accessible for the average school social worker in practice. This is a characteristic that is unfortunately too common in our field, that only 60% of the interventions that have been rigorously evaluated are also easy to access and implement. For Dads for Life (DFL) and ODS-II, it would be hard to advise practitioners at this point how to do these interventions with fidelity until those materials are readily available.

Outcome Evaluation. In some respects, it is very challenging to evaluate progress with these children because of the host setting where school social workers first encounter these students. Students who are referred for a divorce group or intervention may also have other comorbidities that make them eligible for help from the school social worker. They may have an IEP for emotional, behavioral, or learning problems. They may already be in trouble with the school disciplinarian and are referred for anger problems that can be traced back to their experience living as a child of divorce. These other factors need not be a barrier to evaluating these students' progress; rather, it argues for a flexible approach to designing individual evaluation strategies to measure the effectiveness of these interventions.

CONCLUSION

The evidence from this search was encouraging in that it showed that there are several interventions for school social workers to choose from when they want to direct clinical interventions to children dealing with divorce. There are some cautions from the literature that emerged. Aside from the New Beginnings intervention, little was found that seemed to be effective at reaching high school-age adolescents, and this was concerning given all the potential relationship and emotional risk factors present for adolescents and the potential devastating impact parents' divorce could have on them. Finally, the search was useful in forcing us to clarify more what we mean by 'treating" children of divorce: with nearly 50% of all marriages ending in divorce, many students in the nation's schools are likely dealing with the ramifications of divorce. Better screening tools for the impacts of divorce are needed to separate out the impacts of divorce on their social/emotional/behavioral well-being from other more long-standing psychological problems that may have been present prior to the student's parents divorced (e.g. anxiety or depression).

While divorce is a pervasive reality our students have to deal with, it is something that school social workers can directly and effectively address in their day-to-day practice. Whether it's leading groups with students, reaching out in groups or family-based counseling interventions to parents, or discussing the impacts of divorce in individual counseling, there appear to be a number of well-supported interventions and strategies that school social workers can turn to (especially for school social workers in elementary school settings).

Kids we have worked with were often susceptible to depression, anxiety, difficulty forming good peer relationships, and poor academic achievement as they struggled to cope with their loss and the disruption divorce had caused in their lives. Longitudinal research shows that between 20-25% of students exhibit serious mental health problems related to their parents' divorce (Hetherington & Stanley-Hagan 2000) and for some studies claim that the risk of adult mental health problems can be increased by as much as 40% (National Marriage Project, 2006). While there is still controversy about how much of a long-term negative impact divorce has on children (for a good review, see Amato, 2000), clearly school social workers in my sample saw it as a major stressor that they felt they needed to address with their students and families.

9

PREVENTING BULLYING IN SCHOOLS

Both national and cross-national estimates indicate that bullying and victimization are fairly prevalent among school-age children and adolescents, with prevalence estimates varying for 3% to 37% for bullies and from 9% to 32% for victimization (Stassen Berger, 2007). Moreover, recent estimates suggest that such rates may have increased since 1999 and subsequently stabilized, with an average estimate of about 10% (Nansel et al., 2001). Both children who are bullies and children who are victims of bullying show elevated rates of various indicators of psychosocial distress (Smith, J. D. et al., 2004; Vreeman & Carroll, 2007). Some schools and districts increasingly focus on bullying and victimization rates as part of compliance with the Safe and Drug-Free School component of No Child Left Behind. The Office of Safe and Drug-Free Schools houses a significant set of directives and resources to prevent school violence. We offer a brief vignette to show how bullying can impact a school here in Box 9.1

BOX 9.1 BULLYING VIGNETTE

You are a social worker at a suburban elementary school. Overall, your school shows high achievement scores, has high levels of parent involvement, and is well known for its excellent teachers, especially in the early grades. On your caseload, you have two girls—a first grader, Bess, and a third grader, Nina. Nina, receives pull-out services for a severe emotional disturbance and she is well known to school personnel. Nina's mother has been diagnosed with bipolar

---

(continued)

disorder and Nina has shown a pattern of very bizarre behaviors in the past, potentially indicative of a thought disorder. School personnel have worked closely with Nina and her mother to maintain Nina in a regular classroom for part of the day; her academic progress is good. Nina does report that she has trouble making friends. You note that she sometimes wears atypical clothing combinations and often hugs other children inappropriately. Bess, on the other hand, is a new referral. Her teacher notes that she appears anxious and frustrated in class and will sometimes start to cry and hide under her desk during lessons. The teacher is eager to hear your impressions of Bess. Like Nina, Bess presents as a little odd. Her appearance is disheveled and she has very large, very chapped lips. Your classroom observations of both girls are unremarkable. Both teachers have very well-managed classrooms and both classroom teachers appear to care deeply for each girl, respectively.

At your school, all children in the school (including kindergartners through fifth graders) eat lunch at the same time. The playground is supervised by one male classroom aide. During a playground observation, you first note and are, at first, pleasantly surprised that a great majority of children appear to be engaged in a large game of tag. You then notice that both Nina and Bess are "it" and their "it" status never changes. The children run frantically away from both girls, screaming that they have "disgusting cooties." If Nina or Bess tag someone, the children engage in a mass "inoculation" wherein a small group of fifth graders administer "shots" (a brisk punch on the shoulder that appears to sting). The playground attendant says that the kids play tag all the time and remarks, "Isn't it great how all the kids play together so well?" As children line up after the recess period is over, children actively avoid Bess and Nina. When lining up, you notice that children immediately proceeding and following Nina maintain a noticeably wider distance from Nina than is characteristic in other parts of the line. Two girls whisper and point at Beth as they walk back to their class.

Current conceptual frameworks suggest that bullying has multiple correlates at individual, family, peer, and school levels (Olweus, 2005; Smith, J. D. et al., 2004)., Schools have been implicated as a key point of intervention (Olweus, 2005; Rigby, 2002; Smith et al., 1999; Smith, P. K. et al., 2004).

CONCEPTUAL DEFINITIONS

Recent scholarship suggests that an operational definition of bullying/victimization includes incidents that are harmful, repetitive, and imbued with unequal power; bullying can take on one or more of several forms, including physical, behavioral, verbal, and/or relational types (Stassen Berger, 2007). More recently, attention has been placed on cyber-bullying (Diamanduros et al., 2008). Note that while bullying does represent a form of school violence/victimization and aggressive behavior, neither all incidents of school violence nor of school-based aggression would necessarily be defined as bullying.

ORGANIZING AND INTERPRETING THE EVIDENCE

Given the relatively high rates of bullying and related forms of victimization, we asked the following question: What are effective school-based strategies to reduce bullying and bullying-related incidents of victimization? Results of search strategies are summarized in Table 9.1.

Meta-analyses, clearinghouses and books reviewed were remarkably consistent in identifying three overall approaches to preventing school-based bullying. These include so-called whole-school approaches (incorporating whole-school awareness and response to bullying and victimization); curricular approaches delivered in single classrooms or with selected groups of students; and group, social-cognitive skills approaches (Vreeman & Carroll, 2007). Virtually all of the whole-school approaches drew from Dan Olweus's school bullying program (see Olweus, 2005) and include cross-national and mostly quasi-experimental and nonexperimental, large-scale longitudinal designs (the recent studies, including randomized controlled trials, also draw upon similar program logic). Overall, meta-analytic reviews of whole-school approaches generally find weak overall effect sizes on student-reported incidents of bullying and victimization (Smith, J. D. et al., 2004; Merrell et al., 2008). In addition, differential effects for bullying versus victimization-related outcome domains are also found (Smith, J. D. et al., 2004). It is notable that Olweus's own work generates the largest effect sizes and these effect sizes have not been replicated in other studies (Smith, J. D. et al., 2004); a minority of whole-school anti-bullying interventions have yielded negative effect sizes (Merrell et al., 2008). Whole-school approaches may yield larger effects in elementary versus secondary settings and yield relatively larger effects for more high-risk groups than others (Ferguson et al., 2007; Smith, P. K. et al., 2004). Finally, effect sizes differ by reporting source: student self-report versus direct observations of incidents.

In other words, the existing evidence generally supports whole-school approaches as having positive, albeit not always clinically significant, effects on actual rates of bullying and victimization. Authors of meta-analytic reviews speculate that these relatively weak intervention effects may be due to some combination of underpowered research/evaluation designs, uneven implementation of Olweusian programmatic components (including targets at the

TABLE 9.1 INTERVENTION APPRAISAL GRID: INTERVENTIONS FOR SCHOOL BULLYING AND VICTIMIZATION

Intervention	Research Design	Participants (Child/Adoles)	Test Site	Researcher Groups	Follow-Up Period	Review Process	Feasibility
Whole school programs/strategies** Specific Representative Programs: Olweus Bullying Prevention Program** Steps to Respect (STR)**	Four meta-analytic reviews; 1 systematic review; 1 recent randomized trial (STR; Frey, Hirschstein, Snell, Edstrom, MacKenzie, & Broderick, 2005)	K-12 graders@Includes children in both U.S., European, and Asian (Japan and Korean) contexts	School	3+ Note that while most programs theoretically consistent with Olweus; approach is highly variable	Ranges from 3 to 36 months	Blind peer review	Olweus: Materials and training available http://www.clemson.edu/olweus/costs.html: Manuals $19.95–$89.95 per manual); surveys cost approximately $34.50 per every 30 administered. Additional training costs range from $2000 to $3000. Steps to Respect: $749 for materials
Classroom-based approaches* Youth Matters (YM)*	Four meta-analytic reviews; 1 systematic review; 1 recent randomized trial (YM; Jensen & Dieterich, 2007)	Ages 9–16	School	3+	Up to 24 months	Blind peer review	NA

Note:
* Indicates that the strategy was rated "recommended";
** Indicates that the strategy was rated "recommended";

school, parent, class, peer, and individual levels), and sensitization of subjects (i.e., increased reports of bullying may actually reflect increased awareness of the incidents of bullying). Programs may have better effects on knowledge and awareness of bullying and victimization than on actual incidents of bullying and victimization (Ferguson et al., 2007; Merell et al., 2008; Smith, P. K. et al., 2004).

The second key approach draws upon classroom-based curricular approaches, often focusing on social cognitive skills training, but not necessarily delivered as a part of a whole-school package. These approaches yield a mixed pattern of effects (Vreeman & Carroll, 2007).

The third approach includes selective social skills groups. Overall, the effects of these programs (four studies) on bullying and victimization yield null results but in some cases yield desirable results on aggressive and pro-social behaviors (Vreeman & Carroll, 2007).

RECOMMENDED AND EMERGING PROGRAMS AND APPROACHES

Based on search results, none of the studies extracted from the literature met our criteria for *highly recommended*. This is because there are no specific, replicated programs using methods of randomized control. However, the search yielded two recommended strategies, two specific *recommended* programs, and one *emerging* program. Recommended (*Olweus Bullying Program*: Steps to Respect) and emerging programs and strategies (Youth Matters) are presented in Table 9.1.

Specifically, the *Olweus Bullying Program* (see http://www.clemson.edu/olweus/) represents a school wide strategy that consists of three intervention components delivered at school, classroom and individual levels. Key school components include the convening of a "Bullying Prevention Coordinating Committee," administration of student surveys aimed at describing the nature and extent of bullying, development of school wide awareness of bullying, school norms related to behavior, teacher training, as well as parent involvement. Key classroom components include efforts to reinforce knowledge of bullying as well as school norms and rules. Finally, there are individual interventions with students who are directly involved in bullying incidents, as well as their parents. It is recommended that the implementation of the program unfold over a two-year period.

The Steps to Respect Program—generally focused on elementary schools—also represents a school wide approach, delivered in three phases—(1) efforts to gain school-wide "buy-in," (2) teacher training, and (3) a teacher-delivered classroom curriculum (including 11, 30 minute skills lessons and two literature unit selections (7-10 40 minute lessons each). Supplementary family trainings and materials are also available.

PROCESS REFLECTIONS

Overall, our search strategy generated a fairly consistent and easy-to-find set of results because of the substantial number of recent, school-specific systematic reviews and meta-analyses that had already been conducted on the topic. Thus, in this case, the forest view was directly aligned with the tree view of the literature. In addition, chosen books (chapters of which also were revealed in searches) held comprehensive and extensive treatment of the range of programs, assessment issues, and fidelity issues. Thus, an important conclusion is that relevant information on this topic is relatively easily located at very little initial cost.

CONTENT REFLECTIONS

On the other hand, the relatively modest results of whole-school anti-bullying programs are important to consider. A key unanswered question is why these programs show such modest effects. There are at least three competing hypotheses: poor school staff commitment and consistency using the approach; problematic methodological issues (underpowered designs, problematic measures of bullying and victimization); and, perhaps most disconcerting, it may be that the Olweusian model is not transportable to other school conditions. Most of the literature yielded in the search focused on the whole-school elements of these programs; however, it was less clear how to approach children at risk for bullying and victimization and, perhaps, most critically, how to approach work with individual bullies and victims. Given the psychosocial risk of both bullies and victims, other sets of evidence-based interventions for internalizing and externalizing conditions may have to be added to the whole-school package.

LOCATING THE CONTENT WITHIN AN RTI FRAMEWORK

From the perspective of response to intervention (RTI), available treatment strategies cluster on the preventative end—Tier 1—of the continuum. Although the *Olweus Bullying Program* and key programs derived from this approach all contain targeted interventions for students who are bullies or who are victimized, the literature located in this search typically highlights the requisite school community components (e.g., school policies and curricular activities and parent components). Thus, the nature of the continuum in this approach and the step down to more indicated and intensive efforts is not transparent.

ADAPTING AND APPLYING THE EVIDENCE

DEVELOPMENTAL ADAPTATIONS

The literature extracted in this search clearly indicates that bullying programs have been tested at all grade levels. It is important to remember, however, that incidents of bullying and victimization, especially in physical and verbal domains, tend to decrease as children age (Benbenishty & Astor, 2005).

CULTURAL VARIATIONS

Overall, bullying interventions have been tested with diverse student populations, by age, gender and race/ethnicity, and national origins. The search did not locate any specific evidence informing culturally specific adaptation of program content. Recent conceptual work in this area would suggest that school cultural context is an essential variable to consider in understanding school-based victimization (Benbenishy & Astor, 2005). Merrell et al. (2008) found that the modal participant in school bullying programs reviewed is a student in the United Kingdom. U.S.-based participants constitute about 17% of all participants in evaluated bullying programs, raising some questions about the transportability of these approaches to the United States cultural context.

CONTEXTUAL ADAPTATIONS

Although it is clear that the Olweusian model has played a critically important role in school bullying programming worldwide, there are not many research-based guidelines on specific school considerations in adopting these programs. However, original programmers of the *Olweus Bullying Program* and Steps to Respect spend a considerable amount of time (up to a year) in gaining "buy-in" from key stakeholders (e.g., staff and parents). This suggests that such programming cannot be dropped into a school without significant preparation. Evers, Prochaska, Van Marter, Johnson, and Prochaska (2007) describe a trans-theoretical model of bullying that may help dismantle and distill particular program components, should buy-in be an issue. On a final cautionary note, particular school contextual (e.g., disorderliness and attendance rates) and organizational conditions (principal support) influence the intensity of the delivery of school-based prevention programs, which would be a potential consideration (Payne et al., 2006).

EVALUATION

As noted in prior chapters, evaluation should be done on two levels. First, practitioners should conduct a process evaluation to determine whether the interventions were employed as intended. Second, practitioners should conduct an outcome evaluation to determine whether the students responded as hoped.

PROCESS EVALUATION

As alluded to above in the contextual adaptation, program fidelity and integrity is likely a critical component to understanding the weak overall effects of whole-school programs. Indeed, many studies include some form of integrity measures (typically questionnaires of activity checklists developed by Olweus, 2005; see also Smith, J. D. et al., 2004). Smith, J. D. et al. (2004) find that no whole-school programs include a full package of school, parent, classroom, peer, and targeted interventions for individuals. Further, it is not exactly clear what particular program inputs at these levels produce the most marked results. Several themes emerge including a long-term commitment and consistency of school staff to understand and address the problem, raising awareness of these issues in the larger school community, developing a set of clear and consistent policies around these issues that are compatible with the school community, providing education to students about how to handle incidents of bullying and victimization, and developing methods that address specific incidents of bullying and victimization that are compatible with school community norms (Hazler & Carney, 2006; Rigby, 2006; Smith, P. K. et al., 2004). Specific school factors related to intervention integrity include various indicators of teacher commitment and engagement in the program as well as a school culture characterized by collegiality (Limber, 2006).

OUTCOME EVALUATION

The evidence yielded by this search would likely focus a practitioner on group methodologies, given the whole-school nature of the intervention. One of the books searched contains an entire chapter devoted to assessment (Cornell et al., 2006) and discusses the difficulty of measuring the complex set of behaviors that constitute bullying and victimization. Student self-reports of bullying are commonly employed but have critical limitations. Thus, multiple measures from multiple sources of bullying and victimization (including reports from students and staff, peer nomination, and observational strategies) may be necessary to understand the scope of the problem in a school and intervention effects. Given the time to implementation, longitudinal methods may be especially critical. Olweus (2005) provides a quasi-experimental strategy that may be particularly useful for evaluating whole-school approaches (Olweus, 2005).

RELIABLE AND VALID MEASURES

Given concern about limitations of student self reports, some commonly used student self-report measures include include Olweus's Bullying Questionnaire, which contains 42 questions (Olweus, 2005; psychometric details are unpublished) and Reynold's Bully Victimization Scale (Reynolds, 2003).

CONCLUSION

This search allows us to conclude that there are empirically supported strategies for school social workers to use for bullying and victimization, but that effects may be weak and/or mixed. Strategies cluster toward Tier 1 strategies and, as such, are unlikely to work without a strong focus on garnering school staff and parent commitment and consistency over time. Search results would lead to the expectation that results generated from these efforts would show modest effects on bullying and victimization indicators and would likely compel practitioners to layer on supplementary programs.

10

EMPIRICALLY SUPPORTED SOCIAL SKILLS INTERVENTIONS

This chapter discusses how to locate, appraise, adapt, and apply empirically supported social skills interventions. It also demonstrates how to monitor the progress of students receiving social skills instruction and evaluate the effectiveness of interventions employed using an evidence-based practice (EBP) perspective.

Most students who are identified as being at risk for or classified as having an emotional disturbance display social skills deficits. In fact, the current definition for emotional disturbance in the Individuals with Disabilities Education Act (IDEA) contains two social skills problems: (1) an inability to build or maintain satisfactory interpersonal relationships with peers or teachers, and (2) the expression of inappropriate behavior or feelings under normal circumstances (Gresham et al., 2004). Not surprisingly, social skills interventions are the "bread and butter" of school social workers. It almost seems strange to address a chapter about social skills here because so many social skills programs claim that they are evidence-based. We would, however, urge readers to have a healthy dose of skepticism about such claims. Many are really just "authority-based" promotions of products that have limited or mixed research about their effectiveness.

CONCEPTUAL DEFINITION

There is also a wide variety of behaviors that get lumped together in the social skills category (Merrell & Gimpel, 1998; Rao et al., 2008). To have any meaningful discussion of social skills, it is important to begin with a conceptual definition. It may be helpful to begin with the second half of this term: *skills* refer to discrete learned abilities, proficiencies, or competencies for a specific task (Sheridan et al., 1999). In the case of social skills, the specific task is the initiation, development, repair, and eventual termination of interpersonal relationships. In simpler words, social skills enable us to begin, grow, fix, and end a variety of friendships and affiliations. Furthermore, these skills must be sufficiently generalized so that they occur across a variety of settings from simple community interactions to long-term employment (Chadsey-Rusch, 1992). Thus, Sheridan and colleagues (1999) developed the following conceptual definition:

> We define social skills as "goal-directed, learned behaviors that allow one to interact and function effectively in a variety of social contexts." This definition recognizes the importance of discrete acts, but also recognizes the role of the ecological environment within which the behaviors occur. (p. 86)

Gresham, Van, and Cook (2006) state that another important distinction in the conceptualization of social skills is the difference between acquisition deficits and performance deficits. Acquisition deficits occur when students have a lack of knowledge about a particular skill or when they do not know which skill to employ in a specific situation. Performance deficits occur when students fail to exercise a skill that they already know how to perform. Accordingly, Gresham and associates call acquisition deficits "can't do" problems and performance deficits "won't do" problems. Thus performance deficits can be conceptualized as competing behaviors that interfere with the demonstration of social skills. This distinction is important because interventions for acquisition deficits will center on coaching, direct instruction, modeling, and rehearsal while interventions for performance deficits will focus on prompting, shaping, contracting, and reinforcement (Gresham et al., 2004).

The importance of social skills in schools can hardly be overstated. Caprara and colleagues (2000) conducted a longitudinal study that found that third grade prosocial behaviors were a better predictor of eighth grade academic achievement than was third grade academic achievement. This should not be a surprise since social skills, such as active listening, asking questions, and following directions, naturally lead to academic success (Walker et al., 1992).

ORGANIZING AND INTERPRETING THE EVIDENCE

Good intervention planning begins with locating empirically supported interventions. Gibbs (2003) recommends that practitioners formulate an answerable question before exploring the current research. For the following search, we used this question: What are the empirically supported interventions for students with a lack of social skills? Results from this search are found in Table 10.1.

TABLE 10.1 INTERVENTION APPRAISAL GRID: SOCIAL SKILLS

Intervention	Research Design	Participants (Child/ Adolescent)	Test Site	Researcher Groups	Follow-Up Period	Review Process	Feasibility (Cost & Time)
ACCEPTS Curriculum	RCTs	Children (ages 6–12)	Schools	2	N/A	Blind Peer Review	$67/program 27 skills
ACCESS Curriculum	RCTs	Adolescents (ages 12–18)	Schools	2	N/A	Blind Peer Review	$72/program 29 skills
Aggression Replacement Training	RCTs	Adolescents (ages 12–18)	Schools & Corrections	3+	6 months	Blind Peer Review	$27/book $17/CD-Rom $125/DVD 10 Weeks
ASSET program	RCTs	Adolescents (ages 13–18)	Schools & Corrections	2	12 months	Blind Peer Review	$800/program 32 Lessons
Good Behavior Game	RCTs	Children	Schools	3+	12 months	Blind Peer Review	$Negligible Daily, entire school year
I Can Problem Solve	RCTs	Children (grades Pre-K–6)	Schools & Foster Care	3+	60 months	Blind Peer Review	$108/set 83 lessons
Incredible Years	RCTs	Children (ages 2–12)	Schools	3+	12 months	Blind Peer Review	$1600/parents18–20 weeks $1300/children 20–30 weeks$1250/teachers 14–20 weeks
Prepare Curriculum	RCTs	Adolescents (ages 12–18)	Schools	2	N/A	Blind Peer Review	$40/book 10 weeks

TABLE 10.1 INTERVENTION APPRAISAL GRID: SOCIAL SKILLS (CONT'D)

Intervention	Research Design	Participants (Child/Adolescent)	Test Site	Researcher Groups	Follow-Up Period	Review Process	Feasibility (Cost & Time)
Primary Project	RCTs	Children (ages 4–9)	Schools	3+	N/A	Blind Peer Review	$200/manuals & videos 10–14 weeks
Second Step	RCTs	Children (grades Pre-K–9)	Schools	3+	N/A	Blind Peer Review	$879/grade-level kits (1–5) 20–25 lessons $879/grade-level kits (6–9) 15–23 lessons
Skillstreaming	RCTs	Children & Adolescents	Schools	3+	N/A	Blind Peer Review	$72/set $13/student60 Skills

Note: RCT = randomized controlled trial.

The most surprising part of these multiple searches was the diversity of interventions found. There were only four common citations found across the various searches: DeRosier (2004); Feindler, Marriott, and Iwata (1984); Fisher, Masia-Warner, and Klein (2004); and Toplis and Hadwin (2006).

HIGHLY RECOMMENDED

Five of the programs found meet the criteria for *highly recommended*. These strategies include the following five interventions. *The Good Behavior Game* (Barrish, Saunders, & Wolf, 1969) is a simple classroom management strategy, in which intraclass teams compete to earn privileges or rewards for appropriate behavior. Of Rathvon's (2008) seven recommended interventions, this one has the most research support (Embry, 2002). I Can Problem Solve (Shure, 2000) is a manualized, interpersonal, cognitive problem-solving program for young children through early adolescents. The preschool version contains 59 lessons, the kindergarten-primary version contains 83 lessons, and the intermediate version contains 77 lessons. Each lesson includes purposes, materials, and a teacher script. The program is available in English and Spanish and has been evaluated by multiple teams of researchers. Incredible Years (www.incredibleyears.com) is described by SAMHSA as follows:

> Incredible Years is a set of comprehensive, multifaceted, and developmentally based curricula targeting 2- to 12-year-old children and their parents and teachers. The parent, child, and teacher training interventions that compose Incredible Years are guided by developmental theory on the role of multiple interacting risk and protective factors in the development of conduct problems. The three program components are designed to work jointly to promote emotional and social competence and to prevent, reduce, and treat behavioral and emotional problems in young children. The parent training intervention focuses on strengthening parenting competencies and fostering parents' involvement in children's school experiences to promote children's academic and social skills and reduce delinquent behaviors. The Dinosaur child training curriculum aims to strengthen children's social and emotional competencies, such as understanding and communicating feelings, using effective problem-solving strategies, managing anger, practicing friendship and conventional skills, and behaving appropriately in the classroom. The teacher training intervention focuses on strengthening teachers' classroom management strategies, promoting children's prosocial behavior and school readiness, and reducing children's classroom aggression and noncooperation with peers and teachers. The intervention also helps teachers work with parents to support their school involvement and promote consistency between home and school. In all three training interventions, trained

facilitators use videotaped scenes to structure the content and stimulate group discussions and problem solving. (SAMHSA, 2008)

Positive Action (www.positiveaction.net) is a K–12 program that encourages character development, academic achievement, and social-emotional skills and works to reduce disruptive or problem behavior. The program is based on the philosophy that students feel good about themselves when they do positive actions, and there is always a positive path to take. The curriculum includes six to seven units. All lessons are scripted and use classroom discussion, role-play, games, songs, and activity sheets or text booklets. Finally, Second Step (www. cfchildren.org) is described by SAMHSA as follows:

> Second Step is a classroom-based social-skills program for children 4 to 14 years of age that teaches socio-emotional skills aimed at reducing impulsive and aggressive behavior while increasing social competence [Frey, Hirschstein, & Guzzo, 2000]. The program builds on cognitive behavioral intervention models integrated with social learning theory, empathy research, and *social information-processing* theories. The program consists of in-school curricula, parent training, and skill development. Second Step teaches children to identify and understand their own and others' emotions, reduce impulsiveness and choose positive goals, and manage their emotional reactions and decision-making process when emotionally aroused. The curriculum is divided into two age groups: preschool through 5th grade (20 to 25 lessons per year) and 6th through 9th grade (15 lessons in year-1 and 8 lessons in the following 2 years). Each curriculum contains five teaching kits that build sequentially and cover empathy, impulse control, and anger management in developmentally and age-appropriate ways. Group decision-making, modeling, coaching, and practice are demonstrated in the Second Step lessons using interpersonal situations presented in photos or video format. (SAMHSA, 2008)

RECOMMENDED (WITH CAUTION)

Four of the interventions found meet the criteria for *recommended* and are described below.

The ASSET (Hazel et al., 1995) program is a video-based program that includes two DVDs, a facilitator's guide, and reproducible student materials. Students are asked to discuss, role-play, and complete homework assignments on the social situations portrayed in the video. The leader's manual has three sections. The first section provides an overview of group preparation, teaching social skills, conducting meetings, and evaluating the program. The second section covers eight social skills (e.g., giving feedback, accepting feedback, resisting peer pressure, problem solving). The third section contains an appendix of consent forms, skill sheets, home notes, checklists, and questionnaires for pre- and posttests. The main drawbacks of the program are the lack of multiple research teams and the initial expense (see Table 10.1).

Aggression Replacement Training (ART; Goldstein et al., 1998) is a multi-component program that includes a leader's manual, CD-rom for forms, and a training video (DVD or VHS). The manual covers eight topics, including (1) aggression (sources, scope, and solutions); (2) an overview of ART; (3) skill-streaming (behavioral rehearsal); (4) anger control training (emotional restraint); (5) moral reasoning (values); (6) motivation and resistance; (7) generalization; and (8) application and evaluation of effectiveness. The program focuses primarily on performance of social skills and is meant to be delivered over 10 weeks, but this could be changed by increasing or decreasing the frequency of the sessions. There is some question about whether ART works as well with females as it does with males (Cleare, 2000; Leenaars, 2005).

The Primary Project (www.childrensinstitute.net) is described by SAMHSA as follows:

> Primary Project is a school-based program designed for early detection and prevention of school adjustment difficulties in children 4-9 years old (preschool through 3rd grade). The program begins with screening to identify children with early school adjustment difficulties (e.g., mild aggression, withdrawal, and learning difficulties) that interfere with learning. Following identification, children are referred to a series of one-on-one sessions with a trained paraprofessional who utilizes developmentally appropriate child-led play and relationship techniques to help adjustment to the school environment. Children generally are seen weekly for 30–40 minutes for 10–14 weeks. During the session, the trained child associate works to create a nonjudgmental atmosphere while establishing limits on the length of sessions, aggression toward self or others, and destruction of property. Targeted outcomes for children in Primary Project include increased task orientation, behavior control, assertiveness, and peer social skills. The program is suitable for implementation in a specially designed place on a school campus equipped with expressive toys and materials. (SAMHSA, 2008)

The major negative aspect of the research for the Primary Project is the lack of consistent fidelity measures.

Skillstreaming (McGinnis & Goldstein, 2003) is a set of manualized cognitive-behavioral social skills programs for three different age groups: early childhood, elementary school, and adolescents. There is a training video available (DVD or VHS) and each program comes with leader's manual, student manual (except the early childhood version), program forms, skill cards, and video (except early childhood). The focus of this program is on acquiring social skills. For example, the elementary version has 60 lessons in five units: (1) classroom survival skills, (2) friendship skills, (3) affective skills, (4) alternatives to aggression, and (5) stress management skills. There are mixed results regarding the efficacy of the adolescent version of the program, perhaps because of its emphasis on skill acquisition rather than skill performance (Boberg, 2001).

EMERGING

Four of the programs found meet the criteria for *emerging*. These interventions included the following: ACCEPTS (Walker et al., 1988), Connect with Kids (www.connectwithkids.com), Prepare (Goldstein, 1999), and Too Good for Violence (www.mendezfoundation.org). Most of the other interventions failed to qualify due to a lack of at least three-month follow-up results.

REFLECTIONS

It is helpful to view the interventions through the response to intervention (RTI) framework. Most of the effective programs are Tier 1 interventions. The meta-analyses demonstrate the weakness of providing traditional pull-out social skills programs separated from the classroom and the primary teacher. Both ASSET and Aggression Replacement Training would be regarded as Tier 2 interventions since they are normally delivered to a group of targeted students.

ADAPTING AND APPLYING THE INTERVENTIONS

Raines (2008b) argues that school social workers should take three primary factors into account when adapting scientifically based interventions. These include developmental considerations, cultural sensitivity, and contextual constraints of working in schools.

DEVELOPMENTAL ADAPTATIONS

We should always take into consideration the developmental level of the child. It is important to remember that, especially in relation to social skills, age is not always equal to stage. Some interpersonally gifted children are mature beyond their years and some emotionally disturbed students will be immature for their age. A common adaptation for teaching social skills to young children is to use puppets (Kazura & Flanders, 2007; Verschueren et al., 2001), even across other cultures (Otsui & Tanaka-Matsumi, 2007). For example, the Incredible Years program offers up to five puppets as supplementary materials.

CULTURAL VARIATIONS

We should always address the issue of cultural sensitivity. American customs and programs do not always translate readily to other cultures.

Among Asian families, for example, Lak and colleagues (2004) found that common scenarios in American social skills modules needed adaptation for Chinese clients. For example, Chinese people seldom have "parties" where small talk is initiated by discussing the weather. Instead, they are more likely to gather for dim sum [brunch], drink tea, and talk about the food. Likewise, the importance of family in such collectivist cultures requires that therapists intentionally engage parents to promote social competence and problem solving for their children (Ahn, 1998; Siu, 2003).

Working with Hispanic families, Cardemil and colleagues (2002) were careful to adapt the Penn Resiliency Program (PRP). They utilized a method that would be useful for many school-based professionals:

> Particular care was taken to prevent intervention providers from imposing suburban, middle-class values or perspectives on the participants. The group nature of the PRP allowed the students to assist each other in searching for useful cognitive and behavioral solutions to problems, allowing the solutions to come from *within the culture of the children* as much as possible. In addition, given the fact that many of the children faced very difficult real problems, considerable time was spent helping students to develop and enhance their problem-solving skills, in addition to improving their thinking skills. (p. 6, emphasis added)

Cardemil and colleagues were also careful to change the race and/or ethnicity of the characters in the examples they used and were more likely to discuss single-parent families than traditional intact families. Lopez and associates (2002) note that it is especially important to recognize that Hispanic families are a very diverse group and that practitioners should assess English language fluency as well as the degree of acculturation prior to determining which adaptations to make. They have developed a helpful rubric for examining the cultural appropriateness of prevention (and intervention) programming with five components: (1) understanding the cultural context of the problem, (2) distinguishing between cultures and between cultural variables, (3) developing a culturally appropriate delivery system, (4) facilitating culturally sensitive evaluation, and (5) disseminating research findings to all stakeholders.

Knox (1992) addresses issues of social skills training with high-risk African American adolescents. She raises six issues about culturally sensitive social skills intervention with this population. First, what behaviors are being singled out for change? For example, are adolescents with aggressive behaviors referred while shy or withdrawn teens are overlooked? Second, is the adolescent's behavior viewed as an acculturation deficit? If so, what are the consequences of such training for the adolescent's functioning within his or her own community? Third, how much is the adolescent's own desires for change considered? For instance, will the intervention enable the teen to negotiate both cultures (mainstream and minority)? Fourth, are practitioners willing to bring in role models from the minority community, such as clergy, musicians, or sports figures? Fifth, how comfortable are the trainers with aggression? For example, would the group be allowed to determine what is acceptable or unacceptable within their community? Finally, are the practitioners willing to help youth channel their anger into social activism so that they can be advocates for their causes regardless of whether it gains dominant culture approval? Knox goes on to suggest that class role-plays could address ways to manage racist or sexist behaviors that students are likely to encounter.

CONTEXTUAL ADAPTATIONS

Fortunately, the vast majority of social skills programs were originally developed for school-based programs. Therefore, there is little reason to adapt these curricula for contextual reasons. The most important choices to be made in schools are these: (1) Is the program part of a universal (Tier 1) prevention program? (2) Will the curriculum be taught by the classroom teacher or a pupil services provider or a combination? (3) How will social validity be determined—for example, does the curriculum address skills relevant to the participants, not just the adults? (4) How will program integrity be maintained—for example, how will the process be monitored to ensure that core components are implemented with fidelity?

EVALUATION

Evaluation should be done on two levels. First, social workers should perform a process evaluation to determine whether the interventions were implemented as intended. Second, social workers should carry out an outcome evaluation to determine whether the students made progress.

PROCESS EVALUATION

There are eight questions to answer in order to know whether the social skills program was carried out with integrity.

1. Did the intervention include the regular education teacher (as solo, lead, or collaborating instructor)?
2. Was the curriculum provided to all children in the grade level as a Tier 1 intervention?

3. Was the curriculum a regular part of the class schedule?
4. Were the lessons reinforced (through reminders or prompts) during the rest of the week?
5. Did the teacher deliver at least 80% of the curriculum?
6. Was student progress regularly monitored throughout the program?
7. If the emphasis was on the *acquisition* of skills, did the instructor provide coaching, direct instruction, modeling, and rehearsal of skills?
8. If the emphasis was on the *performance* of skills, did the instructor provide prompting, shaping, contracting, and reinforcement of skills?

OUTCOME EVALUATION

After reviewing the meta-analytic studies, it was concluded that traditional social skills programs were only modestly effective at best. (Some further thoughts on how to interpret effect sizes of meta-analyses can be found in Box 10.1) Meadows (2009) agreed and posited six plausible explanations for these discouraging results. First, the social skills targeted for intervention may not have been socially valid for the students. They may be important to the teachers and school administrators, but adults often fail to inquire whether these skills really "work" in the students' social milieu. Second, performance ("won't do") deficits are often confused with skill ("can't do") deficits. It is essential to distinguish between the two problems and adjust the intervention accordingly. Third, most social skills interventions lack intensity—they were taught once a week rather throughout the day. This is an excellent argument for including teachers as part of instructional team for social skills training. Fourth, most commercially available programs were designed for certain types of students but employed with all students. Therefore, it is imperative to determine the original participants for the program selected rather than assume that "one size fits all." Fifth, many social skills "replacement behaviors" may not work because they fail to accomplish the student's social goal. Functional assessment is necessary to determine the purpose of a student's antisocial behavior before attempting to replace it with a prosocial behavior (Raines, 2002). Finally, the social skills may have been taught in contexts that were irrelevant for students. For example, many social skills groups are conducted on a "pull-out" basis and thus separated from the regular classroom where the skills need to be exercised. This makes generalization of the social skills more difficult for the training participants.

Demaray and Ruffalo (1995) reviewed six social skills scales and found that the most comprehensive instrument was the Social Skills Rating System (SSRS; Gresham & Elliott, 1990). It has been used in nearly 250 studies and recently updated (Elliott et al., 2008) as the Social Skills Improvement System (SSIS;

BOX 10.1 INTERPRETING EFFECT SIZE(ES) AND PERCENTAGE
OF NONOVERLAPPING DATA (PND)

An effect size (ES) can be interpreted like a z-score. A positive ES shows the level of improvement correlated with an intervention. Thus, an ES of +1.00 indicates a +1 standard deviation for the treatment group compared to the control group. In other words, it means that 84% of the participants receiving the intervention improved more than the control group participants. Another way to think of this is that if the "average" control group child remained at the 50th percentile, then the average participant in the treatment group moved up to the 84th percentile— a 34 percentile rank increase. In the case of Kavale and associates' (1997) study, an ES of .20 means that the average recipient of social skills training advanced to only the 58th percentile or an 8 percentile rank increase.

The percentage of nonoverlapping data points (PND) can be described as follows. If the intervention is intended to increase a skill, the researcher would draw a dashed line from the highest baseline score across the treatment phase and count the number of data points (measurements) above this line. This number is divided by the total number of intervention data points and multiplied by 100. Thus, a PND of +100% would mean that all of the intervention data points are above the highest baseline data point. A PND of +75% or higher indicates a beneficial intervention because the behavior shows a substantially better result over the baseline performance. A PND of +50, however, demonstrates an intervention that only haphazardly produces the desired effect about 50% of the time. In an ABAB design (baseline$_1$; treatment$_1$; baseline$_2$; treatment$_2$), the researcher would draw two dashed lines (from each baseline) and count the total number of data points above each line, assuming that the same treatment has occurred during both treatment phases. Again, this number would be divided by the total number of intervention data points and multiplied by 100 (Scruggs & Mastropieri, 1998). The example below demonstrates how to perform this simple calculation:

PND = 4/6 or 66.7%   PND = 3/6 or 50%   Total PND = 7/12 or 58.3%

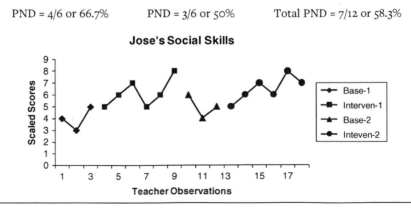

Gresham & Elliott, 2008). Both scales depend upon cross-informant raters, but users of rating scales have known for 20 years not to expect different raters to converge on the same rating (Achenbach et al., 1987). There are three reasons for this phenomenon. First, many social behaviors are situation specific: how the student responds will depend on who is present, where the situation occurs, and even what time of day it happens. Second, all measures of social behavior include some degree of error; at best they are rough estimates of the target student's behavior. Third, "rating scales primarily use rather simple frequency response categories for quantifying behaviors that may vary widely in their frequency, intensity, duration, and social importance" (Elliott et al., 2008, p. 17). With these caveats in place, it is important to monitor students' progress regularly and adapt social skills training according to students' needs.

LESSONS LEARNED

A foray into the scientific literature is always interesting and sometimes even surprising. Here the strengths and weaknesses of empirically supported social skills programs are addressed.

STRENGTHS

The answerable question led to a number of useful research-based programs for children and adolescents. Most of these are accompanied by treatment manuals or program guides that practitioners can readily employ and gradually adapt to fit the needs of students in their schools. Some programs, such as *the Good Behavior Game*, are very inexpensive to start and, with Rathvon's (2008) variations, easy to adapt. It was harder to find materials aimed specifically for urban minority youth, but most of the newer programs have embraced multiculturalism and have altered their materials accordingly.

WEAKNESSES

It was discouraging at first to read the meta-analyses of social skills interventions until one realizes that most of the early social skills programs were pull-out programs divorced from the life of the classroom. The stronger programs are clearly meant to be integrated into the classroom and rely on the leadership (or cooperation) of the teacher to reinforce lessons throughout the week. It has also become frustrating to be inundated with the advertisement that programs are "evidence-based" when precious little research has been done by anyone not connected to the program developer. This is one of the reasons that the authors of this text chose to have our criteria align with the What Works Clearinghouse's insistence that programs be tested by more than one group of researchers. Finally, there has been insufficient attention to treatment fidelity as a critical variable in the effectiveness of social skills programs. It is hoped that the criteria introduced here can be used with a wide assortment of programs.

CONCLUSION

There are many different empirically supported social skills program for every grade level. Most are relatively inexpensive and flexible to use with a variety of youth. Novice social workers can use the programs right out of the box while more experienced practitioners will feel comfortable adapting the lessons to fit their personal style and the needs of their clients. As social-emotional learning becomes more valued and assimilated in schools, it is anticipated that future meta-analyses will demonstrate stronger effects.

11

HELPING STUDENTS WITH ANXIETY IN SCHOOLS

In recent survey research conducted by the authors (Kelly, 2008; Kelly et al., 2009), anxiety disorders stood out as one of the most significant mental health problems school social workers face in their practice. In this chapter, we use an evidence-informed process (EIP) to search for the best available evidence to help students with anxiety disorders in schools.

CONCEPTUAL DEFINITION OF THE ISSUE: STUDENT ANXIETY

Anxiety disorders affect roughly 13 out of 100 young people, affecting girls more than boys (SAMHSA, 2007a). While this chapter focuses on generalized anxiety disorder (GAD) and ways to treat it in a school setting, a number of other anxiety disorders in childhood present in school settings, including panic attacks, separation anxiety disorder, and phobias (Camacho & Hunter, 2006). The characteristics of these other anxiety disorders as well as GAD are having excessive worry about everyday events, difficulty concentrating, somatic complaints, sleep disturbances, and refusal to go to school (Kelly, 2008). Students who have untreated anxiety disorders are at risk for school underachievement, poor social relationships, and eventual substance abuse as they try to self-medicate and cope with their anxiety (Masia-Warner et al., 2005).

For this chapter we chose an effectiveness question: what are effective school-based interventions for students with generalized anxiety disorder (GAD) and/or social anxiety disorder? We consulted a range of evidence-informed literature, including two databases of peer-reviewed articles (PsycInfo and Academic Search Premier/EBSCO), three online EIP clearinghouses (SAMHSA's NREEP, Colorado's Blueprints, and the What Works Clearinghouse), described in more detail in Appendix B. The results of these searches are also collected in our Appraisal Grid in Table 11.1.

TABLE 11.1 HELPING STUDENTS MANAGE ANXIETY DISORDERS: INTERVENTION APPRAISAL GRID

Intervention	Research Design	Participants (Child/Adolescent)	Test Site	Researcher Groups	Follow-Up Period	Review Process	Feasibility
*Coping Cat and C.A.T. (Kendall et al., 1994 and 1997)	Experimental design with random assignment	2nd graders-High School (CAT Project for high school students)	Schools	2+	1-year follow-up	Peer-Review	Workbooks and materials easy to find and buy
*FRIENDS (Lowry-Webster et al., 2003)	Experimental design, with random assignment	1st grade-High School	Schools	2+	1-year follow-up	Peer-Review	Resources available
**Cool Kids Program (Mifsud & Rapee, 2005)	Experimental design, with random assignment	3rd-4th Graders	Schools	1	4-month follow-up	Peer-Review	Resources available
*School-Based CBT Treatment (Bernstein et al., 2005)	Experimental design with random assignment	2nd-5th Graders	Schools	3+	1-year follow-up	Peer-Review	A variety of affordable books on CBT for schools are available
**SASS (Skills for Social and Academic Success) (Maisa-Warner et al., 2005)		9th-11th graders	Schools	1	9-month follow-up	Peer-Review	Resources available

Note:
* indicates that the intervention was rated "highly recommended";
** indicates that the intervention was rated "recommended (with caution)" CBT = cognitive behavioral therapy.

ORGANIZING AND INTERPRETING THE EVIDENCE

Table 11.1 indicates that there are several effective and emerging interventions that school social workers can begin using immediately to help students with anxiety symptoms. This is in addition to the growing use of selective serotonin reuptake inhibitors (SSRIs) and other psychiatric medications that are being used to treat anxiety in children, though there is still some concern among some parents because the Food and Drug Administration hasn't formally approved their use for children (Bentley & Collins, 2006). The best thing about much of the research on anxiety treatments, based on the EIP search conducted for this chapter, was the relatively large number of well-controlled studies that had been completed in school settings. All of the five interventions noted in the EIP search rated as either *highly recommended* (meaning that they met all of our evidentiary criteria) or *recommended* (*with caution*), indicating that they fell short in only one or two areas. All five interventions draw on basic cognitive-behavioral therapy (CBT) ideas, and with the appropriate training (which was offered either directly from the researcher's own Web sites or in training manuals that were easy to find online), a school social worker can quickly begin to offer these interventions to his or her student clients.

DETAILS ON SELECTED INTERVENTIONS FOR CHILDREN WITH ANXIETY DISORDERS

For example, the *Coping Cat* intervention is described by the National Registry of Evidence-based Programs and Practices (NREPP) in its 2006 review of the intervention:

> *Coping Cat* is a cognitive behavioral treatment that assists school-age children in (1) recognizing anxious feelings and physical reactions to anxiety; (2) clarifying cognition in anxiety-provoking situations (i.e., unrealistic expectations); (3) developing a plan to help cope with the situation (i.e., determining what coping actions might be effective); and (4) evaluating performance and administering self-reinforcement as appropriate. The intervention uses behavioral training strategies with demonstrated efficacy, such as modeling real-life situations, role-playing, relaxation training, and contingent reinforcement. Throughout the sessions, therapists use social reinforcement to encourage and reward the children, and the children are encouraged to verbally reinforce their own successful coping. *Coping Cat* consists of 16 sessions. The first eight sessions are training sessions in which each of the basic concepts are introduced individually and then practiced and reinforced. In the second set of eight sessions, the child practices the new skills in both imaginary and real-life

situations varying from low stress/low anxiety to high stress/high anxiety, depending on what is appropriate for each child.

This same review described some of the key findings on the randomized trials of studies of *Coping Cat*, showing reduction of anxiety symptoms:

> In one study, the number of children receiving the *Coping Cat* model of CBT who were diagnosed with overanxious disorder or separation anxiety disorder decreased (p < .0001 and p < .01, respectively) from pretreatment to 1 year and 3.5 years posttreatment ... In another study, the anxiety diagnosis was no longer primary for more than 92% of former *Coping Cat* participants at 7.4 years posttreatment, based on client and parent interviews.... Another evaluation that compared individual and group formats of *Coping Cat* with a wait-list control condition found that 81% of participants in the individual format no longer met criteria for their primary anxiety disorder at 1-year follow-up. The percentage was slightly lower (77%) for the group format. (NREPP, 2006)

The FRIENDS intervention (Lowry-Webster et al., 2003) uses 10 sessions and two follow-up sessions for students at school (students from ages 6 to 11 and 12 to 16 have FRIENDS program materials prepared for them at their developmental level). FRIENDS teaches students CBT techniques to give them tools to reframe their anxious responses, to learn ways to appreciate their own bodies' anxiety responses, and to make a wider social network to help them find support for their anxiety. FRIENDS also contains a parent component that encourages parents to practice the FRIENDS skills at home with their child. Randomized controlled trials of FRIENDS indicate that significant decrease of anxiety symptoms (to the point of being diagnosis-free) were present for almost 70% of the treatment group at one-year follow-up (compared to 6% of the control group).

The Cool Kids Program was initially developed by Australian researchers and practitioners and is described by its creators on their Web site in this way:

> This (Cool Kids) package describes an adaptation of the Cool Kids treatment program for anxious youth to the school setting. Designed to be run within school by school counsellors and related mental health workers, the program includes up to 8 sessions to be run with young people and an additional 2 parent information evenings. The therapist's manual describes in detail how to conduct each session of the program including exercises and comments to assist successful implementation as well as overheads for the parent evening. (Macquarie University Anxiety Research Unit, 2009)

Cool Kids has been evaluated with third through fifth graders using a randomized clinical trial (Mifsud & Rapee, 2005). The key components of Cool Kids are rooted in group-based cognitive-behavioral therapy (CBT) techniques and students are encouraged to learn to dispute the automatic thoughts they have and to counter those thoughts with ideas that allow them to decrease their anxious responses. Cool Kids was shown to maintain clinically significant gains compared to control groups at a four-month follow-up (Mifsud & Rapee, 2005).

ADAPTING AND APPLYING THE EVIDENCE

DEVELOPMENTAL AND CONTEXTUAL VARIATIONS

Though there are a host of complicating issues (students who have comorbid disorders such as attention deficit/hyperactivity disorder [ADHD] or depression, or who also have learning problems), anxiety is one area of school-based mental health that might be addressed fairly quickly and affordably for a broad range of ages and population groups in American schools (Oswald & Mazefsky, 2006). Just as with ADHD, it is important that school social workers work closely with the client system (including the student's health care providers) to help establish that the diagnosis of anxiety is a correct and solid one. There are several clinical interview scaled instruments to help school social workers identify whether a student is suffering from anxiety (for a recent summary of good anxiety assessment scales, see Camacho and Hunter, 2006, and Balon, 2007). In addition to offering these scales to students and their parents, it is important for school social workers to develop linkages with child psychiatrists and pediatric neurologists who might be able to help with the diagnostic work necessary to establish that the student has an anxiety disorder. Additionally, because the vast majority of students are unlikely to get outside psychological counseling for their anxiety disorders (Essau et al., 1999), the more school social workers can provide to students at school, the more potential benefit the interventions noted in this chapter might have for students.

Assuming that a diagnosis of anxiety has been established, it is important to then work to adapt the intervention to the developmental level of the school population and to specific school contextual factors. Fortunately, as we see in Table 11.1, a number of options are available across ages and developmental levels for school social workers to choose from. Additionally, the interventions, while squarely located in Tier 3, could be adapted to a Tier 2 classroom level if the school social worker determined that the class as a whole was experiencing symptoms of anxiety about specific events (we're thinking of test anxiety as one good example). That said, a major limitation of this EIP search was the deliberate choice to focus on two of the "milder" versions of anxiety disorder and not focus on symptoms associated with panic attacks or posttraumatic stress disorder (PTSD). A separate EIP search would be indicated in those instances, for while we found some evidence of school-based treatments that had been tested in the wake of terrorist attacks or natural disasters, such as Hurricane

Katrina, or living in the midst of the Palestinian-Israeli conflict, they were not included in this review.

CULTURAL VARIATIONS

One additional (and in our view, highly significant) limitation of the studies involved in this EIP search is their relative lack of cross-cultural and multi-cultural content. Understanding the specific cultural context of one's school and the way the racial/ethnic/religious groups may express (or not express) anxiety will be crucial to delivering these interventions in a culturally competent manner. Additional EIP searches we conducted yielded three articles that discussed school-based anxiety interventions for specific culturally diverse populations. One article (Wilson & Rotter, 1986) found in an experimental design that a middle-school sample of predominantly African American males struggling with test anxiety was helped by the CBT techniques outlined in several of the interventions highlighted in this chapter. Another study found that African American fifth graders responded well to anxiety management interventions that had previously only been tested with a largely white student population (Cooley & Boyce 2004). An exploratory study using folk tales and narrative therapy to treat anxiety in Hispanic children was noted and showed some initially positive outcomes on anxiety and phobia symptoms (Costantino et al., 2005). One well-designed study that compared two clinical trials for CBT involving Anglo and Hispanic American youth found little difference in treatment outcomes for reduction in anxiety symptoms, leading the researchers to conclude that these two trials showed that CBT could achieve similar outcomes with both Anglo and Hispanic American youth (Pina et al., 2003). Other researchers argue that issues of language, acculturation, and culture-related cognitive schemas need to be considered when evaluating the feasibility of using anxiety assessment tools and treatments with culturally diverse student populations (Cooley & Boyce, 2004; Wood et al., 2008).

EVALUATION

In all of the studies described in this EIP search, a treatment manual and workbooks were used to enhance the effectiveness of the treatment and also demonstrate treatment fidelity. Assuming that those materials can be secured easily and for relatively low cost, the actual content of these manuals does not appear to require a high degree of new training beyond a school social worker's familiarity with basic CBT ideas. In the event that a school social worker isn't familiar with CBT (or frankly, is uncomfortable practicing from that perspective), treatment fidelity will be a significant challenge without further training.

OUTCOME EVALUATIONS AND RELIABLE AND VALID MEASURES FOR PRACTICE

There are multiple quick and efficient ways to assess progress on the treatment of anxiety in schools, most obviously the behavior and emotion scales used in the studies themselves. A number of good anxiety screening tools can then be used to assess progress on the student's anxiety symptoms at three-, six-, and nine-month intervals. Teachers and parents are often able to complete these same scales or other ones commonly used in school assessment and treatment (e. g., the BASC, Conner's Rating Scale, Child Behavior Checklist). These scales, when integrated with naturally occurring data (student grades, attendance, discipline referrals) can give school social workers a good set of tools with which to develop a baseline for their student and then engage in one of the intervention strategies from this search and measure progress.

CONCLUSION

We were happy to see that generalized anxiety disorder has lots of well-supported treatments. Many of them had been evaluated repeatedly within a school setting, heightening the possibility that these interventions might have a high level of social validity for school social workers. That said, it was a concern that so much of the research done in this area was grounded solely in CBT treatments, as many of our colleagues in the field are not trained in CBT and have expressed doubts about how realistic such a manualized treatment would be in their school practices. It will be interesting to see in the coming decade if other intervention programs and strategies (perhaps some involving relaxation techniques or solution-focused brief therapy) might also be tested and compared to the well-established CBT treatments noted in this chapter.

Anxiety is a pervasive and treatable condition for our students. School social workers, provided they have been trained in basic CBT concepts, have a wealth of empirically supported resources to draw on in designing interventions for their students. Culturally diverse populations are also increasingly being included in the testing of school-based anxiety interventions, which is encouraging. As anxiety problems appear to figure prominently in a large portion of the caseloads school social workers carry, we hope this chapter will help allay some of their anxiety as they work to meet the needs of their students.

12

PROBLEMS WITH ADHD IN A SCHOOL SETTING

Characterized by developmentally atypical levels of inattention, activity, and impulsivity, attention deficit/hyperactivity disorder (ADHD) is a prevalent disorder (5%–8% of the school-age population, American Psychiatric Association, 2000). The condition is often first manifested and identified in school settings (DuPaul & Stoner, 2003; Sax & Kautz, 2003; Snider et al., 2000). Children diagnosed with the condition exhibit significant impairment in academic and social functioning as well as risk for accidental injury (Hinshaw, 2002). It is not surprising, then, that recent national and state survey data indicate that a significant number of school social worker respondents indicate that children with ADHD are often referred for social work services.

Notably, some controversy surrounds the diagnosis and treatment of ADHD. There appears to be significant variation in diagnosis, which may be attributable to differences in physician practices (Jensen et al., 1999). A growing body of research indicates significant heterogeneity in psychostimulant use and prescription rates. In a national sample of insured children, Cox, Mothera, Henderson, and Mager (2003) found that being a white male from a smaller family increase the odds of receiving psychostimulants, as did living in an affluent community, urban area, and particular region (the South or Midwest). A complicated pattern of both over- and underdiagnosis as well as over- and underprescribing probably contributes to this variation (Jensen et al., 1999).

Of particular relevance to school social work practitioners, students with ADHD show specific impairments in school functioning, and school factors have been implicated in the diagnosis and treatment of ADHD. Relative to their peers without the condition, children with ADHD earn lower grades

(Barkley et al., 1990) and achievement test scores; they also experience higher rates of grade retention and school dropout (Hansen, Weiss, & Last, 1999; Hinshaw, 1992a, 1992b). For several of these outcomes, most notably those focusing on poor educational attainment in adolescence (grade retention, poor grades, low test scores), robust linkages exist between childhood ADHD and such educational failure. That is, the longitudinal association holds even with statistical control of childhood comorbidities that may accompany ADHD (e.g., oppositional defiant disorder) as well as socio-demographic factors and IQ scores (Hinshaw, 2002), implying that early ADHD is an independent academic risk factor. Moreover, ADHD is often comorbid with other learning disorders (see Hinshaw, 1992b). It is also notable that children with ADHD show marked impairment in peer relationships (Hinshaw, 2002).

Teachers report that children with ADHD are difficult to instruct (Bussing et al., 2002). And it is implied that affected children may have the potential to overwhelm classroom and school resources in both general and special education settings (DuPaul & Stoner, 2003; Forness & Kavale, 2002). DuPaul and Stoner (2003), in particular, argue that teachers need to be supported in their efforts to educate children with ADHD, implying that the nature and quality of classroom supports needed by this population exceed teacher capacities in general education classrooms. Special education service utilization among these children is quite high; estimates indicate that 45% of children with ADHD receive special education services (Forness & Kavale, 2002). Because there is considerable variation in whether and how affected children are identified for and served by special education programs, Forness and Kavale (2002) raise questions about the appropriateness and adequacy of these services. As a whole, these findings suggest that the higher numbers of pupils identified with ADHD may relate to the abilities of teachers or the capacity of special education programs and/or schools to deliver quality instruction and supportive services. There is marked regional variation in ADHD diagnosis rates and psychostimulant usage, and school-related policies and practices are implicated in such variation, as evidenced by recent state and local legislation prohibiting local school personnel from discussing or recommending psychostimulant evaluation and treatment (Fine, 2001). We offer a story about "Jasper," a first-grade boy, to help illustrate the ways that ADHD presents in a school setting in Box 12.1

CONCEPTUAL DEFINITION OF THE ISSUE

Barkley (2006a) argues that the weight of theoretical and empirical evidence to date supports the classification of "a developmental disorder of probable neuro-genetic origins" (p. 121) and highlights specific sets of neurocognitive deficits

---

BOX 12.1 ATTENTION DEFICIT/HYPERACTIVITY DISORDER (ADHD) VIGNETTE

Jasper's mother contacted a school social worker for help in October. Her son, who was currently a first grader, had long-standing difficulties with impulsive and hyperactive behaviors starting in preschool. In the early fall of his kindergarten year, Jasper was evaluated by a physician specializing in ADHD, who confirmed that Jasper met criteria for attention deficit/hyperactivity disorder, combined subtype. Because of his age, the fact that he showed few peer-related difficulties, and performed well academically, the physician advocated a "wait and see" approach toward medication but strongly recommended that Jasper's parents work closely with his teacher to support him in the classroom. Based on his experience in kindergarten, Jasper functioned well under the following conditions: (1) when he was seated in such a way that allowed him to occasionally stand, so long as he completed assigned work; (2) when the teacher sent home a daily report card, based on specific ratings on work completion taken at 15 minute intervals; and (3) when the teacher prepared him (by providing specific directives) prior to transitions (between lesson segments, before and after recess and lunch). Jasper's mother discussed these supports with his new first grade teacher at the beginning of the school year and the teacher enthusiastically agreed to adhere to these plans. Over time, however, Jasper's mother noticed that daily report cards were being sent home filled out sporadically (entire rating intervals were missing) and infrequently (sometimes up to every third or fourth day). The teacher then began calling to complain that Jasper was "difficult to manage" and "a real handful" and "hinted that Jasper's mother should "really consider a reevaluation for medication." When the school social worker followed up to ask the teacher for her perspective, she said that she "simply didn't have the time fill out all that paperwork." The teacher also suggested that if Jasper needed such support, maybe the school social worker should help the mother start the process for a special education evaluation, because she was unsure that Jasper's behaviors could be maintained in a general education setting.

---

characterizing the condition, including verbal and nonverbal working memory and internalization and self-regulation of affect. The core symptoms and specific impairments of the disorder may manifest in complex ways in a given child or adolescent in a given setting (e.g., school). Thus, for purposes of this chapter, the focus of the search was on school-based, psychosocial, or academic interventions for children affected by ADHD, cross-cutting children whose symptoms cluster around (1) inattentive, (2) hyperactive/impulsive, and/or (3) combined subtypes.

ORGANIZING AND INTERPRETING THE EVIDENCE

What are effective school-based, psychosocial, or academic interventions for students with attention deficit/hyperactivity disorder? In this chapter, we do not cover psychostimulant treatments or parent training in behavior management methods, although these would both be considered an evidence-informed treatment strategy (for a review and current practice parameters on these subjects, see Pliszka and AACAP Work Group on Quality Issues, 2007, and Barkley, 2006a, 2006b). The efficacy of psychostimulant medication in controlling the core symptoms of the disorder is well established (MTA Cooperative Group, 1999) and would meet criteria for a *highly recommended* intervention; behavioral methods in general also constitute an empirically supported intervention strategy (Fabiano et al., in press; Hinshaw et al., 2007). Table 12.1 summarizes the search results.

None of the studies extracted from the literature met our criteria for *highly recommended*. This is because there are no specific, replicated programs using methods of randomized control. However, the search yielded a set of both *recommended* and *emerging* strategies falling into one of four general classes: school-based contingency management, self-management/organizational training, consultation-based methods, and tutoring. Less supportive results have been generated for attention training methods, cognitive-behavioral methods, and social skills training. Key studies and reviews are summarized in Table 12.1.

There are several important thematic issues that cut across existent research studies. First, multimodal treatment of ADHD is asserted to (and this is congruent with meta-analytic findings; Schachar et al., 2002) constitute a best practice (Barkley, 2006a; DuPaul & Stoner, 2003; MTA Cooperative Group, 1999). In the context of this literature, multimodal refers to a combination of "modes of intervention": medication, home and school-based contingency management, and inclusion of supportive school services that are provided to students over time. Second, the overall efficacy of treatment effects are dependent on the outcomes assessed (core symptoms of ADHD, social, academic outcomes). Reporter source (e.g., parent versus teacher versus child) also appears to matter. Overall, psychostimulant treatment garners the greatest effect sizes for core disorder-specific symptomatology and social outcomes (Schachar et al., 2002) and multimodal treatments yield the largest effect sizes for social outcomes (MTA Cooperative Group, 1999; Schachar, 2002). On the other hand, school-centered interventions (e.g., contingency management, tutoring, and consultation) to date show the largest effects on cognitive outcomes (Purdie et al., 2002). Among school-based interventions, contingency management and tutoring show higher effect sizes than self-management strategies (DuPaul & Eckert, 1997). Regardless of modality, effects of any of these treatments fade without sustained follow-up (Barkley, 2006a, 2006b; Hinshaw et al., 2007). It should also be noted that a single

TABLE 12.1 INTERVENTION APPRAISAL GRID: INTERVENTIONS FOR CHILDREN WITH ATTENTION DEFICIT/HYPERACTIVITY DISORDER (ADHD) IN SCHOOLS

Intervention	Research Design	Participants	Test Site	Researcher Groups	Follow-Up Period	Review Process	Feasibility
School-based contingency management**	RCT; Meta-analysis	Elementary schoolers	Schools	3+	Variable	Blind Peer Review	N/A
Self-Management Training**	RCT; Meta-analysis	7-13 years	Schools	3+	Variable	Blind Peer Review	N/A
Classroom and peer tutoring*	RCT	Elementary schoolers	Schools	1	15-month follow-up	Blind Peer Review	N/A
Consultation*	RCT	Elementary schoolers	Schools	1	15 month follow-up	Blind Peer Review	N/A

Note:

** indicates that the strategy was rated "recommended";

* indicates that the intervention was rated "emerging"; RCT = randomized controlled trial.

randomized trial (the MTA study) contributes to a large majority of research findings in this area and results of meta-analyses include a preponderance of single subject and within-subject designs. Finally, the literature searched also identifies strategies that do not demonstrate efficacy in the treatment of ADHD. These appear in a narrative review and include bio-feedback and related therapies, dietary intervention, play therapy, cognitive behavioral therapy, and social skills training (Barkley, 2006b).

Recommended (with caution). DuPaul & Weyandt (2006a) divide behavioral and contingency management methods into either proactive and reactive approaches. It is recommended that these methods include both rewards/ incentives as well as consequences for behaviors (Barkley, 2006b; DuPaul & Weyandt, 2006a; 2006b). Specific proactive approaches (designed to prevent undesirable and promote desirable behaviors) include peer tutoring and class-wide peer tutoring. Such approaches combine intensive one-on-one interaction, continuous prompting of and immediate feedback on performance. Reactive approaches (those which occur after a behavior has occurred) included specific and non-punitive reprimands, school or home based reward systems. For example, a recent randomized trial of a home-school coordinated behavior modification system showed positive academic achievement effects for children with inattentive-type ADHD (Pfiffner et al., 2007).

In summary, school-based contingency management refers to a set of strategies—rather than a particular program per-se, thus readers are instructed to gain familiarity with these approaches in general. These interventions are typically delivered by teachers in classroom settings. These strategies, broadly defined, set of individualized plans for children that (1) specifically define desired and undesired behaviors and (2) provide reinforcers for the positive behaviors (which are typically defined by the student) and that may be delivered by a teacher or parent. Conversely, there are often a set of consequences for negative behaviors. Such strategies may also include "ignoring" particular, non-disruptive behaviors. For specific guidelines in developing contingency management interventions, including decisions about the number of behaviors to be targeted, how to identify child-level reinforcers, the nature and timing of rewards and consequences, as well as guidelines in deciding how to include both teachers and parents, readers are directed to DuPaul & Stoner, 2003.

Emerging. Three emerging strategies were identified. The first included self-management, self-monitoring and organizational strategies (Langberg et al., 2008; Gureasko-Moore et al., 2007; Gureasko-Moore et al., 2006). Generally speaking, such interventions focus on student goal setting and developing specific self-monitoring and self-reinforcing strategies tailored to specific student situations. Self-management/ organizational training (see Gureasko-Moore, DuPaul, & White, 2006) is related to contingency management training but the affected child self monitors and reports on progress toward a set of desired behaviors, under the guidance of a key adult (e.g., teacher, therapist). With the key adult, a student typically works to identify problems, sets goals as well as strategies for monitoring results. Students then evaluate their own progress and administer their own reinforcers/consequences (Snyder and Bambara, 1997). Such approaches are typically conducted with older students and are thought to place less demands on teachers, especially in terms of monitoring and administering reinforcers (Gureasko-Moore, DuPaul, & White, 2006).

The second included teacher-centered consultation. One recent trial found that both general and student-specific teacher consultation approaches related to child achievement growth over a 15 month period (DuPaul et al., 2006). Interestingly, the extent to which the consultation approach included behavioral methods did not show many additional benefits. The generic consultation approach, which in this case involved doctoral students in psychology or special education as consultants included a total of two interviews with the teacher. During the first interview the teacher described specific student difficulties and goals. At the second interview, the consultant provided the teacher a menu of potential intervention plans. After the teacher chose a plan, the consultant provided further details on the specific components of the plan.

Finally, classroom and peer tutoring encompasses a final set of strategies. As a representative example, after a particular skill is taught, student-peer dyads are formed whereby one assumes the role of tutor and the other of quizee. Dyads are supervised and then roles may be reversed (that is, the tutor and quizee change roles).

On a final note, results from a long term prevention trial, FastTrack, which targeted externalizing behaviors and combining a teacher delivered curricula (PATHS), parent training and home visiting, social skills training and friendship enhancement, and tutoring beginning in first grade showed no relationship to a later diagnosis of ADHD, but was predictive of fewer core symptoms of the disorder relative to controls (Bierman et al., 2007).

RECOMMENDED

DuPaul and Weyandt (2006a) divide behavioral and contingency management methods into proactive and reactive approaches. It is recommended that these methods include both rewards/incentives and consequences for behaviors (Barkley, 2006b; DuPaul & Weyandt, 2006a, 2006b). Specific proactive approaches (designed to prevent undesirable and promote desirable behaviors) include peer tutoring and classwide peer tutoring. Such approaches combine intensive one-on-one interaction, continuous prompting of and immediate feedback on performance. Reactive approaches (those that occur after a behavior has occurred) included specific and nonpunitive reprimands as well as school- or home-based reward systems. For example, a recent randomized trial of a home–school coordinated behavior modification system showed positive academic achievement effects for children with inattentive-type ADHD (Pfiffner et al., 2007).

EMERGING

Two emerging strategies were identified. The first included self-management, self-monitoring, and organizational strategies (Langberg et al., 2008; Gureasko-Moore et al., 2007; Gureasko-Moore et al., 2006). Generally, such interventions focus on student goal setting and development of specific self-monitoring and self-reinforcing strategies tailored to specific student situations. The second included teacher-centered consultation. One recent trial found that both general and student-specific teacher consultation approaches related to child achievement growth over a 15-month period (DuPaul et al., 2006).

On a final note, results from a long-term prevention trial, FastTrack, showed no relationship to a later diagnosis of ADHD. FastTrack targeted externalizing behaviors and combined a teacher-delivered curriculum (PATHS), parent training and home visiting, social skills training and friendship enhancement, and tutoring beginning in first grade. However, the program was predictive of fewer core symptoms of the disorder relative to controls (Bierman et al., 2007).

REFLECTIONS

PROCESS REFLECTIONS

Overall, a substantial number of school-specific meta-analyses have already been conducted on the topic. Moreover, recent research almost exclusively relies on randomized controlled trials, so it is clear that there is a trend toward a strengthened knowledge base specific to ADHD as is it is manifested in schools. If ADHD is best conceptualized as a neurobiologically based, chronic condition that children will have to manage throughout life as well as a condition that is manifested through a very heterogeneous presentation of symptoms and functional impairments, an individualized and intensive intervention approach would be warranted and appropriate.

CONTENT REFLECTIONS

There are still areas in which research is still emerging. Indeed, the evidence base on methods of parent behavior management is better established than the evidence base of methods implemented in classroom and school settings (Fabiano et al., in press). There is an urgent need for emphasis on better standardizing the behavioral methods in ways that are accessible to practitioners as well as for replicating promising strategies. The lack of strategies directly tested on students in mid- and late adolescence is also of concern, especially given the poor long-term academic performance outcomes as manifested in school dropout among affected adolescents.

LOCATING THE CONTENT WITHIN A RESPONSE TO INTERVENTION FRAMEWORK

From the perspective of this framework, available treatment strategies cluster on the intensive end—Tier 3—of the continuum. That is, these strategies have been developed for children who have already been identified for treatment. Indeed, this intensive focus may be warranted in that an intensive prevention trial encompassing curricular, parent, peer, and child components did not influence whether a child met the criteria in the *Diagnostic and Statistical Manual of Mental Disorders* (*DSM-IV*; American Psychological Association, 2000) by third grade (Bierman et al., 2007). Given the nature of the condition, sustained supports with recommended practices may help optimize and sustain child functioning over time.

Response to intervention approaches, which highlight the importance of a continuous, data-driven focus on problem identification, implementation, and evaluation of intervention efforts (see Chapter 10, this volume) dovetails very neatly with the literature retrieved, which underscores the importance of identifying child-specific behavioral targets, specifically intervening on those targets, and assessing the extent to which children meet these targets (Barkley 2006a, 2006b; DuPaul & Stoner, 2003).

ADAPTING AND APPLYING THE EVIDENCE

Given the variability in diagnosis and psychostimulant rates related to children with ADHD, a first step for school social workers is to assess and advocate adequate diagnostic and treatment methods. Recent evidence-based practice parameters discuss recommended evaluation methods and measures (including structured and unstructured child, parent, school reports of symptoms and comorbid conditions as well as child bio-psychosocial history). These parameters also specify guidelines for pharmacological intervention and agents as well as the ordering of other empirically supported treatment strategies (see Pliszka & AACAP Work Group on Quality Issues, 2007, and Barkley, 2006a, 2006b). Other adaptations and applications follow.

DEVELOPMENTAL ADAPTATIONS

The literature extracted in our search reaffirms that much of the weight of the evidence has been generated from elementary school and middle school–aged samples of children, leaving unclear the extent to which findings are generalizable to older adolescents. DuPaul and Stoner (2003) suggest several guidelines for modifying contingency management by a focus on developing study skills and using contingency contracting, peer coaching, and a greater reliance on both self-monitoring and self-evaluation strategies. Barkeley (2006b) suggests that cognitive-behavioral methods may play an important role for older adolescents, although there is not yet evidence to support this claim.

CULTURAL ADAPTATIONS

Note that most research studies have been conducted on samples of boys, although these have been somewhat heterogeneous on race-ethnicity and socio-economic status. A good deal of evidence indicates that minority children are less likely to receive psychostimulant medication—in some cases a proportion as low as 4% of those diagnosed (Schneider & Eisenberg, 2006). This probably represents both cultural preferences (Perry et al., 2005;) and problematic access to necessary services as well as the extent to which these disparities relate to other relevant service modalities (Hervey-Jumper et al., 2006). A study of African American parents found that 71% were initially hesitant to use stimulant medications based on what they had learned from the popular press. Specifically, 22% believed that stimulants were overprescribed, 21% worried about negative side effects, and 17% thought that taking stimulants might lead to future drug abuse (dosReis et al., 2007). A qualitative follow-up study (dosReis et al., 200) found that parents went through four stages toward acceptance of stimulant medication. First, they formed a variety of sometimes contradictory opinions about ADHD. Second, they contemplated the origin of the problem (e.g., parental substance abuse, heredity, or parenting). Next, they reevaluated their child's self-control. Finally, they conceptualized ADHD as a medical illness and sought health care services. With Spanish-speaking parents, it is essential that information be readily available in their native language (e.g., http://www.help4adhd.org/espanol.cfm). It is reasonable to conclude that when intervening with racial and ethnic minorities it is imperative to assess caregiver expectations and engagement in recommended strategies and to offer multimodal approaches, consisting of both medication and behavioral training (Arnold et al., 2003; DuPaul & Weyandt, 2006a).

CONTEXTUAL ADAPTATIONS

Contextual factors can unduly influence the number of referrals for attention problems. Havey and colleagues (2005) found that larger classroom size contributed to teachers identifying more children as having ADHD. They suggest two possible explanations for this phenomenon. First, larger classrooms may contain more distractions and ADHD children may behave better in smaller classes with fewer distractions. Second, teachers with larger class sizes may have less time to devote to students with disruptive behavior, thereby increasing the likelihood of presuming that the "cause" for misbehavior is internal to the child rather than the environment. The researchers also found that the highest proportion of teachers felt that attentional problems were biochemical in nature and therefore needed medication. Part of this is probably due to a knee-jerk reaction on the part of teachers to assign all attentional problems the diagnosis of ADHD because they simply do not know that these can be associated with a number of other causes, including anxiety disorders, conduct disorders, mood disorders, and thought disorders (Kauffman, 2005). DuPaul and associates (2006) caution that school-based helping professionals are not necessarily uniformly trained in behavioral theory and approaches. Thus, the knowledge and skills of both teachers and other learning support professionals should be considered and supplemented. Disruptive school contextual factors can undermine the effectiveness of cognitive-behavioral interventions for children with disruptive behaviors (Gottfredson et al., 2002; Hunter, 2003).

EVALUATION

As noted in prior chapters, evaluation should be done on two levels. First, practitioners should conduct a process evaluation to determine whether the interventions were employed as intended. Second, practitioners should conduct an outcome evaluation to determine whether the students responded as hoped.

PROCESS EVALUATION

Because the weight of evidence is based on general strategies (versus program or intervention packages), a key limitation in this area is the lack of readily available manualized treatments (for exceptions, see Langberg et al., 2008). There are, however, available guides for typical target domains relevant to children with ADHD (Barkley, 2006a, 2006b). DuPaul and

Stoner (2003) provide general guidelines in constructing behavioral plans; they recommend Gresham (1989) as a measure of treatment fidelity in a response cost format as a useful fidelity framework. Gresham (1989) provides an observational rating scale that rates the extent to which the system is described and displayed, whether relevant materials are in place (e.g., tokens), whether contingencies are applied, and whether reinforcers are actually offered.

OUTCOME EVALUATION

The evidence yielded by this search would likely focus a practitioner on single subject or within-subject methodologies. This assertion is based three key themes gleaned from this review: (1) the relatively small number of affected children a practitioner would likely see in a given school (estimated at about one child in a class of 20; DuPaul & Stoner, 2003), (2) the nature of outcomes sought (which are probably more readily visualized and assessed through methods such as rates of off-task behavior and/or work completion, and accuracy), and (3) the likely heterogeneity in behavioral plans across affected students.

RELIABLE AND VALID MEASURES

Three sets of measures are widely used in assessing and evaluating children with ADHD. These include (1) broad and narrow band measures of symptoms from teacher perspectives, (2) ratings and observational measures of school performance, and (3) school or teaching records, work completion, and curriculum-related assessments. Measures of symptoms include the Behavioral Assessment System of Children (BASC-2; Reynolds & Kamphaus, 2004) and the ADHD Rating Scale-IV (DuPaul et al., 1998. School performance rating scales from teacher perspectives include the School Situations Scale-Revised (SSQ-R; DuPaul & Barkley, 1992) and the Academic Performance Rating Scale (APRS; DuPaul et al., 1991). In addition, the Behavior Observation for Students in Schools (BOSS; Shapiro, 1996) is an observational measure of student performance.

CONCLUSION

This review allows us to conclude that there are empirically supported strategies for school social workers to use for children affected with ADHD. Most of these strategies would be classified as falling into more intensive and indicated forms of intervention, and this may be appropriate given the nature of the disorder- and child-specific symptom patterning and impairments. Findings from this chapter strongly emphasize the need for school social practitioner proficiency in functional behavior assessment and a variety of behavioral and contingency management methods.

13

IATROGENIC INTERVENTIONS IN SCHOOLS

As school social work scholars concerned with seeing our work make a direct impact on practice in schools, we would be remiss if we didn't consider the more painful and problematic notions of evidence-informed practice, that is, interventions that have the potential to harm school clients. The idea that interventions can (and do) cause harm for the children who make up the majority of our school clients isn't easy to contemplate. No school social worker we've ever met has indicated that he or she had consciously chosen interventions or ideas knowing they would harm clients. Such a person would be in such direct contravention of our profession's code of ethics that we would have taken action to stop that individual from continuing to practice in schools. Rather than demonize individual practitioners (which is not our intention with this chapter), we wish to show how good intentions, "authority-based practice," and poor understanding of what makes an intervention potentially harmful have come together in several situations to create what we call here "iatrogenic school-based interventions."

CONCEPTUAL DEFINITION: DEFINING AN IATROGENIC INTERVENTION

For this chapter, iatrogenic interventions are defined as interventions that have the unintended consequence of causing harm to the very clients the school social worker or other school professionals were trying to help. *Iatrogenic* is a term that comes from medicine and is originally from the Greek for physician (*iatros*) and product of (*gennan*). Medical history is full of interventions and procedures once considered to be effective and legitimated by expert opinion that have now been clearly shown to be harmful to most patient—such as bloodletting for severe illness, thalidomide for morning sickness in pregnant women (Greenhalgh, 2006).

With this understanding, we would expect a school-based iatrogenic intervention to directly impact student educational, emotional, or behavioral outcomes in a negative manner and to do so despite the stated intention of doing exactly the opposite. As we show in our search and appraisal process, practitioners using interventions that we judged to be iatrogenic were often infused with the best of intentions (reducing teen drug use, preventing teen pregnancy and sexual activity, protecting schools from gun violence) but in failing to achieve their desired outcomes, seemingly resisted the competing evidentiary claims on the intervention's efficacy and simply pressed on, ignoring any disconfirming evidence.

As readers can identify by now, the use of iatrogenic interventions can be an unintended consequence of "authority-based practice," which privileges the practitioner's (or researcher's) view of the intervention and its potential efficacy over any evidence that may argue against the intervention's claims of efficacy. While not all authority-based practice is iatrogenic, the risk that practitioners might employ iatrogenic interventions is heightened when they fail to stay current with the research literature, and the risk can be heightened further when practice contexts (such as the ones we've been discussing in schools) simply declare certain interventions to be policy and not open for discussion or debate. Finally, authority-based practice always increases the possibility that in asserting the intervention's value and claims of effectiveness, clients' voices will be minimized if they express concern about the potential benefits of the intervention.

By our definition, iatrogenic interventions are those that do harm on an outcome of interest and not necessarily interventions that show null findings. While this definition delimits our focus, we are also aware that there is a continuum of harm and that we might more broadly define harm issues. Implementing an intervention with null effects on outcomes of interest (e. g., dietary restrictions to reduce symptoms among children with ADHD) would not be iatrogenic in this sense. We elected for this chapter to separate these interventions for three main reasons. First, we wanted to focus attention here on interventions that have been shown by at least some evidence to have demonstrable and enduring harmful effects for at least some of the clients the interventions were designed to help. Second, the neutral/no effect intervention findings may be a function of poorly designed intervention studies or small sample sizes for the studies already conducted, and may prove upon further examination (using more rigorous evaluative methodologies) to actually be effective. Finally, in our previous nine chapters we have already identified a number of interventions that had neutral/no effect, and readers may examine these more critically as they engage in their own evidence-informed work.

ORGANIZING AND INTERPRETING THE EVIDENCE

For this chapter, we were looking for any and all interventions both in schools and typically used with school-age clients (students) and people directly connected to students, such as parents, teachers, school administrators. We chose this question as the basis for our search: What are potentially harmful treatments (PHTs) that might be employed to directly address academic, behavioral, and/or emotional problems that present in a pre-K through 12th grade setting, with PHTs being defined as interventions or therapies that produce demonstrable and relatively enduring negative effects in school clients.

Tables 13.1 and 13.2 contains a provisional list of PHTs. Building on the work of Lilienfeld (2007), we divided our tables into Level 1 (interventions that are probably harmful for at least some school-based clients) and Level 2 (interventions that are possibly harmful for at least some school-based clients).

TABLE 13.1 POTENTIALLY HARMFUL TREATMENTS (LEVEL 1: POSSIBLY HARMFUL FOR AT LEAST SOME SCHOOL CLIENTS)

Intervention/Strategy	Potential Harm	Primary Source of Evidence
Grouping of aggressive youth	Deviance Training effects	3+ RCTS; deviancy training effects also seen in mixed groups
Aggression and violence prevention strategies	Social skills programs that don't account for age or baseline levels of aggression, or peer status	Meta-analysis
Grade retention	Rates of achievement growth lower for retained (versus matched socially promoted youth)	2 high quality QEDS
Substance abuse prevention and harm reduction	Treated more likely to report use; effects pronounced among high users and never used	Narrative review, 2 + RCTS
Critical Incident Stress Debriefing (CISD)	Heightened risk for PTSD symptoms	RCTs
Individual grief therapy or counseling for students with normal grief reactions	Increase in depressive symptoms	Meta-analysis

Note: PTSD = posttraumatic stress disorder; RCT = randomized controlled trials; QED = quasi-experimental design.

TABLE 13.2 POTENTIALLY HARMFUL TREATMENTS (LEVEL 2: POSSIBLY HARMFUL FOR AT LEAST SOME SCHOOL CLIENTS)

Intervention	Potential Harm	Primary Source of Evidence
Abstinence Education Programs	Potentially inaccurate information; providing confusing messages about sexual activity that might inadvertently encourage some adolescents to become sexually active; results from studies are mixed on whether abstinence education harms	Systematic Review RCT (large-scale federally funded study)
Zero Tolerance	Disproportionate rates of suspension and expulsion among minority and special education students; negative effects on schoolwide academic achievement	QEDs

Note: RCT = randomized controlled trial; QED = quasi-experimental design.

Interventions were included in Table 13.1 if they had at least one independent evaluation by outside investigators that showed harm and used either a randomized controlled trial (RCT), systematic review, or meta-analysis to evaluate the outcomes. Level 2 interventions (Table 13.2) had the same independent evaluation component but drew on findings from less rigorous designs (quasi-experimental designs or replicated single subject designs).

DESCRIPTIONS OF IATROGENIC INTERVENTIONS

Grouping Aggressive Youth

The first intervention in our Table 13.1 is one of the most common interventions we have seen in our school practices. Schools often group students with aggressive behavior first in special education classrooms if they meet the Individuals with Disabilities Education Act (IDEA) criteria for behavior disorder. The school social worker often then involves some of those same students in a group treatment setting (in the school social worker's office) and tries to teach social skills and anger management techniques to these students. Our evidence-informed practice (EIP) search indicates that grouping these students this way can produce more behavior problems, as students will compare notes and may become more skilled at the very behaviors that got them referred to the group in the first place (often referred to as the "deviancy training" hypothesis). While a number of references in Table 13.1 argue for this potentially iatrogenic result of grouping aggressive youth, a fierce debate is raging in the empirical literature on whether this hypothesis actually holds and whether group treatment professionals should be concerned about grouping aggressive youth in this manner (Weiss et al., 2005).

Aggression and Violence Prevention Strategies

Many schools today are concerned with how to put violence prevention/anger management programs into place, and to do this quickly. Results from our EIP search indicates that schools and school social workers should slow down and make sure that their violence prevention programs and intervention choices are developmentally appropriate actually calibrated to the students' levels of aggression at baseline. The above concern about grouping students who already exhibit aggressive behavior also applies.

Grade Retention Programs

Students having significant academic problems have historically been threatened with being held back in their current grade level for another year. Grade retention programs appear to go in and out of fashion, though it is estimated that for the past 14 years, overall grade retention rates have remained constant at about 10% of all K–8 public school children (Institute for Education Sciences, 2009). The problems with retention are significant: (1) students who are retained do not perform better academically as a result of the retention; (2) retaining students does not prevent them from dropping out; and (3) retention is an intervention that is disproportionately applied to male students, poor students, and African American students (Institute for Educational Sciences, 2009).

Critical Incident Stress Debriefing (CISD)

This intervention is a component of Critical Incident Stress Management (CISM) and is applied to entire organizations, schools, or communities after a significant traumatic event (e.g., natural disaster, school shooting). The debriefing takes place usually soon after the traumatic event and involves a group discussion of the negative emotions group members are associating with the traumatic event, its potential impacts for causing posttraumatic stress disorder (PTSD), and ways to recognize the symptoms of PTSD. A number of recent meta-analyses and randomized controlled trials have challenged the premise that such intensive (and often compulsory) treatment is effective (Rose et al., 2001). In some situations, CISD has increased anxiety in clients and has failed to prevent the eventual onset of PTSD, leading the Cochrane review by Rose and colleagues (2001) to state flatly that compulsory use of CISD for clients should stop altogether. Proponents of CISD point to their own earlier meta-analyses and argue that the program has to be applied more selectively and tailored to specific clients (Everly & Boyle, 1999). Perhaps most important for this volume, we were not able to find any rigorous evaluation of CISD for a school-age population (or for faculty working with students), heightening our sense that at best, this is a highly problematic intervention to consider using in school contexts.

Individual Grief Therapy for Students Having Normal Grief Reactions

A common problem faced by school social workers involves helping children and families deal with grief issues related to the death of a parent, sibling, or other important person. While it is well known that complicated grief can produce potential pathology in children including depression, anxiety, or even PTSD, little is known about what is beneficial in treating children who appear to be experiencing normal grief reactions (defined here as sadness, confusion, and increased anxiety that persists for roughly six months) as many children and adults appear to spontaneously recover within six months (Dyregrov, 2008; Lilienfeld, 2007). However, given the above emphasis noted via CISD, some school social workers may feel that they have to counsel students going through normal grief reactions with intensive counseling intervention. While to date no rigorous studies have been conducted on this question with children, the evidence on individual grief therapy for adults experiencing normal grief reactions is at best modest; in some cases it may hamper clients in navigating out of their grief on their own (Neimeyer, 2000). We encourage school social workers to conduct a thorough psychosocial assessment of the grieving student and family system before embarking on any individual grief therapy.

Substance Abuse Prevention Programs

Just as with violence prevention, most schools we've worked in have had a goal of providing at least some health education to try to prevent substance abuse by their students. Programs like D.A.R.E. (Drug Abuse Resistance Education) are widely used and are often considered to be "effective," despite long-standing concerns raised by researchers and policy makers about its ability to affect student behavior and attitudes toward drugs. Our EIP search lists substance abuse prevention programs as a "Level 1" PHT, and any definitive conclusion drawn from this chapter on its status as an iatrogenic intervention would be premature. However, any intervention that is likely to be widely adopted and that causes at least some students harm (in this case, the increased likelihood of using drugs) is understandably a cause for concern. It is notable here too that there has been a recent reanalysis of D.A.R.E. program data suggesting that its results may not be as negative as initially estimated (Gorman, 2005). Confusing matters further, there may be important limitations and biases in clearinghouses synthesizing these programs (Gorman, Conde, & Huber, 2007).

Abstinence-Only Sex Education Programs

While the early sexual behavior of American teens and high rates of sexually-transmitted infections (STIs) continue to persist, sex education programs continue to cause controversy, particularly in communities where conservative religious values predominate. Interestingly, despite a strong federal push for abstinence-only education curricula that dates back to the 1990s and the Clinton administration (Arsneault, 2001), there is still no conclusive evidence that abstinence-only curricula delay student sexual activity and prevent risky sexual behavior (Trenholm et al., 2007). Rather, the opposite is increasingly proving to be the case, as the following recent studies argue that abstinence education actually hurts students by giving them incomplete and/or inaccurate information and may actually increase their risky sexual behavior (Santelli et al., 2006). An overwhelming number of professional and scientific health organizations recommend "comprehensive" sex education, which, while including an emphasis on abstinence, also involves information about contraception and the prevention of STIs if students choose to be sexually active (Committee on Psychosocial Aspects of Child and Family Health and Committee on Adolescence, 2001).

"Zero Tolerance" Discipline Policies

In part a reflection of the increasing anticrime policies of states and federal authorities in the 1990s, and in part a response to the high-profile incidences of school violence during that same decade, "zero tolerance" policies have come to K–12 public education. While these policies differ across districts and regions, they essentially set up standards of behavior that result in students being removed (usually expelled) if they violate the standards of behavior one time—for example, bring a weapon or drugs to school, or engage in a physical fight on campus. While we would not deny that schools have the right to act decisively to combat behavior problems, the question of whether immediate expulsion of students for rule violations "works" is one that was scarcely examined when zero tolerance policies took root across the United States in the 1990s (Cameron, 2006). Now with more than a decade of implementation, recent reviews of zero tolerance policies indicate that, similar to grade retention policies, zero tolerance does not prevent further behavior problems with other students who remain at school, and they are disproportionately applied to students of color (Casella, 2003).

LOCATING THE CONTENT WITHIN AN RTI FRAMEWORK

Because response to intervention puts such a premium on examining the potential value of universal interventions first, the notion that some universal interventions (aggression and violence prevention strategies, substance abuse prevention, abstinence education, zero tolerance policies, grade retention) may actually make students worse would give any evidence-informed RTI team strong motivation to critically appraise what universal strategies they are selecting to help their students. Interventions on the other tiers (groups for aggressive youth, boot camp treatments, grief counseling) are also concerning, but the preponderance of iatrogenic interventions we found tended to focus on larger groups of students than on students who had already been identified by more intensive supports.

CONCLUSION

As uncomfortable and even angry as iatrogenic interventions might make us as researchers and practitioners, this chapter is not trying to point fingers or cast aspersions on school faculty or administration. Self-righteous indignation might make us feel better, but it won't make our school practice environments any more effective. The interventions we discuss in this chapter are a concern in part because they are, in our experience, so common: they have been chosen freely by a wide variety of well-intentioned and hard-working educators trying to do the best they can to help some of the most challenging students in their schools. We applaud their good intentions, but we humbly hope that the evidence we cite in this chapter (as well as the evidence in the remainder of this book) might begin to raise questions for both school social workers and administrators when they are eager to simply "do something" about the latest major problem in their school. Not all interventions work, and sometimes they can do harm. It's up to all of us to continue to encourage the kind of evidence-informed processes we showcase in this book so that all school stakeholders (school social workers, teachers, parents, students, administrators) feel they can consult the best available evidence to help them avoid doing harm in the name of doing good.

14

LESSONS LEARNED FROM OUR EVIDENCE-INFORMED PRACTICE PROCESS AND FINAL REFLECTIONS

In this chapter the reflections offered in Chapters 4–12 are synthesized and integrated. Thus, our collective successes and challenges are delineated. These lessons learned are organized around the eight-step EIP process for school social workers detailed in Chapter 3.

POSING AN ANSWERABLE QUESTION

In some ways, posing an answerable question was simultaneously the most important and the least "real" part of our process. Because we as researchers were using recent survey data to generate our list of important practice issues, we knew that these 10 topics were relevant to a large number of school social workers around the country. However, because none of us are presently working full time in a school, we had to create our answerable questions out of examples from our prior cases and our best sense of what typical school social workers might want to investigate further with their school clients. In some ways this is not a problem for our book, which was designed to teach an evidence-informed practice process to students and practitioners who want to be effective in a school setting. But for actual clients, this would reveal immediately how context-driven and specific questions can become in an evidence-informed school practice. For example, some of the questions we asked for chapters in this book were the following:

- What are the empirically supported interventions for students with a lack of social skills?
- What is the state of evidence supporting the use of BIPs?

- What prevention or intervention programs or strategies are effective for improving compliance with teacher requests or classroom rules within the classroom setting?

These three examples show the diverse directions that an EIP question can take, and they also offer plenty of ammunition for EIP scholars who might want to critique the way we went about designing our answerable questions. After all, despite our making nods to types of EIP questions in our review of previous EIP scholarship (such as the Population-Intervention-Comparison-Outcomes (PICO) method or Client Oriented Practical Evidence Search (COPES) or question sequence), when it came time for us to actually "do" the reviews, those ways of posing questions did not resonate with us as we struggled to approximate what practitioners might actually want to know in co-constructing a question with their school clients.

And sometimes the effort to pose an answerable question itself can reveal the limitations of the present EIP process we've demonstrated here. Our (unsuccessful) attempt to fashion a meaningful chapter on effective interventions to help youth manage the transition to adulthood is instructive. Based on our national survey data, we knew that 30% of school social workers told us they were involved with transition planning for their students, and 50% of that time was being completed outside of the IEP process (Kelly et al., 2009). What we didn't know was that the ability to pose an answerable question that sufficiently covered the diversity of programs and specific student populations would prove to be so difficult. For example, our initial searches found many separate literatures related to the transition to adulthood. Here is a partial list of them: helping students get into college (e.g., Rosenbaum, 2002), helping minority and low-income students get into college (e.g., Fashola & Slavin, 2001), helping students with chronic illness transition into adulthood (e.g., Callahan et al., 2001), helping youth aging out of the child welfare system make the transition to adulthood (e.g., Masinga et al., 2004), and helping students with IEPs for emotional disturbance transition successfully into adulthood (e.g., Lehman, 2002 2002). Some of these literatures had more descriptive studies using longitudinal data (e.g., Berzin, 2008); still other literatures seemed to focus mostly on the risk factors and negative outcomes students experienced after entering adulthood (e.g., Barth & Jonson-Reid, 2000).

In discussing these initial searches with our team, we decided that the transition to adulthood literature represented an example of the potential difficulty of posing answerable questions about problems that present in schools. The overall problem of "helping adolescents with the transition to adulthood" lacked sufficient conceptual definition and coherence across the many student populations we wished to address with this book. Clearly, we could have written a chapter in which we posed multiple questions related to transition issues, such as

"What programs are most effective in helping youth transitioning out of the child welfare system find employment ?" or "What interventions have the best likelihood of helping students from low-socioeconomic families enter and graduate from four-year colleges?" In some ways, however, this would have defeated our goal for this book: writing chapters that showed how overarching topics can help form answerable questions that address some particularly salient school/student issues. To adequately address the evidence for "transition to adulthood" would have required us to write five or six mini-chapters, a task that proved to be too daunting. Additionally, what evidence we did find was not particularly promising, as few programs appear to have been rigorously evaluated (Collins, 2001), and fewer still seem to be actually located in school settings and conducted by school social workers (Anderson-Butcher et al., 2006).

INVESTIGATING THE EVIDENCE

It was enormously helpful to create a set of permanent searches in the OVID databases. The OVID databases include ERIC, PsycINFO, and Social Work Abstracts. A permanent search set saved in one database could be accessed and rerun in the others in just a few minutes. The three most helpful search sets were *Children* (adolescen*, boys, children, girls, teen*, or youth); *Counseling* (counseling, intervention, mental health program, psychotherapy, or treatment); and *Scientifically-based indicators* (clinical trial, comparison group, control group, effectiveness, efficacy, quasi-experimental, or random*). The reason these sets were so useful as permanent saved searches was the number of terms saved in each set that did not have to be reentered each time we went to the database. Another helpful search set was *Meta-analysis* (meta-analysis, quantitative synthesis, or systematic review). Looking back, it probably would have helped to share one person's personal account name and password to facilitate the use of the search sets by everyone on the research team. Unfortunately, this did not occur to one of us [Raines] until he was writing his last chapter.

In one sense, the use of search sets represents a balance between effectiveness and efficiency. Ideally, search sets would allow a researcher to locate all of the articles that demonstrate effective practice regarding the clinical issue. Exhaustive search sets, however, are inefficient. They lead to what might be called a Type I error where the databases return false positives in response to our search criteria. Efficient search sets save us time, but they may be ineffective. They lead to what might be called a Type II error where the databases screen out false negatives in response to our search criteria. The solution to finding a good balance is to always map the search term to the subject heading. The subject headings enable investigators to determine what terms the database uses to categorize certain topics. For example, ERIC uses the phrase "educational environment" to categorize school or classroom climate issues, but PsycINFO uses the term "school environment" for the same topic. There is no shortcut to the gradual refinement of search terms; it takes a certain amount of trial and error before it works as expected.

A regular problem with the abstracts was that some of them were written more as advertisements for the article than genuine summaries of the article. The advertisements tended to obfuscate the actual findings of the study so that researchers had to look through the entire journal article to discover whether the intervention actually worked. For example, one abstract from PsycINFO contained this amorphous description:

> Conducted a quasi-experimental study of the effectiveness of a multidimensional intervention program with 3 cohorts of secondary school students at risk of dropping out of school. Human subjects: 84 male and female Canadian adolescents and adults (ages 15–18 yrs) (secondary school students) (1993–1994) (Cohort 1). 61 male and female Canadian adolescents and adults (aged 15–18 yrs) (secondary school students) (1994–1995) (Cohort 2). 81 male and female Canadian adolescents and adults (aged 15–18 yrs) (secondary school students) (1995–1996) (Cohort 3). A pretest-posttest design was used. Dependent variables were behavior problems, social delinquency, anxiety and withdrawal, psychotic behaviors, motor activity, social skills, and academic skills. The intervention lasted 3 years and emphasized acquisition of academic knowledge, the development of personal and social skills, and practical knowledge for use on the job. Repeated measures ANOVAs were performed. Test used: The Revised Behavior Problem Checklist and the Social Skills Rating System. (Fortin & Picard, 1998, p. 125)

Note that nowhere in this 150-word abstract is there a clue about whether this long-term program actually worked! In the case of journals that were not electronically available in full text, we were required to go to the library stacks to find the correct volume and then be disappointed (e.g., Toldson et al., 2006). While this is clearly an author problem, it is more extensive. Journal editors should have edited the abstracts just as carefully as the texts of the articles.

The quest to balance exhaustive and efficient search strategies clearly privileges results of intervention research over more basic knowledge about a given topic. Virtually all the topics covered in this book are undergirded with literature that describes the issue, discusses relevant factors that are related to the issues, and theories or conceptual frameworks that help delineate causes of the issue. At the other end of the continuum lie process or formative studies that describe the logic of often novel intervention strategies and how these were initially received by key stakeholders (e.g., school staff, parents). From the perspective of at least a couple of the authors, this kind of knowledge is also critically important for at least two reasons. First, it helps us understand the who and what of an issue: who or what is likely to be affected, how should we conceptualize the issue (as an individual or a contextual problem), and what are best guesses (theories) as to why the issue emerges in the first place. This additional lens would ultimately suggest another perspective on appraisal: Does a given intervention address the factors thought to strongly contribute to and maintain a given issue? Second, we are also aware that just because an intervention has not been tested for efficacy does not mean that it is not potentially efficacious. We would hope that, should a practitioner decide to implement an untested strategy (for example, in the case of null findings from a search), the process of searching would (1) underscore the need for a transparent account to the client about why an untested strategy was being implemented and potential risks to the client, (2) identify potential evaluation methods (e.g., measures), and (3) underscore the need for a practitioner-initiated evaluation strategy such as a single subject design to track progress toward hoped-for outcomes.

Another lesson related to the investigation of evidence was locating interventions that appeared to be misrepresented by the evidence. While consistently an issue, two examples are offered here. First, the First Step to Success intervention was recognized by a single text and was categorized as an *emerging* practice after we completed the EIP search process for our chapter on compliance. However, because we were aware of several studies that were not identified in the search process, we elevated its status to a *highly recommended* practice. In a second example, the Rainbows intervention for children dealing with divorce is one of the most popular and widely adopted programs in schools, yet the only published study on the program (from the 1990s) showed the program was ineffective. These examples are provided because we were aware of evidence that was not revealed by our search process (indeed, in the case of Rainbows, that program didn't come up in initial EIP searches at all). It is difficult to hypothesize how frequently our search process misrepresented the actual evidence for a particular topic.

ORGANIZING AND INTERPRETING THE EVIDENCE

Another regular problem occurs with meta-analyses. Some researchers apparently begin with a favorite intervention rather than a specific problem and conduct a synthesis of the literature on the intervention. This illustrates what I refer to as the "cart before the horse" problem (Raines, 2008b). The particular intervention review we discovered this time was about drama therapy for youth with acquired brain injuries (Goyal & Keightly, 2008). The problem with such studies lies in the presumption of effectiveness and the apparent ignorance of publication bias by journals dedicated to promoting specific techniques (including the one that published their review). It would have been far better if the meta-analysis authors had asked an answerable question, such as "What are the most effective treatments for youth with acquired brain injuries?" This inquiry would have led them to multiple interventions rather than just the one that they already preferred.

In addition to the limitations we identified in our searches for meta-analyses, we found a challenge in appraising the other different levels of evidence we found. For instance, a well-done randomized controlled trial (RCT) that was not replicated (but showed successful outcomes maintained at six-month and twelve-month follow-ups) is not as effective an argument for an intervention than a well-done systematic review or meta-analysis (which often includes aggregations of studies that have used a wider range of less rigorous designs). But what if that RCT was all our search found? Or what if the only empirical evidence we found was a quasi-experimental design or a pre- and posttest of the intervention? Another example involved the behavior intervention planning chapter. Because this intervention, by definition, is unique for each child, it lends itself to single subject design methodology. The single subject methodology has been implemented in special education for over 40 years (Horner et al., 2005). Whether this methodology is capable of establishing a definitive causal relationship between dependent and independent variables is a question that has been debated for decades. Because of the criteria we had set up in advance, an intervention could not receive our highest endorsement if it had not been subjected to a randomized controlled trial or quasi-experimental design, which may be impossible for behavior intervention planning. Looking back we should have included the phrase "multiple baseline" in our search set for scientifically based indicators. This would have allowed us to uncover well-designed single subject research.

Another problem with appraising the evidence was either the lack of or highly variable time frames leading to follow-up results. It seems that most of the efficacy and effectiveness research conducted simple pretest and posttest assessments. Few of the studies we examined discussed long-term results of three-, six-, or twelve-month duration. If students get better only to regress after treatment is over, there does not seem to be much of a reason to ever terminate treatment. Somewhat surprisingly, even the Internet clearinghouses did not report this information about the interventions they endorsed. This required us to go back to the databases to combine the name of the intervention with the term *follow-up* to determine whether such research even existed.

ADAPTING AND APPLYING THE EVIDENCE

One of the difficulties with adapting the evidence is locating rigorous empirical research conducted by or for minority groups. This may have two explanations. First, there is evidence that most of the treatments that are effective for dominant culture youth are effective for minority youth with few differences in effect (Arnold et al., 2003; Kazdin, 2002; Pina et al., 2003). This does not mean that everyone is the same but that differences are likely to be minor, not major (Deffenbacher & Swaim, 1999). In other words, one is more likely to find differences of degree (how well an intervention works) rather than differences of type (whether it works). Second, there may be cultural conflicts about the definition of evidence. Chorpita (2003) notes, "Defining evidence is not a simple task, and yet the arguments outlined thus far suggest that the definition of evidence may in fact make or break the connection to local practice and policy, which in turn can drive systems to change or not to change" (p. 48). It is certainly possible, then, that minority groups that object to positivism as a Eurocentric philosophy would also refuse to carry out such research on their own populations and reject such research carried out by others (Sundarararjan, 2002). This is one of the reasons that it is so important for authors of systematic reviews to include single subject designs and qualitative research in their examination of the scientific literature. While some qualitative research proponents have rejected any grounds for determining scientific rigor (Schwandt, 1996; Shank & Villella, 2004; Wolcott, 1994), others have argued that it is not only possible but necessary on pragmatic grounds alone (Lincoln, 2001; McNeill, 2006; Raines, 2008b). Failure to apply any criteria to culturally sensitive research inevitably leads to the Dodo bird verdict that "all have won and all must have prizes" (Luborsky et al., 1975). One solution to this problem is to adopt a communitarian perspective in which the participants have an active voice in the design, collection, and dissemination of the research (Denzin, 2003).

A major problem with applying the evidence is that few practitioners write or publish in professional journals (Raines & Massat, 2004; Staudt et al , 2003). One of the reasons that most articles are written by academics is because of the "publish or perish" dilemma that university professors face (Wilson, 2001). To the degree that practice research is seen as an ivory tower exercise, this leads to a social validity problem. Social validity is the acceptability of a treatment or evaluation method across multiple constituents, including parents, students, and teachers (Daunic et al., 2006; Frey et al., 2006; Lyst et al., 2005). The acceptability of an intervention can be defined as the degree to which the method is perceived by those involved as appropriate, effective, efficient, and fair (Finn & Sladeczek, 2001). Another possible reason for the lack of practitioner research may lie in the lack of research technology skills (Edmond et al., 2006).

Obviously, one of the ways this situation can be overcome is to create more partnerships between academic researchers and school-based practitioners (Barlow et al., 1993; Franklin & McNeil, 1992; Hess & Mullen, 1995). One barrier to these partnerships, however, is that most of the benefits accrue to the researcher, not to the practitioner (Christians, 2005). Therefore, it behooves researchers to find and negotiate ways to demonstrate benefit to their clinical partners.

QUADRANTS AND RTI

As described in Chapter 1, the clinical quadrant can be used as a tool to assess the fit between school social work practice, the ecological perspective, and the school-based prevention and intervention literature (Frey & Dupper, 2005). In the first two chapters we argued, largely based on a recent national survey of school social workers (Kelly et al., 2009), that a substantial gap exists between the school-based intervention literature and response to intervention and schoolwide positive behavior support (SWPBS), both education-specific frameworks that promote the organization of prevention and intervention services within the context of a three-tiered structure, and the practice choices of school social workers. Results of this survey suggest that school social workers' practice choices are primarily located within quadrant C, with many spending a disproportionate amount of time engaged in psychotherapy or counseling and small group work to address social skill deficits. The school social workers in this sample also indicated that the majority of their time is focused on a few students with the most significant behavior concerns and a relatively small percentage indicated that they engage in activities that could be described as capacity building, or working with parents and teachers in small groups (quadrant A) or across an entire school or district (quadrant B) to indirectly affect the children whom they serve.

In Chapters 4 through 13 we discussed the findings of our respective searches in relation to the three-tiered framework. In this chapter we discuss the results of our searches in the context of the clinical quadrant[1] to better understand whether the type of presenting problem should moderate school social workers' practice choices with respect to the quadrant model. Table 14.1 provides a summary of the interventions and programs identified through this search process by type (strategy or manualized program), evidence for program or strategy (*Highly recommend*, *Recommend*, *Emerging*, or *Ineffective*), and the quadrant(s) the strategy or program represents.

The search on Tier 2 interventions (Chapter 4) indicates that the majority of the interventions would fall under quadrant C—interventions that involve and target individuals, small groups, and families. One of the interventions would fall

TABLE 14.1 THE CLINICAL QUADRANTS FOR PARENT INVOLVEMENT

A. Programs	B. Programs
	• *Incredible Years—Teacher Component*
	• *Iowa Strengthening Families Program*
	• *Comer School Development Program*
INTERVENTION STRATEGIES	**INTERVENTIONS**
• **Direct or indirect parent tutoring or training**	• **Direct or indirect parent tutoring or training**
	• Encouragement of parent visiting
C. Programs	D. Programs
• *FAST*	• *FAST*
INTERVENTION STRATEGIES	**INTERVENTION STRATEGIES**
• **Direct or indirect parent tutoring or training**	• **Direct or indirect parent tutoring or training**
• **Nonspecific family support**	• **Nonspecific family support**
• *Direct encouragement of parent-teacher communication*	
• ***Prevention-oriented, task-centered casework***	

Note: Highly recommended programs or strategies shown in bold, recommended with caution programs or strategies shown in italics, emerging programs or strategies shown in underline, and strategies for which evidence suggests they are ineffective shown in capitals.

under quadrants B and D since it involves large groups and targets both systemic and student change. This is the *Check & Connect* program that identifies student, family, peers, school, and community contributions to students' dropping out. For example, some of the school policy barriers include out-of-school suspensions, administrative transfers, and limited parent outreach (Evelo et al., 1996). Three of the interventions, however, would fall under quadrant D. These are Accelerated Middle Schools, the Behavior Education Program, and *Early Risers*. Accelerated Middle Schools is a schoolwide intervention that enables students who are struggling academically to catch up with their grade-level peers. The Behavior Education Program involves *all* teachers in monitoring the behavior of at-risk students and reporting to the students' monitors. The *Early Risers* program is a multicomponent program that offers a community-based six-week summer component to help students maintain academic and behavioral skills over the summer break.

As shown in Table 14.1, the search related to parental involvement identified five strategies and four programs. Direct parent training of academic skills, depending on how it is implemented, can fall into any of the four quadrants and is the only strategy that fills the quadrant among those reviewed. Formal intervention programs most frequently populate quadrant B. FAST interventions are best characterized as falling in either quadrant C or D.

HELPING STUDENTS COPE WITH DIVORCE

The search related to divorce identified interventions that fit nicely within quadrant C (individual work with clients and their families), with the parent groups also having implications for quadrants A and D. It is easy for us to imagine that a school district that committed to using the CODIP or Children's Support Group interventions could be implementing them in classrooms building or districtwide to teach children how to handle their feelings about divorce (and to arguably empower others to learn new ways to understand and empathize with what their peers are going through, in the event that their parents aren't divorced or separated). It's also possible to imagine the other parent–group-based interventions being included as a Tier 2 intervention strategy that all parents in a school district could participate in, possibly offered at the school site in partnership with a local community mental health agency. What stands out in our evidence-based practice process is how little we can say we know about school-based individual and group interventions for students that are having acute symptoms as a result of their parents' divorce. It is possible that some of the interventions related to anxiety (see Chapter 11) might address some of the issues associated with divorce, as well as other effective interventions for children and adolescents dealing with depression, but that would be a question for another review.

As shown in Table 14.2, the search related to bullying prevention identified one strategy and three programs. Interestingly, all three programs were *recommended* or *recommended with caution* after the evidence was weighed. The First Step to Success and Youth Matters programs span three quadrants and the Olweus program spans all four. Thus, these approaches target the school community (including parents) with outcomes focused on multiple and multilevel targets of change (for example, including individual and school aggregate rates of bullying). The only strategy, social skills groups, represented only quadrant C and was also determined to be ineffective in preventing bullying. This literature base suggests that interventions to prevent bullying must address changes at the child level and within the environment; thus, multiquadrant approaches are essential.

As shown in Table 14.3, the search related to social skills interventions identified a large number of programs across all the quadrants Most of the effective programs fall in quadrant A as they aim at large groups of students, but they do not attempt to change the system. Two exceptions

TABLE 14.2 THE CLINICAL QUADRANTS FOR BULLYING PREVENTION

A. Programs	B. Programs
• *Olweus Bullying Program*	• *Olweus Bullying Program*
• *First Step to Success*	• *First Step to Success*
• Youth Matters	
INTERVENTION STRATEGIES Whole school or curriculum-based, classroom approaches	
C. Programs	D. Programs
• *Olweus Bullying Program*	• *Olweus Bullying Program*
• *First Step to Success*	• *First Step to Success*
• Youth Matters	• Youth Matters
INTERVENTION STRATEGIES • SOCIAL SKILLS GROUPS	

Note: Highly recommended programs or strategies shown in bold, recommended with caution programs or strategies shown in italics, emerging programs or strategies shown in underline, and strategies for which evidence suggests they are ineffective shown in capitals.

TABLE 14.3 THE CLINICAL QUADRANT FOR SOCIAL SKILLS TRAINING

A. Programs	B. Programs
• **Incredible Years (parent and teacher components)**	• *School-wide positive behavior support*
• ***Early Risers* (family and school component)**	**INTERVENTION STRATEGIES** • *Ecology/climate*
• **First Step to Success (family and school components)**	• *Establishing and communicating high and clear expectations*
• *Schoolwide positive behavior support*	• *Incentives and motivational strategies*
INTERVENTION STRATEGIES • *High probability requests/behavioral momentum*	• *In-service training*
• *Ecology/climate*	• *Cooperative learning strategies (e.g., Good Behavior Game)*
• *Establishing and communicating high and clear expectations*	• *Matching academic programming with skill levels of low-performing students*
• *Incentives and motivational strategies*	• *Home school communication*
• *Establishing clear and predictable routines*	
• *Reducing transition time*	

TABLE 14.3 THE CLINICAL QUADRANT FOR SOCIAL SKILLS TRAINING (CONT'D)

* *Cooperative learning strategies (e.g., Good Behavior Game)*
* *Matching academic programming with skill levels of low-performing students*
* *Home school communication*
* *Behavioral consultation*
* *Assisting families to manage behavior in the home setting*
* *In-service training*

C. Programs

* **Incredible Years (child component)**
* **Early Risers (child component)**
* **First Step to Success (school component)**
* *School-wide positive behavior support*

Intervention strategies
* **Systematically teaching social skills**
* **Anger control training**
* **Stress inoculation training**
* **Group assertiveness training**
* **Cognitive-behavioral therapy**
* **Contracting**
* Self-monitoring
* PHARMACOLOGICAL INTERVENTIONS
* PSYCHOTHERAPY AND COUNSELING

D. Programs

* *School-wide positive behavior support*

Intervention strategies
* **Systematically teaching social skills**

Note: Highly recommended programs or strategies shown in bold, recommended with caution programs or strategies shown in italics, emerging programs or strategies shown in underline, and strategies for which evidence suggests they are ineffective shown in capitals.

to this would be the ASSET and Aggression Replacement Training that would fall in quadrant C as they aim to help select students who have already demonstrated problems with social skills. Another exception is the Incredible Years that would fall in quadrant A since it targets parents and teachers as well as children.

The search related to anxiety identified a range of effective manualized treatments for students struggling with anxiety. Additionally, the interventions, while squarely located in quadrant C, could be adapted to classroom-level content if the school social worker determined that the class as a whole was experiencing symptoms of anxiety about specific events (test anxiety is a good example).

Noncompliance can be attributed to deficits in children's behavioral self-regulation, social skills, or social competence which would necessitate an intervention plan associated with quadrant C if applied with a single child or in a small group setting and quadrant D if applied in the context of an entire classroom or schoolwide. Noncompliance can also be attributed to a poor fit between the child and his environment (e.g., classroom, home, or school). Whether the poor fit is structural or relational, it necessitates interventions in quadrant A if applied with a single child or in a small group setting and quadrant B if applied in the context of an entire classroom or schoolwide. It also is possible that distal risk factors, such as the neighborhood environment, affect compliance in the classroom setting.

Our search related to compliance identified 21 strategies and four programs. Twelve strategies focus on the environment and target teacher behavior, parent behavior, or the classroom environment and are applied to individuals or small groups; these represent quadrant A. Seven of the 12 strategies from quadrant A can be applied school- or districtwide and are therefore listed in quadrant B as well. Nine strategies focus on change in the child, and therefore are listed in quadrant C; of these, only one, systematically teaching social skills, can be implemented schoolwide and is therefore included in quadrant D. Of the four programs, the Incredible Years program has the potential to span all four quadrants, schoolwide positive behavior support spans all four quadrants by definition, and the *Early Risers* and First Step to Success programs both represent quadrants A and C.

With respect to the weight of the evidence, one could reasonably conclude that no single strategy is likely to be effective at improving compliance; none of the 21 strategies exceeded the *emerging* distinction, and two (psychopharmocology and counseling/psychotherapy) were determined to be ineffective. Conversely, three of the programs were *highly recommended* and one (schoolwide positive behavior support) was *recommended with caution*. All of the programs represent multiple quadrants. Thus, they target multiple intervention agents (child, parent, teacher) and multiple risk factors (e.g., social skills, parent-child conflict, connectedness with family and school, classroom management). Importantly, each of the *highly recommended* programs target fairly young children and therefore represent early intervention strategies that would be dependent on an effective early screening system to identify appropriate candidates for services. These programs are essentially well-packaged combinations of the individual intervention strategies presented in this chapter. Thus, it is clear that no single intervention strategy or reliance on a single quadrant, appears advisable. It is also worth noting that the only interventions that appear ineffective are those that represent quadrant C only.

For our searches related to iatrogenic interventions, these interventions mapped onto all of the four quadrants. Grouping aggressive youth or youth with conduct problems (typically a quadrant C intervention in a school) stood out as an intervention that we've seen again and again in our consultations with schools and school social workers. Grief counseling with students going through normal grief reactions was another iatrogenic intervention that would most likely be in quadrant C, though it conceivably could be employed in tandem with critical incident stress debriefing (CISD) groups that would be in quadrant A (again, we've seen this used as a standard intervention in several schools we've worked with that have responded to a traumatic event in the community with grief therapy and CISD for all the affected students and faculty). There were also several quadrant A and D interventions here (behavior "boot camps," substance abuse prevention curriculum, anger management and aggression prevention curricula) and these also were unfortunately quite familiar (one of us worked for almost 10 years in two school districts that used the drug prevention program D.A.R.E., which has been shown in some cases to actually increase drug use with youth).

Interestingly, many of the iatrogenic interventions in our tables had their roots in quadrant B. Whether the iatrogenic intervention involved grade retention, zero tolerance policies, or simply the approval of the curriculum mentioned above, many iatrogenic interventions appear to get their start and their support at the district level. This is both discouraging and hopeful, because though widespread harm may be perpetrated by well-intentioned school leadership, the ability to advocate evidence-informed interventions that aren't iatrogenic may be easier to do at a whole-school or districtwide level than to change specific classroom or practitioner habits. Still, the notion that many American schools may have essentially iatrogenic interventions that are mandated school policies is a cause for concern.

A main thrust of this book was also to locate interventions with clinical quadrant and response to intervention frameworks. We found a variety of interventions that mapped into the four quadrants, with Table 14.3 showing quadrant A, B, C, and D interventions for social skills training. In many cases, we found a predominance of quadrant C and intensive interventions populating our searches. (For example, see Table 14.4 for how we mapped the quadrants for interventions for students with ADHD.) Interestingly, this was particularly true for professional texts edited or authored by social workers. Professional texts authored or edited by those from other disciplines were far more likely to promote interventions or strategies from quadrants A and D, and generally only promoted quadrant C interventions as one component of multicomponent

TABLE 14.4 THE CLINICAL QUADRANT FOR INTERVENTIONS FOR STUDENTS WITH ATTENTION DEFICIT/HYPERACTIVITY DISORDER (ADHD)

A.	B.
No interventions mapped into quadrant **A**	Intervention strategies • **Classwide peer tutoring**
C.	D. Programs
Intervention strategies • Teacher/staff implemented proactive and reactive contingency/behavioral management • Home-school coordinated behavioral methods • Tutoring • **Self-management training** • **Teacher consultation**	• **FastTrack** Intervention strategies • **Teacher consulation**

Note: Highly recommended programs or strategies shown in bold, recommended with caution programs or strategies shown in italics, emerging programs or strategies shown in underline, and strategies for which evidence suggests they are ineffective shown in capitals.

intervention strategies. In general, there was more evidence to support interventions that represented multiple quadrants, a finding that was cited in Chapter 2. It is one thing to critique practitioners for practicing in quadrant C, but if professional texts authored or edited by school social workers promote these practices can the findings be considered surprising?

We interpret this pattern in several ways. First, it is our strong suspicion that there is a tendency for the literature to generate more quadrant C interventions because these interventions are likely more amenable to evaluation (focusing on students versus classrooms or schools obviously necessitates simpler research designs). Second, in light of numerous *highly recommended* and *recommended* strategies available for work in quadrant C across a variety of practitioner concerns, there would have to be compelling reasons for practitioners not to utilize these strategies. Many of these strategies, moreover, show strong roots in behavioral methods, suggesting strongly the need for practice knowledge in this area. Third, how one frames the answerable question has a great deal to do with the evidence that is found. For example, if a *DSM* diagnosis, which implies a Tier 3 intervention and generally an internal cause (e.g., anxiety, depression, ADHD), is used to frame the question, one should not be surprised to identify interventions that represent Tier 3 and target risk factors at the individual level.

At the same time, even though there is a predominance of such intervention strategies, we did find interventions and strategies that covered the range of quadrants and multiple points of the response to intervention continuum. We were also struck by the rapid pace at which such evidence appears to be accumulating. We hope the search techniques modeled underscore the need for practitioners to be continuously scanning knowledge as more and more evidence accumulates on these topics. As such, our book is a starting point, not an end point.

EVALUATION OF RESULTS

For many of our chapters, this final section proved to be quite challenging. Just as calling interventions "research-based" is virtually meaningless without providing some standard for what is considered research (and what is good research, at that), the blithe comments we hear again and again that school social workers should be evaluating their practice tend to make practitioners' eyes glaze over. What we tried for in this book was to help practitioners identify both process and outcome evaluation tools, and to be introduced to why both modes of evaluation matter. Our own survey research indicates that school social workers aren't yet using either process or outcome evaluation ideas regularly in their practice (Kelly et al., 2009) and this has been a challenge for other school-based mental health professions as well (Kratochwil & Stoiber, 2002; Romano & Kachgal, 2004).

Fortunately, for most of our chapter topics, we found that intervention researchers have paid significant attention to developing process and outcome measures to help guide school social workers who want to use them in their practice. There was also the overall RIOT (Review Records, Interview Informants, Observations, and Testing) rubric to guide practitioners as well, and we tried to use that rubric in several of our chapters as a model.

Unfortunately, we found two common problems with the outcome measures. First, there are few outcome measures for the environment in which students must function. Since social workers are trained to use a person-in-environment approach, this scarcity limits the ability of practitioners to monitor ecological factors. Two recent scales have been developed to evaluate the teacher's contribution to behavioral problems in the classroom. The Questionnaire on Teacher Interaction (Mellor & Moore, 2003) measures teacher communications with students along two orthogonal dimensions: Dominance-Submission and Cooperation-Opposition. This assessment results in eight different styles of instructional behavior that can be modified through mentoring or consultation. The Teacher Performance Rate and Accuracy Scale (Ross, Singer-Dudek, & Greer, 2005) evaluates the teacher's ability to correctly carry out an individualized functional behavior improvement plan. Teachers are graded on their ability to implement constructive antecedents and consequences for student behavior.

There are also two useful scales that measure the classroom environment. These are the My Class Inventory for elementary grades (Sink & Spencer, 2005, 2007) and the Classroom Environment Scale for secondary grades. There are also three assessment tools that measure the social-emotional aspects of the educational environment. Laxton (2005) compared three school safety measures and found that the Oregon School Safety Survey (Sprague et al., 1995) was the most useful. Furlong and associates (2005) developed a short form of the California School Climate and Safety Survey. Most recently, Tarshis and Huffman (2007) have created the Peer Interactions in Primary School (PIPS) questionnaire to measure bullying and victimization for elementary students. Second, many of the student outcome measures are pathology oriented rather than strengths-based. Two strengths-based scales are worth mentioning. First, the Social Skills Improvement System (SSIS; Gresham & Elliott, 2008) measures positive social skills (communication, cooperation, assertion, responsibility, empathy, engagement, and self-control) as well as problem behaviors (externalizing, bullying, hyperactivity, internalizing, and autism spectrum). Second, the Behavior and Emotional Rating System, second edition (BERS-2, Epstein, 2004) measures six areas of strengths (interpersonal, family, intrapersonal, school, affective, and career) (Epstein et al., 2004; Mooney et al., 2005).

SOCIAL VALIDITY

In Chapter 2, the social validity of the EIP process was acknowledged as a barrier to practitioners adopting an evidence-based orientation. One strategy we proposed when we initially began writing this book was to recruit and train school social work practitioners to engage in the EIP process proposed here and complete it independently. We hoped then to compare their conclusions with ours. Despite some initial interest at several conference workshops we led on EIP in schools, most of the school social workers who had contacted us initially ultimately decided that they did not have the time to learn the approach and expressed regret that they would have to wait for our book's publication to learn the skills involved in using this evidence-informed approach. This served as a reminder that school social workers are both attracted to and intimidated by the notion of becoming more involved in evidence-informed practice. They know that it's "good" to be using things in their school practice that are "evidence-based," but they're also not really sure what that means and they are deeply skeptical of any external authority that tries to tell them that something "works." In the workshops we lead, once they get past that initial skepticism, they see that becoming evidence informed is something that they can do and that can even validate some of the work they're already doing with their clients. But they're still concerned about the time commitment involved and how they could fit this into their jam-packed days of students, meetings, and crises. And they may be right. Certainly for this book we were able to take all the time we needed to do our EIP process well. And though we all tried to keep our actual search and appraisal times to within a few hours, that understandably couldn't fully capture the many revisions and edits we eventually gave to the chapters in which we presented our eight-step process. So as much as we hope that this book will meet the "Is this practical?" threshold that many students and practitioners will hold it to, there are still some questions we have about how practical the search process itself will ultimately prove to be for most school social workers.

One obvious reason that so many school-based mental professionals don't evaluate the outcomes of their interventions is lack of time. High caseloads and constant crises are two reasons school social workers have indicated as barriers to doing more primary prevention (Kelly, 2008). These would also partially explain why they don't systematically measure the outcomes of the interventions they implement with their school clients. Even if school social workers can find time, do they know how to evaluate their own practice efficiently and clearly? While the literature is replete with calls for school social workers to evaluate their practice and document what they do, it's clear that most school social workers still do not do this systematically. Could it be that school social workers avoid this key part of the EIP process because they aren't sure how to do it? In our own trainings and teaching, we have seen again and again that the learning curve on these issues can be long for students and veteran practitioners alike, particularly if they are operating in schools that have largely required them to simply document the time they spend and have not taught them how to evaluate outcomes. It's possible that the emphasis in both PBS and RTI on data-driven decision making might begin to expose school social workers to more systematic strategies for incorporating process and outcome evaluation into their day-to-day practices, but evidence is limited at this point about the impact that the RTI/PBS movement is having on school social work practice.

FUTURE DIRECTIONS

While changing the culture and practice of school social workers may be an uphill battle, schools of social work do have influence over the next generation of practitioners, and this book may offer a starting place to prepare them for these new practice realities. In many ways, this idea inspired the book, and we hope that our efforts might inform future school social work practice courses. The complexity and enormity of this task did not escape us as we worked on this volume, however; our national survey data indicate that while more states than ever are requiring an MSW and some state certification to practice in a school, there is no clear national consensus on what skills a school social worker must have to practice in a school. Looking at the state school social work standards for Illinois (where two of us teach), a whole standard is devoted to a nice description of knowledge and performance indicators for "Assessment and Evaluation," but a review of our own syllabi indicates that little if any consistent attention is paid to teaching these specific process and outcome evaluation skills to practitioners In our own courses, we try to build these ideas into assignments and class content, but even there, we haven't rigorously evaluated whether our students are actually practicing the skills we've taught them in their field placements. As educators, the question of how best to prepare school social workers to use the tools of evidence-informed practice is one we intend to continue working on both at our own schools and in national and state-level contexts such as our state school social work associations as well as national organizations such as NASW and SSWAA. It is our hope that this book, with its "warts and all" approach to teaching and doing evidence-informed practice, might constitute a small contribution to moving this discussion forward.

CONCLUSION

The aim of this book was to provide students and practitioners with interventions that they could start using immediately to help their schools. To do this, we wanted to model an EIP framework to help them extract evidence from the literature and to shed light on effective intervention strategies for some of the most common problems they face. Overall, our searches—with the limitations described herein—did yield information on the extent of efficacy and effectiveness across a wide variety of strategies. We realize that the social validity of this process could be questioned by many, particularly the very practitioners we are trying to reach. That said, we believe many trends will improve this process over the next decade. First, we stand committed to listening to those emboldened to try it, and we will revise the process based on their feedback. Second, we hope the public sector will eventually have access to resources that are currently available only to those associated with universities. Third, as the knowledge base expands, this process will offer more support for those seeking guidance from the available evidence.

NATIONAL SCHOOL SOCIAL WORK SURVEY INSTRUMENT

SCHOOL SOCIAL WORK SURVEY 2008

Michael S. Kelly, Loyola University Chicago
Stephanie C. Berzin, Boston College
Andy Frey, University of Louisville
Michelle Alvarez, University of Minnesota-Mankato
Gary Shaffer, University of North Carolina-Chapel Hill
Kimberly O' Brien, Boston College (doctoral student)

Thank you for taking the time to complete this survey, which is designed to better understand the important role school social workers play across the country in removing barriers to learning. Your perspective is important, and the results of this study will be used to inform and advocate for school social work practice.

Please skip any question you do not feel you are able to answer accurately. This survey is intended to be completed by school social workers or those who have been trained in social work whose primary role in the school is to provide services to students and their families. If you do not fit this description (e.g., academics, principals), we would encourage you to submit the survey with the questions that are not relevant to you blank.

SECTION 1

In this section we are primarily interested in how you spend your time, how you select the specific interventions, programs, or modalities you rely on to serve clients, and how you evaluate the effectiveness of your services.

1. Please read the following category descriptions and estimate the percentage of time you have actually spent and the percentage of time

you would have ideally spent in the last full academic year for each category. Your totals for each column (actual and ideal) should each add up to 100%.

Category	Actual time (%)	Ideal time(%)
1. Primary prevention work This includes work (direct or indirect/ administrative) at the classroom, school, or district level aimed at all students to remove risk factors or promote resiliency factors for all students. The goal can also to be to prevent the need for further intervention by school social workers for additional services.		
2. Tertiary prevention: This includes work (direct or indirect/administrative) at the individual, family, or classroom level to help specific students who have already been referred for school social work services and reduce the severity of those students' problems at school		
3. Other		

2. We would also like to know what percentage of your time you spend on these administrative tasks overall. Please indicate what percentage of your average workweek you spend writing reports, progress, notes, case notes, or other paperwork related to the services you provide? If you do not feel you can accurately estimate the answer to this question, please leave it blank.
___ %

3. If there is a significant discrepancy between your actual and ideal percentages, could you help us understand this discrepancy by indicating how the following reasons might contribute to the discrepancy.

	Accounts for nearly all	Accounts for most	Accounts for approximately half	Accounts for some	Accounts for a little
I serve too many students/ schools to engage in prevention activities	5	4	3	2	1
My role is largely proscribed for me by my district/ administration	5	4	3	2	1
I have not been trained to do these activities	5	4	3	2	1
Other (specify below)	5	4	3	2	1

4. When working to support children prior to having them referred for school social work services, to what extent do you rely on the following approaches?

	All of the time	Most of the time	Sometimes	Occasionally	Rarely
Increasing parental involvement/engagement	5	4	3	2	1
Enhancing community involvement/engagement	5	4	3	2	1
Delivering teacher professional development (e.g., inservices on prevention/intervention strategies, legal issues)	5	4	3	2	1
Developing prevention or intervention protocols	5	4	3	2	1
Improving school-wide culture/climate (unified discipline systems; bully prevention; behavioral expectations; supervision)	5	4	3	2	1
Delivering classroom- or school- wide social skills curriculum	5	4	3	2	1
Facilitating small groups as prevention activities (e.g., social skill, organizational, etc.)	5	4	3	2	1
Analyzing data to support school decision-making and presenting that data to school administrators	5	4	3	2	1
Participating on school or district committees or task forces	5	4	3	2	1

Other (specify)

5. When you are working with students who have been referred for school social work services, to what extent do you rely on the following approaches?

	All of the time	Most of the time	Sometimes	Occasionally	Rarely
Individual counseling	5	4	3	2	1
Group counseling	5	4	3	2	1
Classroom groups	5	4	3	2	1
Family-based practice	5	4	3	2	1
Sessions with the student and his/her teacher	5	4	3	2	1
Other (specify)	5	4	3	2	1

6. Of the students you serve after they have been referred, what percentage of students receive social work services as part of a special education Individualized Education Plan (IEP)?

    —% of students I serve regularly

7. What resources do you consult most often for information to apply to your work? Rate these 1-5, with 1 being rarely and 5 being all of the time.

	All of the time	Most of the time	Sometimes	Occasionally	Rarely
Online databases of research articles	5	4	3	2	1
Journals and scholarly books	5	4	3	2	1
Trainings/Workshops	5	4	3	2	1
Supervision	5	4	3	2	1
Peer Consultation Other (please specify)	5	4	3	2	1

8. How do you determine if your interventions/services are effective? Rate these 1-5, with 1 being rarely and 5 being all of the time.

	All of the time	Most of the time	Sometimes	Occasionally	Rarely
Standardized outcome measures e.g. rating scales	5	4	3	2	1
Observations	5	4	3	2	1
Student/teacher self-report	5	4	3	2	1
Data collected at the school level e.g. attendance, discipline records, grades	5	4	3	2	1
Other (please specify)	5	4	3	2	1

SECTION 2

For this section, we are primarily interested to learn about the students and families you serve at your school, as well as some other questions related to collaboration with teachers and post-high school transition planning. Please answer the following questions by making an X or check mark next to the response that best describes your work and your experience.

9. From which source do you receive the most referrals? (Pick one)

— Student (Self-referral)
— Another student (a friend)
— Teacher
— Counselor
— Attendance officer
— Administrator
— Parent
— The special education diagnostic team (for IEP services)
— Other (Please specify below)

10. Please indicate the proportion of students that are referred for school social work services for the reasons listed below. Rate these 1-5, with 1 being few of the students and 5 being all of the students

	All	Most	Approximately half	Some of the students	Few of the students
Behavior problems at home or school (Externalizing Problems e.g. fighting, refusal to follow directions)	5	4	3	2	1
Emotional problems at home or school (Internalizing problems e.g. depression and anxiety)	5	4	3	2	1
Academic problems	5	4	3	2	1
Attendance	5	4	3	2	1
Other (specify)	5	4	3	2	1

11. What proportion of the following risk factors would you say helps explain the causes of the student problems you noted in the previous question?

	All	Most	Approximately half	Some	Few
Poor learning of related social skills (listening, staying on task, organizational skills)	5	4	3	2	1
Social behavior problems (social interaction with peers or adults)	5	4	3	2	1
Parent-child conflict	5	4	3	2	1
Lack of connectedness with peers, family, school, and community	5	4	3	2	1
Limited school resources	5	4	3	2	1
Inconsistent classroom management	5	4	3	2	1
Unhealthy school or classroom climate	5	4	3	2	1
Weak, inconsistent adult leadership from parents, teachers, and other important adults	5	4	3	2	1
Overrellance on physical security measures	5	4	3	2	1

12. How do you help teachers? (Check all that apply)

— Work directly with disruptive students (e.g. not following class rules, fighting with other students and the teacher)

— Work directly with emotionally overwhelmed students who are not disruptive (e.g. depressed, anxious)

— Follow up with families and/or community agencies after students make a serious disclosure to the teacher (e.g. disclosing abuse in the family, suicidal ideation, pregnancy)

— Work with teachers on ways to improve classroom management techniques for challenging students

— Work directly with teachers to implement behavior management plans for specific students

— Provide inservices and additional training to teachers on a variety of mental health and education-related topics

— Provide teachers with community resources and referrals to help children/parents in their classroom

— Other (please specify)

13. What percentage of your time do you spend with students planning for their transition out of high school?

    —— %
    —— I don't work with students at this age level

14. Please indicate the proportion of students you work with on each of the following domains of the transition to adulthood?

	All students	Most students	Approximately half	Some students	Few students
Mental health	5	4	3	2	1
Education plans and college readiness	5	4	3	2	1
Job readiness and placement	5	4	3	2	1
Housing	5	4	3	2	1
Marital and dating issues	5	4	3	2	1
Contraception and family planning	5	4	3	2	1
Health services	5	4	3	2	1
Independent living skills	5	4	3	2	1
Connection to community resources	5	4	3	2	1
Other (please describe)	5	4	3	2	1

15. Of the work described above related to the transition to adulthood, how much of this work is done outside of the IEP process? (Check one)

    —— Most
    —— Some
    —— A little
    —— None

16. Of the families/children you work with regularly, what proportion of them receive services from government social welfare programs (for example, Medicaid, SSI, TANF, free/reduced school lunch)? Rate these 1-5, with 1 being few families/children and 5 being all children. If you are not confident you can estimate the answer to this question accurately, please leave it blank.

All	Most	Approximately half	Some	Few
5	4	3	2	1

17. Of the children you work with regularly, what proportion of them receive counseling or therapeutic services from an outside agency or professional (e.g., foster care, mental health system, private therapist)? Rate these 1-5, with 1 being few children and 5 being all children. If you are not confident you can estimate the answer to this question accurately, please leave it blank.

All	Most	Approximately half	Some	Few
5	4	3	2	1

SECTION 3

For this final section, we are interested in learning more about you and the context of the setting in which you provide your services.

18. What is your gender?

—— Female
—— Male

19. What is your racial/ethnic background? (Check all that apply)

—— African-American
—— Asian-American
—— Hispanic/Latino
—— Native American
—— White/European-American
—— Other

20. In what state do you practice?

21. Which degrees/certifications/licenses do you currently hold? (Check all that apply)

—— Bachelor's Degree in Social Work
—— Other Bachelor's Degree (Please specify ——)
—— Master's in Social Work
—— Other Master's Degree (Please specify: ——)

—— Doctorate in Social Work (PhD, DSW)
—— Other Doctorate (Please specify: ———)

22. Which of the following certificates and licenses do you have? (Check all that apply)

—— State issued School Social Work Certificate or License
—— Licensed Clinical Social Work or Certificate
—— Academy of Clinical Social Workers (NASW)
—— School Social Work Specialists (NASW)
—— Other (please specify below)

23. How many schools do you work in each year?

——

24. Which description best characterizes your employer?:

—— A local education agency (public school district)
—— A private educational system (parochial school, private school, etc.)
—— A social service agency that (delivers) contracts to provide services in a school setting
—— School-based health clinic
—— Other (Please specify:

25. Is your position primarily funded through a grant, contract, or other time-limited project?

—— Yes
—— No

25a. If you said yes, what is your specific funding source? (Check all that apply)

—— Federal grants
—— State grants
—— Foundation funding
—— Agency contracts with local school districts
—— Other (please specify)

26. How many years have you been practicing as a school social worker?

—— Years

27. Does your position require you to have state social work licensure/certification to start in a school social work position?

—— Yes
—— No

28. How would you characterize the school or schools in which you're employed?

—— Rural
—— In a small town (less than 20,000 people)
—— In a mid-size city (50,000-500,00)
—— Suburban
—— Urban (large city, 500,000+)

29. Which grade levels are you most involved in serving? (Check one)

—— Pre-kindergarten/Early childhood
—— Elementary (K-6)
—— Junior high/Middle school
—— High school
—— Other grade level arrangements (Please specify below)

One final question:

30. Can you comment on what you see as the future for the field of school social work?

THANK YOU!!!!!

APPENDIX B

HOW WE INVESTIGATED THE EVIDENCE

INVESTIGATING THE EVIDENCE: TIER 2 INTERVENTIONS (CHAPTER 4)

Plan development begins with locating empirically supported interventions. Raines (2008a) suggests three major sources for school social workers investigating the scientifically based research.

CLEARINGHOUSES

The first and most easily accessible sources are the Internet clearinghouses, including the Campbell Collaboration, the Substance Abuse and Mental Health Services Administration's (SAMHSA) National Registry of Evidence-Informed Programs and Practices, and the What Works Clearinghouse. Exceptions, however, do occur, such as the Campbell Collaboration's review of school-based *Social Information Processing* (Wilson & Lipsey, 2006a,b); SAMHSA's reviews of the *Coping Cat* program (SAMHSA, 2006) and the Incredible Years (SAMHSA, 2007a); and the What Works Clearinghouse's review of Accelerated Middle Schools (Dynarski et al., 1998; U.S. Dept. of Education, 2008a), a program designed to help students who were at least one year behind grade level catch up to their peers before high school, and *Check & Connect*, a dropout prevention program (Evelo et al., 1996; Sinclair et al., 1998; U.S. Dept. of Education, 2008a).

DATABASES

The second, and most difficult type of source to access, is the proprietary scholarly databases. Using these databases requires skills in combining Boolean operators and wildcard characters (*) to define the search parameters. This search was conceptua-lized as discovering the overlap for four intersecting circles (see Figure 4.2).

PsycINFO is the oldest and largest of the scholarly databases. Raines (2008a) recommends obtaining a broad "forest" view of the literature before looking for specific "trees" or interventions. The forest or general view was obtained by searching for three terms: meta-analysis, quantitive synthesis, or systematic review. These results provided a good overview of the effectiveness of group therapy for children and adolescents. Tillitski (1990) conducted the oldest meta-analysis of nine studies and found that group therapy was definitely better than no therapy control groups and superior to individual therapy for adolescents, but not for children. Hoag and Burlingame (1997) conducted a meta-analysis of 56 studies and found that group treatment participants improved more than 73% of the participants in no treatment control groups.

Several more focused meta-analyses determined that group treatment was generally effective for imparting life skills for youth with disabilities (Kingsnorth et al., 2007) and for treating youth with anger management problems (Lavenberg, 2007), bereavement issues (Sharpnack, 2001), mood disorders (Grossman & Hughes, 1992), sexual abuse (Hetzel-Riggin et al., 2007; Reeker et al., 1997), and social phobia. Group therapy, however, was not as effective as family therapy for youth with substance abuse problems (Schurink et al., 2004). An identical search for systematic reviews in Social Work Abstracts led to just one meta-analytic review for sexually abused chil-dren (Reeker et al., 1997).

The search for specific "trees" or interventions resulted in 10 scientifically based group interventions for adolescents and seven group interventions for children. Effective group treatments were found for adolescents with aggressive behavior and poor classroom behavior (Jackson-Sinegar, 2001), adolescents with poor classroom behavior (Jackson-Sinegar, 2001, adolescents exposed to com-munity violence (Layne et al., 2008; Saltzman et al., 2001; Stein et al., 2003), adolescents coping with stress (Butke, 2006; Stewart, 1998); adolescents with depression (Phillips, 2004; Ralph & Nicholson, 1995; Rohde et al., 2005), adoles-cents with off-task behaviors (Davis-Williams, 2004), adolescents who are preg-nant or parenting (Harris & Franklin, 2003, 2007), adolescents with risk-taking behavior (Glodich et al., 2001), adolescents with social anxiety disorders (Masia et al., 2001), and adolescents with weight problems (Melnyk et al., 2007). Effective group interventions were also found for children with anxiety disorders (Bernstein et al., 2005; Dadds, et al., 1997; Lowry-Webster et al., 2001), children with behavioral problems (Muris et al., 2005), children being bullied (DeRosier, 2004), children with depression (Stark et al., 2005), children with divorcing parents (Alpert-Gillis et al., 1989), children with low physical activity (Wilson et al., 2005), and children with violence-related trauma (Ehntholt et al., 2005).

An identical search for interventions in Social Work Abstracts led to three scientifically based group interventions for adolescents and one for children. Effective group interventions were found for adolescents coping with stress (Butke, 2006), adolescents who are pregnant or parenting (Harris & Franklin, 2003, 2007), and early adolescents with school behavior problems (Dupper, 2003). One effective group intervention was found for children at risk for future chemical dependency that improved their assertiveness, frustration tolerance, and locus of control (DeMar, 1994, 1997).

A third search was also conducted in PsycINFO for "targeted" interventions that may not be group interventions but are still aimed at selected groups of students (see Chapter 1). This search resulted in two effective Tier 2 interventions. The first program is a check-in, check-out intervention (Filter et al., 2007; Hawken & Horner, 2003; Todd et al., 2008) that uses a daily behavior report card for elementary students as part of the Behavior Education Program (Crone et al., 2004). For examples of both daily and weekly behavior report cards, see Chapter 7 in Raines (2008b). The second intervention is the *Early Risers* program for elementary students with aggressive behavior (August et al., 2001; August et al., 2003; August et al., 2007; Bernat et al., 2007). An identical search in Social Work Abstracts yielded no further interventions.

BOOKS

The third source for locating empirically supported intervention is scholarly books. Unfortunately, most books about psychosocial treatments for child and adolescent problems assume that practitioners will use individual therapy. Fortunately, there are three new books available that do focus on groups.

First, Massat et al. (2009) have published a new edition of *School Social Work* that has a chapter on Tier 3 interventions. Lindsey and White (2008) identify six effective programs, including The Journey, a six-week group for students with attention deficit/hyperactivity disorder (Webb & Myrick, 2003); Challenging Horizons, an after school program for disruptive youth (Evans et al., 2004); Kids Together, a play therapy for students with attentional problems (Hansen et al., 2000); Peer-Pairing, a pair therapy for children with poor social skills (Mervis, 1998); the Behavior Education Program, a check-in, check-out program using daily behavioral logs (Hawken et al., 2007); and the Anger Management Group, a pet therapy program (Hanselman, 2002). Second, Macgowan's (2008) book on evidence-informed group work, identifies four interventions for children and youth, including treatment for victims of childhood sexual abuse (Reeker et al., 1997); social skills training for antisocial youth (Ang & Hughes, 2002); multiple family group treatment for children with emotional disorders (McDonnell & Dyck, 2004); and social problem skills for children (Fraser et al., 2000).

Finally, Franklin, Harris, and Allen-Meares's (2006) *School Services Sourcebook* has a section (VIII) on effective group work. Three of the chapters within this section offer suggestions for empirically supported interventions. First, Garvin's (2006) chapter on groups for adolescents identifies effective programs for six issues: anger/class disruption (Feindler et al., 1984; Lochman et al., 2003), anxiety (Masia et al., 2001), depression (Clarke et al., 2003), empowerment of minority youth (Malgady & Costantino, 2003; Scott, 2001), substance abuse (Curry et al., 2003; Wagner & Macgowan, 2006), and trauma (Glodich et al., 2001; Saltzman et al., 2001; Tellerman, 2001). Second, LeCroy's (2006) chapter on groups for children identifies effective interventions for five common problems: aggressive behavior (Conduct Problems Prevention Research Group, 1992), divorce (Pedro-Carroll et al., 1992), peer mediation (Hawkins et al., 1992), social competence (Elias & Tobias, 1998; LeCroy, 2004), and withdrawn behavior (Weiss & Harris, 2001). Finally, Dupper's (2006) chapter identifies five effective life skills programs: Life Skills Training (Botvin et al., 1998; www.lifeskillstraining.com), Promoting Alternative Thinking Strategies (PATHS; Greenberg et al., 2006; www.colorado.edu/cspv/blueprints), School Survival Group (Dupper & Krishef, 1993; Dupper, 2003); Second Step (www.cfchildren.org), and Social Skills Group Intervention (S.S. GRIN; DeRossier, 2004).

INVESTIGATING THE EVIDENCE: PARENT INVOLVEMENT (CHAPTER 5)

CLEARINGHOUSES

Three clearinghouses were identified that could potentially provide relevant information about parent involvement in schooling: National Network of Partnership Schools at Johns Hopkins University, the Harvard Family Project, and the Campbell and Cochrane Collaborations. The National Network of Partnership Schools provides technical assistance to schools and districts attempting to increase what are termed "Type II" forms of parent involvement (school- and district-initiated efforts to involve parents) and includes a number of research studies based on the description of these partnerships as well as surveys to assess various types of parent involvement. Perusal of research available on this site, however, yielded only a few intervention studies using nonexperimental designs (on interactive homework assignments, Van Voorhis, 2003; attendance raising efforts, Sheldon & Epstein, 2002). The Harvard Family Project also conducted a literature review related to family involvement in schooling (Caspe et al., 2007). In addition, it identified four specific interventions: Families and Schools Together (FAST), Parent Institute for Quality Education (PIQE), Generacion Diez (G-10), and the Math and

Parent Partnership (MAPPS). One additional review was also extracted from this source (Fishel & Ramirez, 2005).

Finally, the Campbell Collaboration was searched for relevant reviews and yielded one specifically related to this search (Nye et al., 2006). In addition, there is a pending Campbell review focusing on synthesizing effects of the FAST program including five randomized controlled trials and pilot studies (Soydan et al., 2005).

DATABASES

Two databases were searched, including the Sage Education Full Text database and ERIC using the following sets of keyword search terms:

Set 1 terms: parent* or famil* or caregiv* (yielding 25,206 and 1887 abstracts, respectively)

Set 2 terms: school* or educat* or academic* or academics (yielding 54,281 and 2474 abstracts, respectively)

Set 3 terms: communicat* or involve* or engage* or collaborat* or partner* or empower* or invit* or resource* or program* or inteven* or cooperat* or enhanc* (yielding 64,024 and 9807 abstracts respectively)

Set 4 terms: meta-analy* or metaanaly* or "systematic review" (yielding 3937 and 266 abstracts, respectively)

Combining these four sets of search terms yielded 134 and 152 abstracts, respectively, from which 12 relevant meta-analyses and a systematic review were culled, including subject matter related to the overall effects of parent involvement in schooling (Fan & Chen, 1999; Jeynes, 2003, 2005, 2007; Kim & Choi, 2002; Rosenzweig, 2000; Strom & Boster, 2007), parent tutoring and child literacy development (Erion, 2006; Senechal, 2006; Mol et al., 2008), general effects of family support programs (Layzer et al., 2001), and specific programs of parent involvement in schools (Mattingly et al., 2002).

Finally, to locate additional empirical evidence, an additional search on the following terms was conducted: intervention or evaluation or random or randomized or trial or experiment or experimental or quasi-experiment or quasi-experimental or control group or comparison group or pretest or posttest or effectiveness or efficacy (yielding 4921 abstracts and 6 abstracts, respectively). As both search engines identified overlapping citations, we decided that searching 4921 abstracts and all the time frames of the available multiple meta-analyses was too unwieldy, so we narrowed our search to the publication year 2003, a decision that yielded 4485 and 6 abstracts. A final search for the most rigorous study designs (including only the operators randomized or trial or experiment* or quasi-experiment* yielded 368 and 4 studies, respectively. A hand search of these abstracts yielded 14 relevant studies (12 and 2 abstracts, respectively). Studies were deemed irrelevant if they concerned only children in preschool settings, if promoting parent involvement was not a key aim or outcome of the intervention, or if the research involved only process or formative evaluation studies.

BOOKS

Three books were selected for review, including *The Field Guide to Comer Schools in Action* (comer et al., 2004), the *School Services Sourcebook* (Franklin et al., 2006), and *Schools and Families: Creating Essential Connections for Learning* (Christensen & Sheridan, 2002). No additional intervention studies were gleaned from these sources. However, they did yield two independently conducted quasi-experimental designs showing mixed support for the Comer Model (Cook et al., 2000).

INVESTIGATING THE EVIDENCE: INCREASING STUDENT COMPLIANCE (CHAPTER 6)

For the purpose of this chapter, intervention programs or strategies for which the *primary* outcome is to improve compliance in the classroom were investigated. Since noncompliance is a gateway behavior that can lead to more severe and potentially chronic behavior problems (Walker et al., 2004), it is common for noncompliance within the classroom to be addressed by intervention packages that are framed as substance abuse, violence, dropout, or bully prevention programs. To be sure, there would be substantial overlap in evidence-based practice (EBP) searches framed by any of these perspectives. However, since the topic was framed narrowly within the referral (e.g., rule following in classroom settings), interventions in which getting along with peers or social competence in general was the primary focus, even if they included components related to compliance that were not included in this search. Additionally, interventions that were framed as substance abuse prevention, bullying prevention, or character education were excluded. Interventions that were considered violence prevention were included only if compliance in the classroom setting represented the main focus of the program or intervention strategy. Relevant clearinghouses, databases, and academic texts were examined in relation to the answerable question.

CLEARINGHOUSES

The Campbell Collaboration, SAMHSA, and the What Works clearinghouses were determined relevant to the search question. A Campbell Collaboration search yielded 19 titles under the category of "education." None of the interventions identified in this clearinghouse were narrowly focused on improving compliance in the classroom. Next, a search of SAMHSA's National Registry of Evidence-Informed Programs and Practices resulted in 26 interventions categorized as violence prevention. Two interventions were judged to focus somewhat narrowly on compliance in the classroom: Early Risers "Skills for Success" (August et al., 2006) and Incredible Years (Reid & Webster-Stratton, 2001). The What Works Clearinghouse could be searched only by topics that were determined too broad for the search question (e.g., character education and dropout prevention).

DATABASES

Two databases, PsycINFO (through EBSCOHost) and ERIC, were utilized for this search. As recommended by Raines (2008b), an effort was made to examine the problem by obtaining the "forest" view of the literature by combining three sets of searches. The first set included the words "compliance" OR "following rules." The PSYCH info search using these words and the Boolean operator OR resulted in 17,508 abstracts. The second set identified "meta-analysis" OR "systematic review"; this search yielded 10,738 abstracts. Set three included "school-based," which resulted in 8,137 abstracts. These three sets of words were then combined with the Boolean operator AND, resulting in a single abstract that focused on smoking cessation. A search using set one and set two, combined with a set of terms for identifying scientifically based research (clinical trial OR control group OR effectiveness OR efficacy OR quasi-experimental OR comparison group OR random*) was conducted. This search yielded 14 abstracts and three strategies including behavioral momentum (Oliver & Skinner, 2002), schoolwide positive behavior support (Leedy et al., 2004; Sprague & Horner, 2006), and high-probability requests (Banda & Kubina, 2006).

A similar search was also conducted in the ERIC database. In this database the first set resulted in 7,959 abstracts, and the second in 2793 abstracts. These two sets of terms were then combined with the Boolean operator AND resulting in nine abstracts. One of these nine, a meta-analysis of high-probability requests, was deemed relevant. Set one was then combined with a set of terms for identifying scientifically based research and the results yielded 965 abstracts. As this number was deemed unmanageable, the search was narrowed by adding the word "classroom"; this search resulted in 100 abstracts. The Boolean operator NOT was used with "Federal Legislation," resulting in 83 abstracts. To further narrow the scope of the search, years of publication were limited to 1990-2008, resulting in 52 abstracts. These abstracts were reviewed and seven strategies were judged relevant. Specifically, two abstracts were related to schoolwide positive behavior support, two were related to high-probability requests, two described classroom management programs, and one described an interpersonal skills training program. These studies are presented in Table 6.1 in Chapter 6.

The third source for locating empirically supported interventions for improving compliance or following classroom rules was scholarly books. Eight books were consulted for this review. The first two, *Antisocial Behavior in School: Evidence-Informed Practices* (Walker et al., 2004) and *Best Practices in School Psychology IV* (Thomas & Grimes, 2002), represent the literature from other related service disciplines (e.g., school psychology, counseling psychology, clinical psychology, and special education). Five books represented school social work literature: *The School Services Sourcebook* (Franklin et al., 2006), *Social Work Services in Schools* (Allen-Meares, 2007), *School Social Work: Theory to Practice* (Bye & Alvarez, 2007), *School Social Work: Practice, Policy, and Research* (Massat et al., 2009), and *School Social Work: Skills & Interventions for Effective Practice* (Dupper, 2002). Each of the books was scanned to identify chapters that appeared relevant to compliance or following rules within the classroom.

Walker et al. (2004) identify 13 "proven strategies" and one "proven" program relevant to the reason for referral. The 13 strategies were establishing a positive ecology; keeping teacher reactions as neutral as possible; establishing and communicating high clear expectations; reducing transition time; employing cooperative learning strategies; systematically teaching social skills; matching academic programming with skill levels of low-performing students; teaching assertiveness; using difficult situations at "teachable moments;" offering praise and encouragement; communicating a genuine interest in students' progress; using individualized instruction, cues, prompts, debriefing, coaching, and positive incentives for task completion and accuracy; and assisting families to manage behavior effectively. Additionally, Walker et al. indicate that medications such as Ritalin substantially reduce the overall rate of impulsive and disruptive behavior and increase compliance, but they suppress behavior rather than produce enduring changes. The authors also offer the following commentary on the effectiveness of counseling and psychotherapy: "Regrettably, counseling is among the least effective options available to us if the goal is to produce reliable, meaningful changes in student behavior" (p. 159). One intervention program, First Step to Success (Walker et al., 1997), was highlighted.

Bear, Cavalier, and Manning (2002) identify a number of "best practices" for developing self-discipline and preventing behavior problems. They categorize strategies as schoolwide and classroom strategies. Schoolwide strategies include developing a positive school climate and clearly articulating and consistently enforcing rules/expectations with appropriate sanctions for rule infractions. Bear et al. (2002) also recommend ensuring that physical facilities are well designed and monitored and providing ongoing staff development as schoolwide strategies. Classroom strategies consist of prevention and corrective strategies. Prevention strategies recommended include arranging the physical environment in ways that reduce congestion and facilitate the smooth and quiet movement of students, establishing clear and predictable routines, actively involving students in the establishment of rules and consequences in the first week of school, frequently discussing rules and behaviors in class, using a variety of teaching methods, promoting cooperation rather than competition, and offering opportunities for students to voice needs and opinions. Corrective approaches include developing positive reductive techniques, behavioral momentum, school-home contingency notes, group contingencies, and self-management.

Linseisen (2006) suggests that no individual interventions are effective for working with children with oppositional defiant disorder, which is largely defined by an unwillingness to comply with adult requests. She does, however, indicate that skilled practitioners discuss the positive effects of relational, cognitive-behavioral, and supportive individual work. Additionally, Linseisen indicates that play therapy is supported by practice wisdom and suggests that some evidence is available in the literature to support the use of the following interventions: problem solving and social skills training groups, anger control and stress inoculation training, and group assertiveness training. Finally, Linseisen indicates that "quite a bit" of evidence supports the use of parent training approaches, recommends that rational-emotive therapy be used with caution, and reports no evidence base for the use of pharmacological interventions with children diagnosed with oppositional defiant disorder.

Tracy and Usaj (2007) recommend a number of strategies for a range of issues and populations, including children who do not follow rules. These include self-management (e.g., self-monitoring, self-instruction), differential reinforcement, contracting, classroom behavior management procedures, cognitive behavioral therapy, and social skills training.

Dupper (2002) provides a partial list of programs that are successful in minimizing or preventing classroom behavior problems in general. These include *The Good Behavior Game,* Consistency Management and Cooperative Discipline, behavioral consultation, and the Effective Classroom Management in-service training course for teachers.

Franklin and Harris (2007) offer medication management and contingency management as effective practices for children and adolescents to increase compliance in the classroom, and they also recommend the Incredible Years program (Reid & Webster-Stratton, 2001).

Finally, Frey and Walker (2007) recommend developing caring relationships, establishing a democratic classroom climate, defining and clearly communicating class rules to students and parents, providing direct instruction for expected behaviors, and providing incentives and motivational strategies based on operant learning strategies (e.g., privileges, social rewards, and tangible rewards).

INVESTIGATING THE EVIDENCE: BEHAVIOR INTERVENTION PLANS (CHAPTER 7)

CLEARINGHOUSES

The Campbell Collaboration, SAMHSA, and the What Works clearinghouses were determined relevant to these search questions. A Campbell Collaboration title search using "intervention plan," "support plan," "behavior plan," and "consultation" yielded zero titles under the category of "education." Next, a search of SAMHSA's National Registry of Evidence-Informed Programs and Practices using the same key words resulted in one abstract for "intervention plan," zero abstracts for "behavior plan" or "support plan," and 28 abstracts for "consultation." None of the abstracts related to behavior intervention planning (BIP). A search under the "dropout prevention" topic and "staying in school" subtopic was conducted in the What Works Clearinghouse. Twenty-one interventions were found, but none were relevant to the search question.

DATABASES

Two databases, PsycINFO (through EBSCOHost) and ERIC, were utilized for this search. As recommended by Raines (2008b), an effort was made to examine the problem by obtaining the "forest" view of the literature by combining three sets of searches. The first set included the words "behavior plan" OR "intervention plan," "support plan." "Consultation" was dropped as a search term because it was assumed that BIP would include consultation, and consultation alone would yield excessive hits that were not relevant to BIP. This search using these terms and the Boolean operator OR resulted in 88 abstracts. The second set identified "meta-analysis" OR "systematic review"; this search yielded 7866 abstracts. Set three included the term "school-based," which resulted in 8256 abstracts. These three sets of terms were then combined with the Boolean operator AND, resulting in zero abstracts. A search using set one combined with a set of terms for identifying scientifically based research (clinical trial OR control group OR effectiveness OR efficacy OR quasi-experimental OR comparison group OR random*) yielded 55 abstracts, which were reviewed. Seven abstracts were relevant. Of these, three were conceptual, and two were empirical studies of effectiveness (see Table 7.1 in Chapter 7). The other two empirical studies, discussed later in this chapter, addressed the fidelity of BIP rather than effectiveness.

A similar search was also conducted in the ERIC database. In this database the first set resulted in 369 abstracts, and the second set resulted in 2856 abstracts. These two sets of terms were then combined with the Boolean operator AND resulting in zero abstracts. Set one was then combined with a set of terms for identifying scientifically-based research and the results yielded 77 abstracts. These abstracts were reviewed and 13 were judged relevant. Of these three were conceptual articles addressing the second question and 10 were empirical. Of the empirical studies, three assessed fidelity and seven assessed effectiveness (see Table 7.1); one was identified in the prior search.

BOOKS

The third source for investigating the evidence of behavior intervention planning was scholarly books. Eight books were consulted for this review: The first four—*Antisocial Behavior in School: Evidence-Informed Practices*(Walker et al., 2004), *Best Practices in School Psychology IV* (Thomas & Grimes, 2002), *Handbook of Positive Behavior Support*(Sailor et al., 2009), and *Evidence-Informed Practices for Educating Students with Emotional and Behavior Disorders* (Drasgow et al., 2009)—represent the literature from related service disciplines (e.g., school psychology, counseling psychology, clinical psychology, and special education). Five books represented school social work literature: *The School Services Sourcebook* (Franklin et al., 2006); *Social Work Services in Schools* (Allen-Meares, 2007); *School Social Work: Theory to Practice* (Bye & Alvarez, 2007); *School Social Work: Practice, Policy, and Research* (Massat et al., 2009); *School Social Work: Skills and Interventions for Effective Practice* (Dupper, 2002). Three of the four related services texts had chapters dedicated to behavior intervention planning. All of these chapters describe a very similar process and there is widespread agreement on the content. Specifically, each of these texts refers to a team-based process in which the results of a functional behavioral assessment (FBA) drive the content of the BIP. One of the school social work texts (Massat et al., 2009) had a chapter dedicated to planning, of which behavior intervention planning is one type. However, when referring to behavior intervention planning, Constable (2007a) makes no mention of the functional behavioral assessment (FBA) process that is to drive intervention selection. Dupper (2002) includes a paragraph on BIP based on FBA, and Allen-Meares (2007) and Sabatino (2009) each have chapters specific to consultation, which is clearly relevant to BIP, but do not identify BIP specifically.

INVESTIGATING THE EVIDENCE: HELPING STUDENTS COPE WITH THEIR PARENTS' DIVORCE (CHAPTER 8)

For this evidence-informed practice (EIP) process, we consulted the following databases: Academic Premier/EBSCO Host and PsycInfo, searching from the start of the database history to 2008 for peer-reviewed articles addressing the EIP question. We consulted the following three EIP databases: the Promising Practices Network (http://www.promisingpractices.net/default.asp), the Campbell Collaboration (http://www.campbellcollaboration.org/) and SAMHSA's National Registry of Evidence-Informed Programs and Practices (http://www.nrepp.samhsa.gov/). We also consulted the following three school social work textbooks to help identify potential interventions, which are also summarized here in Table 8.1.

DATABASES

As recommended by Raines (2008b), an effort was made when possible to examine the problem by obtaining the "forest" view of the literature by combining three sets of scarches. The first set included the terms "divorce" OR "separation" or "mediation." The PSYCH info search using these terms and the Boolean operator OR resulted in 37, 316 abstracts. The second set identified "meta-analy* or metaanaly* or systematic review" (12,026 abstracts). Set three included the term "group counseling or group therapy or group treatment" (16, 972 abstracts). The final set included adolescen* OR boys OR girls OR children OR teen* and yielded 407,639abstracts. These four sets of terms were then combined with the Boolean operator AND, resulting in zero abstracts that related to the evidence-informed question. A second PSYC Info search was attempted, using a similar method but using different terms. Using "divorce" OR "separation" OR "mediation" for one set, and using AND to combine it with "group counseling" OR "group therapy" OR "group treatment" and using AND to combine those two with "effective" OR "efficacious" OR "promising" yielded 32 abstracts, seven of which were directly relevant to the evidence-informed question.

A different search process was used in Academic Search Premier/EBSCO Host, this time using "divorce" AND "schools" AND "interventions," yielding 31 abstracts, nine of which appeared to be directly related to the evidence-informed question. These abstracts were then combined with the resources found in the above databases and augmented by literature cited in the three school social work textbooks used for this search (Dupper, 2003; Franklin et al., 2006; Massat et al., 2008).

CLEARINGHOUSES

For the clearinghouses, no divorce-specific programs were evaluated and described by Campbell, NREEP, or Promising Practices, though elements of programs alluded to interventions designed to address depression, violence, and anxiety, three issues that can be described as regularly experienced by some children of divorce. The three school social work textbooks were consulted searching the book indexes for "divorce," "family-based," or "families" as starting points for reviewing the book's contents.

BOOKS

Of the three books, only one chapter addressing group work with children in schools in the *Sourcebook* by LeCroy specifically mentioned two "group programs with empirical support." (LeCroy, 2006, p. 597).

INVESTIGATING THE EVIDENCE: PREVENTING BULLYING IN SCHOOLS (CHAPTER 9)

DATABASES

Two "forest" searches (see Raines, 2008b) were conducted in PsycINFO and WilsonWeb/Education Full-Text databases, using the following search criteria and Boolean operators: "bully or bullying or bullies" (yielding 2434 and 1105 abstracts, respectively), school* (yielding 25,0061 and 30,1370 abstracts, respectively), and "meta-analy* or systematic review" (yielding 11,468 and 302 abstracts, respectively). Combination of these terms yielded eight and one abstracts, respectively. From these, four relevant meta-analyses were located (Derzon, 2006; Ferguson et al., 2007; Livingston, 2008; Merrell et al., 2008). The remaining five abstracts were either not meta-analyses or not meta-analyses related to interventions (e.g., a meta-analysis on the relationship between bullying and risk for suicide; Kim and Leventhal, 2008). Dropping the last search set and confining results to the years after 2006 (given the time frames of the meta-analytic reviews) and adding the search set "randomiz* or experiment* or quasi-experiment* or trial or intervention or evaluation" (yielding 51,4046 and 74,596 abstracts, respectively) resulted in 221 and 156 abstracts, respectively. These sets were hand searched for intervention studies, yielding nine additional intervention studies (Andreou et al., 2007; Black & Jackson, 2007; ErtesvÅg & Vaaland, 2007; Evers et al., 2007; Hunt, 2007; Jenson & Dieterich, 2007; McLaughlin et al., 2006; Minton & O'Moore, 2008; Slee & Mohyla, 2007).

CLEARINGHOUSES

Three clearinghouses were consulted, including the National Registry of Evidence-Informed Programs and Practices (http://nrepp.samhsa.gov/find.asp), the U.S. Department of Education What Works Clearinghouse (http://www.whatworks. ed.gov/), and Campbell and Cochrane Collaboration databases. Search of these databases yielded no additional intervention studies. However, the Campbell Collaboration is currently conducting a school bullying review. A reference hand search of this source located two additional reviews-one meta-analytic (Smith, J. D. et al., 2004a) and one systematic review (Vreeman & Carroll, 2007).

BOOKS

Three texts were searched: *The School Services Sourcebook* (Franklin et al., 2006), the *Handbook of School Safety and Violence* (Jimerson & Furlong, 2006) and *Bullying Prevention and Intervention: Realistic Strategies for Schools* (Swearer et al., 2009). Overall, these sources provide ample descriptions of relevant school-based intervention programs. In addition, they identify one universal program, Steps to Respect, that has shown effects on bullying (Frey et al., 2005) and two others that show effects on social competence-related skills as well as reducing aggressive and disruptive behaviors (though not primarily focused on bullying): Second Step and the PATHS curriculum.

INVESTIGATING THE EVIDENCE: SOCIAL SKILLS INTERVENTIONS (CHAPTER 10)

Raines (2008b) suggests three major sources for school social workers investigating the scientifically based research. These include Internet clearinghouses, computer databases, and scholarly books.

CLEARINGHOUSES

The first and most accessible type of source to find interventions is the Internet clearinghouses, including the Campbell Collaboration, Substance Abuse and Mental Health Services Administration's (SAMHSA) National Registry of Evidence-Based Programs and Practices, and the What Works Clearinghouse. Users will find that these clearinghouses provide excellent reviews of interventions that should be categorized as universal prevention programs. This is fortunate in the case of social skills since remediation is much more difficult than primary prevention.

One intervention review was found in the Campbell Collaboration using the words "social" AND "education." This was a meta-analytic review of social information processing (Wilson & Lipsey, 2006a,b). *Social information processing* interventions aim to change cognitive patterns among children to improve their ability to accurately interpret and respond to cues from those around them. According to the *social information processing* model, social behavior is the result of five related steps: (1) encoding situational cues, (2) correctly interpreting the cues, (3) clarifying a goal, (4) generating possible responses to meet the goal, and (5) selecting the best response. Antisocial behavior, such as aggression, is considered to be the result of cognitive distortions at one or more of these steps. As such, *social information processing* interventions are distinct from behavioral interventions. Behavioral social skills programs focus primarily on the social (or antisocial) behaviors themselves rather than the underlying thought processes. The reviewers examined 73 studies and found that the average effect size was low (ES = .21; see Box 10.1). Nevertheless, they did identify five studies with an effect size greater than 1.00 (Etscheidt, 1991; Fcindler et al., 1984; Johnson, 2001; Shapiro, 1998; Shure & Spivack, 1980). Only one of these studies, however, used a widely available manual for practitioners—the I Can Problem Solve curriculum (Shure, 2000).

The SAMHSA registry was checked and resulted in eight interventions. Three of the interventions addressed social skills: Incredible Years, Primary Project, and Second Step.

The What Works Clearinghouse (WWC) contains a set of nine reviews on character education and explains that these interventions are intended to improve student outcomes related to positive character development, prosocial behavior, and academic performance. Programs are ranked by three criteria: an improvement index, evidence rating, and extent of the evidence. The improvement index is the difference between the percentile rank of the average student in the treatment group and the percentile rank of the average student in the control group. The WWC found three programs that had an improvement index of 15 percentile points or more. The highest ranked intervention was Positive Action (see the description below). The second highest intervention was Too Good for Violence, a K-8 program that supports character values, social-emotional skills, and healthy beliefs. The program includes seven lessons per grade level for elementary school (K-5) and nine lessons per grade level for middle school (6-8). All lessons are scripted and engage students through role-playing and cooperative learning games, small group activities, and classroom discussions. Students are encouraged to generalize these skills to different contexts. The third highest intervention was Connect with Kids, -third to twelfth grade programs that aim to promote prosocial attitudes and positive behavior of upper elementary (grades 3-5) and secondary (grades 6-12) students by teaching character values. Lesson plans include realistic videos, story summaries, discussion questions, student games, and activities for character traits.

The second and most difficult type of source to access is the computerized databases. Using these databases requires skills in combining Boolean operators (AND, OR, & NOT) as well as wildcard characters (*) to define the search parameters.

ERIC (Education Resources Information Center) is sponsored by the Institute of Education Sciences of the U.S. Department of Education. ERIC covers a wide variety of materials, including conference reports, dissertations, and peer-reviewed articles, back as far as 1965. The "forest" search for social skills interventions resulted in only 14 abstracts that met all three criteria.

Schneider and Byrne (1985) examined 51 studies to compare four major approaches to social skills training. First, modeling: using filmed, videotaped, or live demonstration worked best with preschool children and older adolescents (ages 14-19). Second, operant conditioning: using social or material reinforcement worked best with both preschoolers and school-age children through age 13. Third, coaching using direct instruction followed by discussion worked best with preschoolers and older adolescents, but not as well with school-age children. Finally, cognitive approaches were the least effective with all of the age groups. Kavale and colleagues (1997) focused on students with behavior disorders and compared 35 group-design studies and 64 single subject design studies. For the group-design studies, they found a relatively small effect size of only .20, but for the single subject designs, they found that the average percentage of nonoverlapping data points (PND) from baseline to intervention phases was 62%, a low effect size (see Box 10.1). Interestingly, commercially available programs, such as ACCEPTS (Walker et al., 1988), ASSET (Hazel et al., 1995), Skillstreaming (McGinnis & Goldstein, 2003), Prepare (Goldstein, 1999), and Aggression Replacement Training (ART; Goldstein et al., 1998) fared no better than generic programs that also employed the same core elements of direct instruction, modeling, rehearsal, feedback, discussion, and role-playing. Furthermore, efficacy was not affected by participant age or length of training. In fact, a shorter training period of 12 weeks or less did slightly better than longer training periods (ES = .214 vs. ES = .183).

Social skills improvement was most likely to be noticed by teachers (ES = .223) and least likely to be observed by parents (ES = .153). Finally, social skills training had the best results on social anxiety (ES = .42) and the lowest results on social aggression (ES = .12), an effect so low that social skills training might be considered ineffective for students with conduct disorders. Ang and Hughes

(2002) conducted a meta-analysis of social skills training with antisocial youth. Their effect size across 38 studies was considerably better at .62, meaning that children receiving treatment outperformed 73% of children who received no treatment. An important result of their systematic review was that group composition affected outcome. They found that the effect size for homogeneous groups of antisocial youth (ES = .55) was significantly lower than for heterogeneous groups (ES = .70). Interestingly, of the eight negative outcomes, seven involved homogeneous groups. Lösel and Beelmann (2003) examined 84 randomized controlled trials of social skills programs aimed at preventing antisocial behavior and found a small effect size (ES = .38) that became even smaller at follow-up (ES = .28). Nonetheless, they concluded that "well-implemented, cognitive-behavioral programs targeting high-risk youngsters who already exhibit some behavioral problems seem to be particularly effective" (p. 102). Another meta-analysis by Gansle (2005) reviewed interventions that aimed to reduce inappropriate displays of anger, with social skills being one outcome. Again, the weighted mean effect size for social skills was small (ES = .34).

A meta-analysis search in PsycINFO yielded just 18 abstracts. Whipple (2007) found that social skills training for children with externalizing behaviors was only slightly more effective when it included a parent training component (ES = .24) than when it did not (ES = .20). Similarly, the number of treatment agents (clinician, parent, teacher, peers) had only nonsignificant differences in effect. Like Kavale and colleagues (1997), Whipple found no differences based on treatment duration. Bellini and Hopf (2007) examined school-based social skills training for children with autism spectrum disorders. Using the percentage of nonoverlapping data points (PND) method for single subject designs, they found a result of only 70%, meaning that in nearly one-third of the measurements participants did not display the desired outcomes (see Box 10.1). Reynhout and Carter (2006) looked at social stories as an intervention for children with autism spectrum disorder. They calculated a PND of only 51% in the 12 studies they examined, meaning that participants demonstrated improved behavior in only about half of the observations. Renk and Phares (2004) determined that much of the problem with measurement is that it depends on the perception of the informant (self, parent, teacher, or peer) and these often have little correlation with each other. Overall, we must conclude that the effectiveness of traditional (pull-out) social skills programs has generally been modest at best.

A search of ERIC resulted in 54 abstracts and produced three scientifically based interventions for adolescents and 10 interventions for children. Specifically, effective social skills interventions were found for adolescents with delinquency (Feindler et al., 1984), adolescents with mild intellectual disabilities (O'Reilly & Glynn, 1995), and adolescents with social anxiety (Fisher et al., 2004; Masia-Warner et al., 2007). Effective social skills interventions were also found for children with aggressive behavior (August et al., 2004; DeRosier, 2004), children of alcoholics (Nastasi & DeZolt, 1994; Riddle et al., 1997), children with anxiety (Wood, 2007), children with autism (Toplis & Hadwin, 2006), children at risk for behavioral disorders (Gresham et al., 2006), children who were disruptive (Abdul-Latif, 1998), children at risk for drug abuse (Hahn et al., 2007), children with learning disabilities (Utay & Lampe, 1995), children in poverty (Reid et al., 2007; Tolan et al., 2004), and children in urban communities (Hennessey, 2007).

A search in PsycINFO generated six scientifically based interventions for adolescents and 11 for children. Specifically, effective social skills interventions were found for adolescent bystanders of bullying (Merrell, 2004), adolescents at risk for drug abuse (Sun et al., 2006; Wagner & Beaumont, 2007; Williams et al., 2005), adolescents at risk for HIV (Givaudan et al., 2007), adolescents with learning disabilities, Hispanic adolescents who were pregnant or parenting (Harris & Franklin, 2003, 2007), and adolescents with social anxiety (Fisher et al., 2004). Effective interventions were also found for children with aggressive behavior (DeRosier, 2004), children with autism (Kalyva & Avramidis, 2005; Toplis & Hadwin, 2006), child bystanders of bullying (Frey et al., 2005), children in foster care (Pears et al., 2007), child victims of maltreatment (Fantuzzo et al., 2005), children with oppositional behavior (Muris et al., 2005), children in poverty (Domitrovich et al., 2007; Izard et al., 2008), children with reactive aggression (Louwe et al., 2007), children's social-emotional skills (Linares et al., 2005), children in urban communities (Mokrue et al., 2005), and children at risk for committing violence (Vazsonyi et al., 2004).

BOOKS

For this topic, a statewide consortium of 76 academic and research libraries was searched and this resulted in seven books. The tables of contents were perused to determine which ones had a chapter on social skills. Three books met this criterion.

Mitchell's (2008) book contains a chapter on social skills training. He identifies six steps for teaching social skills. First, the teacher should describe and discuss why the skills are important. Second, the teacher should break each skill down to its component parts and model the skill for the students. Third, students should be given an opportunity to practice the skill in a structured situation (e.g., role-play) with explicit feedback. Fourth, the students should be provided with prompts and praises for good behavior. Fifth, the students should be encouraged to reinforce each other's skills. Finally, other staff should encourage prosocial behavior by students. Mitchell also provides two important cautions. First, he notes that special social skills classes have limited value and argues that social skills should be taught in natural (whole classroom) contexts. Second, he warns that students need consistent messages from all the educators in the school and their parents. In summary, Mitchell focuses primarily on the core components of social skills training without any specific program suggestions.

Rathvon's (2008) book contains a lengthy chapter titled "Interventions to Improve Behavior and Enhance Social Competence." The chapter is divided into two main sections: (1) interventions for improving social competence in the classroom and (2) interventions for improving behavior in other school settings (e.g., lunchroom, playground, and hallways). Like Gresham and colleagues (2006), Rathvon distinguishes between acquisition deficits and performance deficits. Her emphasis is on performance deficits.

Rathvon identifies seven classroom interventions for improving prosocial conduct. Each strategy is described in detail, and variations are provided. The first intervention she discusses is *the Good Behavior Game* (Barrish et al., 1969). The second classroom intervention is Three Steps to Self-Managed Behavior (Dalton et al., 1999), a strategy that includes three components: (1) self-monitoring (using a form), (2) self-evaluation (comparing oneself to the class criterion), and (3) self-correction (modifying one's own behavior). Third, she describes the use of Randomized Group Contingencies (Kelshaw-Levering et al., 2000), an intervention that provides the whole class randomized reinforcements for randomly selected behaviors. Fourth, Rathvon explains the Response Cost Raffle (Proctor & Morgan, 1991), which involves taking away a reinforcer for inappropriate behavior. Fifth, she describes Positive Peer Reporting (Moroz & Jones, 2002), wherein the teacher uses daily brief sessions for peers to give positive comments about their classmates' behavior. The sixth strategy is Peer-Monitored Self-Management (Davies & Witte, 2000), where students are seated in groups of four or five and disruptive students are dispersed among these groups with each group monitoring members' behavior to earn rewards. The final classroom strategy is a Multicomponent Intervention to Reduce Disruptive Behavior (Mottram et al., 2002) that combines elements from both the Randomized Contingencies and the Response Cost Raffle. Practitioners will appreciate Rathvon's explicit directions, flexible variations, and useful forms.

Yell and associates' new book contains a chapter titled "Social Skills Instruction" by Meadows (2009). For preschoolers, she recommends My Friends & Me (Davis, 1988). For elementary-age children, she endorses I Can Problem Solve (Shure, 1982), Skillstreaming (McGinnis & Goldstein, 2003), and Tribes (Gibbs, 2001). For middle-school and junior high youth, she commends Prepare (Goldstein, 1999), ACCESS (Walker et al., 1988), and ASSET (Hazel et al., 1995). For high school youth, she suggests ASSET (Hazel et al., 1995), Learning to Get Along (Jackson et al., 1991), and LCCE: Life Centered Career Education (Brolin, 1997).

INVESTIGATING THE EVIDENCE: ANXIETY IN SCHOOLS (CHAPTER 11)

DATABASES

In PsycINFO, we did a "forest search" (see Raines, 2008b, for more detail on this search technique) using Boolean OR categories as follows: "anxiety OR separation anxiety OR panic attacks" (101,780 abstracts), combined with "schools OR high school OR elementary school" (144, 529 abstracts), combined with "adolescen* or boys or girls or children or teen* (410,664 abstracts), finally combined with "meta-analy* or metaanaly* or systematic review(12,026 abstracts) to produce a total of three abstracts, all of which were directly related to the evidence-informed practice question. We also conducted a search with PsycINFO that attempted to target anxiety treatments more specifically, searching for "anxiety OR separation anxiety OR panic attacks" combined with "clinical trial or control group or effectiveness or efficacy or quasi-experimental or comparison group or random* "(225, 254 abstracts), "school-based or in-school or school setting or school counseling" (28,758 abstracts) and "(adolescen* OR boys OR girls OR children OR teen*)." This second search produced 37 abstracts, 12 of which were directly relevant to the question for this chapter. For Academic Search Premier/ EBSCO Host, we used the search "(anxiety) AND (children) AND (school-based)" and found 68 abstracts, 12 of which had direct implications to the EIP question. With the 20 remaining abstracts, we hand searched them, and the findings from these studies and the others from PsycInfo are part of the Intervention Appraisal Grid in Table 11.1.

CLEARINGHOUSES

For the three online clearinghouses, the National Registry of Evidence-Informed Programs and Practices (located at http://nrepp.samhsa.gov/find.asp), the U.S. Department of Education What Works Clearinghouse (located at http://www.what-works.ed.gov/), and the University of Colorado's Center for the Study and Prevention of Violence Blueprints for Violence Prevention site (located at http://www.colorado.edu/cspv/blueprints/) were consulted. Of these databases, we only found items at the NREPP (22 programs) and after hand searching them, found only one that was directly relevant to the EIP question.

BOOKS

The three school social work textbooks (Dupper, 2003; Franklin et al., 2006; Massat et al., 2009) yielded a range of empirically-supported interventions and we pursued the citations in those books to learn more about the specific interventions (in the case of the *"Coping Cat"* intervention, both our NREPP search and the textbooks matched up in their discussion of this intervention's potential effectiveness).

INVESTIGATING THE EVIDENCE: PROBLEMS WITH ATTENTION DEFICIT/HYPERACTIVITY DISORDER (ADHD) IN A SCHOOL SETTING (CHAPTER 12)

DATABASES

Two forest searches (see Raines, 2008b) were conducted in PsycINFO and PubMed, using the following search criteria and Boolean operators: attention deficit hyperactivity disorder or ADHD or ADD" combined with "school* or educat* or academic*" and "intervention or counseling or program" and "meta-analysis or meta-analytic review or systematic review meta-analyses." Combination of these terms yielded 7 and 144 abstracts, respectively. These were hand searched, yielding four relevant meta-analyses (DuPaul, & Eckert, 1997, Purdie et al., 2002; Reid et al., 2005; Schachar et al., 2002). Dropping the last search set and adding the search set "intervention or randomized or trial or evaluation or quasi-experiment* or experiment* or pre-test or post-test" yielded 477 and 424 abstracts, respectively. These sets were hand searched. After removal of general reviews, studies on preschool populations, those not incorporating empirical research, those not conducted in school settings, and those not covered in prior meta-analyses, this search located six additional abstracts (Bierman et al., 2007; Gureasko-Moore et al., 2006, 20072008a; Langberg et al., 2008; Pfiffner et al., 2007) and two additional narrative reviews deemed relevant to chapter aims (DuPaul & Weyandt, 2006a, 2006b).

CLEARINGHOUSES

Three clearinghouses were consulted, including the National Registry of Evidence-Informed Programs and Practices (http://nrepp.samhsa.gov/find.asp), the U.S. Department of Education What Works Clearinghouse (http://www.whatworks.ed.gov/), and the Campbell and Cochrane Collaboration databases. Search of these databases yielded no relevant interventions.

BOOKS

Three texts were searched, including *Psychosocial Treatments for Child and Adolescent Disorders: Empirically Based Strategies for Clinical Practice* (Hibbs & Jensen, 2007); *ADHD in the Schools* (DuPaul & Stoner, 2003) and, finally, one school social work source, the *School Services Sourcebook* (Franklin et al., 2006).

INVESTIGATING THE EVIDENCE: IATROGENIC INTERVENTIONS IN SCHOOLS (CHAPTER 13)

DATABASES

Searches were conducted in both the Psychinfo and ERIC databases using the following sets of keyword terms:

1. harmful* OR iatrogenic OR wORse* OR deteriORat* OR "negative effect*" yielding 35,644 and X abstracts, respectively
2. treatment* OR intervention* OR counseling* OR therap* OR psychotherap* OR psycho-therap* OR KW=prevention*, yielding 65,2107 and X abstracts, respectively
3. school* OR educat* OR academic*, yielding 48,1664 and X abstracts, respectively
4. adolescen* OR boys OR girls OR child* OR teen*, yielding 502148 and X abstracts, respectively
5. meta-analy* OR metaanaly* OR "systematic review" (yielding 11,591 and X abstracts, respectively)

Combining these sets of terms yielded four irrelevant abstracts in PsychInfo and zero abstracts in ERIC. Dropping the fifth search set produced 1103 and 303 abstracts, respectively. Deeming the PsychInfo set too large to search, we narrowed this search in two ways: (1) confining the search to publication years between 2000 and the present, and (2) using only the terms "iatrogenic and (school* OR educat* or academic*)." The first yielded 423 abstracts and the latter 86 abstracts. All these sets were hand searched and yielded 12 narrative review articles and nine empirical studies. The reviews included topics on deviant peer influences (Dishion et al., 2002; Gifford-Smith et al., 2005), school-based substance abuse prevention (Werch & Owen, 2002), youth gangs and school violence prevention (Flannery et al., 1998; Guerra et al., 2006; Skiba et al., 2004), health education programming (Greenberg, 1985; Lamarine, 1989), school discipline policies (Cameron, 2006; Cameron & Sheppard, 2006; Skiba et al., 2004), grade retention (Meisels, 1992), and high-stakes testing and standards-based reform (Hedrick, 2007; Baines & Stanley, 2006).

BOOKS

The following books that directly addressed potentially iatrogenic effects of programs, treatments, or strategies that are typically directed toward schools and/or children were consulted. These include an edited volume on peer contagion effects, *Deviant Peer Influences in Programs for Youth: Problems and Solutions* (Dodge et al., 2006) and the *School Services Sourcebook* (Franklin et al., 2006).

NOTES

CHAPTER 1 THE NEED FOR AN EVIDENCE-INFORMED PRACTICE APPROACH IN SCHOOLS

The U.S. Department of Education's (2006a) definition of the term *scientifically based research* as follows:

a. means research that involves the application of rigorous, systematic, and objective procedures to obtain reliable and valid knowledge relevant to education activities and programs; and

b. includes research that –

1. Employs systematic, empirical methods that draw on observation or experiment;
2. Involves rigorous data analyses that are adequate to test the stated hypotheses and justify the general conclusions drawn;
3. Relies on measurements or observational methods that provide reliable and valid data across evaluators and observers, across multiple measurements and observations, and across studies by the same or different investigators;
4. Is evaluated using experimental or quasi-experimental designs in which individuals, entities, programs, or activities are assigned to different conditions and with appropriate controls to evaluate the effects of the condition of interest, with a preference for random assignment experiments, or other designs to the extent that those designs contain within-condition or across-condition controls;
5. Ensures that experimental studies are presented in sufficient detail and clarity to allow for replication or, at a minimum, offer the opportunity to build systematically on their findings; and
6. Has been accepted by a peer-reviewed journal or approved by a panel of independent experts through a comparably rigorous, objective, and scientific review (§ 300.35).

REFERENCES

Abdul-Latif, D. L. (1998). *Improving the social-adaptive behavior of chronically disruptive students in an elementary school setting.* Ed.D. practicum I report. Nova Southeastern University. (ERIC Document Reproduction Service No. ED425847)

Abel, R. E., and Lyman W. N. (Eds.). (2002). *Scholarly publishing: Books, journals, publishers, and libraries in the twentieth century.* New York: John Wiley.

Achenbach, T. M. (1991). *Manual for the Child Behavior Checklist/4-18 and the 1991 profile.* Burlington: University of Vermont, Department of Psychiatry.

Achenbach, T. M., McConaughy, S. H., & Howell, C. T. (1987). Child/adolescent behavioral and emotional problems: Implications of cross-informant correlations for situational specificity. *Psychological Bulletin, 101*(2), 213–232.

Addo, L. A. (1997). Oppositional behavior in black male early adolescents. Ph.D. dissertation, Boston University, Massachusetts. Retrieved February 10, 2009, from Dissertations and Theses: Full Text database. (Publication No. AAT 9713656)

Ahn, S. (1998). Maternal beliefs and management strategies of peer interactions as correlates of social competence in Korean children. *Dissertation Abstracts International Section A: Humanities & Social Sciences, 58*(11-A), 4180.

Allen-Meares, P. (1977). Analysis of tasks. *Social Work, 22*(3), 196–201.

Allen-Meares, P. (1993). Pull and push: Clinical or macro interventions in schools. *Social Work in Education, 15*(1), 3–5.

Allen-Meares, P. (1994). Social work services in schools: A national study of entry level tasks. *Social Work, 39*(5), 560–565.

Allen-Meares, P. (Ed.). (2007). *Social work services in schools* (5th ed.). Boston: Pearson Education.

Alpert-Gillis, L. J., Pedro-Carroll, J. L., & Cowen, E. L. (1989). The Children of Divorce Intervention Program: Development, implementation, and evaluation of a program for young urban children. *Journal of Consulting Psychology, 57*(5), 583–589.

Amato, P.R. (2000). The consequences of divorce for adults and children. *Journal of Marriage and the Family, 62*, 1269–1287.

American Psychological Association (APA), Division 12. (1993). Task force on promotion and dissemination of psychological procedures. Retrieved August 6, 2009, from http://www.apa.org/divisions/div12/chamble2.pdf.

American Psychological Association (APA). (2000). *Diagnostic and statistical manual of mental disorders*, Fourth Edition, Text Revision. Washington, DC: Author.

American Psychological Association (APA). (2005). Evidence-based practice in psychology. *American Psychologist, 61*(4), 271–285. Also available as the *Report of the 2005 Presidential task force on evidence-based practice*. Washington, DC: Author. Retrieved August 6, 2009, from http://www.apa.org/practice/ebpreport.pdf.

Anderson, A. R., Christenson, S. L., Sinclair, M. F., & Lehr, C. A. (2004). Check & connect: The importance of relationships for promoting engagement with school. *Journal of School Psychology, 42*(2), 95–113.

Anderson-Butcher, D., Stetler, E.G., & Midle, T. (2006). A case for expanded school-community partnerships in support of positive youth development. *Children & Schools, 28*, 155–163.

Andreou, E., Didaskalou, E., & Vlachou, A. (2007). Evaluating the effectiveness of a curriculum-based anti-bullying intervention program in Greek primary schools. *Educational Psychology, 27*(5), 693–711.

Ang, R. P., & Hughes, J. N. (2002). Differential benefits of skills training with antisocial youth based on group composition: A meta-analytic investigation. *School Psychology Review, 31*(2), 164–185.

Angold, A., Costello, E. J., Farmer, E. M. Z., Burns, B. J., & Erkanli, A. (1999). Impaired but undiagnosed. *Journal of the American Academy of Child and Adolescent Psychiatry, 38*(2), 129–137.

Arnold, L. E., Elliott, M., Sachs, L., Bird, H., Kraemer, H. C., Wells, K. C., Abikoff, H. B., Comarda, A., Conners, C. K., Elliott, G. R., Greenhill, L. L., Hechtman, L., Hinshaw, S. P., Hoza, B., Jensen, P. S., March, J. S., Newcorn, J. H., Pelham, W. E., Severe, J. B., Swanson, J. M., Vitiello, B., & Wigal, T. (2003). Effects of ethnicity on treatment attendance, stimulant response/ dose, and 14-month outcome in ADHD. *Journal of Consulting and Clinical Psychology, 71*(4), 713–727.

Arnold, M. E., & Hughes, J. N. (1999). First do no harm: Adverse effects of grouping deviant youth for skills training. *Journal of School Psychology, 37*(1), 99–115.

Arsneault, S. (2001). Values and virtue: The politics of abstinence-only education. *American Review of Public Administration, 31*(4), 436–454.

Astor, R. A., Behre, W., Wallace, J., & Fravil, K. (1998). School social workers and school violence: Personal safety, violence programs, and training. *Social Work, 43*, 223–232.

Astor, R., Benbenishty, R., & Marachi, R. (2003). Violence in schools. In P. Allen-Meares (Ed.), *Social work services in schools*. New York: Allyn & Bacon.

Astor, R., Benbenishty, R., & Meyer, H.A. (2004). Monitoring and mapping student victimization in schools. *Theory into Practice, 43*(1), 39–49.

August, G. J., Bloomquist, M. L., Realmuto, G. M., & Hektner, J. M. (2006). An integrated components prevention intervention for aggressive elementary school children: The Early Risers program. *Journal of Consulting and Clinical Psychology, 69*(4), 614–626.

August, G. J., Bloomquist, M. L., Realmuto, G. M., & Hektner, J. M. (2007). The Early Risers "Skills for Success" program: A targeted intervention for preventing conduct problems and substance abuse in aggressive elementary school children. In P. Tolan, J. Szapocznik, & S. Sambrano (Eds.), *Preventing youth substance abuse: Science-based programs for children and adolescents* (pp. 137–158). Washington, DC: American Psychological Association.

August, G. J., Egan, E. A., Realmuto, G. M., & Hektner, J. M. (2003). Four years of the Early Risers' age-targeted prevention intervention: Effects on aggressive children's peer relations. *Behavior Therapy, 34*(4), 453–470.

August, G. J., Lee, S. S., Bloomquist, M. L., Realmuto, G. M., & Hektner, J. M. (2004). Maintenance effects of an evidence-based prevention innovation for aggressive children living in culturally diverse urban neighborhoods: The Early Risers effectiveness study. *Journal of Emotional & Behavioral Disorders, 12*(4), 194–205.

August, G. J., Realmuto, G. M., Winters, K. C., & Hektner, J. M. (2001). Prevention of adolescent drug abuse: Targeting high-risk children with a multifaceted intervention model–The Early Risers "skills for success" program. *Applied & Preventive Psychology, 10*(2), 135–153.

Bagley, C., & Pritchard, C. (1998). The reduction of problem behaviours and school exclusion in at-risk youth: An experimental study of school social work with cost benefit analyses. *Child and Family Social Work, 3*(4), 219–226.

Baines, L. A., & Stanley, G. K. (2006). The iatrogenic consequences of standards-based education. *Clearing House: A Journal of Educational Strategies, Issues and Ideas, 79*(3), 119–123.

Balon, R. (2007). Rating scales for anxiety/anxiety disorders. *Current Psychiatry Reports, 9*(4), 271–277.

Banda, D. R., & Kubina, R. M. (2006). The effects of high-probability request sequencing technique in enhancing transition behaviors. *Education and Treatment of Children, 29*(3), 507–516.

Barkham, M., & Mellor-Clark, J. (2003). Bridging evidence-based practice and practice-based evidence: Developing rigorous and relevant knowledge for the psychological therapies. *Clinical Psychology & Psychotherapy, 10*(6), 319–327.

Barkley, R. A. (2006a). *Attention-deficit hyperactivity disorder: A handbook for diagnosis and treatment* (3rd ed). New York: Guilford Press.

Barkley, R. A. (2006b). Attention-deficit/hyperactivity disorder. In D. A. Wolfe & E. J. Mash (Eds.), *Behavioral and emotional disorders in adolescents: Nature, assessment, and treatment* (pp. 91–153). New York: Guilford Press.

Barkley R. A., Fischer, M., Edelbrock, C. S., & Smallish, L. (1990). The adolescent outcome of hyperactive children diagnosed by research criteria: I. An 8-year prospective follow-up study. *Journal of the American Academy of Child & Adolescent Psychiatry, 29,* 546–557.

Barlow, D. H., Morrow-Bradley, C., Elliot, R., & Phillips, B. N. (1993). Relationship between the scientist and the practitioner. In J. A. Mindell (Ed.), *Issues in clinical psychology* (pp. 11–35). Madison, WI: Brown & Benchmark.

Barnett, D. W., Daly, E. J., III, Jones, K. M., & Lentz, F. E., Jr. (2004). Response to intervention. *Journal of Special Education, 38*(2), 66–79.

Barrett, P. M., Dadds, M. R., & Rapee, R. M. (1991). *The coping koala: Treatment manual.* Unpublished manuscript, University of Queensland, Queensland, Australia.

Barrett, P. M., Lowry-Webster, H. M., & Holmes, J. M. (1999a). *FRIENDS program for children–Group leader's manual* (2nd ed.). Brisbane, Australia: Australian Academic Press.

Barrett, P. M., Lowry-Webster, H. M., & Holmes, J. M. (1999b). *FRIENDS program for children–Parents supplement* (2nd ed.). Brisbane, Australia: Australian Academic Press.

Barrett, P. M., Lowry-Webster, H. M., & Holmes, J. M. (1999c). *FRIENDS program for children–Participant workbook* (2nd ed.). Brisbane, Australia: Australian Academic Press.

Barrish, H. H., Saunders, M., & Wolf, M. M. (1969). Good Behavior Game: Effects of individual contingencies for group consequences on disruptive behavior in a classroom. *Journal of Applied Behavior Analysis, 2*(2), 119–124.

Barth, R. P., & Jonson-Reid, M. (2000). Outcomes after child welfare services: Implications for the design of performance measures. *Children and Youth Services Review, 22* (9–10), 763.

Batsche, G., Elliot, J., Graden, J. L., Grimes, J., Kovaleski, J. F., Prasse, D., Reschly, D. J., Schrag, J., & Tilly, W. D. (2006). *Response to intervention: Policy considerations and implementation.* Alexandria, VA: National Association of State Directors of Special Education.

Bear, G. G., Cavalier, A. R., & Manning, M. A. (2002). Best practices in school discipline. In A. Thomas & J. Grimes (Eds.), *Best practices in school psychology IV* (Vols. 1 and 2). Bethesda, MD: National Association of School Psychologists.

Beard, K. Y., & Sugai, G. (2004). First Step to Success: An early intervention for elementary children at risk for antisocial behavior. *Behavioral Disorders, 29*(4), 396–409.

Beelmann, A., Pfingsten, U., & Losel, F. (1994). Effects of training social competence in children: A meta-analysis of recent evaluation studies. *Journal of Clinical Child Psychology, 23*(3), 260–271.

Bellini, S., & Hopf, A. (2007). The development of the autism social skills profile: A preliminary analysis of psychometric properties. *Focus on Autism and Other Developmental Disabilities, 22* (2), 80–87.

Benazzi, L., Horner, R. H., & Good, R. H. (2006). Effect of behavior support team composition on the technical adequacy and contextual fit of behavior support plans. *Journal of Special Education, 40*(3), 160–170.

Benbenishty, R., & Astor, R.A. (2005). *School violence in context.* New York: Oxford University Press.

Bentley, K. J., & Collins, K. S. (2006). Psychopharmacological treatment for child and adolescent mental disorders. In C. Franklin, M. B. Harris, & P. Allen-Meares (Eds.), *School services sourcebook.* New York: Oxford University Press.

Bernat, D. H., August, G. J., Hektner, J. M., & Bloomquist, M. L. (2007). The Early Risers preventive intervention: Testing for six-year outcomes and mediational processes. *Journal of Abnormal Child Psychology, 35*(4), 605–617.

Bernstein, G. A., Layne, A. E., Egan, E. A., & Tennison, D. M. (2005). School-based interventions for anxious children. *Journal of the American Academy of Child & Adolescent Psychiatry, 44*(11), 1118–1127.

Berzin, S. C. (2008). Difficulties in the transition to adulthood: Using propensity scoring to understand what makes foster youth vulnerable. *Social Service Review, 82*(2), 171.

Bierman, K. L., Coie, J. D., Dodge, K. A., Foster, E. M., Greenberg, M. T., Lochman, J. E., McMahon, R.J., & Pinderhughes, E. (2007). Fast track randomized controlled trial to prevent externalizing psychiatric disorders: Findings from grades 3 to 9. *Journal of the American Academy of Child & Adolescent Psychiatry, 46*, 1250–1250.

Bird, H. R., Canino, G. J., Davies, M., Zhang, H., Ramirez, R., & Lahey, B. B. (2001). Prevalence and correlates of antisocial behaviors among three ethnic groups. *Journal of Abnormal Child Psychology, 29*(6), 465–478.

Black, S. A., & Jackson, E. (2007). Using bullying incident density to evaluate the Olweus bullying prevention programme. *School Psychology International, 28*(5), 623–638.

Bloom, M., Fischer, J., Orme, JG. (2005). Evaluating Practice: Guidelines for the accountable professional (2ndEd.). Boston: Allyn & Bacon.

Boberg, M. J. (2001). The effects of a social skills training program on preadolescents' prosocial behavior and self-control. Ph.D. dissertation, Ball State University, Indiana. Retrieved August 7, 2009, from Dissertations and Theses: Full text database. (Publication no. AAT 3029854)

Botvin, G. J., Mihalic, S. F., & Grotpeter, J. K. (1998). *Life skills training.* Boulder: University of Colorado, Center for the Study and Prevention of Violence, Institute of Behavioral Science.

Bowen, G. L., & Richman, J. M. (2001). *School Success Profile.* Chapel Hill: University of North Carolina at Chapel Hill, Jordan Institute for Families, School of Social Work.

Bowen, N. K. (1999) A role for school social workers in promoting student success through school-family partnership. *Social Work in Education, 21,* 34–47.

Briar-Lawson, K., Lawson, H., Collier, C., & Joseph, A. (1997). School-linked comprehensive services: Promising beginnings, lessons learned, and future challenges. *Social Work in Education, 19*(3), 136–149.

Brint, S. (1994). *In an age of experts: The changing role of professionals in politics andpublic life.* Princeton, NJ: Princeton University Press.

Briones, J. (2007). A stress management and coping skills classroom guidance program for elementary school students. *Dissertation Abstracts International Section A: Humanities and Social Sciences, 68* (4-A), 1337.

Brolin, D. (1997). *LCCE: Life centered career education* (5th ed.). Reston, VA: Council for Exceptional Children.

Broota, A., & Sehgal, R. (2004). Management of conduct disorders through cognitive behavioural intervention. *Psychological Studies, 49*(1), 69–72.

Broussard, A. (2003). Facilitating home-school partnership for multiethnic families: School social workers collaborating for success. *Children & Schools, 25,* 211–222.

Browder, D. M., & Cooper-Duffy, K. (2003). What is special about special education? Evidence-based practices for students with severe disabilities and the requirement for accountability in "No Child Left Behind." *Journal of SpecialEducation, 37*(3), 157–164.

Brown, K. J., Morris, D., & Fields, M. (2005). Intervention after grade 1: Serving increased numbers of struggling readers effectively. *Journal of Literacy Research, 37*(1), 61–94.

Buck, G. H., Polloway, E. A., Smith-Thomas, A., & Cook, K. W. (2003). Pre-referral intervention processes: A survey of state practices. *Exceptional Children, 69*(3), 349–360.

Burke, M. D., Hagan-Burke, S., & Sugai, G. (2003). The efficacy of function-based interventions for students with learning disabilities who exhibit escape-maintained problem behaviors: Preliminary results from a single-case experiment. *Learning Disabilities Quarterly, 26*(1), 15–25.

Burns, M. K., & Gibbons, K. A. (2008). *Implementing response-to-intervention in elementary and secondary schools: Procedures to assure scientific-based practices.* New York: Routledge.

Burns, M. K., Vanderwood, M. L., & Ruby, S. (2005). Evaluating the readiness of pre-referral intervention teams for use in a problem solving model. *School Psychology Quarterly, 20*(1), 89–105.

Bussing, R., Gary, F. A., Leon, C. E., Wilson Garvan, C., & Reid, R. (2002). General classroom teachers' information and perceptions of attention deficit hyperactivity disorder. *Behavioral Disorders, 27,* 327–339.

Butke, M. (2006). Cultivating hardiness: Group therapy research with urban adolescent girls. Ph. D. dissertation, Smith College School for Social Work, Massachusetts. Retrieved October 30, 2008, from Dissertations and Theses: Full Text database. (Publication No. AAT 3248939)

Bye, L., & Alvarez, M. (Eds.). (2007). *School social work: Theory to practice.* Belmont, CA: Thompson Brooks/Cole.

Cadieux, A., & Boudreault, P. (2005). The effects of a parent-child paired reading program on reading abilities, phonological awareness and self-concept of at-risk pupils. *Reading Improvement, 42*(4), 224–237.

Caldarella, P., & Merrell, K. (1997). Common dimensions of social skills of children and adolescents: A taxonomy of positive behaviors. *School Psychology Review, 26*(2), 264–279.

Callahan, S. T., Winitzer, R. F., & Keenan, P. (2001) Transition from pediatrics to adult-oriented care: A challenge for patients with chronic illness. *Current Opinion in Pediatrics, 13*(4), 310–316.

Camacho, M., & Hunter, L. (2006). Effective interventions for students with separation anxiety disorder. In C. Franklin, M. Harris, & P. Allen-Meares (Eds.), *School services sourcebook.* New York: Oxford University Press.

Cameron, M. (2006). Managing school discipline and implications for school social workers: A review of the literature. *Children & Schools, 28*(4), 219–227.

Cameron, M., & Sheppard, S. M. (2006). School discipline and social work practice: Application of research and theory to intervention. *Children & Schools, 28*(1), 15–22.

Caprara, G. V., Barbaranelli, C., Pastorelli, C., Bandura, A., & Zimbardo, P. G. (2000). Prosocial foundations of children's academic achievement. *Psychological Science, 11*(4), 302–305.

Cardemil, E. V., Reivich, K. J., & Seligman, M. E. P. (2002). The prevention of depressive symptoms in low-income minority middle school students. *Prevention & Treatment, 5*(article 8), posted May 8, 2002 [Electronic journal]. Retrieved January 11, 2009, from http://journals. apa.org/prevention/volume5/pre0050008a.html.

Casella, R. (2003). Zero tolerance policy in schools: Rationale, consequences, and alternatives. *Teachers College Record 105*(5), 872–892.

Caspe, M., Lopez, M. E., & Wolos, C. (2007). *Family involvement in elementary school children's education. Family involvement makes a difference.* Cambridge, MA: Harvard University, Harvard Family Research Project.

Chadsey-Rusch, J. (1992). Toward defining and measuring social skills in employment settings. *American Journal on Mental Retardation, 96*(4), 405–418.

Chamberlain, P., Leve, L. D., & Smith, D. K. (2006). Preventing behavior problems and health-risking behaviors in girls in foster care. *International Journal of Behavioral Consultation and Therapy, 2*(4), 518–530.

Chambless, D. L., & Hollon, S.D. (1998). Defining empirically supported therapies. *Journal of Consulting and Clinical Psychology, 66,* 7–18

ChildStats. (2007). America's children: Key national indicators of well-being, 2007. Retrieved on August 18, 2007, from http://www.childstats.gov/americaschildren/.

Cho, H., Hallfors, D. D., & Sanchez, V. (2005). Evaluation of a high school peer group intervention for at-risk youth. *Journal of Abnormal Child Psychology, 33*(3), 363.

Chorpita, B. F. (2003). The frontier of evidence-based practice. In A. E. Kazdin & J. R. Weisz (Eds.), *Evidence-based psychotherapies for children and adolescents* (pp. 42–59). New York: Guilford Press.

Christensen, L., Young, K. R., & Marchant, M. (2007). Behavioral intervention planning: Increasing appropriate behavior of a socially withdrawn student. *Education and Treatment of Children, 30*, 81–103.

Christenson, S. L., & Sheridan, S. M. (2002). *Schools and families: Creating essential connections for learning.* New York: Guildford Press.

Christians, C. (2005). Ethics and politics in qualitative research. In N. K. Denzin & Y. S. Lincoln (Eds.), *Handbook of qualitative research* (3rd ed., pp. 139–164). Thousand Oaks, CA: Sage.

Clark, J. P. (1990). The challenge of demonstrating the outcomes of school social work intervention. *Journal of School Social Work, 4*(2), 55–66.

Clarke, G. N., DeBar, L. L., & Lewisohn, P. M. (2003). Cognitive-behavioral group treatment for adolescent depression. In A. E. Kazdin, & J. R. Weisz (Eds.), *Evidence-based psychotherapies for children and adolescents* (pp. 120–134). New York: Guildford Pres.

Cleare, M. J. (2000). Effects of social cognitive skills training with angry, aggressive adolescent females. Psy.D. dissertation. Antioch University/New England Graduate School, New Hampshire. Retrieved August 7, 2009, from Dissertations and Theses: Full text database. (Publication no. AAT 9988021)

Cohen, J. (1988). *Statistical power analysis for the behavioral sciences* (2nd ed.). Hillsdale, NJ: Lawrence Earlbaum.

Cohen, J. S., & St. Clair, S. (2008, April 20). Emotional struggles detailed in essays. *Chicago Tribune*, Sec. 1, pp. 1, 14.

Collaborative on Social and Emotional Learning (CASEL). (2007). List of best practices for social-emotional learning in schools. Retrieved January 10, 2007, from www.casel.org.

Collins, M. E. (2001). Transition to adulthood for vulnerable youths: A review of research and implications for policy. *Social Service Review* (Chicago), *75*(2), 271–291.

Colvin, J., Lee, M., Magnano, J., & Smith, V. (2008). The partners in prevention program: Further development of the task-centered case management model. *Research on Social Work Practice, 18*(6), 586–595.

Comer, J. P., Joyner, E. T., & Ben-Avie, M. (Eds.). (2004). *The field guide to Comer schools in action.* Thousand Oaks, California: Corwin Press.

Committee on Psychosocial Aspects of Child and Family Health and Committee on Adolescence. (2001). Sexuality education for children and adolescents. *Pediatrics, 108*, 498–502.

Conduct Problems Prevention Research Group. (1992). A developmental and clinical model for the prevention of conduct disorders: The FAST Track program. *Development & Psychopathology, 4*(4), 509–527.

Conner, N. W. (2006). "Making Choices" and "Strong Families": A pilot study of a preschool preventive intervention program. Ph.D. dissertation, University of North Carolina at Chapel

Hill. Retrieved August 7, 2009, from Dissertations and Theses: Full text database. (Publication No. AAT 3190233)

Constable, R. (2007a). Planning and setting goals: Behavioral intervention plans, the individualized education program, and the individualized family service plan. In C. R. Massat, R. Constable, S. McDonald, & J. P. Flynn (Eds.), *School social work: Practice, policy, and research* (7th ed., pp. 494–521). Chicago: Lyceum.

Constable, R. (2007b). The role of school social workers. In C. R. Massat, R. Constable, S. McDonald, & J. P. Flynn (Eds.), *School social work: Practice, policy, and research* (7th ed., pp. 3–29). Chicago: Lyceum.

Constable, R., & Alvarez, M. (2006, Summer). Specialization in school social work: The Indiana example. *School Social Work Journal* (Special Issue), 116–132.

Constable, R., & Massat, C. R. (2008). Evidence-based practice: Implications for school social work. In C. R. Massat, R. Constable, S. McDonald, & J. P. Flynn (Eds.), *School social work: Practice, policy, and research* (7th ed., pp. 94–105). Chicago: Lyceum.

Cosntantino, G., Malgady, R. G., & Cardalda, E. (2005). TEMAS narrative treatment: An evidence-based culturally competent therapy modality. In Euthymia D. Hibbs & Peter S. Jensen (Eds.), *Psychosocial treatments for child and adolescent disorders: Empirically based strategies for clinical practice* (2nd ed., pp. 717–742). Washington, DC: American Psychological Association.

Constantino, G., Malgady, R. G., & Rogler, L. H. (1984). Cuentos folkloricos as a therapeutic modality with Puerto Rican children. *Hispanic Journal of Behavioral Sciences, 6*(2), 169–178.

Cook, T. D., Habib, F., Phillips, M., Settersten, R. A., Shagle, S. C., & Degirmencioglu, S. M. (1999). Comer's school development program in Prince George's County, Maryland: A theory-based evaluation. *American Educational Research Journal, 36*(3), 543–597.

Cook, T. D., Hunt, H. D., & Murphy, R. F. (2000). Comer's school development program in Chicago: A theory-based evaluation. *American Educational Research Journal, 37*, 535–597.

Cooke, M. B., Ford, J., Levine, J., Bourke, C., Newell, L., & Lapidus, G. (2007). The effects of city-wide implementation of "Second Step" on elementary school students' prosocial and aggressive behaviors. *Journal of Primary Prevention, 28*(2), 93–114.

Cookston, J., Braver, S.L., Griffin, W.A., De Luse, S.L., & Miles, J. C. (2007). Effects of the Dads for Life intervention on interparental conflict and co-parenting in the two years after divorce. *Family Process, 46*(1), 123–137.

Cooley, M. R., & Boyce, C. A. (2004). An introduction to assessing anxiety in child and adolescent multiethnic populations: Challenges and opportunities for enhancing knowledge and practice. *Journal of Clinical Child and Adolescent Psychology, 33*(2), 210–215.

Cooper, H. (2001). *The battle over homework: Common ground for administrators, teachers, and parents*. Thousand Oaks, CA: Corwin.

Corcoran, J. (1998). Solution-focused practice with middle and high school at-risk youths. *Social Work in Education, 20*(4), 232–243.

Cornell, D. G., Sheras, P. L., & Cole, J. C. M. (2006). Assessment of bullying. In S. R. Jimerson & M. Furlong (Eds.), *Handbook of school violence and school safety: From research to practice* (pp. 191–210). Mahwah, NJ: Lawrence Erlbaum.

Costin, L. (1969a). School social work: An analysis of function. *Psychology in the aSchools, 6*(4), 347–352.

Costin, L. B. (1969b). A historical review of school social work. *Social Casework, 50*, 439–453.

Costin, L. (1975). School Social Work Practice: A New Model. *Social Work, 20*(2), 135–39.

Cox, E., Mothera, B., Henderson, R., & Mager, D. (2003). Geographic variation in the prevalence of stimulant medication use among children 5 to 14 years old: Results from a commercially insured sample. *Journal of Pediatrics, 111,* 237–243.

Crespi, T. D., Gustafson, A. L., & Borges, S. M. (2005). Group counseling in the schools: Considerations for child and family issues. *Journal of Applied Psychology, 22*(1), 67–85.

Crick, N. R., & Dodge, K. A. (1994). A review and reformulation of social information-processing mechanisms in children's social adjustment. *Psychological Bulletin, 115*(1), 74–101.

Crone, D. A., & Horner, R. H. (2003). *Building positive behavior support systems in schools.* New York: Guilford Press.

Crone, D. A., Horner, R. H., & Hawken, L. S. (2004). *Responding to problem behavior in schools: The Behavior Education Program.* New York: Guilford Press.

Currie, J., & Stabile, M. (2006). Child mental health and human capital accumulation: The case of ADHD. *Journal of Health Economics, 25,* 1094–1118.

Curry, J. E., Wells, K. C., Lochman, J. E., Craighead, W. E., & Nagy, P. D. (2003). Cognitive-behavioral intervention for depressed, substance-abusing adolescents: Development and pilot testing. *Journal of the American Academy of Child & Adolescent Psychiatry, 42*(6), 656–665.

Dadds, M. R., Spence, S. H., Holland, D. E., Barrett, P. M., & Laurens, K. R. (1997). Prevention and early intervention for anxiety disorders: A controlled trial. *Journal of Consulting Psychology, 65* (4), 627–635.

Dalton, T., Martella, R. C., & Marchand-Martella, N. E. (1999). The effects of a self-management program in reducing off-task behavior. *Journal of Behavioral Education, 9*(3/4), 157–176.

Dane, B. O., & Simon, B. L. (1991). Resident guests: Social workers in host settings. *Social Work 36* (3), 208–213.

Daunic, A. P., Smith, S. W., Brank, E. M., & Penfield, R. D. (2006). Classroom-based cognitive-behavioral intervention to prevent aggression: Efficacy and social validity. *Journal of School Psychology, 44*(2), 123–139.Davies, P. (1999). What is evidence-based education? *British Journal of Educational Studies 47* (2), 108–121.

Davies, S., & Witte, R. (2000). Self-management and peer-monitoring within a group contingency to decrease uncontrolled verbalizations of children with attention-deficit/hyperactivity disorder. *Psychology in the Schools, 37*(2), 135–147.

Davis, D. E. (1988). *My friends and me.* Circle Pines, MN: American Guidance Service.

Davis-Williams, B. M. (2004). The effects of self-monitoring on off-task behaviors of African-American male adolescents with emotional and behavioral disorders: A school-based family service approach. Unpublished doctoral dissertation, Union Institute, OH. University Microfilms International (UMI) number: 3118687.

Deffenbacher, J. L., & Swaim, R. C. (1999). Anger expression in Mexican-American and white non-Hispanic adolescents. *Journal of Counseling Psychology 46*(1), 61–69.

DeGarmo, D. S., & Forgatch, M. S. (2005). Early development of delinquency within divorced families: Evaluating a randomized preventive intervention trial. *Developmental Science 8*(3), 229–239.

DeLucia-Waack, J. L., & Gerrity, D. (2001). Effective group work for elementary school-age children whose parents are divorcing. *Family Journal, 9*(3), 273–284.

DeMar, J. (1994). A study of a school-based preventive group intervention with latency age children at risk. Ph.D. dissertation, Barry University School of Social Work, Miami, Florida.

Retrieved November 29, 2008, from Dissertations and Theses: Full Text database. (Publication No. AAT 9425347)

DeMar, J. (1997). A school-based group intervention to strengthen personal and social competencies in latency-age children. *Social Work in Education, 19*(4), 219–230.

Demaray, M. K., & Ruffalo, S. L. (1995). Social skills assessment: A comparative evaluation of six published rating scales. *School Psychology Review, 24*(4), 648–672.

Denzin, N. K. (2003). *Performance ethnography: Critical pedagogy and the politics of culture.* Thousand Oaks, CA: Sage.

DeRosier, M. E. (2004). Building relationships and combating bullying: Effectiveness of a school-based social skills group intervention. *Journal of Clinical & Adolescent Psychology, 33*(1), 196–201.

Derzon, J. (2006). How effective are school-based violence prevention programs in preventing and reducing violence and other antisocial behaviors? A meta-analysis. In S. R. Jimerson & M. Furlong (Eds.), *Handbook of school violence and school safety: From research to practice* (pp. 429–441). Mahwah, NJ: Lawrence Erlbaum.

Diamanduros, T., Downs, E., & Jenkins, S. J. (2008). The role of school psychologists in the assessment, prevention, and intervention of cyberbullying *Psychology in the Schools 45*(8), 693–704.

Dibble, N. (2004, Spring). Revenues generated for school districts by school social work services. *School Social Work Connection, 1*, 11–12.

DIBELS. (2007). Introduction to DIBELS. Retrieved August 11, 2007, from http://dibels.uoregon.edu/index.php.

Diken, I. H., & Rutherford, R. B. (2005). First Step to Success early intervention program: A study of effectiveness with Native-American children. *Education and Treatment of Children, 28*(4), 444–465.

Diperna, J.C., & Elliott, S. N. (2002). Promoting academic enablers to improve student achievment: An introduction to the mini-series. *School Psychology Review. 31*(3), 293–297.

Dishion, T. J., Bullock, B. M., & Granic, I. (2002). Pragmatism in modeling peer influence: Dynamics, outcomes and change processes. *Development and Psychopathology, 14*(4), 969–981.

Dishion, T., McCord, J., & Poulin, F. (1999). When interventions harm: Peer groups and problem behavior. *American Psychologist, 54*(9), 755–764.

Dishion, T. J., & Stormshak, E. A. (2007). The ecology of the child and family therapist. In *Intervening in children's lives: An ecological, family-centered approach to mental health care* (pp. 219–239). Washington, DC: American Psychological Association.

Dodge, K. A., Dishion, T. J., & Lansford, J. E. (Eds.). (2006). *Deviant peer influences in programs for youth problems and solutions.* New York: Guildford Press.

Domitrovich, C. E., Cortes, R. C., & Greenberg, M. T. (2007). Improving young children's social and emotional competence: A randomized trial of the preschool "PATHS" curriculum. *Journal of Primary Prevention, 28*(2), 67–91.

Donovan, M. S., & Cross, C. T. (Eds.). (2002). *Minority students in special and gifted education.* Washington, DC: National Academy Press.

dosReis, S., Mychailyszyn, M. P., Myers, M. A., & Riley, A. W. (2007). Coming to terms with ADHD: How urban African-American families come to seek care for their children. *Psychiatric Services, 58*(5), 636–641.

Drasgow, E., Martin, C. A., O'Neill, R. E., & Yell, M. L. (2009). Functional behavioral assessments and behavior intervention plans. In M. L. Yell, N. B. Meadows, E. Drasgow, & J. G. Shriner (Eds.), *Evidence-informed practices for educating students with emotional and behavior disorders* (pp. 92–123). Upper Saddle River, NJ: Pearson.

Duchnowski, A. J., & Kutash, K., (2007). *Family-driven care.* Tampa: University of South Florida, Louis de la Parte Florida Mental Health Institute, Department of Child & Family Studies.

Duncan, B. Hubble, M., & Miller, S. (Eds.). (1999). *Heart and soul of change: What works in therapy.* Washington, DC: APA Press.

Dunlap, G., Sailor, W., Horner, H. F., & Sugai, G. (2009). Overview and history of positive behavior support. In W. Sailor, G. Dunlap, G. Sugai, & H. F. Horner (Eds.), *Handbook of positive behavior support: Issues in clinical child psychology* (pp. 3–16). New York: Springer.

DuPaul, G. J., & Barkley, R. A. (1992). Situational variability of attention problems: Psychometric properties of the revised home and school situations questionnaires. *Journal of Clinical Child Psychology, 21,* 178–188.

DuPaul, G. J., & Eckert, T. L. (1997). The effects of school-based interventions for attention deficit hyperactivity disorder: A meta-analysis. *School Psychology Review, 26,* 5–25.

DuPaul, G. J., Jitendra, A. K., Volpe, R. J., Tresco, K. E., Lutz, J. G., Junod, R. E. V., Cleary, K.S., Flammer, L. M., & Manella, M. C. (2006). Consultation-based academic interventions for children with ADHD: Effects on reading and mathematics achievement. *Journal of Abnormal Child Psychology, 34*(5), 635–635.

DuPaul, G. J., Power, T. J., & Anastopoulos, A. D. (1999). *The ADHD Rating Scale-IV: Checklists, norms, and clinical interpretations.* New York: Guilford Press.

DuPaul, G. J., Rapport, M. D., & Periello, L. M. (1991). Teacher ratings of academic skills: The development of the Academic Performance Rating Scale. *School Psychology Review, 20,* 284–300.

DuPaul, G., & Stoner, G. (2003). *ADHD in the schools: Assessment and intervention strategies* (2nd ed.). New York: Guilford Press.

DuPaul, G. J., & Weyandt, L. L. (2006a). School-based intervention for children with attention deficit hyperactivity disorder: Effects on academic, social, and behavioural functioning. *International Journal of Disability, Development and Education, 53,* 161–161.

DuPaul, G. J., & Weyandt, L. L. (2006b). School-based interventions for children and adolescents with attention-deficit/hyperactivity disorder: Enhancing academic and behavioral outcomes. *Education & Treatment of Children, 29,* 341–341.

Dupper, D. R. (2002). *School social work: Skills and interventions for effective practice.* Hoboken, NJ: John Wiley.

Dupper, D. R. (2003). *School social work: Skills and interventions for effective practice.* Hoboken, NJ: Wiley.

Dupper, D. R. (2006). Design and utility of life skills groups in schools. In C. Franklin, M. B. Harris, & P. Allen-Meares (Eds.), *The school services sourcebook: A guide for school-based professionals* (pp. 603–612). New York: Oxford University Press.

Dupper, D. R., & Krishef, C. H. (1993). School-based social-cognitive skills training for middle school students with school behavior problems. *Children & Youth Services Review, 15*(2), 131–142.

Dynarski, M., Gleason, P., Rangarajan, A., & Wood, R. (1998). *Impacts of dropout prevention programs: Final report. A research report from the School Dropout Demonstration Assistance Program evaluation.* Princeton, NJ: Mathematica Policy Research.

Dyregrov, A. (2008). *Grief in children* (2nd ed.). Philadelphia: Jessica Kingsley.

Early, T., & Vonk, M. E. (2001). Effectiveness of school social work from a risk and resilience perspective. *Children & Schools, 23*(1) 9–31.

Eddy, J. M., Reid, J. B., Stoolmiller, M., & Fetrow, R. A. (2003). Outcomes during middle school for an elementary school-based preventive intervention for conduct problems: Follow-up results from a randomized trial. *Behavior Therapy, 34*(4), 535–552.

Eddy, J.M., Reid, J.B., & Curry, V. (2002). The etiology of youth antisocial behavior, Delinquency, and violence and a public health approach to prevention. In M. Shinn, H. Walker, & G. Stoner (Eds.) *Interventions for academic and behavior problems: PreventiveAnd remedial approaches* (pp. 27–51). Washington, D.C.: National Association of School Psychologists.

Edmond, T., Megivern, D., Williams, C., Rochman, E., & Howard, M. (2006). Integrating evidence-based practice and social work field education. *Journal of Social Work Education, 42*(2), 377–396.

Ehntholt, K. A., Smith, P. A., & Yule, W. (2005). School-based cognitive-behavioral therapy group intervention for refugee children who have experienced war-related trauma. *Clinical Child Psychology & Psychiatry, 10*(2), 235–250.

Elias, M. J., & Tobias, S. E. (1998). *Social problem-solving: Interventions in the schools*. New York: Guildford Press.

Elkin, I. (1999). A major dilemma in psychotherapy outcome research: Disentangling therapists from therapies. *Clinical Psychology: Science & Practice, 6*(1), 10–32.

Elliot, D. S. (1998). Blueprints for violence prevention. Boulder: University of Colorado, Center for the Study and Prevention of Violence.

Elliott, S. N., Gresham, F. M., Frank, J. L., & Beddow P. A., III. (2008). Intervention validity of social behavior rating scales: Features of assessments that link results to treatment plans. *Assessment for Effective Intervention, 34*(1), 15–24.

Embry, D. D. (2002). The Good Behavior Game: A best practice candidate as a universal behavioral vaccine. *Clinical Child & Family Psychology Review, 5*(4), 273–297.

Engels, R. J., & Schutt, R. K. (2008). Conceptualization and measurement. In R. M. Grinnell, Jr., & Y. A. Unrau (Eds.), *Social work research and evaluation: Foundations of evidence-based practice* (8th ed., pp. 105–156). New York: Oxford University Press.

Ennett, S. T., Tobler, N. S., Ringwalt, C. L., & Flewelling, R. L. (1994). Resistance education? A meta-analysis of Project D.A.R.E. outcome evaluations. *American Journal of Public Health, 84* (9), 1394–1401.

Epstein, J. L., & Sanders, M. G. (2002). Family, school, and community partnerships. In M. H. Bornstein (Ed.), Handbook of parenting: Vol. 5. *Practical issues in parenting* (pp. 407–437). Mahwah, NJ: Erlbaum.

Epstein, M. H. (2004). *Behavioral and Emotional Rating Scale* (2nd ed.). Austin, TX: Pro-Ed.

Epstein, M. H., Mooney, P., Ryser, G., & Pierce, C. D. (2004). Validity and reliability of the Behavioral and Emotional Rating Scale (2nd ed.): Youth Rating Scale. *Research on Social Work Practice, 14*(5), 358–367.

Erickson, C. L., Mattaini, M., & McGuire, M. (2004). Constructing nonviolent cultures in schools: The state of the science. *Children & Schools, 26*(2), 102–117.

Erion, J. (2006). Parent tutoring: A meta-analysis. *Education and Treatment of Children, 29*(1), 79–106.

Ertesvåg, S. K., & Vaaland, G. S. (2007). Prevention and reduction of behavioural problems in school: An evaluation of the respect program. *Educational Psychology, 27*(6), 713–736.

Esposito, S., Sweeney, A., Spak, K., Brown, M., & Herrmann, A. (2008, February 17). Portrait of a killer. *Chicago Sun Times*. Retrieved February 18, 2008, from http://www.suntimes.com/news/metro/798150,021708niu.article.

Essau, C. A., Conradt, J., & Petermann, F. (1999). Frequency of panic attacks and panic disorder in adolescents. *Depression & Anxiety, 9,* 19–26.

Etscheidt, S. L. (1991). Reducing aggressive behavior and improving self-control: A cognitive-behavioral training program for behaviorally disordered adolescents. *Behavioral Disorders, 16* (2), 107–115.

Evans, C., Connell, J. Barkham, M., Marshall, C., & Mellor-Clark, J. (2003). Practice-based evidence: benchmarking NHS primary care counselling services at national and local levels. *Clinical Psychology & Psychotherapy, 10 (6),* 374–388.

Evans, S., Axelrod, J., & Langberg, J. (2004). Efficacy of a school-based treatment program for middle school youth with ADHD. *Behavior Modification, 28*(4), 528–547.

Evans, S. W., Timmins, B., Sibley, M., Sibley, L., White, C., Serpell, Z. N., & Schultz, B. (2006). Developing coordinated, multimodal, school-based treatment for young adolescents with ADHD. *Education and Treatment of Children, 29*(2), 359–378.

Evelo, D., Sinclair, M., Hurley, C., Christenson, S., & Thurlow, M. (1996). *Keeping kids in school: Using Check & Connect for dropout prevention*. Minneapolis: University of Minnesota, Institute on Community Integration. Retrieved October 30, 2008, from http://ici.umn.edu/checkandconnect/KeepingKidsInSchool.pdf.

Everhart, K. D. (2001). Promoting resiliency in at-risk children through an integrated adult-child mentoring and character development program: An analysis of mentoring strategies with regard to outcomes. *Dissertation Abstracts International: Section B: The Sciences and Engineering, 62* (2-B), 1075.

Everly, G. S., & Boyle, S. H. (1999). Critical incident stress debriefing (CISD): A meta-analysis. *International Journal of Emergency Mental Health, 3,* 165–168.

Evers, K. E., Prochaska, J. O., Van Marter, D. F., Johnson, J. L., & Prochaska, J. M. (2007). Transtheoretical-based bullying prevention effectiveness trials in middle schools and high schools. *Educational Research, 49*(4), 397–414.

Fabiano, G. A., Pelham, W. E., Coles, E. K., Gnagy, E. M., Chronis-Tuscano, A., & O'Connor, B. (in press). A meta-analysis of behavioral treatments for attention-deficit/hyperactivity disorder. *Clinical Psychology Review*.

Fairbanks, S., Sugai, G., Guardino, D., & Lathrop, M. (2007). Response to intervention: An evaluation of a classroom system of behavior support for second grade students. *Exceptional Children, 73,* 288–310.

Fan, X., & Chen, M. (1999, April 19–23). *Parental involvement and students' academic achievement: A meta-analysis*. Paper presented at the annual meeting of the American Educational Research Association, Montreal, Quebec, Canada.

Fantuzzo, J., Manz, P., Atkins, M., & Meyers, R. (2005). Peer-mediated treatment of socially withdrawn maltreated preschool children: Cultivating natural community resources. *Journal of Clinical Child & Adolescent Psychology, 34*(2), 320–325.

Farber, M. (2006). *Empirical evaluation of program evaluations for Rainbows participants.* Retrieved February 4, 2009, from http://www.rainbows.org/sumresults.html.

Fashola, O. S., & Slavin, R. E. (2001). Effective dropout prevention and college attendance programs for Latino students. In R. E. Slavin & M. Calderon (Eds.), *Effective programs for Latino students* (pp. 67–100). New York: Lawrence Erlbaum.

Fasko, S. N. (2006). Special education services and response to intervention: What, why, and how? *Third Education Group Review/Essays, 2*(9). Retrieved May 10, 2009 from http://www.thirdeducationgroup.org/Review/Essays/v2n9.htm

Faubel, G. (1998) An efficacy assessment of a school-based intervention program for emotionally handicapped students. Psy.D. dissertation, Miami Institute of Psychology of the Caribbean Center for Advanced Studies, Florida. Retrieved January 9, 2009, from Dissertations and Theses: Full Text database. (Publication No. AAT 9815257)

Federal Bureau of Investigation. (2000). The school shooter: A threat assessment perspective. Retrieved July 3, 2005, from www.fbi.gov/publications/school/school2.pdf.

Feil, E.G., Severson, H.G., Walker, H.M. (1998). Screening for emotional and behavioral delays. *Journal of Early Intervention 21* (3), 252–266.

Feindler, E. L., Marriott, S. A., & Iwata, M. (1984). Group anger-control training for junior high school delinquents. *Cognitive Therapy & Research, 8*(3), 299–311.

Ferguson, C. J., San Miguel, C., Kilburn, J. C., Jr., & Sanchez, P. (2007). The effectiveness of school-based anti-bullying programs: A meta-analytic review. *Criminal Justice Review, 32*(4), 401–401.

Filter, K. J., McKenna, M. K., Benedict, E. A., Horner, R. H., Todd, A. W., & Watson, J. (2007). Check in/Check out: A post-hoc evaluation of an efficient, secondary-level targeted intervention for reducing problem behaviors in schools. *Education & Treatment of Children, 30*(1), 69–84.

Fine, L. (2001). New laws leave ritalin decisions to parents and doctors, *Education Week, 20*(43), 31.

Fink, A., & Kosecoff, J. (1985). *How to conduct surveys: A step-by-step guide.* London: Sage.

Finn, C. A., & Sladeczek, I. E. (2001). Assessing the social validity of behavioral interventions: A review of treatment acceptability measures. *School Psychology Quarterly, 16*(2), 176–206.

Fischer, J., & Corcoran, K. (2007). *Measures for clinical practice and research: A sourcebook, Vol. 1: Couples, families, and children* (4th ed.). New York: Oxford University Press.

Fishel, M., & Ramirez, L. (2005). Evidence-based parent involvement interventions with school-aged children. *School Psychology Quarterly, 20*, 371–402.

Fisher, P. H., Masia-Warner, C., & Klein, R. G. (2004). Skills for social and academic success: A school-based intervention for social anxiety disorder in adolescents. *Clinical Child & Family Psychology Review, 7*(4), 241–249.

Fitzgerald, P. K. & Van Schoiack Edstrom, L. (2006) Second Step: A violence prevention curriculum. In S. R. Jimerson & M. Furlong (Eds.), *Handbook of school violence and school safety: From research to practice* (pp. 429–441). Mahwah, NJ: Lawrence Erlbaum.

Follette, W. C., & Beitz, K. (2003). Adding a more rigorous scientific agenda to the empirically supported treatment movement. *Behavior Modification* (Special Issue): *Empirically Supported Treatments, 27*(3), 369–386.

Fonagy, P., Target, M., Cottrell, D., Phillips, J., & Kurtz, Z. (2002). *What works for whom? A critical review of treatments for children and adolescents.* New York: Guildford Press.

Forness, S. M., & Kavale, K. A. (2002). Impact of ADHD on school systems. In P. S. Jensen & J. R. Cooper (Eds.), *Attention-deficit hyperactivity disorder: State of the science, best practices* Chapter. 24, pp.1–16). Kingston, NJ: Civic Research Institute.

Fortin, L., & Picard, Y. (1998). The effects of a multidimensional intervention program for secondary school students at risk of dropping out of school [French]. *Revue Quebecoise de Psychologie, 19*(2), 125–145.

Flannery, D. J., Huff, C. R., & Manos, M. (1998). Youth gangs: A developmental perspective. In T. P. Gullotta, G. R. Adams, & R. Montemayor (Eds.), *Delinquent violent youth: Theory and interventions* (pp. 175–204). Thousand Oaks, CA: Sage.

Franklin, C. (1999). Research on practice: Better than you think? *Social Work in Education, 21*(1), 3–9.

Franklin, C. (2001a). The effectiveness of solution-focused therapy with children in a school setting. *Research on Social Work Practice, 11*(4), 411–434.

Franklin, C. (2001b). Now is the time for building the infrastructure of school social work practice. *Children & Schools, 23*, 67–71.

Franklin, C., & Gerlach, B. (2006, Summer). One hundred years of linking schools with communities: Current models and opportunities. *School Social Work Journal, 44*–62.

Franklin, C., & Harris, M. B. (2007). The delivery of school social work services. In P. Allen-Meares (Ed.), *Social work services in schools* (5th ed., pp. 317–360). Boston: Pearson Education.

Franklin, C., Harris, M. B., & Allen-Meares, P. (2006). *The school services sourcebook: A guide for school-based professionals.* New York: Oxford University Press.

Franklin, C., & Hopson, L. (2004). Into the schools with evidence-based practices. *Children & Schools, 26*(2), 67–70.

Franklin, C., & Hopson, L. (2007). Facilitating the use of evidence-based practice in community organizations. *Journal of Social Work Education 43*(3), 377–405.

Franklin, C. & Kelly, M.S. (2009). Becoming evidence-informed in the real world of school social Work practice. *Children & Schools 31* (1), 46–56.

Franklin, C., & McNeil, J. S. (1992). The Cassata project: A school-agency partnership for practice research integration. *Arete, 17*(1), 47–52.

Franklin, C., & Streeter, C. L. (1996). School reform: Linking public schools with human services. *Social Work, 40*, 773–782.

Franklin, C., Streeter, C. L., Garner, J. A., Kim, J., Hopson, L., & Tripodi, S. (2004). *Solution-focused alternatives for education: An evaluation of Gonzalo Garza Independence High School.* Retrieved May 1, 2005, from http://www.utexas.edu/school social workers/faculty/franklin/.

Fraser, M. W., Day, S. H., Galinsky, M. J., Hodges, V. G., & Smokowski, P. R. (2004). Conduct problems and peer rejection in childhood: A randomized trial of the Making Choices and Strong Families programs. *Research on Social Work Practice, 14*(5), 313–324.

Fraser, M. W., Nash, J. K., Galinsky, M. J., & Darwin, K. M. (2000). *Making choices: Social problem-solving skills for children.* Washington, DC: NASW Press.

Freeman, E. M., Franklin, C., Fong, R., Shaffer, G., & Timberlake, E. M. (Eds.). (1998). *Multisystem skills and interventions in school social work practice.* Washington, DC: NASW Press.

Freidson, E. (1986). *Professional powers: A study of the institutionalization of formalknowledge.* Chicago: University of Chicago Press.

Frey, A., & Dupper, D. R. (2005). A broader conceptual approach to clinical practice for the 21st century. *Children & Schools, 27*(1), 33–44.

Frey, A., Lingo, A., & Nelson, C. M. (in press). Implementing positive behavior support in elementary schools. In H. Walker & M. K. Shinn (Eds.), *Interventions for achievement and behavior problems: Preventive and remedial approaches,*. National Association for School Psychologists. Washington, DC.

Frey, A. J., Lingo, A., & Nelson, C. M. (2008). Positive behavior support: A call for leadership. *Children & Schools, 30* (4), 5–14.

Frey, A. J., Boyce, C. A., & Tarullo, L. B. (2009). Implementing a positive behavior support approach within Head Start. In W. Sailor, G. Dunlap, G. Sugai, & H. F. Horner (Eds.), *Handbook of positive behavior support: Issues in clinical child psychology* (pp. 125–148). New York: Springer.

Frey, A., Faith, T., Elliott, A., & Royer, B. (2006). A pilot study examining the social validity and effectiveness of a positive support model in Head Start. *School Social Work Journal, 30*(2), 22–44.

Frey, K. S., Hirschstein, M. K., & Guzzo, B. A. (2000). Second step: Preventing aggression by promoting social competence. *Journal of Emotional & Behavioral Disorders, 8*(2), 102–113.

Frey, K. S., Hirschstein, M. K., Snell, J. L., Edstrom, L. V., MacKenzie, E. P., & Broderick, C. J. (2005). Reducing playground bullying and supporting beliefs: An experimental trial of the Steps to Respect program. *Developmental Psychology, 41*(3), 479–491.

Frey, A. J., & Walker, H. (2007). School social work at the school organization level. In L. Bye & M. Alvarez (Eds.), *School social work: theory to practice* (pp. 82–104). Belmont, CA: Brooks/Cole.

Friedman, E. (2008, February 15). Who was the Illinois school shooter? *ABC News.* Retrieved February 18, 2008, from http://abcnews.go.com/.

Fuchs, L. S., & Fuchs, D. (1998). Treatment validity: A unifying concept for reconceptualizing the identification of learning disabilities. *Learning Disabilities Research & Practice, 13*, 204–219.

Fuchs, L. S., & Fuchs, D. (2001). Principles for sustaining research-based practice in the schools: A case study. *Focus on Exceptional Children, 33*(1), 1–14.

Furlong, M. J., Greif, J. L., Bates, M. P., Whipple, A. D., Jimenez, T. C., & Morrison, R. (2005). Development of the California School Climate and Safety Survey–Short form. *Psychology in the Schools, 42*(2), 137–149.

Gable, R. A., Quinn, M. M., Rutherford, R. B., Howell, K. W., & Hoffman, C. C. (2000). *Addressing student problem behavior–Part III: Creating positive behavioral intervention plans and supports.* Washington, DC: American Institute for Research.

Gambrill, E. (2001). Social work: An authority-based profession. *Research on Social Work Practice, 11*(2), 166–175.

Gambrill, E. (2003). Evidence-based practice: Sea change or the emperor's new clothes? *Journal of Social Work Education, 39*(1), 3–23.

Gambrill, E. (2005). *Critical thinking in clinical practice: Improving the quality of judgments and decisions* (2nd ed.). Hoboken, NJ: John Wiley.

Gambrill, E. (2006). *Social work practice: A critical thinker's guide* (2nd ed.). New York: Oxford University Press.

Gansle, K. (2005). The effectiveness of school-based anger interventions and programs: A meta-analysis *Journal of School Psychology, 43*(4), 321–341.

Garvin, C. D. (2006). Designing and facilitating support groups and therapy groups with adolescents: Importance of the topic for schools. In C. Franklin, M. B. Harris, &

P. Allen-Meares (Eds.), *The school services sourcebook: A guide for school-based professionals* (pp. 587–594). New York: Oxford University Press.

Gerber, M. M. (2003, December 4–5). *Teachers are still the test: Limitations of response to intervention strategies for identifying children with learning disabilities.* Paper presented at the National Research Center on Learning Disabilities Responsiveness-to-Intervention Symposium, Kansas City, MO.

Germain, C. B. (1979). *Social work practice: People and environments, an ecological perspective.* New York: Columbia University Press.

Ghandi, A. G., Murphy-Graham, E., Petrosino, A., Chrismer, S. S., & Weiss, C. H. (2007). The devil is in the details: Examining the evidence for "proven" drug abuse prevention programs. *Evaluation Review 31*(1), 43–74.

Gibbs, J. (2001). *Tribes: A new way of learning and being together.* Windsor, CA: Center Source Systems.

Gibbs, L. (2003). *Evidence-based practice for the helping professions: A practical guide with integrated multimedia.* Pacific Grove, CA: Thomson-Brooks/Cole.

Gibelman, M. (1999). The search for identity: Defining social work–past, present, future. *Social Work, 44*(4), 298–311.

Gifford-Smith, M., Dodge, K. A., Dishion, T. J., & McCord, J. (2005). Peer influence in children and adolescents: Crossing the bridge from developmental to intervention science. *Journal of Abnormal Child Psychology, 33*(3), 255.

Gilgun, J. F. (2005). The four cornerstones of evidence-based practice in social work. *Research on Social Work Practice, 15*, 52–61.

Gilman, J., Schneider, D., Shulak, R. (2005) Children's ability to cope post-divorce the effects of kids' turn intervention program on 7 to 9 year olds. *Journal of Divorce & Remarriage 42*(3), 109–126.

Gitterman, A., & Miller, I. (1989). The influence of the organization on clinical practice. *Clinical Social Work Journal, 17*(2), 151–164.

Givaudan, M., Van de Vijver, F. J. R., Poortinga, Y. H., Leenen, I., & Pick, S. (2007). Effects of a school-based life skills and HIV-prevention program for adolescents in Mexican high schools. *Journal of Applied Social Psychology, 37*(6), 1141–1162.

Glasgow, R. E., Klesges, L. M., Dzewaltowski, D. A., Bull, S. S., & Estabrooks, P. A. (2004). The future of health behavior change research: What is needed to improve translation of research into health promotion practice? *Annals of Behavioral Medicine, 27*, 3–12.

Glisson, C. (1992). Structure and technology in human service organizations. In Y. Hershenfeld (Ed.), *Human services as complex organizations.* Thousand Oaks, CA: Sage.

Glisson, C. (2000). Organizational culture and climate In R. Patti (Ed.), *The handbook of social welfare management* (pp.195–218). Thousand Oaks, CA: Sage.

Glisson, C., & Hemmelgarn, A. (1998). The effects of organizational climate and interorganizational coordination on the quality and outcomes of children's service systems. *Child Abuse & Neglect, 22*(5), 401–421.

Glodich, A., Allen, J. G., & Arnold, L. (2001). Protocol for a trauma-based psychoeducational group intervention to decrease risk-taking, reenactment, and further violence exposure: Application to the public high school setting. *Journal of Child & Adolescent Group Therapy, 11*(2–3), 87–107.

Goldman, R. D., & Macpherson, A. (2006). Internet health information use and e-mail access by parents attending a pediatric emergency department. *Emergency Medicine Journal, 23*, 345–348.

Goldstein, A. P. (1999). *The Prepare curriculum: Teaching prosocial competencies* (rev. ed.). Champaign, IL: Research Press.

Goldstein, A. P., Glick, B., & Gibbs, J. C. (1998). *Aggression replacement training: A comprehensive intervention for aggressive youth* (rev. ed.). Champaign, IL: Research Press.

Goleman, D. (1997). *Emotional intelligence: Why it can matter more than IQ*. New York: Bantam.

Golly, A., Sprague, J., Walker, H. M., Beard, K., & Gorham, G. (2000). The First Step to Success program: An analysis of outcomes with identical twins across multiple baselines. *Behavioral Disorders, 25*(3), 170–182.

Golly, A. M., Stiller, B., & Walker, H. M. (1998). First Step to Success: Replication and social validation of an early intervention program. *Journal of Emotional and Behavioral Disorders, 6*(4), 243–250.

Gonzales, N. A., Dumka, L. E., Deardorff, J. C., McCray, A. (2004). Preventing poor mental health and school dropout of Mexican-American adolescents following the transition to junior high school. *Journal of Adolescent Research, 19*(1), 113–131.

Goopman, J. (2004, January 26). The grief industry: How much does crisis counseling help––or hurt? *The New Yorker*.

Gorman, D. M. (2005). Drug and violence prevention: Rediscovering the critical rational dimension of evaluation research. *Journal of Experimental Criminology 1*(1), 39–62.

Gorman DM, Conde E, & Huber JC. (2007). The Creation of Evidence in 'Evidence-Based' Drug Prevention: A Critique of the Strengthening Families Program Plus Skills Training Evaluation. *Drug and Alcohol Review, 26*, 585–593.

Gottfredson, G., & Gottfredson, D. (1999). Development and applications of theoretical measures for evaluating drug and delinquency prevention programs. Elliot City, MD: Gottfredson.

Gottfredson, G. D., Jones, E. M., & Gore, T. W. (2002). Implementation and evaluation of a cognitive-behavioral intervention to prevent problem behavior in a disorganized school. *Prevention Science, 3*, 43–56

Goyal, A., & Keightly, M. L. (2008). Expressive art for the social and community integration of adolescents with acquired brain injuries: A systematic review. *Research in Drama Education, 13* (3), 337–352.

Graham, S. (2003). The role of perceived responsibility in nurturing morality. *LSS Review, 2*(3), 6–8.

Greenberg, J. S. (1985). Iatrogenic health education disease. *Health Education, 16*(5), 4–6.

Greenberg, M., Weissberg, R. P., O'Brien, M. U., Fredericks, L., Elias, M. J., Resnik, H., Zins, J. E.. (2003). Enhancing school-based prevention and youth development through coordinated social, emotional, and academic learning. *American Psychologist, 58*(6/7), 466–474.

Greenberg, M. T., & Kusch, C. A. (2006). Building social and emotional competence: The PATHS Curriculum. In S. R. Jimerson & M. Furlong (Eds.), *Handbook of school violence and school safety: From research to practice* (pp. 394–412). Mahwah, NJ: Lawrence Erlbaum.

Greenhalgh, T. (2006). *How to read a paper: The basics of evidence-based medicine* (3rd ed.). Oxford, UK: Blackwell.

Greenwood, E. (1962). Attributes of a profession. In S. Nosow & W. Form (Eds.), *Man, work, and society*. New York: Basic Books.

Gresham, F.M. (1989). Assessment of treatment integrity in school and prereferral intervention. *School Psychology Review, 18*, 37–50.

Gresham, F. M. (2002). Responsiveness to intervention: An alternative approach to the identification of learning disabilities. In R. Bradley, L. Danielson, & D. P. Hallahan (Eds.), Identification of learning disabilities: Response to treatment (pp. 467–519). Mahwah, NJ: Erlbaum.

Gresham, F. M. (2004). Current status and future directions of school-based behavioral interventions. *School Psychology Review, 33(3), 326–343.*.

Gresham, F. M., Cook, C. R., Crews, S. D., & Kern, L. (2004). Social skills training for children and youth with emotional and behavioral disorders: Validity considerations and future directions. *Behavior Disorders, 30(1), 32–46.*

Gresham, F. M., & Elliott, S. N. (1990). *Social Skills Rating System.* Circle Pines, MN: American Guidance Service.

Gresham, F. M., & Elliott, S. N. (2008). *Social Skills Improvement System.* Minneapolis, MN: Pearson Assessments.

Gresham, F. M., Van, M. B., & Cook, C. R. (2006). Social skills training for teaching replacement behaviors: Remediating acquisition deficits in at-risk students. *Behavioral Disorders, 31(4),* 363–377

Grolnick, W. S., & Slowiaczek, M. L. (1994). Parents' involvement in children's schooling: A multidimensional conceptualization and motivation model. Child Development, 65, 237–252.

Grossman, D. C., Neckerman, H. J., Koepsell, T. D., Liu, P. Y., Asher, K. N., Beland, K., Frey, K., & Rivara, F. P. (1997). Effectiveness of a violence prevention curriculum among children in elementary school: A randomized controlled trial. *Journal of the American Medical Association, 277,* 1605–1611.

Grossman, P. B., & Hughes, J. N. (1992). Self-control interventions with internalizing disorders: A review and analysis. *School Psychology Review, 21(2),* 229–245.

Guerra, N. G., Boxer, P., & Cook, C. R. (2006). What works (and what does not) in youth violence prevention: Rethinking the questions and finding new answers. *New Directions for Evaluation, 110,* 59–71.

Gureasko-Moore, S., DuPaul, G. J., & White, G. P. (2006). The effects of self-management in general education classrooms on the organizational skills of adolescents with ADHD. *Behavior Modification, 30(2),* 159–183.

Gureasko-Moore, S., DuPaul, G. J., & White, G. P. (2007). Self-management of classroom preparedness and homework: Effects on school functioning of adolescents with attention deficit hyperactivity disorder. *School Psychology Review, 36(4),* 647–664.

Hahn, E. J., Hall, L. A., Rayens, M. K., Myers, A. V., & Bonnel, G. (2007). School- and home-based drug prevention: Environmental, parent, and child risk reduction. *Drugs: Education, Prevention & Policy, 14(4),* 319–331.

Haine, R. A., Sandler, I. N., Wolchik, S. A., Tein, J.-Y., & Dawson-McClure, S. R. (2003). Changing the legacy of divorce: Evidence from prevention programs and future directions. *Family Relations, 52,* 397–405.

Hall, C. J. (2008). A practitioner's application and deconstruction of evidence-based practice. *Families in Society, 89(3),* 385–393.

Hamilton, G., Cross, D., Resnicow, K., & Shaw, T. (2007). Does harm minimisation lead to greater experimentation? Results from a school smoking intervention trial. *Drug and Alcohol Review, 26(6),* 605–613.

Han, S. S., Catron, T., Weiss, B., & Marciel, K. K. (2005). A teacher-consultation approach to social skills training for pre-K children: Treatment model and short-term outcome effects. *Journal of Abnormal Child Psychology, 33*(6), 681–693.

Hanselman, J. (2002). Coping skills interventions with adolescents in anger management using animals in therapy. *Journal of Child & Adolescent Group Therapy, 11*(4), 159–195.

Hansen, C., Weiss, D., & Last, C.G. (1999). ADHD boys in young adulthood: Psychosocial Adjustment. *Journal of the American Academy of Child and Adolescent Psychiatry, 38* (2), 165–171.

Hansen, S., Meissler, K., & Owens, R. (2000). Kids Together: A group play therapy model for children with ADHD symptomatology. *Journal of Child & Adolescent Therapy, 10*(4), 191–211.

Harris, M. B., & Franklin, C. G. (2003). Effects of a cognitive-behavioral, school-based, group intervention with Mexican American pregnant and parenting adolescents. *Social Work Research, 27*(2), 71–83.

Harris, M. B., & Franklin, C. G. (2007). *Taking charge: A school-based life skills program for adolescent mothers.* New York: Oxford University Press.

Havey, J.M., Olson, J.M., McCormick, C., Cates, G.L. (2005). Teachers' perceptions of the incidence and management of attention-deficit hyperactivity disorder. *Applied Neuropsychology, 12* (2), 120–127.

Hawken, L. S., & Horner, R. H. (2003). Evaluation of a targeted group intervention within a school-wide system of behavior support. *Journal of Behavioral Education, 12*(3), 225–240.

Hawken, L. S., MacLeod, K. S., & Rawlings, L. (2007). Effects of the Behavior Education Program on office discipline referrals of elementary school students. *Journal of Positive Behavior Interventions, 9*(2), 94–101.

Hawkins, J. D., Catalano, R. F., Kosterman, R., Abbott, R. D., & Hill, K. G. (1999). Preventing adolescent health-risk behaviors by strengthening protection during childhood. *Archives of Pediatrics & Adolescent Medicine, 153,* 226–234.

Hawkins, J. D., Catalano, R. F., Morrison, D., O'Konnell, J., Abbott, R., & Day, L. (1992). The Seattle Social Development Project: Effects of the first four years on protective factors and problem behaviors. In J. McCord & R. Tremblay (Eds.), *The prevention of antisocial behavior in children* (pp. 139–161). New York: Guilford Press.

Hawkins, J. D., Von Cleve, E., & Catalano, R. F. (1991). Reducing early childhood aggression: Results of a primary prevention program. *Journal of American Academy of Child Adolescent Psychiatry, 30,* 208–217.

Haynes, R., Devereaux, P., & Guyatt, G. (2002). Editorial: Clinical expertise in the era of evidence-based medicine and patient choice. *ACP Journal Club, 136,* A11–14.

Hazel, J. S., Schumaker, J. B., Sherman, J. A., & Sheldon-Wildgen, J. (1995). *ASSET: A social skills program for adolescents.* Champaign, IL: Research Press.

Hazler, R. J. & Carney, J. V. (2006). Critical characteristics of effective bullying programs. In S. R. Jimerson & M. Furlong (Eds.), *Handbook of school violence and school safety: From research to practice* (pp. 275–292). Mahwah, NJ: Lawrence Erlbaum.

Hedrick, W. B. (Ed.). (2007). Test madness. *Voices from the Middle, 15*(2), 64–65.

Hemmeter, M.L., & Fox, L. (2009). The Teaching Pyramid: A model for the implementation of classroom practices within a program-wide approach to behavior support. *NHSA Dialog 12* (2), 133–147.

Hennessey, B. A. (2007). Promoting social competence in school-aged children: The effects of the Open Circle Program. *Journal of School Psychology, 45*(3), 349–360.

Hervey-Jumper, H., Douyon, K., Franco, K.N. (2006). Deficits in diagnosis, treatment and continuity of care in African-American children and adolescents with ADHD. *Journal of the National Medical Association, 98* (2), 233–238.

Hess, P. M., & Mullen, E. J. (Eds.). (1995). *Practitioner-researcher partnerships: Building knowledge from, in, and for practice.* Washington, DC: NASW Press.

Hetherington, E. M., and Stanley-Hagan, M. (2000). Diversity among stepfamilies. In D. H. Demo, K. R. Allen, & M. A. Fine (Eds.), *Handbook of family diversity* (pp. 173–196).. New York: Oxford University Press.

Hetzel-Riggin, M. D., Brausch, A. M., & Montgomery, B. S. (2007). A meta-analytic investigation of therapy modality outcomes for sexually abused children and adolescents: An exploratory study. *Child Abuse & Neglect, 31*(2), 125–141.

Heward, W. L. (2003). Ten faulty notions about special education. *Journal of Special Education, 36* (4), 186–205.

Hiatt-Michael, D. B. (2006). Reflections and directions on research related to family-community involvement in schooling. *School Community Journal, 16*(1), 7–30.

Hibbs, E. D., & Jensen, P. S. (2007). *Psychosocial treatments for child and adolescent disorders: empirically based strategies for clinical practice.* Washington, D.C.: American Psychological Association.

Hinshaw, S. P. (1992a). Academic underachievement, attention deficits, and aggression: Comorbidity and implications for intervention. *Journal of Consulting and Clinical Psychology, 60,* 893–903.

Hinshaw, S. P. (1992b). Externalizing behavior problems and academic underachievement in childhood and adolescence: Causal relationships and underlying mechanisms. *Psychological Bulletin, 111,* 127–155.

Hinshaw, S. P. (2002). Is ADHD an impairing condition in childhood and adolescence? In P. S. Jensen & J. R. Cooper (Eds.), *Attention-deficit hyperactivity disorder: State of the science, best practices* (Chapter 5, pp. 1–21). Kingston, NJ: Civic Research Institute.

Hinshaw, S. P., Klein, R., & Abikoff, H. (2007). Childhood attention-deficit hyperactivity disorder: Nonpharmacologic treatments and their combination with medication. In P. E. Nathan & J. Gorman (Eds.), *A guide to treatments that work*(3rd ed., pp. 3–27). New York: Oxford University Press.

Hirschstein, M., & Frey, K. (2006). Promoting behavior and beliefs that reduce bullying: The Steps to Respect program. In S. R. Jimerson & M. Furlong (Eds.), *Handbook of school violence and school safety: From research to practice* (pp. 383–394). Mahwah, NJ: Lawrence Erlbaum.

Hoag, M. J., & Burlingame, G. M. (1997). Evaluating the effectiveness of child and adolescent group treatment. *Journal of Clinical Child Psychology, 26*(3), 234–246.

Hoagwood, K. (2000). Research on youth violence: Progress by replacement, not addition. *Journal of Emotional & Behavioral Disorders, 8*(2), 67–70.

Hoagwood, K. E., Olin, S. S., Kerker, B. D., Kratochwill[Q1], T. R., Crowe, M., & Saka, N. (2007). Empirically based school interventions targeted at academic and mental health functioning. *Journal of Emotional & Behavioral Disorders, 15*(2), 66–92.

Hong, G., & Yu, B. (2007). Early-grade retention and children's reading and math learning in elementary years. *Educational Evaluation and Policy Analysis, 29*(4), 239–261.

Hoover-Dempsey, K. V., Walker, J. M. T., Sandler, H. M., Whetsel, D., Green, C. L., Wilkins, A. S., & Closson, K. (2005). Why do parents become involved? Research findings and implications. *Elementary School Journal, 106*(2), 105–130.

Horn, W. F., & Tynan, D. (2001, Summer). Revamping special education. *Public Interest, 144,* 36–53.

Horner, R. H., Todd, A. W., Lewis-Palmer, T., Irvin, L. K., Sugai, G., & Boland, J. (2004). The school-wide evaluation tool: A research instrument for assessing school-wide positive behavior support. *Journal of Positive Behavior Interventions, 6*(1), 3–12.

Horner, R. H., Sugai, G., Todd, A. W., & Lewis-Palmer, T. (2005). Schoolwide positive behavior support. In L. Bambara & L. Kern (Eds.), *Individualized supports for students with problem behaviors* (pp. 359–377). New York: Guilford Press.

Jensen, L. (2001). The demographic diversity of immigrants and their children. In R. G. Rumbaut & A. Portes (Eds.), *Ethnicities: Children of immigrants in America* (pp. 21–56). Berkeley: University of California Press.

Howard, M. O., McMillen, C. J., & Pollio, D. E. (2003). Teaching evidence-based practice: Toward a new paradigm for social work education. *Research on Social Work Practice, 13*(2), 234–259.

Hubble, M., Duncan, B., & Miller, S. (1999). *The heart and soul of change.* Washington, DC: APA Press.

Hughes, J., & Kwok, O. (2007). Influence of student-teacher and parent-teacher relationships on lower achieving readers' engagement and achievement in the primary grades. *Journal of Educational Psychology, 99*(1), 39–51.

Hunsberger, P. (2007) "Where am I?" A call for "connectedness" in literacy. *Reading Research Quarterly, 42*(3), 420–424.

Hunt, C. (2007). The effect of an education program on attitudes and beliefs about bullying and bullying behaviour in junior secondary school students. *Child and Adolescent Mental Health, 12* (1), 21–26.

Hunter, L. (2003). School psychology: A public health framework: III. Managing disruptive behavior in schools: The value of a public health and evidence-based perspective. *Journal of School Psychology, 41*, 39–59.

Huxtable, M. (2006). International network for school social work: The Status of School Social Work Results of 2006 survey. Retrieved on June 1, 2007, from http://www.hkcss.org.hk/cy/Final%20Report%20International%20Network%202006.pdf.

Illinois Association of School Social Workers. (2005). The history of school social work in Illinois. Retrieved January 3, 2005, from www.iaschoolsocialworkers.org.

Illinois State Board of Education. (2005). Standards for school service personnel. Retrieved June 1, 2005, from www.isbe.state.il.us.

Individuals with Disabilities Education Act. (2004). Questions and answers on RTI. Retrieved July 3, 2007, from http://idea.ed.gov/explore/view/p/%2Croot%2Cdynamic%2CQaCorner%2C8%C.

Institute for Education Sciences, National Center for Education Statistics. (2009). Student effort and educational progress: Grade retention. Retrieved August 2, 2009, from http://nces.ed.gov/programs/coe/2009/section3/indicator18.asp.

Irvin, L. K., Horner, R. H., Ingram, K., Todd, A. W., Sugai, G., Sampson, N. K., & Boland, J. B. (2006). Using office discipline referral data for decision making about student behavior in elementary and middle schools: An empirical evaluation of validity. *Journal of Positive Behavior Interventions, 8*(1), 10–23.

Izard, C. E., King, K. A., Trentacosta, C. J., Morgan, J. K., Laurenceau, J-P., Krauthamer-Ewing, E. S., & Finlon, K. J. (2008). Accelerating the development of emotion competence in Head Start children: Effects on adaptive and maladaptive behavior. *Development & Psychopathology, 20*(1), 369–397.

Jackson, D., Jackson, N., Bennett, M., Bynum, D., & Faryna, E. (1991). *Learning to get along: Social effectiveness training for people with developmental disabilities.* Champaign, IL: Research Press. Jackson-Sinegar, M. (2001). The effects of a cognitive-behavioral group counseling intervention on the classroom behavior and self-efficacy of middle school students [Sample daily log in Appendix]. Unpublished doctoral dissertation, Department of Educational Leadership, University of New Orleans, LA. UMI: 3009266.

Jayaratne, S., & Levy, R. L. (1979). *Empirical clinical practice.* New York: Columbia University Press.

Jenson, J. M., & Dieterich, W. A. (2007). Effects of a skills-based prevention program on bullying and bully victimization among elementary school children. *Prevention Science, 8*(4), 285–296.

Jensen, L. (2001). The demographic diversity of immigrants and their children. In R. G. Rumbaut & A. Portes (Eds.), *Ethnicities: Children of immigrants in America* (pp. 21–56). Berkelcy: University of California Press.

Jensen, P. S., Kettle, L., Roper, M. T., Sloan, M. T., Dulcan, M. K., Hoven, C., Bird, H. R., Bauermeister, J. J., & Payne, J. D. (1999). Are stimulants overprescribed? Treatment of ADHD in four U.S. communities. *Journal of the American Academy of Child and Adolescent Psychiatry, 38,* 797–804.

Jeynes, W. H. (2003). A meta-analysis: The effects of parental involvement on minority children's academic achievement. *Education and Urban Society, 35*(2), 202–218.

Jeynes, W. H. (2005). A meta-analysis of the relation of parental involvement to urban elementary school student academic achievement. *Urban Education, 40*(3), 237–269.

Jeynes, W. H. (2007). The relationship between parental involvement and urban secondary school student academic achievement: A meta-analysis. *Urban Education, 42*(1), 82–110.

Jeynes, W. H. (2007). The relationship between parental involvement and urban secondary school student academic achievement: A meta-analysis. *Urban Education, 42*(1), 82–110.

Jimerson, S. R., & Furlong, M. J. (2006). *Handbook of school violence and school safety: From research to practice.* Mahwah, NJ: Lawrence Erlbaum Associates.

Johnson-Reid, M., Kontak, D., Citerman, B., Essma, A., & Fezzi, N. (2004). School social work case characteristics, services, and dispositions: Year one results. *Children & Schools, 26*(1), 5–22.

Joint Commission on Accreditation of Healthcare Organizations. (2004). *Assessment: Nutritional, functional, and pain assessment and screens.* Oakbrook Terrace, IL: Author.

Kalyva, E., & Avramidis, E. (2005). Improving communication between children with autism and their peers through the "Circle of Friends": A small-scale intervention study. *Journal of Applied Research in Intellectual Disabilities, 18*(3), 253–261.

Kataoka, S., Zhang, L., & Wells, K. (2002). Unmet need for mental health care among U.S. children: Variation by ethnicity and insurance status. *American Journal of Psychiatry, 159*(9), 1548–1555.

Kauffman, J.M. (2005). How we prevent the prevention of emotional and behavioral difficulties in education. In P. Clough, *Handbook of Emotional and Behavioral Difficulties* (pp. 429–440). Thousand Oaks, CA: Sage Books.

Kavale, K. A., Mathur, S. R., Forness, S. R., Rutherford, R. B., & Quinn, M. M. (1997). Effectiveness of social skills training for students with behavior disorders: A meta-analysis. *Advances in Learning and Behavior Disabilities, 11*, 1–26.

Kazdin, A. E. (2002). Psychosocial treatments for conduct disorder in children and adolescents. In P. E. Nathan & J. M. Gorman (Eds.), *A guide to treatments that work* (2nd ed., pp. 57–85). New York: Oxford University Press.

Kazura, K., & Flanders, R. (2007). Preschool children's social understanding: A pilot study of goals and strategies during conflict situations. *Psychological Reports, 101*(2), 547–554.

Kelly, M. S. (2008). *The demands and domains of school social work.* New York: Oxford University Press.

Kelly, M. S., Berzin, S. C., Frey, A., Alvarez, M., Shaffer, G., & O'Brien, K. (2009). *The state of school social work: Findings from the National School Social Work Survey.* Manuscript submitted for publication.

Kelly, M. S., & Stone, S. (2009). An analysis of factors shaping interventions used by school social workers. *Children & Schools 31*(3), 163–176.

Kelshaw-Levering, K., Sterling-Turner, H. E., Henry, J. R., & Skinner, C. H. (2000). Randomized interdependent group contingencies: Group reinforcement with a twist. *Psychology in the Schools, 37*(6), 523–533.

Kendall, P. C. (1994). Treating anxiety disorders in children: Results of a randomized clinical trial. *Journal of Consulting and Clinical Psychology, 62*, 100–110.

Kendall, P. C. (2003). Child-focused treatment of anxiety. In A. E. Kazdin & J. R. Weisz (Eds.), *Evidence-based psychotherapies for children and adolescents* (pp. 81–100). New York: Guilford Press.

Kendall, P. C., Aschenbrand S. G., & Hudson, J. L (2003). Child-focused treatment of anxiety. In A. E. Kazdin & J. R. Weisz (Eds.), *Evidence-based psychotherapies for children and adolescents.* New York: Guilford Press.

Kendall, P. C., Flannery-Schroeder, E., Panicelli-Mindel, S. M., Southam-Gerow, M. A., Henin, A., & Warnam, M. (1997). Therapy for youths with anxiety disorders: A second randomized clinical trial. *Journal of Consulting and Clinical Psychology, 65*, 366–380.

Kern, L., Gallagher, P., Starosta, K., Hickman, W., & George, M. (2006). Longitudinal outcomes of functional behavioral assessment-based intervention. *Journal of Positive Behavior Interventions, 8*(2), 67–78.

Kerr, M.M. & Nelson, C.M. (2006). *Strategies for addressing behavior problems in the classroom.* Upper Saddle River, NJ: Pearson/Merrill/Prentice Hall.

Franklin, C., Kim, J., & Tripodi, S. (2009). A meta-anlaysis of published school social work studies: 1980–2007. *Research on Social Work Practice, 19*(16), 667–677.

Kim, J. (2006). Effects of a voluntary summer reading intervention on reading achievement: Results from a randomized field trial. *Educational Evaluation and Policy Analysis, 28*(4), 335–355.

Kim, S., & Choi, S. Y. (2002). A meta-analysis of parental involvement and gifted development. *Journal of the Korean Association for Research in Science Education, 22*(3), 671–681.

Kim, S., Kverno, K., Lee, E. M., Park, J. H., Lee, H. H., & Kim, H. L. (2006). Development of a music group psychotherapy intervention for the primary prevention of adjustment difficulties in Korean adolescent girls. *Journal of Child & Adolescent Psychiatric Nursing, 19*(3), 103–111.

Kim, Y. S., & Leventhal, B. (2008). Bullying and suicide. A review. *International Journal of Adolescent Medicine and Health, 20*(2), 133–154.

King, N. J., & Heyne, D. (2000). Promotion of empirically validated psychotherapies in counselling psychology. *Counseling Psychology Quarterly, 13* (1), 1–12.

Kingery, J. N., Roblek, T. L., Suveg, C., Grover, R. L., Sherrill, J. T., & Bergman, R. L. (2006). They're not just "little adults": Developmental considerations for implementing cognitive-behavioral therapy with anxious youth. *Journal of Cognitive Psychotherapy, 20*(3), 263–273.

Kingsnorth, S., Healy, H., & MacArthur, C. (2007). Preparing for adulthood: A systematic review of life skills programs for youth with physical disabilities. *Journal of Adolescent Health Care, 41* (4), 323–332.

Knoster, T. P., & McCurdy, B. (2002). Best practices in functional behavioral assessment for designing individualized student programs. In A. Thomas & J. Grimes (Eds.), *Best practices in school psychology IV* (Vol. 2, pp. 1007–1028). Bethesda, MD: National Association of School Psychologists.

Knox, T. (1992). A framework for understanding high-risk Black adolescents' social interactive issues. In I. G. Fodor (Ed.), *Adolescent assertiveness and social skills training: A clinical handbook* (pp. 82–98). New York: Springer.

Kramer, L., Laumann, G., & Brunson, L. (2000). Implementation and diffusion of the Rainbows program in rural communities. *Journal of Educational & Psychological Consultation, 11*(1), 37–55.

Kratochwil, T. R., & Stoiber, K.C. (2002, Winter). Evidence-based interventions in school psychology: Conceptual foundations of the Procedural and Coding Manual of Division 16 and the Society for the Study of School Psychology Task Force. *School Psychology Quarterly 17* (4), 341–389.

Kroeger, S. D., & Phillips, L. J. (2007). Positive behavior support assessment guide: Creating student-centered behavior plans. *Assessment for Effective Intervention, 32*(2), 100–112.

Kyriakides, L. (2005). Evaluating school policy on parents working with their children in class. *Journal of Educational Research, 98*(5), 281–281.

Ladner, M., & Hammons, C. (2005). Special but unequal: Race and special education. Retrieved August 22, 2007, from http://www.edexcellence.net/library/special_ed/special_ed_ch5.pdf.

Lak, D. C. C., Tsang, H. W., Liberman, R. P., & Kopelowicz, A. (2004). Cultural adaptation of the basic conversational skills module for a Chinese population. *Hospital & Community Psychiatry, 55*(9), 988–990.

Lamarine, R. J. (1989). First, do no harm. *Health Education, 20*(4), 22–25.

Langberg, J. M., Epstein, J. N., Urbanowicz, C. M., Simon, J. O., & Graham, A. J. (2008). Efficacy of an organization skills intervention to improve the academic functioning of students with attention-deficit/hyperactivity disorder. *School Psychology Quarterly, 23*(3), 407–417.

Lansford, J. E., Malone, P. S, Dodge, K. A., Crozier, J. C., Pettit, G. S., & Bates, J. E. (2006). A 12-year prospective study of patterns of social information processing problems and externalizing behaviors. *Journal of Abnormal Child Psychology, 34*(5), 715–724.

Larson, M. S, (1977). *The rise of professionalism: A sociological analysis.* Berkeley: University of California Press.

Lavenberg, J. G. (2007). Effects of school-based cognitive-behavioral anger interventions: A meta-analysis. Ph.D. dissertation, University of Pennsylvania. Retrieved October 30, 2008, from Dissertations & Theses: Full Text database. (Publication No. AAT 3271850)

Laxton, T. C. (2005) Refining the construct of school safety: An exploration of correlates and construct validity of school safety measures. Ph.D. dissertation, University of Oregon Retrieved January 28, 2009, from Dissertations & Theses: Full Text database. (Publication No. AAT 3181107)

Layne, C. M., Saltzman, W. R., Poppleton, L., Burlingame, G. M., Pasalic, A., Durakovic, E., Music, M., Campara, N., Dapo, N., Arslanagic, B., Steinberg, A. M., & Pynoos, R. S. (2008). Effectiveness of a school-based group psychotherapy program for war-exposed adolescents: A randomized controlled trial. *Journal of the American Academy of Child & Adolescent Psychiatry*, 47(9), 1048–1062.

Layzer, J. I., Goodson, B. D., Bernstein, L., & Price, C. (2001). National evaluation of family support programs. Final report, Volume A: The meta-analysis. Retrieved January 10, 2009, from http://www.acf.dhhs.gov/programs/core/pubs_reports/famsup/fa m_sup_vol_a.pdf.

LeCroy, C. W. (2006). Designing and facilitating groups with children. In C. Franklin, M. B. Harris, & P. Allen-Meares (Eds.), *The school services sourcebook: A guide for school-based professionals* (pp. 595–602). New York: Oxford University Press.

LeCroy, C. W. (2004). Experimental evaluation of "Go Grrrls" preventive intervention for early adolescent girls. *Journal of Primary Prevention, 25*(4), 457–473.

Lee, D. L. (2005). Increasing compliance: A quantitative synthesis of applied research on high-probability request sequences. *Exceptionality 13*(3), 141–154.

Lee, W. C. (2007). The many facets in the role of a school social worker. In M. Alvarez & L. Bye (Eds.), *School social work: Theory to practice* (pp. 51–64). Belmont, CA: Thompson Brooks/Cole.

Leedy, A., Bates, P., & Safran, S. P. (2004). Bridging the research-to-practice gap: Improving hallway behavior using positive behavior support. *Behavioral Disorders, 29*(2), 130–139.

Leenaars, P. E. M. (2005). Differences between violent male and violent female forensic psychiatric outpatients: Consequences for treatment. *Psychology, Crime & Law, 11*(4), 445–455.

Lehman, C. M. (2002). Transition from school to adult life: Empowering youth through community ownership and accountability. *Journal of Child and Family Studies 11*(1), 127.

Lehr, C. A., Sinclair, M. F., & Christenson, S. L. (2004). Addressing student engagement and truancy prevention during the elementary school years: A replication study of the Check & Connect model. *Journal of Education for Students Placed at Risk, 9*(3), 279–301.

Leithwood, K., & Jantzi, D. (1999). The relative effects of principal and teacher sources of leadership on student engagement with school. *Educational Administration Quarterly, 35*(5), 679–706.

Lewis, C. P. (2004). The relation between extracurricular activities with academic and social competencies in school-age children: A meta-analysis. Ph.D. dissertation, Texas A&M University. Retrieved December 30, 2008, from Dissertations & Theses: Full Text database. (Publication No. AAT 3189504)

Lilienfeld, S. O. (2007). Psychological treatments that cause harm. *Perspectives on Psychological Science, 2*(1), 53–70.

Limber, S. (2006). The Olweus bullying prevention program: An overview of its implementation and research basis. In S. R. Jimerson & M. Furlong (Eds.), *Handbook of school violence and school safety: From research to practice* (pp. 293–308). Mahwah, NJ: Lawrence Erlbaum.

Linares, L. O., Rosbruch, N., Stern, M. B., Edwards, M. E., Walker, G., Abikoff, H. B., & Alvir, J. M. J. (2005). Developing cognitive-social-emotional competencies to enhance academic learning. *Psychology in the Schools, 42*(4), 405–417.

Linseisen, T. (2006). Effective interventions for youth with Oppositional Defiant Disorder. In C. Franklin, M.B. Harris, & P. Allen-Meares (Eds.)The School Services Sourcebook (pp. 57–67). New York: Oxford University Press.

Lincoln, Y. S. (2001). Varieties of validity: Quality in qualitative research. In J. C. Smart & W. G. Tierney (Eds.), *Higher education: Handbook of theory and research* (Vol. 16, pp. 25–72). New York: Agathon Press.

Lindsey, B., & White, M. (2008). Tier 2 behavioral interventions for at-risk students. In C. R. Massat, R. Constable, S. McDonald, & J. P. Flynn (Eds.), *School social work: Practice, policy, and research* (7th ed., pp. 665–673). Chicago, IL: Lyceum.

Linseisen, T. (2006). Effective interventions for youth with oppositional deviant disorder. In C. G. Franklin, M. B. Harris, & P. Allen-Meares (Eds.), *The school services sourcebook: A guide for school-based professions* (pp. 57–68). New York: Oxford University Press.

Litner, B. (2003). Teens with ADHD: The challenge of high school. *Child & Youth Care Forum, 32,* 137–158.

Littell, J., Corcoran, J., & Pillai, V. (2008). *Systematic reviews and meta-analysis.* New York: Oxford University Press.

Livingston, P. K. (2008). A meta-analysis of the effectiveness of anti-bullying programs on students. *Dissertation Abstracts International Section A: Humanities and Social Sciences, 69*(3-A).

Lo, Y., & Cartledge, G. (2006). FBA and BIP: Increasing the behavior adjustment of African American boys in schools. *Behavioral Disorders, 31*(2), 147–161.

Lochman, J. E., Barry, T. D., & Pardini, D. A. (2003). Anger control training for aggressive youth. In A. E. Kazdin & J. R. Weisz (Eds.), *Evidence-based psychotherapies for children and adolescents* (pp. 263–278). New York: Guilford Press.

Lomonaco, S., Scheidlinger, S., & Aronson, S. (2000). Five decades of children's group treatment–An overview. *Journal of Child and Adolescent Group Therapy, 10*(2), 77–96.

Lopez, S. J., Edwards, L. M., Teramoto-Pedrotti, J., Ito, A., & Rasmussen, H. N. (2002). Culture counts: Examinations of recent applications of the Penn Resiliency Program or toward a rubric for examining cultural appropriateness of prevention programming. *Prevention & Treatment, 5*(Article 12). Posted May 8, 2002 [Electronic journal]. Retrieved January 11, 2009, from http://journals.apa.org/prevention/volume5/pre0050012u.html.

Lösel, F., & Beelmann, A. (2003). Effects of child skills training in preventing antisocial behavior: A systematic review of randomized evaluations. *Annals of the American Academy of Political & Social Science, 587,* 84–109.

Losen, D. J., & Orfield, G. (Eds.). (2002). *Racial inequity in special education.* Cambridge, MA: Harvard University Press.

Louwe, J. J., Van Overveld, C. W., Merk, W., DeCastro, B. O., & Koops, W. (2007). The effect of the PATHS-curriculum on reactive and proactive aggression [Dutch]. *Pedagogische Studien, 84* (4), 277–292.

Lowry-Webster, H. M., Barrett, P. M., & Dadds, M. R. (2001). A universal prevention trial of anxiety and depressive symptomatology in childhood: Preliminary data from an Australian study. *Behaviour Change, 18*(1), 36–50.

Lowry-Webster, H. M., Barrett, P., & Lock, S. (2003). A universal prevention trial of anxiety symptomatology during childhood: Results at one-year follow-up. *Behaviour Change, 20*(1), 25.

Luborsky, L., Singer, B., & Luborsky, L. (1975). Comparative studies of psychotherapies: Is it true that everyone has won and all must have prizes? *Archives of General Psychiatry, 32*(8), 996–1008.

Luiselli, J. K., Putnam, R. F., Handler, M. W., & Feinberg, A. B. (2005). Whole-school positive behavior support: Effects on student discipline and academic performance. *Educational Psychology, 25*(2/3), 183–199.

Lyst, A. M., Gabriel, S., O'Shaughnessy, T. E., Meyers, J., & Meyers, B. (2005). Social validity: Perceptions of Check & Connect with early literacy support. *Journal of School Psychology, 43* (3), 197–218.

MacDonald, K. M. (1995). *The sociology of professions.* London: Sage.

Macquarie University Anxiety Research Unit. (2009). Description of Cool Kids Program. Retrieved July 15, 2009, from http://www.psy.mq.edu.au/MUARU/books/prof.htm.

Macgowan, M. J. (2008). *A guide to evidence-based group work.* New York: Oxford University Press.

Mager, W. M. (2004). Effects of intervention group composition on young adolescents at-risk for externalizing behavior problems. *Dissertation Abstracts International: Section B: The Sciences and Engineering, 64* , 4049.

Mager, W., Milich, R., Harris, M. J., & Howard, A. (2005). Intervention groups for adolescents with conduct problems: Is aggregation harmful or helpful? *Journal of Abnormal Child Psychology, 33*, 349.

Malecki, C. K., & Demaray, M. K. (2007). Social behavior assessment and response to intervention. In S. R. Jimerson, M. K. Burns, & A. M. VanDerHeyden (Eds.), *Handbook of response to intervention: The science and practice of assessment and intervention* (pp. 161–171). New York: Springer.

Malgady, R. G., & Costantino, G. (2003). Narrative therapy for Hispanic children and adolescents. In A. E. Kazdin & J. R. Weisz (Eds.), *Evidence-based psychotherapies for children and adolescents* (pp. 425–438). New York: Guilford Press.

March, R. E., & Horner, R. H. (2002). Feasibility and contributions of functional behavioral assessment in schools. *Journal of Emotional and Behavioral Disorders, 10*(3), 158–170.

Marks, I. M. (1974). Empirical psychotherapeutic methods. *Psychotherapy and Psychosomatics, 24* (4–6), 222–237.

Masia, C. L., Klein, R. G., Storch, E. A., & Corda, B. (2001). School-based behavioral treatment for social anxiety disorder in adolescents: Results of a pilot study. *Journal of the American Academy of Child & Adolescent Psychiatry, 40*(7), 780–786.

Masia-Warner, C., Fisher, P. H., Shrout, P. E., Rathor, S., & Klein, R. G. (2007). Treating adolescents with social anxiety disorder in school: An attention control trial. *Journal of Child Psychology & Psychiatry, 48*(7), 676–686.

Masia-Warner, C., Klein, R. G., Dent, H. C., Fisher, P., Alvir, J., Albano, A. M., & Guardino, M. (2005). School-based intervention for adolescents with social anxiety disorder: Results of a controlled study. *Journal of Abnormal Child Psychology, 33*(6), 707–722.

Massat, C., Orenstein, E., & Moses, H. (2006). Mental health and school social work. In R. Constable, C. Massat, S. McDonald, & J. Flynn (Eds.), *School social work: Practice, policy, and research.* Chicago: Lyceum.

Massat, C. R., Constable, R., McDonald, S., & Flynn, J. P. (Eds.). (2009). *School social work: Practice, policy, and research* (7th ed.). Chicago, IL: Lyceum.

Massinga, R., & Pecora, P. J. (2004). Providing better opportunities for older children in the child welfare system. *The Future of Children/Center for the Future of Children, the David and Lucile Packard Foundation, 14*(1), 150–173.

Mattingly, D. J., Prislin, R., & McKenzie, T. L. (2002). Evaluating evaluations: The case of parent involvement programs. *Review of Educational Research, 72*(4), 549–576.

McCart, M. R., Priester, P. E., Davies, W. H., & Azen, R. (2006). Differential effectiveness of behavioral parent training and cognitive-behavioral therapy for anti-social youth: A meta-analysis. *Journal of Abnormal Child Psychology, 34*(4), 527–543.

McDonnell, M. G., & Dyck, D. G. (2004). Multiple-family group treatment as an effective intervention for children with psychological disorders. *Clinical Psychology Review, 24*(6), 685–706.

McGinnis, E., & Goldstein, A. P. (2003). *Skillstreaming the elementary school child: New strategies and perspectives for teaching prosocial skills* (rev. ed). Champaign, IL: Research Press.

McGlynn, E. A., Asch, S. M., & Adams, J. (2003). The quality of health care delivered to adults in the United States. *New England Journal of Medicine, 348*, 2635–2645.

McKay, M. M., Nudelman, R., McCadem, K., & Gonzalez, J. (1996). Evaluating a social work engagement approach to involving inner-city children and their families in mental health care. *Research on Social Work Practice, 6*(4), 462–472.

McLaughlin, L., Laux, J. M., & Pescara-Kovach, L. (2006). Using multimedia to reduce bullying and victimization in third-grade urban schools. *Professional School Counseling, 10*(2), 153–160.

McNeill, T. (2006). Evidence-based practice in an age of relativism: Toward a model for practice. *Social Work, 51*, 147–156.

McRae, M. W. (1993). *The literature of science: Perspectives on popular scientific writing.* Athens: University of Georgia Press.

Meadows, N. B. (2009). Social skills instruction. In M. L. Yell, N. B. Meadows, E. Drasgow, & J. G. Shriner (Eds.), *Evidence-based practices for educating students with emotional and behavioral disorders* (pp. 155–175). Upper Saddle River, NJ: Merrill/Pearson.

Megill, A. (1994). *Re-thinking objectivity.* Durham, NC: Duke University Press.

Meiland, J. (1999). Category mistake. *Cambridge Dictionary of Philosophy.* Cambridge, UK: Cambridge University Press.

Meisels, S. J. (1992). Doing harm by doing good: Iatrogenic effects of early childhood enrollment and promotion policies. *Early Childhood Research Quarterly* (Special Issue): *Research on Kindergarten, 7*(2), 155–174.

Mellard, D. F., & Johnson, E. (2008). *RTI: A practitioner's guide to implementing response to intervention.* Thousand Oaks, CA: Corwin/NAESP.

Mellor, D. J., & Moore, K. A. (2003). The Questionnaire on Teacher Interaction: Assessing information transfer in single and multi-teacher environments. *Journal of Classroom Interaction, 38*(2), 29–35.

Melnyk, B. M., Small, L., Morrison-Beedy, D., Strasser, A., Spath, L., Kreipe, R., Crean, H., Jacobson, D., Kelly, S., & O'Haver, J. (2007). The COPE Healthy Lifestyles TEEN program: Feasibility, preliminary effects, and lessons learned from an after school group intervention with overweight adolescents. *Journal of Pediatric Health Care, 21*(5), 315–322.

Merrell, K. W., & Gimpel, G. (1998). *Social skills of children and adolescents: Conceptualization, assessment, and treatment.* Mahwah, NJ: Lawrence Erlbaum.

Merrell, K. W., Gueldner, B. A., Ross, S. W., & Isava, D. M. (2008). How effective are school bullying intervention programs? A meta-analysis of intervention research. *School Psychology Quarterly, 23*(1), 26–26.

Merrell, R. (2004) *The impact of a drama intervention program on the response of the bystander to bullying situations.* Ed.D. dissertation, University of Rochester, New York. Retrieved January 9, 2009, from Dissertations & Theses: Full Text database. (Publication No. AAT 3139437)

Mervis, B. (1998). The use of peer-pairing in schools to improve socialization. *Child & Adolescent Social Work Journal, 15*(6), 467–477.

Metropolitan Area Child Study. (2007). FCRG publication list. Retrieved August 10, 2007, from http://www.psych.uic.edu/fcrg/publications.html.

Meyer, J. R., Reppucci, N. D., & Owen, J. A. (2006). Criminalizing childhood: The shifting boundaries of responsibility in the justice and school systems. In K. Freeark & W. S. Davidson, II (Eds.), *The crisis in youth mental health: Critical issues and effective programs, Vol. 3: Issues for families, schools, and communities* (pp. 219–247). Westport, CT: Praeger/Greenwood.

Michael, S., Dittus, P., & Epstein, J.L. (2007). Family and community involvement in schools: Results from the School Health Policies and Programs Study, 2006. *Journal of School Health, 77,* 567–587.

Mifsud, C., & Rapee, R. M. (2005). Early intervention for childhood anxiety in a school setting: Outcomes for an economically disadvantaged population. *Journal of American Academy Child Adolescent Psychiatry, 44*(10), 996–1004.

Miller, L. A. (2006) *Interventions targeting reciprocal social interaction in children and young adults with autism spectrum disorders: A meta-analysis.* Ph.D. dissertation, University of Utah. Retrieved December 30, 2008, from Dissertations & Theses: Full Text database. (Publication No. AAT 3217476)

Millerson, G. (1964). *The qualifying associations.* London: Routledge.

Millsap, M., Chase, A., Obeidallah, D., Perez-Smith, A., Brigham, N., Johnston, K., Cook, T., & Hunt, D. (2000). *Evaluation for Detroit's Comer Schools and Families Initiative.* Cambridge, MA: Abt Associates for the Skillman Foundation.

Minton, S. J., & O'Moore, A. M. (2008). The effectiveness of a nationwide intervention programme to prevent and counter school bullying in Ireland. *International Journal of Psychology & Psychological Therapy, 8*(1), 1–12.

Mitchell, D. (2008). *What really works in special and inclusive education: Using evidence-based teaching strategies.* New York: Routledge/Taylor & Francis.

Mitchell, G. (1958). When to prescribe the school social worker. *Elementary School Journal, 58*(8), 439–444.

Mokrue, K., Elias, M. J., & Bry, B. H. (2005). Dosage effect and the efficacy of a video-based teamwork-building series with urban elementary school children. *Special Services in the Schools, 21*(1), 67–97.

Mol, S. E., Bus, A. G., de Jong, M. T., & Smeets, D. J. H. (2008). Added value of dialogic parent-child book readings: A meta-analysis. *Early Education and Development, 19*(1), 7–26.

Monette, D. R., Sullivan, T. J., & DeJong, C. R. (2008). *Applied social research: Tool for the human services* (7th ed.). Belmont, CA: Thomson/Wadsworth.

Montgomery, K. (2000). Classroom rubrics: Systematizing what teachers do naturally. *The Clearing House, 73*(6), 324–328.

Mooney, P., Epstein, M. H., Ryser, G., & Pierce, C. D. (2005). Reliability and validity of the Behavioral and Emotional Rating Scale-second edition: Parent Rating Scale. *Children & Schools, 27*(3), 147–155.

Moore-Brown, B. J., Montgomery, J. K., Bielinski, J., & Shubin, J. (2005). Responsiveness to intervention: Teaching before testing helps avoid labeling. *Topics in Language Disorders, 25* (2), 148–167.

Moroz, K. B., & Jones, K. M. (2002). The effects of positive peer reporting on children's social involvement. *School Psychology Review, 31*(2), 235–245.

Morrison, V. (May, 2004). School social work in Illinois. *IASSW News.*

Mottram, L. M., Bray, M. A., Kehle, T. J., Broudy, M., & Jenson, W. R. (2002). A classroom-based intervention to reduce disruptive behavior. *Journal of Applied School Psychology, 19* (1), 65–74.

MTA Cooperative Group. (1999). A 14-month randomized clinical trial of treatment strategies for attention-deficit/hyperactivity disorder. *Archives of General Psychiatry, 56,* 1073–1086.

Mullen, E. J., & Dumpson, J. R. (Eds.). (1972). *Evaluation of social intervention.* San Francisco: Jossey-Bass.

Muris, P., Meester, C., Vincken, M., & Eijkelenboom, A. (2005). Reducing children's aggressive and oppositional behaviors in the schools: Preliminary results of a social-cognitive group intervention program. *Child & Family Behavior Therapy, 27*(1), 17–32.

Murphy, J. (1999). Common factors of school-based change. In S. Miller & B. Duncan (Eds.), *Heart and soul of change: What works in therapy.* Washington, DC: American Psychological Association.

Murphy, J. I. (2005). How to learn, not what to learn: Three strategies that foster lifelong learning in clinical settings. *Annual Review of Nursing Education, 3,* 37–55.

Mytton, J. A., DiGuiseppi, C., Gough, D. A., Taylor, R.S., & Logan, S. (2002). School-based violence prevention trials: Systematic review of secondary prevention trials. *Archives of Pediatric Adolescent Medicine, 156,* 752–762.

Nansel, T. R., Overpeck, M., Pilla, R. S., Ruan, W., Simons-Morton, B., & Scheidt, P. (2001). Bullying behaviors among US youth: Prevalence and association with psychosocial adjustment. *Journal of the American Medical Association, 285,* 2094–2100.

Nastasi, B. K., & DeZolt, D. M. (1994). *School interventions for children of alcoholics.* New York: Guilford Press.

National Association of Social Workers. (1999). Code of ethics. Retrieved August 28, 2003, from http://www.socialworkers.org/pubs/code/code.asp.

National Association of Social Workers. (2002). NASW Standards for school social work practice. Retrieved July 10, 2007, from http://www.socialworkers.org/practice/standards/NASW_SSWS.pdf.

National Association of Social Workers. (2003). Preventing school attacks in the United States: A final report of the Safe School Initiative. Retrieved August 1, 2003, from www.naswdc.org.

National Longitudinal Transition Study. (1993). First wave data. Retrieved July 15, 2007, from http://www.nlts2.org/links.html.

National Marriage Project. (2006). The state of our unions: The social health of marriage in America, 2005. Retrieved July 20, 2007, from http://marriage.rutgers.edu/Publications/SOOU/SOOU2006.pdf.

National Registry of Evidence-Based Programs and Practices (NREPP). (2006, October). *Coping Cat Review*. Retrieved on May 3, 2009 from http://www.nrepp.samhsa.gov/programfulldetails.asp?PROGRAM_ID=82.

National Registry of Evidence-Based Programs and Practices (NREPP). (2007, September). *New Beginnings review*. Retrieved July 2, 2009, from http://www.nrepp.samhsa.gov/programfulldetails.asp?PROGRAM_ID=98.

National Research Council. (2002). *Minority students in special and gifted education*. Washington, DC: National Academy Press.

Neimeyer, R. (2000). Searching for the meaning of meaning: Grief therapy and the process of reconstruction. *Death Studies, 24*, 541–558.

Nelson, J. L., Palonsky, S. B., & McCarthy, M. R. (2004). Critical issues in education: Dialogues and dialectics (5th ed.). Boston: McGraw-Hill.

Nettles, S. M., Caughy, M. O., & O'Campo, P. J. (2008). School adjustment in the early grades: Toward an integrated model of neighborhood, parental, and child processes. *Review of Educational Research, 78*, 3–32.

Newsome, S. (2002). The effectiveness and utility of solution-focused brief therapy (SFBT) with at-risk junior high students: A quasi-experimental study. Unpublished doctoral disssertation, The Ohio State University.

Newsome, S. (2004). Solution-focused interventions with at-risk students: Enhancing the bottom line. *Research on Social Work Practice, 14*(5), 336–343.

Newsome, S., & Kelly, M. (in press). Grandparents raising grandchildren: A solution-focused school-based intervention. *Social Work with Groups*.

Newsome, S., & Kelly, M. (2006). School violence and bullying: Best practice interventions. In J. Waller (Ed.), *Child and adolescent mental health in the classroom*. Thousand Oaks, CA: Sage.

No Child Left Behind. (2002). *Introduction to the NCLB legislation*. Retrieved February 20, 2004, from http://www.ed.gov/nclb/overview/intro/4pillars.html.

No Child Left Behind Act of 2001. (2002). P.L. 107–110. 115 Stat. 1425.

Nock, M. K., Goldman, J. L., Wang, Y., & Albano, A. M. (2004). From science to practice: The flexible use of evidence-based treatments in clinical settings. *Journal of the American Academy of Child & Adolescent Psychiatry, 43*(6), 777–780.

Nolan, E. E., Gadow, K. D., & Sprafkin, J. (2001) Teacher reports of *DSM-IV* ADHD, ODD, and CD symptoms in schoolchildren. *Journal of the American Academy of Child & Adolescent Psychiatry, 40*(2), 241–249.

Norcross, J. C., Beutler, L. E., & Levant, R. E. (Eds.). (2006). *Evidence-based practices in mental health: Debate and dialogue on the fundamental questions*. Washington, DC: American Psychological Association.

Nye, C., Turner, H., & Schwartz, J. (2006). Approaches to parent involvement for improving the academic performance of elementary school age children. In D. Olweus ed., *Bullying at school: What we know and what we can do*. Campbell Collaboration, Campbell Library of Systematic Reviews. Oxford, UK: Blackwell.

Nylund, D. (2000). *Treating Huckleberry Finn: A new narrative approach to working with kids diagnosed ADD/ADHD*. San Francisco: Jossey-Bass.

Oakes, J., & Lipton, M. (1990). Tracking and ability grouping: A structural barrier to access and achievement. In J. I. Goodlad & P. Keating (Eds), *Access to knowledge: An agenda for our nation's schools* (pp. 187–204). New York: College Entrance Examination Board.

Oliver, R., & Skinner, C. H. (2002). Applying behavioral momentum theory to increase compliance: Why Mrs. H. revved up the elementary students with Hokey-Pokey. *Journal of Applied School Psychology, 19*(1), 75–94.

Ollendick, T. H., & Davis, T. E. (2004). Empirically supported treatments for children and adolescents: Where to from here? *Clinical Psychology: Science & Practice, 11*(3), 289–294.

Olweus, D. (2005) A useful evaluation design, and effects of the Olweus Bullying Prevention Program. *Psychology, Crime and Law, 4*, 389–402.

Openshaw, L. (2008). *Social work in schools: Principles and practice*. New York: Guilford Press.

O'Reilly, M. F., & Glynn, D. (1995). Using a process social skills approach with adolescents with mild intellectual disabilities. *Education & Training in Mental Retardation and Developmental Disabilities, 30*(3), 187–198.

Orpinas, P., Horne, A. M., & Staniszewski, D. (2003). School bullying: Changing the problem by changing the school. *School Psychology Review, 32*(3), 431–445.

Oswald, D. P., & Mazefsky, C. A. (2006). Empirically supported psychotherapy interventions for internalizing disorders. *Psychology in the Schools, 43*(4), 439–449.

O'Toole, M. E. (1999, July). *The school shooter: A threat assessment perspective*. Quantico, VA: U.S. Department of Justice/Federal Bureau of Investigation. Retrieved May 19, 2002, from http://www.fbi.gov/publications/school/school2.pdf.

Otsui, K., & Tanaka-Matsumi, J. (2007). Preschoolers' social skills as predicted by perspective taking, regulation of emotion, and social problem solving. [Japanese] *Japanese Journal of Social Psychology, 22*(3), 223–233.

Overton, S., McKenzie, L., & King, K. (2002). Replication of the First Step to Success model: A multiple-case study of implementation effectiveness. *Behavioral Disorders, 28*(1), 40–56.

Pappas, D. (2006). Review of ADHD rating scale-IV: Checklists, norms, and clinical interpretation. *Journal of Psychoeducational Assessment, 24*, 172–178.

Pascopella, A. (2003). The next challenge. *District Administration, 39*(6), 24–30.

Payne, A. A., Gottfredson, D. C., & Gottfredson, G. D. (2006). School predictors of the intensity of implementation of school-based prevention programs: Results from a national study. *Prevention Science, 7*, 225–237.

Payne, C. (2008). *So much reform, so little change: The persistence of failure in urban schools*. Cambridge, MA: Harvard Education Press.

Pears, K. C., Fisher, P. A., & Bronz, K. D. (2007). An intervention to promote social emotional school readiness in foster children. *School Psychology Digest, 36*(4), 665–673.

Pedro-Carroll, J. L., Alpert-Gillis, L. J., & Cowen, E. L. (1992). An evaluation of the efficacy of a preventive intervention for 4th–6th grade urban children of divorce. *Journal of Primary Prevention, 13*(2), 115–130.

Pedro-Carroll, J. L.., Alpert-Gillis, L. J., & Sterling, S. (1997). A procedures manual for conducting divorce support groups for 2nd and 3rd grade children. (2nd ed.). Rochester, NY: Primary Mental Health Project.

Pedro-Carroll, J. L., Sutton, S. E., & Wyman, P.A. (1999). A two-year follow-up evaluation of a preventive intervention for young children of divorce. *School Psychology Review, 28*(3), 467–476.

Perlstadt, H. (1998). Commentary on Turner. *Sociological Perspectives, 41*(2), 259–273.

Perry, C.E., Hatton, D., & Kendall, J. (2005). Latino parents' accounts of Attention-Deficit Hyperactivity Disorder. *Journal of Transcultural Nursing, 16,* (4), 312–321.

Peterson, K. (2002). The professional development of principals: Innovations and opportunities. *Educational Administration Quarterly, 38*(2), 213–232.

Pfiffner, L. J., Mikami, A. Y., Huang-Pollock, C., Easterlin, B., Zalecki, C., & McBurnett, K. (2007). A randomized, controlled trial of integrated home-school behavioral treatment for ADHD, predominantly inattentive type. *Journal of the American Academy of Child & Adolescent Psychiatry, 46,* 1041–1050.

Phillips, J. H. (2004). An evaluation of school-based cognitive-behavioral social skills training groups with adolescents at risk for depression. Ph.D. dissertation, University of Texas at Arlington. Retrieved October 30, 2008, from Dissertations & Theses: Full Text database. (Publication No. AAT 3138791)

Pina, A. A., Silverman, W. K., Fuentes, R. M., Kurtines, W. M., & Weems, C. F. (2003). Exposure-based cognitive-behavioral treatment for phobic and anxiety disorders: Treatment effects and maintenance for Hispanic/Latino relative to European-American youths. *Journal of the American Academy of Child & Adolescent Psychiatry, 42*(10), 1179–1187.

Pliszka, S., & AACAP Work Group on Quality Issues. (2007). Practice parameters for the assessment and treatment of children and adolescents with attention-deficit/hyperactivity disorder. *Journal of the American Academy of Child and Adolescent Psychiatry, 46,* 894–921.

Pollio, D. E. (2006). The art of evidence-based practice. *Research on Social Work Practice, 16*(2), 224–232.

Popper, K. R. (1992). *In search of a better world: Lectures and essays from thirty years.* London: Routledge & Kegan Paul.

Powell, D. R., & Peet, S. H. (2008). Development and outcomes of a community-based intervention to improve parents' use of inquiry in informal learning contexts. *Journal of Applied Developmental Psychology, 29*(4), 259–273.

Powers, M. D. (1985). Behavioral assessment and the planning and evaluation of interventions for developmentally disabled children. *School Psychology Review, 14*(2), 155–161.

Presidential New Freedom Commission on Mental Health. (2002). Final Report. Retrieved August 15, 2007, from http://www.mentalhealthcommission.gov/reports/reports.htm.

President's Commission on Excellence in Special Education. (2002). *A new era: Revitalizing special education for children and their families.* Washington, DC: U.S. Department of Education, Office of Special Education and Rehabilitative Services. Retrieved May 19, 2004, from http://www.ed. gov/inits/commissionsboards/whspecialeducation/reports/images/Pres_Rep.pdf.

Proctor, M. A., & Morgan, D. (1991). Effectiveness of a response cost raffle procedure on the disruptive classroom behavior of adolescents with behavior problems. *School Psychology Review, 20*(1), 97–109.

Purdie, N., Hattie, J., & Carroll, A. (2002). A review of the research on interventions for attention deficit hyperactivity disorder: What works best? *Review of Educational Research, 72*(1), 61–99.

Quong, M. K. (2006). The effectiveness of the Open Minds Peace Signs program (Structured Anger Management and Life Skills Program) in the reduction of aggression and behavior problems in elementary school students in Hana, Maui. Psy.D. dissertation, Argosy University, Hawaii. Retrieved January 9, 2009, from Dissertations & Theses: Full Text database. (Publication No. AAT 3233124)

Raffaele, L. M., & Knoff, H. M. (1999). Improving home-school collaboration with disadvantaged families: Organizational principles, perspectives, and approaches. *School Psychology Review, 28*(3), 448–466.

Rainbows for All God's Children. (2009). Description of program and research on program. Retrieved February 2, 2009, from http://www.rainbows.org/index.asp.

Raines, J. C. (2002). Brainstorming hypotheses for functional behavioral assessment: The link to effective behavioral intervention plans. *School Social Work Journal, 26*(2), 30–45.

Raines, J. C. (2003). Rating the rating scales: Ten criteria to use. *School Social Work Journal, 27*(2), 1–17.

Raines, J. (2004). Evidence-based practice in school social work: A process in perspective. *Children & Schools, 26*(2), 71–85.

Raines, J. C. (2006). SWOT! A strategic plan for school social work in the 21st century. *School Social Work Journal* (Special Issue on the 100th Anniversary of School Social Work), 132–150.

Raines, J. (2007, April). *Evidence-based practice in schools.* Presentation at School Social Work Association of America. Denver, CO.

Raines, J. C. (2008a). *SSWAA ethical guideline series: School social work and group work.* Indianapolis, IN: School Social Work Association of America.

Raines, J. C. (2008b). *Evidence-based practice in school mental health: A primer for school social workers, psychologists, and counselors.* New York: Oxford University Press

Raines, J. C. (2008c). Evaluating qualitative research studies. In R. M. Grinnell, Jr., & Y. A. Unrau (Eds.), *Social work research and evaluation* (8th ed., 445–461). New York: Oxford University Press.

Raines, J. C., & Massat, C. R. (2004). Getting published: A guide for the aspiring practitioner. *School Social Work Journal, 29*(1), 1–17.

Ralph, A., & Nicholson, L. (1995). Teaching coping skills to depressed adolescents in high school settings. *Behaviour Change, 12*(4), 175–190.

Rao, P. A., Beidel, D. C., & Murray, M. J. (2008). Social skills interventions for children with Asperger's syndrome or high-functioning autism: A review and recommendations. *Journal of Autism and Developmental Disorders, 38*(2), 353–361.

Rasinski, T., & Stevenson, B. (2005). The effects of fast start reading: A fluency-based home involvement reading program, on the reading achievement of beginning readers. *Reading Psychology an International Quarterly, 26*(2), 109–125.

Rathvon, N. (2008). *Effective school interventions: Evidence-based strategies for improving school outcomes* (2nd ed.). New York: Guilford Press.

Reeker, J., Ensing, D., & Elliott, R. (1997). A meta-analytic investigation of group treatment outcomes for sexually abused children. *Child Abuse & Neglect, 21*(7), 669–680.

Reid, M. J., & Webster-Stratton, C. (2001). The Incredible Years parent, teacher, and child intervention: Targeting multiple areas of risk for a young child with pervasive conduct problems using a flexible, manualized treatment program. *Cognitive and Behavioral Practice, 8*, 377–386.

Reid, M. J., Webster-Stratton, C., & Hammond, M. (2007). Enhancing a classroom social competence and problem-solving curriculum by offering parent training to families of moderate- to high-risk elementary school children. *Journal of Clinical Child & Adolescent Psychology, 36*(4), 605–620.

Reid, R., Trout, A. L., & Schartz, M. (2005). Self-regulation interventions for children with ADHD. *Exceptional Children, 71*(4), 361–377.

Reid, W. J. (1978). *The task-centered system.* New York: Columbia University Press.

Renk, K., & Phares, V. (2004). Cross-informant ratings of social competence in children and adolescents. *Clinical Psychology Review, 24*(2), 239–254.

Reschly, D. (2004). Commentary: Paradigm shift, outcomes criteria, and behavioral interventions: Foundations for the future of school psychology. *School Psychology Review, 33,* 408–416.

Rey, R. B., Smith, A. L., Yoon, J., Somers, C., & Barnett, D. (2007). Relationships between teachers and urban African American children: The role of informant. *School Psychology International, 28*(3), 346–364.

Reynhout, G., & Carter, M. (2006). Social stories™ for children with disabilities. *Journal of Autism and Developmental Disorders, 36*(4), 445–469.

Reynolds, C. R., & Kamphaus, R. W. (2004). *Behavior assessment system for children* (2nd ed.). Circle Pines, MN: Pearson/American Guidance Service.

Reynolds, W. (2003). *Reynolds Bully Victimization Scales for Schools.* San Antonio, TX: Psychological Corp.

Ribordy, S. C., Camras, L. A., Stefani, R., & Spaccarelli, S. (1988). Vignettes for emotion recognition research and affective therapy with children. *Journal of Clinical Child Psychology, 17*(4), 322–325.

Rich, B. W., Molloy, P., Hart, B., Ginsberg, S., & Mulvey, T. (2007). Conducting a children's divorce group: One approach. *Journal of Child & Adolescent Nursing, 20*(3), 163–175.

Riddle, J., Bergin, J. J., & Douzenis, C. (1997). Effect of group counseling on the self-concept of children of alcoholics. *Elementary School Guidance & Counseling, 31*(3), 192–203. [Appendix includes group activities for 14 sessions.]

Rigby, K. (2002). New perspectives on bullying. Philadephia, PA: Jessica Kingsley.

Rigby, K. (2006). What can we learn from evaluated studies of school-based programs to reduce bullying in schools? In S. R. Jimerson, & M. Furlong (Eds.), *Handbook of school violence and school safety: From research to practice* (pp. 335–338). Mahwah, NJ: Lawrence Erlbaum.

Rimm-Kaufman, S. E., Planta, R. C., & Cox, M. J. (2000). Teachers' judgments of problems in the transition to kindergarten. *Early Childhood Research Quarterly 15*(2), 147–166.

Roberts, A. R., & Yeager, K. (2004). Systematic reviews of evidence-based studies and practice-based research: How to search for, develop, and use them. In A. R. Roberts & K. Yeager (Eds.), *Evidence-based practice manual: Research and outcome measures in health and human services* (pp. 3–14). New York: Oxford University Press.

Robison, L. M., Sclar, D. A., Skaer, T. L., & Galin, R. S. (1999). National trends in the prevalence of attention deficit/hyperactivity disorder and the prescribing of methylphenidate among school-age children: 1990–1995. *Clinical Pediatrics, 38*(4), 209–217.

Rohde, P., Lewinsohn, P. M., Clarke, G. N., Hops, H., & Seeley, J. R. (2005). The Adolescent Coping with Depression course: A cognitive-behavioral approach to the treatment of adolescent depression. In E. D. Hibbs, & P. S. Jensen (Eds.), *Psychosocial treatments for child and adolescent disorders: Empirically based strategies for clinical practice* (2nd ed., pp. 219–237). Washington, DC: American Psychological Association.

Rohrbach, L. A., Ringwalt, C. L., Ennett, S. T., & Vincus, A. A. (2005). Factors associated with adoption of evidence-based substance use prevention curricula in US school districts. *Health Education Research, 20*(5), 514–526.

Romano, J. L., & Kachgal, M. M. (2004). Counseling psychology and school counseling: An underutilized partnership. *The Counseling Psychologist, 32*(2), 184–215.

Romeo, R., Byford, S., & Knapp, M. (2005). Annotation: Economic evaluations of child and adolescent mental health interventions: A systematic review. *Journal of Child Psychology & Psychiatry & Allied Disciplines, 46*(9), 919–930.

Rones, M., & Hoagwood, K. (2000). School-based mental health services: A research review. *Clinical Child & Family Psychology Review, 3*(4), 223–241.

Rose, S., Bisson, J., & Wessely S. (2001). Psychological debriefing for preventing posttraumatic stress disorder (PTSD). Cochrane Review. In *The Cochrane Library, 3*. Oxford, UK: Update Software.

Rosenbaum, J.E. (2002). Beyond empty promises: Policies to improve transitions into college and jobs. Retrieved on July12, 2009 from http://www.ed.gov/offices/OVAE/HS/rosenbaum.doc.

Rosenzweig, C. (2000). A meta-analysis of parenting and school success: The role of parents in promoting students' academic performance. Unpublished doctoral dissertation, Hofstra University, New York.

Ross, D. E., Singer-Dudek, J., & Greer, R. D. (2005). The Teacher Performance Rate & Accuracy Scale (TPRA): Training as evaluation. *Education & Training in Developmental Disabilities, 40*(4), 411–423.

Ross-Fisher, R. L. (2005). Developing effective successful rubrics. *Kappa Delta Pi Record, 41*(3), 131–135.

Rubin, A., & Parrish, D. (2007). Challenges to the future of evidence-based practice in social work education. *Journal of Social Work Education, 43*(3), 405–428.

Saari, C. (1986). *Clinical social work treatment: How does it work?* New York: Gardner Press.

Sabatino, C. A. (2009). School social work consultation and collaboration. In C. R. Massat, R. Constable, S. McDonald & J. P. Flynn (Eds.), *School social work: Practice, policy, and research* (7th ed., pp. 336–402). Chicago, IL: Lyceum.

Sabatino, C. A., Mayer, L. M., & Timberlake, E. M. (2006). The effectiveness of school social work practice. In R. Constable, C. Massat, S. McDonald, & J. Flynn (Eds.), *School social work: Practice, policy, and research.* Chicago: Lyceum.

Sackett, D. L., Rosenberg, W. M. C., Gray, J. A. M., Haynes, R. B., & Richardson, W. D. (1996). Evidence based medicine: What it is and what it isn't. *British Medical Journal, 312,* 71–72.

Sackett, D. L., Strauss, S. E., Richardson, W. S., Rosenberg, W., & Haynes, R. B. (2000). *Evidence-based medicine: How to practice and teach EBM* (2nd ed.). Edinburgh: Churchill Livingstone.

Sailor, W., Dunlap, G., Sugai, G., & Horner, R. (Eds.). (2009). *Handbook of positive behavior support: Issues in clinical child psychology.* New York: Springer.

Saint-Laurent, L., & Giasson, J. (2005). Effects of a family literacy program adapting parental intervention to first graders' evolution of reading and writing abilities. *Journal of Early Childhood Literacy, 5*(3), 253–278.

Saltzman, W. R., Layne, C. M., Steinberg, A. M., & Pynoos, R. S. (2006). Trauma/grief-focused group psychotherapy with adolescents. In L. A. Stein, H. I. Spitz, G. M. Burlingame, & P. R.

Muskin (Eds.), *Psychological effects of catastrophic disasters: Group approaches to treatment* (pp. 609–729). New York: Haworth.

Saltzman, W. R., Steinberg, A. M., Layne, C. M., Aisenberg, E., & Pynoos, R. S. (2001). A developmental approach to school-based treatment of adolescents exposed to trauma and traumatic loss. *Journal of Child & Adolescent Group Therapy, 11*(2–3), 43–56.

SAMHSA (Substance Abuse and Mental Health Services Administration), National Registry of Evidence-based Programs and Practices. (2006, October). [Review of] Coping Cat. Retrieved May 19, 2008, from http://www.nrepp.samhsa.gov/programfulldetails.asp?PROGRAM_ID=82.

SAMHSA (Substance Abuse and Mental Health Services Administration), National Registry of Evidence-based Programs and Practices. (2007a, August). [Review of] Incredible Years. Retrieved May 19, 2008, from http://www.nrepp.samhsa.gov/programfulldetails.asp?PROGRAM_ID=131.

SAMHSA (Substance Abuse and Mental Health Services Administration). (2007b). National mental health information center: Anxiety disorders. Retrieved August 20, 2007, from http://mentalhealth.samhsa.gov/publications/allpubs/ken98–0045/default.asp.

SAMHSA (Substance Abuse and Mental Health Services Administration), U.S. Department of Health & Human Services. (2008). National registry of evidence-based programs and practices. Retrieved January 12, 2009, from: http://nrepp.samhsa.gov/find.asp.

Sanetti, L. M. H. (2006). *The effects of the Treatment Integrity Planning Protocol (TIPP) on the implementation and effectiveness of the Good Behavior Game.* Ph.D. dissertation, University of Wisconsin–Madison. Retrieved January 9, 2009, from Dissertations & Theses: Full Text database. (Publication No. AAT 3234742)

Santelli, J., Ott, M. A., Lyon, M., Rogers, J., Summers, D., & Schleifer, R. (2006). Abstinence and abstinence-only education: A review of U.S. policies and programs. *Journal of Adolescent Health 38*(1), 72–81.

Satake, H., Yamashita, H., & Yoshida, K. (2004). The family psychosocial characteristics of children with Attention-Deficit Hyperactivity Disorder with or without oppositional or conduct problems in Japan. *Child Psychiatry & Human Development, 34*(3), 219–235.

Sax L., & Kautz, K. J. (2003). Who first suggests the diagnosis of attention deficit/hyperactivity disorder? *Annals of Family Medicine, 1,* 171–174.

Schachar, R., Jadad, A. R., Gauld, M., Boyle, M., Booker, L., Snider, A., Kim, M., & Cunnunigham, C. (2002). Attention-deficit hyperactivity disorder: Critical appraisal of extended treatment studies. *Canadian Journal of Psychiatry, 47,* 337–348.

Schippers, A. P. (2005). A self-evaluation instrument for support plans. *Journal of Intellectual Disability Research, 49*(10), 806–808.

Schneider, B. H. (1992). Didactic methods for enhancing children's peer relations: A quantitative review. *Clinical Psychology Review, 12*(3), 363–382.

Schneider, B. H., & Byrne, B. M. (1985). Children's social skills training: A meta-analysis. In B. H. Schneider, K. H. Rubin, & J. E. Ledingham (Eds.), *Children's peer relations: Issues in assessment and intervention* (pp. 175–192). New York: Springer-Verlag.

Schneider, H., & Eisenberg, D. (2006). Who receives a diagnosis of attention-deficit/hyperactivity disorder in the United States elementary school population? *Pediatrics, 117,* 601–609.

School Social Work Association of America. (2005). State-by-state information on school social workers. Retrieved January 10, 2005, from www.schoolsocialworkersaa.org.

Schurink, I., Schippers, G. M., & deWildt, W. A. J. M. (2004). Family therapy in treating adolescents with substance abuse problems: A review of the literature. [Dutch] *Gedrag & Gezondheid: Tijdschrift voor Psychologie en Gezondheid, 32*(3), 203–214.

Schutt, R. K. (2004). *Investigating the social world: The process and practice of research.* Thousand Oaks, CA: Pine Forge Press.

Schutz, A. (2006). Home is a prison in the global city: The tragic failure of school-based community engagement strategies. *Review of Educational Research, 76*, 691–743.

Schwandt, T. A. (1996). Farewell to criteriology. *Qualitative Inquiry, 2*(1), 1–7.

Scott, C. C. (2001). The sisterhood group: A culturally focused empowerment group model for inner city African-American youth. *Journal of Child & Adolescent Group Therapy, 11*(2–3), 77–85.

Scott, T. M., Anderson, C. M., Mancil, R., & Alter, P. (2009). Function-based supports for individual students in school settings. In W. Sailor, G. Dunlap, G. Sugai, & H. F. Horner (Eds.), *Handbook of positive behavior support: Issues in clinical child psychology* (pp. 421–441). New York: Springer.

Scott, T. M., McIntyre, J., Liaupsin, C. J., Nelson, C. M., Conroy, M. A., & Payne, L. D. (2005). An examination of the relation between functional behavior assessment and selected intervention strategies with school-based teams. *Journal of Positive Behavior Interventions, 7*(4), 205–215.

Scruggs, T. E., & Mastropieri, M. A. (1998). Summarizing single-subject research: Issues and applications. *Behavior Modification, 22*(3), 221–242.

Seligman, M. (1995). *The optimistic child.* New York: Harper Paperbacks.

Senechal, M. (2006). *The effect of family literacy interventions on children's acquisition of reading from kindergarten to grade 3. A meta-analytic review.* Washington, DC: National Institute for Literacy.

Shadish, W., & Myers, D. (2004). *Campbell Collaboration research design policy brief.* Retrieved May 19, 2009, from http://camp.ostfold.net/artman2/uploads/1/Research_Design_Policy_Brief.pdf.

Shaffer, G. L. (2006). Promising school social work practices of the 1920s: Reflections for today. *Children & Schools, 28*(4), 243–251.

Shank, G., & Villella, O. (2004). Building on new foundations: Core principles and new directions for qualitative research. *Journal of Educational Research, 98*(1), 46–55.

Shapiro, E. S. (1996). Academic skills problems: Direct assessment and intervention (2nd ed.). New York: Guilford Press.

Shapiro, E. S. (2004). *Academic skills problems workbook* (rev. ed.). New York: Guilford Press.

Shapiro, M. S. (1998). An integrative group approach to enhance social competence in a rural elementary school. *Dissertation Abstracts International, 59/6-B*, 3125. (University Microfilms No. AAT98-36036)

Sharpnack, J. D. (2001). *The efficacy of group bereavement interventions: An integrative review of the research literature.* Unpublished doctoral dissertation, Utah State University, Logan, UT. UMI number: 9999114.

Shechtman, Z., & Nachsol, R. (1996). A school-based intervention to reduce aggressive behavior in maladjusted adolescents. *Journal of Applied Developmental Psychology, 17*(4), 535–552.

Sheldon, S. B., & Epstein, J. L. (2002). Improving student behavior and school discipline with family and community involvement. *Education and Urban Society, 35*, 4–26.

Sheridan, S. M., Hungelmann, A., & Maughan, D. P. (1999). A contextualized framework for social skills assessment, intervention, and generalization. *School Psychology Review, 28*(1), 84–103.

Shlonsky, A., & Gibbs, L. (2006). Will the real evidence-based practice please stand up? Teaching the process of evidence-based practice to the helping professions. In A. R. Roberts & K. R. Yeager (Eds.), *Foundations of evidence-based practice* (pp. 103–121). New York: Oxford University Press.

Sholomskas, D. E., Syracuse-Siewart, G., Rounsaville, B. J., Ball, S. A., Nuro, K. F., & Carroll, K. M. (2005). We don't train in vain: A dissemination trial of three strategies of training clinicians in cognitive-behavioral therapy. *Journal of Consulting & Clinical Psychology, 73*(1), 106–115.

Shriver, T. P., & Weissberg, R. P. (2005, August 16). No emotion left behind. *New York Times,* p. 31.

Shure, M. B. (2000). *I Can Problem Solve: An interpersonal cognitive problem-solving program* (2nd ed.). Champaign, IL: Research Press.

Shure, M. B., & Spivack, G. (1980). Interpersonal problem solving as a mediator of behavioral adjustment in preschool and kindergarten children. *Journal of Applied Developmental Psychology, 1*(1), 29–44.

Shure, M. B., & Spivack, G. (1982). Interpersonal problem-solving in young children: A cognitive approach to prevention. *American Journal of Community Psychology, 10*(3), 341–356.

Sinclair, M. F., Christenson, S. L., Evelo, D. L., & Hurley, C. M. (1998). Dropout prevention for youth with disabilities: Efficacy of a sustained school engagement procedure. *Exceptional Children, 65*(1), 7–21.

Sink, C. A., & Spencer, L. R. (2007). Teacher version of the My Class Inventory-Short Form: An accountability tool for elementary school counselors. *Professional School Counseling, 11*(2), 129–139.

Sink, C. A., & Spencer, L. R. (2005). My Class Inventory-Short Form as an accountability tool for elementary school counselors to measure classroom climate. *Professional School Counseling, 9*(1), 37–48.

Sipple, J. W., & Banach, L. (2006). Helping schools meet the mandates of federal policies: No Child Left Behind and other cutting-edge federal policies. In C. Franklin, M. Harris, & P. Allen-Meares (Eds.), *School services sourcebook*. New York: Oxford University Press.

Sirvani, H. (2007). The effect of teacher communication with parents on students' mathematics achievement. *American Secondary Education, 36*(1), 31–46.

Siu, A. M-H (2003). Interpersonal competence, family functioning, and parent-adolescent conflicts. *Dissertation Abstracts International Section A: Humanities & Social Sciences, 63*(10-A), p. 3733.

Skiba, R., Rausch, M. K., & Ritter, S. (2004). Children left behind: Series summary and recommendations. *Education Policy Briefs, 2,* Center for Evaluation and Education Policy. Indiana University, Bloomington, IN.

Skitka, L. J., & Frazier, M. (1995). Ameliorating the effects of parental divorce: Do small group interventions work? *Journal of Divorce and Remarriage, 24*(3), 159–180.

Slawson, D. C., & Shaughnessy, A. F. (2005). Teaching evidence-based medicine: Should we be teaching information management instead? *Academic Medicine, 80*(7), 685–689.

Slee, P. T., & Mohyla, J. (2007). The peace pact: An evaluation of interventions to reduce bullying in four Australian primary schools. *Educational Research, 49*(2), 103–103.

Sloboda, Z., & David, S. L. (1997). *Preventing drug use among children and adolescents.* Washington, DC: National Institute on Drug Abuse.

Smith, J. D., Schneider, B., Smith, P. K., & Ananiadou, K. (2004). The effectiveness of whole-school anti-bullying programs: A synthesis of evaluation research. *School Psychology Review, 33,* 548–561.

Smith P. K., Morita Y., Junger-Tas J., Olweus D., Catalano R., & Slee, P. (1999). *The nature of school bullying: A cross-national perspective.* London: Routledge.

Smith, P. K., Pepler, D., & Rigby, K. (2004). *Bullying in schools: How successful can interventions be?* Cambridge, UK: Cambridge University Press.

Smith, Rosa. (2004). Saving black boys. *American Prospect, 15*(2), 49–50.

Smokowski, P. R., Fraser, M. W., Day, S. H., Galinsky, M. J., & Bacallao, M. L. (2004). School-based skills training to prevent aggressive behavior and peer rejection in childhood: Evaluating the Making Choices program. *Journal of Primary Prevention, 25*(2), 233–251.

Smolkowski, K., Biglan, A., Barrera, M., Taylor, T., Black, C., & Blair, J. (2005). Schools and homes in partnership (SHIP): Long-term effects of preventive intervention focused on social behavior and reading skill in early elementary school. *Prevention Science, 6* (2), 113–125.

Snider, V. E., Frankenberger, W., & Aspenson, M. R. (2000). The relationship between learning disabilities and attention deficit hyperactivity disorder: A national survey. *Developmental Disabilities Bulletin, 28,* 18–38.

Soydan, H., Nye, C., ChacÓn-Moscoso, S., SÁnchez-Meca, J., & Almeida, C. (2005). Families and Schools Together (FAST) for improving outcomes of school-aged children and their families. Campbell Collaboration, Campbell Library of Systematic Reviews.

Specht, H., & Courtney, M. (1994). *Unfaithful angels: How social work has abandoned its mission.* New York: Free Press.

Spoth, R., Randall, G. K., & Shin, C. (2008). Increasing school success through partnership-based family competency training: Experimental study of long-term outcomes. *School Psychology Quarterly, 23*(1), 70–89.

Sprague, J., Colvin, G., & Irvin, L. (1995). *The Oregon School Safety Survey.* Eugene: University of Oregon.

Sprague, J. R., & Horner, R. H. (2006). Schoolwide positive behavioral supports. In S. Jimerson, R. Furlong, & M. Furlong (Eds.), *Handbook of school violence and school safety: From research to practice* (pp. 413–427). Mahwah, NJ: Lawrence Erlbaum.

Sprott, J. B., Jenkins, J. M., & Doob, A. N. (2005). The importance of school: Protecting at-risk youth from early offending. *Youth Violence and Juvenile Justice, 3*(1), 59–79.

Stallard, P., Simpson, N., Anderson, S., Hibbert, S., & Osborn, C. (2007). The FRIENDS Emotional Health Programme: Initial findings from a school-based project. *Child and Adolescent Mental Health, 12*(1), 32–37.

Stark, K. D., Hoke, J., Ballatore, M., Valdez, C., Scammaca, N., & Griffin, J. (2005). Treatment of child and adolescent depressive disorders. In E. D. Hibbs & P. S. Jensen (Eds.), *Psychosocial treatments for child and adolescent disorders: Empirically based strategies for clinical practice* (2nd ed., pp. 239–265). Washington, DC: American Psychological Association.

Stark, K. D., Schnoebelen, S., Simpson, J., Hargrave, J., Glenn, R., & Molnar, J. (2004a). *Treating depressed children: Therapist manual for ACTION.* Ardmore, PA: Workbook Publishing.

Stark, K. D., Schnoebelen, S., Simpson, J., Hargrave, J., Glenn, R., & Molnar, J. (2004b). *ACTION Workbook*. Ardmore, PA: Workbook Publishing.

Stassen Berger, K. (2007). Update on bullying at school: Science forgotten? *Developmental Review, 27*(1), 90–90.

Staudt, M. (1997). Correlates of job satisfaction in school social work. *Social Work in Education, 19* (1), 43–52.

Staudt, M., Cherry, D. J., & Watson, M. (2005). Practice guidelines for school social workers: A modified replication of a prototype. *Children & Schools, 27*(2), 71–81.

Staudt, M. M., Dulmus, C., & Bennett, G. A. (2003). Facilitating writing by practitioners: Survey of practitioners who have published. *Social Work, 48*(1), 75–83.

Steele, R. G., Elkin, T. D., & Roberts, M. C. (Eds.). (2008). *Handbook of evidence-based therapies for children and adolescents: Bridging science and practice.* New York: Springer.

Stein, B. D., Jaycox, L. H., Kataoka, S. H., Wong, M., Tu, W., Elliott, M. N., & Fink, A. (2003). A mental health intervention for schoolchildren exposed to violence: A randomized controlled trial. *JAMA: Journal of the American Medical Association, 290*(5), 603–611.

Stern, S. B. (2004). Evidence-based practice with antisocial and delinquent youth: The key role of family and multisystemic intervention. In H. E. Briggs & T. L. Rzepnicki (Eds.), *Using evidence in social work practice: Behavioral perspectives* (pp. 104–127). Chicago: Lyceum.

Stevens, J. W. (1999). Creating collaborative partnerships: Clinical intervention research in an inner-city middle school. *Social Work in Education, 21*(3), 151–162.

Stewart, M. S. (1998). The effects of school-based counseling intervention on adolescent stress: An exploratory study. Ph.D. dissertation, Seattle Pacific University, Washington. Retrieved October 30, 2008, from Dissertations & Theses: Full Text database. (Publication No. AAT 9912170)

Stoep, A.V., Weiss, N.S., Kuo, E.S., Cheney, D., Cohen, P. (2003). What proportion of failure to complete secondary school in the US population is attributable to adolescent psychiatric disorder? *Journal of Behavioral Health Research 30* (1), 119–124.

Stolberg, A., & Mahler, J. (1994). Enhancing treatment gains in a school-based intervention for children of divorce. *Journal of Consulting and Clinical Psychology, 62*(1), 147–156.

Stone, S., & Gambrill, E. (2007). Do school social work texts provide a sound guide for practice and policy? *Children & Schools, 29*(2), 109–118.

Strom, R. E., & Boster, F. J. (2007). Dropping out of high school: A meta-analysis assessing the effect of messages in the home and in school. *Communication Education, 56*(4), 433–452.

Sugai, G., & Horner, R. H. (2008). What we know and need to know about preventing problem behavior in schools. *Exceptionality, 16,* 67–77.

Sugai, G., Horner, R. H., Dunlap, G., Hieneman, M., Lewis, T. J., Nelson, C. M., et al. (1999). *Applying positive behavior support and functional behavioral assessment in school: Technical assistance guide.* Center on Positive Behavioral Interventions and Support (OSEP), Washington, DC.. Retrieved on March 15, 2009 from http://www.cde.state.co.us/cdesped/download/pdf/FBA-PBS_TA_Guide.pdf.

Sun, W., Skara, S., Sun, P., Dent, C. W., & Sussman, S. (2006). Project Towards No Drug Abuse: Long-term substance abuse outcomes evaluation. *Preventive Medicine, 42*(3), 188–192.

Sundarararjan, L. (2002). Humanistic psychotherapy and the scientist-practitioner debate: An "embodied" perspective. *Journal of Humanistic Psychology, 42*(2), 34–47.

Swearer, S. M., Espelage, D. L., & Napolitano, S. A. (2009). *Bullying prevention and intervention: Realistic strategies for schools.* New York: Guilford Press.

Sylva, K., Scott, S., Totsika, V., Ereky-Stevens, K., & Crook, C. (2008). Training parents to help their children read: A randomized control trial. *British Journal of Educational Psychology, 78* (3), 435–455.

Tarshis, T. P., & Huffman, L. C. (2007). Psychometric properties of the Peer Interactions in Primary School (PIPS) questionnaire. *Journal of Developmental & Behavioral Pediatrics, 28*(2), 125–132.

Taylor, I., O'Reilly, M., & Lancioni, G. (1996). An evaluation of an ongoing consultation model to train teachers to treat challenging behaviour. *International Journal of Disability, Development, and Education, 43*(3), 203–218.

Teasley, M. (2006). Effective treatments for attention deficit disorder. In C. Franklin, M. Harris, & P. Allen-Meares (Eds.), *School services sourcebook* (pp. 45–55). New York: Oxford University Press.

Teasley, M., Baffour, T. D., & Tyson, E. H. (2005). Perceptions of cultural competence among urban school social workers: Does experience make a difference? *Children & Schools, 27*(4), 227–236.

Tellerman, J. S. (2001). The Solutions Unlimited Now-SUN program: Psychodynamic/cognitive structured groups for teens, pre-teens, and families. *Journal of Child & Adolescent Group Therapy, 11*(4), 117–134.

Terzian, M. A. (2007). Preventing aggressive behavior by promoting information-processing skills: A theory-based evaluation of the Making Choices program. Ph.D. dissertation, University of North Carolina at Chapel Hill. Retrieved August 7, 2009, from Dissertations & Theses: Full text database. (Publication no. AAT 3262618)

Thomas, A., & Grimes, J. (2002). *Best practices in school psychology IV* (Vols. 1 and 2). Bethesda, MD: National Association of School Psychologists.

Thyer, B. A. (2004). Science and evidence-based social work practice. In H. E. Briggs & T. L. Rzepnicki (Eds.), *Using evidence in social work practice: Behavioral perspectives* (pp. 74–89). Chicago: Lyceum.

Thyer, B. A., & Myers, L. L. (1999). On science, antiscience, and the client's right to effective treatment. *Social Work, 44*(5), 501–504.

Tillitski, C. J. (1990). A meta-analysis of estimated effect sizes for group versus individual versus control treatments. *International Journal of Group Psychotherapy, 40*(2), 215–224.

Todd, A. W., Campbell, A. L., Meyer, G. G., & Horner, R. H. (2008). The effects of a targeted intervention to reduce problem behaviors: Elementary implementation of Check In-Check Out. *Journal of Positive Behavior Interventions, 10*(1), 46–55.

Tolan, P., Gorman-Smith, D., & Henry, D. (2004). Supporting families in a high-risk setting: Proximal effects of the SAFEChildren preventive intervention. *Journal of Consulting & Clinical Psychology, 72*(5), 855–869.

Tolan, P., & Guerra, N. (1995). *What works in reducing adolescent violence: An empirical review of the field.* Monograph prepared for the Center for the Study and Prevention of Youth Violence. Boulder: University of Colorado.

Tolan, P., Guerra, N., & Kendall, P. (1995). A developmental-ecological perspective on antisocial behavior in children and adolescents: Toward a unified risk and intervention framework. *Journal of Consulting and Clinical Psychology, 63*(4), 579–584.

Tolan, P., & McKay, M. M. (1996). Preventing serious antisocial behavior in inner-city children: An empirically-based family intervention program. *Family Relations, 45*(2), 148–155.

Toldson, I. A., Harrison, M. G., Perine, R., Carreiro, P., & Caldwell, L. D. (2006). Assessing the impact of family process on rural African American adolescents' competence and behavior using latent growth curve analysis. *Journal of Negro Education, 75*(3), 430–442.

Toplis, R., & Hadwin, J. A. (2006). Using social stories to change problematic lunchtime behaviour in school. *Educational Psychology in Practice, 22*(1), 53–67.

Toren, N. (1969). Semi-professionalism and social work: A theoretical perspective In A. Etzioni (Ed.), *The semi-professions and their organization: Teachers, nurses, and social workers.* New York: Free Press.

Torgerson, C. (2003). *Systematic reviews.* New York: Continuum.

Torres, A. (1998). The status of school social work. In E. Freeman & C. Franklin (Eds.), *Multisystem skills and interventions in school social work practice.* Washington, DC: NASW Press.

Totton, N. (1999). The baby and the bathwater: "Professionalisation" in psychotherapy and counseling. *British Journal of Guidance & Counselling, 27*(3), 313–324.

Tracy, E., & Usaj, K. (2007). School social work with individuals and small groups. In L. Bye & M. Alvarez (Eds.), *School social work: theory to practice* (pp. 141–163). Belmont, CA: Brooks/Cole.

Trenholm, C., Devaney, B., Fortson, K., Quay, L., Wheeler, J., & Clark, M. (2007, April). Impacts of four Title V, Section 510 abstinence education programs: Final report. Retrieved on April 6, 2009 from http://74.125.155.132/scholar?q=cache:9nuLs2ey3LAJ:scholar.google.com/&hl=en

Turner, W. (2000). Cultural considerations in family-based primary prevention programs in drug abuse. *Journal of Primary Prevention, 21*(2), 285–303.

United States House Committee on Education and the Workforce. (2001, October 21). *Overidentification issues within the Individuals with Disabilities Education Act and the need for reform.* (ED Publication No. 473013). Washington, DC: U.S. Government Printing Office.

U.S. Department of Education. (2005). *Information on No Child Left Behind.* Retrieved January 12, 2006, from www.ed.gov.

U.S. Department of Education, Office of Special Education and Rehabilitative Services. (2006a, August 14). Assistance to states for the education of children with disabilities and preschool grants for children with disabilities: Final rule. 34CFR Parts 300 and 301. *Federal Register, 71* (156), 46540–46845.

U.S. Department of Education. (2006b, September 21). [WWC Intervention report] Check & Connect. Retrieved August 28, 2008, from http://ies.ed.gov/ncee/wwc/pdf/WWC_Check_Connect_092106.pdf.

U.S. Department of Education (2008a, July). [WWC Intervention report] Accelerated middle schools. Retrieved August 7, 2008, from http://ies.ed.gov/ncee/wwc/pdf/WWC_AccelMiddleSch_070808.pdf.

U.S. Department of Education, Institute of Education Sciences (2008b, December). What works: Clearinghouse procedures and standards handbook. Retrieved May 19, 2009, from http://ies.ed.gov/ncee/wwc/pdf/wwc_procedures_v2_standards_handbook.pdf.

U.S. Department of Health & Human Services, National Registry of Evidence-based Programs and Practices (2008). *Quality of research,* from http://www.nrepp.samhsa.gov/

Utay, J. M., & Lampe, R. E. (1995). Use of a group counseling game to enhance social skills of children with learning disabilities. *Journal for Specialists in Group Work, 20*(2), 114–120.

Valente, T. W., Ritt-Olson, A., Stacy, A., Unger, J. B., Okamoto, J., & Sussman, S. (2007). Peer acceleration: Effects of a social network tailored substance abuse prevention program among high-risk adolescents. *Addiction, 102*(11), 1804–1815.

Valentine, J. C., & Cooper, H. (2003). *Effect size substantive interpretation guidelines: Issues in the interpretation of effect sizes.* Washington, DC: What Works Clearinghouse. Retrieved September 24, 2007, from http://ies.ed.gov/ncee/wwc/pdf/essig.pdf.

Van Acker, R., Boreson, L., Gable, R. A., & Potterton, T. (2005). Are we on the right course? Lessons learned about current FBA/BIP practices in schools. *Journal of Behavioral Education, 14*(1), 35–56.

Vanderbleek, L. M. (2004). Engaging families in school-based mental health treatment. *Journal of Mental Health Counseling, 26*(3), 211–225.

Van Voorhis, F. L. (2003). Interactive homework in middle school: Effects on family involvement and science achievement. *Journal of Educational Research, 96*, 323–338.

Vazsonyi, A. T., Belliston, L. M., & Flannery, D. J. (2004). Evaluation of a school-based, universal violence prevention program: Low-, medium-, and high-risk children. *Youth Violence & Juvenile Justice, 2*(2), 185–206.

Verschueren, K., Buyck, P., & Marcoen, A. (2001). Self-representations and socioemotional competence in young children: A 3-year longitudinal study. *Developmental Psychology, 37*(1), 126–134.

Volpe, R. J., DiPerna, J. C., Hintze, J. M., & Shapiro, E. S. (2005). Observing students in classroom settings: A review of seven coding schemes. *School Psychology Review, 34*(4), 454–474.

Vreeman, R. C., & Carroll, A. E. (2007). A systematic review of school-based interventions to prevent bullying. *Archives of Pediatrics and Adolescent Medicine, 161*, 78–88.

Wagner, E. F., & Macgowan, M. J. (2006). School-based group treatment for adolescent substance abuse. In H. A. Liddle & C. L. Rowe (Eds.), *Adolescent substance abuse: Research and clinical advances* (pp. 333–356). New York: Cambridge University Press.

Wagner, S. L., & Beaumont, S. L. (2007). Evaluating the efficacy of a social competency program: Reducing adolescents' intentions to use substances during future pregnancy. In A. Columbus (Ed.), *Advances in Psychology Research, 38*, 93–116.

Walker, H. M. (1988). *The Walker social skills curriculum: The ACCESS program, adolescent curriculum for communication & effective social skills.* Austin, TX: Pro-Ed.

Walker, H. M. (1998). First steps to prevent antisocial behavior. *Teaching Exceptional Children, 30* (4) (Special issue on Discipline), 16–19.Walker, H. (2001). *School safety issues and prevention strategies: The changing landscape of what we know.* Eugene, OR: Institute on Violence and Destructive Behavior.

Walker, H. M. (2002). The First Step to Success program: Preventing destructive social outcomes at the point of school entry. In P. S. Jensen (Ed.), *Report on Emotional & Behavioral Disorders in Youth, 3*(1), 3–6, 22–23.

Walker, H. (2004). Commentary: Use of evidence-based interventions in schools: Where we've been, where we are, and where we need to go. *School Psychology Review, 33*(3), 398–407.

Walker, H. M., Golly, A. M., McLane, J. Z., & Kimmich, M. (in press). The Oregon First Step to Success initiative: State-wide results of an evaluation of the First Step to Success program's impact. *Journal of Emotional and Behavioral Disorders.*

Walker, H. M., & Gresham, F. M. (2003). School-related behavior disorders. In W. M. Reynolds & G. Miller (Eds.), *Handbook of psychology: Educational psychology* (Vol. 7, pp. 511–530). New York: Wiley.

Walker, H., Horner, R. H., Sugai, G., Bullis, M., Sprauge, J. R., Bricker, D., et al. (1996). Integrated approaches to preventing antisocial behavior patterns among school-age children and youth. *Journal of Emotional & Behavioral Disorders, 4,* 193–256.

Walker, H. M., Irvin, L., Noell, J., & Singer, G. (1992). A construct score approach to the assessment of social competence: Rationale, technological considerations, and anticipated outcomes. *Behavior Modification, 16*(4), 448–474.

Walker, H. M., Kavanagh, K., Stiller, B., Golly, A., Severson, H. H., & Feil, E. G. (1998). First Step to Success: An early intervention approach for preventing school antisocial behavior. *Journal of Emotional and Behavioral Disorders, 6*(2), 66–80.

Walker, H. M., McConnell, S., Holmese, D., Todis, B., Walker, J., & Golden, N. (1988). *The Walker social skills curriculum: The ACCEPTS program, a curriculum for children's effective peer & teacher skills.* Austin, TX: Pro-Ed.

Walker, H., & Severson, H. H. (1990). *Systematic screening for behavior disorders (SSBD): User's guide and technical manual.* Longmont, CO: Sopris West.

Walker, H. M., Stiller, B., & Golly, A. (1998). First Step to Success: A collaborative home-school intervention for preventing antisocial behavior at the point of school entry. *Young Exceptional Children, 1*(2), 2–6.

Walker, H. M., Stiller, B., Golly, A., Kavanagh, K., Severson, H. H., & Feil, E. G. (1997). *First Step to Success: Helping young children overcome antisocial behavior* (Vol. 6). Longmont, CO: Sopris West.

Walker, H. M., Stiller, B., Severson, H. H., & Golly, A. (1998). First Step to Success: Intervening at the point of school entry to prevent antisocial behavior patterns. *Psychology in the Schools, 35* (3), 259–269.

Walker, H. W., Ramsey, E., & Gresham, F. M. (2004). Antisocial behavior in school: Evidenced-based practices (2nd ed.). Belmont, CA: Wadsworth.

Walker, J. S., Briggs, H. E., Koroloff, N., & Friesen, B. J. (2007). Implementing and sustaining evidence-based practice in social work. *Journal of Social Work Education, 43*(3), 361–375.

Wallerstein, J. S. (1983) Children of divorce: The psychological tasks of the child. *American Journal of Orthopsychiatry 53*(2), 230–243.

Wampold, B. E. (2001). *The great psychotherapy debate: Models, methods and findings.* Mahwah, NJ: Lawrence Erlbaum.

Waterman, J. & Walker, E. (2001). Helping at-risk students: A group counseling approach for grades 6-9. New York: Guilford Press.

Watkins, A., & Kurtz, P. D. (2001). Using solution-focused intervention to address African-American male overrepresentation in special education: A case study. *Children & Schools, 23*(4), 223–234.

Webb, L., & Myrick, R. (2003). A group counseling intervention for children with Attention Deficit Hyperactivity Disorder. *Professional School Counseling, 7*(2), 108–115.

Webb, S. A. (2001). Some considerations on the validity of evidence-based practice in social work. *British Journal of Social Work 31*(1), 57–79.

Webster-Stratton, C., Reid, M. J., & Hammond, M. (2001). Preventing conduct problems, promoting social competence: A parent and teacher training partnership in Head Start. *Journal of Clinical Child Psychology, 30,* 283–302.

Webster-Stratton, C., Reid, M. J., & Stoolmiller, M. (2008). Preventing conduct problems and improving school readiness: Evaluation of the Incredible Years teacher and child training programs in high-risk schools. *Journal of Child Psychology and Psychiatry, 49*(5), 471–488.

Webster-Stratton, C., & Taylor, T. (2001). Nipping early risk factors in the bud: Preventing substance abuse, delinquency, and violence in adolescence through interventions targeted at young children (0–8 years). *Prevention Science, 2*, 165–192.

Weiss, B., Caron, A., Ball, S., Tapp, J., Johnson, M., & Weisz, J. R. (2005). Iatrogenic effects of group treatment for antisocial youth. *Journal of Community and Clinical Psychology, 73*(6), 1036–1044.

Weiss, M., & Harris, S. L. (2001). Teaching social skills to people with autism. *Behavior Modification, 25*(5), 785–802.

Weissberg, R., & Durlak, J. (2007). SEL Meta-analysis. Retrieved August 15, 2007, from http://www.casel.org/sel/meta.php.

Weisz, J. R., Jensen-Doss, A., & Hawley, K. M. (2006). Evidence-based youth psychotherapies versus usual clinical care: A meta-analysis of direct comparisons. *American Psychologist, 61*(7), 671–689.

Weller, A. C. (2001). *Editorial peer review: Its strengths and weaknesses.* Medford, NJ: American Society for Information Science and Technology.

Wendt, D. C., & Slife, B. D. (2007). Is evidence-based practice diverse enough? Philosophy of science considerations. *American Psychologist 62*(6), 613–614.

Werch, C. E., & Owen, D. M. (2002). Iatrogenic effects of alcohol and drug prevention programs. *Journal of Studies on Alcohol, 63*(5), 581–590.

West, S. L., & O'Neal, K. K. (2004). Project D.A.R.E. outcome effectiveness revisited. *American Journal of Public Health, 94*(6), 1027–1029.

Westen, D., Novotny, C. M., & Thompson-Brenner, H. (2005). EBP • EST: Reply to Crits-Christroph et al. (2005) and Weisz et al. (2005). *Psychological Bulletin, 131*(3), 427–433.

Whipple, D. L. (2007) Effectiveness of social competence promotion on disruptive behavior: A quantitative review. Ph.D. dissertation, University of Rhode Island. Retrieved December 30, 2008, from Dissertations & Theses: Full Text database. (Publication No. AAT 3277010)

White, N. J., & Rayle, A. D. (2007). Strong teens: A school-based small group experience for African American males. *Journal for Specialists in Group Work, 32*(2), 178–189.

White, T. G., & Kim, J. S. (2008). Teacher and parent scaffolding of voluntary summer reading. *Reading Teacher, 62*(2), 116–125.

Whitfield, G. W. (1999). Validating school social work: An evaluation of a cognitive-behavioral approach to reduce school violence. *Research on Social Work Practice, 9*(4), 399–426.

Wiggins, J. E. (2005). [Book review] Helping at-risk students: A group counseling approach for grades 6–9. *School Social Work Journal, 30*(1), 85–87.

Williams, C., Griffin, K. W., Macaulay, A. P., West, T. L., & Gronewold, E. (2005). Efficacy of a drug prevention CD-ROM intervention for adolescents. *Substance Use & Misuse, 40*(6), 869–878.

Wilson, S. J., & Lipsey, M. W. (2006a). *The effects of school-based social information processing interventions on aggressive behavior: Part I–Universal programs.* Campbell Collaboration, Norway.

Wilson, S. J., & Lipsey, M. W. (2006b, March 13). The effects of school-based social information processing: Part II, Selected/indicated pull-out programs. Retrieved May 19, 2008, from

http://www.sfi.dk/graphics/Campbell/reviews/social%20information%20processing.pdf%
202.pdf

Wilson, D. K., Evans, A. E., Williams, J., Mixon, G., Sirard, J. R., & Pate, R. (2005). A preliminary test of a student-centered intervention on increasing physical activity in underserved adolescents. *Annals of Behavioral Medicine, 30*(2), 119–124.

Wilson, N. H., & Rotter, J. C. (1986). Anxiety management training and study skills counseling for students on self-esteem and test anxiety and performance. *School Counselor, 34*(1), 18–31.

Wilson, R. (2001, January 5). A higher bar for earning tenure: Junior faculty members find that they must publish more and publish quickly. *Chronicle of Higher Education,* A12–17.

Winslow, E. B., Wolchik, S. A., & Sander, I. (2004). Preventive interventions for children of divorce. *Psychiatric Times, 21*(2), 45–46.

Winters, W. G., & Easton, F. (1983). *The practice of social work in schools: An ecological perspective.* New York: Free Press.

Witkin, S. L., & Harrison, W. D. (2001). Whose evidence and for what purpose? *Social Work, 46* (4), 293–296.

Wolchik, S. A., Sandler, I.N., Millsap, R.E., Plummer, B.A., Greene, S. M., Anderson, E.R., Dawson-McClure, S.R., Hipke, K., Haine, R. A. (2002). Six-year follow-up of preventive interventions for Children of Divorce. *Journal of the American Medical Association, 288* (15), 1874–1881.

Wolcott, H. F. (1994). On seeking–and rejecting–validity in qualitative research. In H. Wolcott (Ed.), *Transforming qualitative data: Description, analysis, and interpretation* (pp. 337–373). Thousand Oaks, CA: Sage.

Wolraich, M. L., Bickman, L., Lambert, E. W., Simmons, T., & Doffing, M. A. (2005). Intervening to improve communication between parents, teachers, and primary care providers of children with ADHD or at high risk for ADHD. *Journal of Attention Disorders, 9*(1), 354–368.

Wolraich, M. L., Wibbelsman, C. J., Brown, T. (2005). ADHD among adolescents. *Pediatrics, 115* (6), 1734–1745.

Wood, J. J. (2007). Effect of anxiety reduction on children's school performance and social adjustment. *Developmental Psychology, 42*(2), 345–349.

Wood, J. J., Chiu, A. W., Hwang, W., Jacobs, J., & Ifekwunigwe, M. (2008). Adapting cognitive-behavioral therapy for Mexican-American students with anxiety disorders: Recommendations for school psychologists. *School Psychology Quarterly, 23*(4), 515–532.

Woolley, M. E., & Bowen, G. L. (2007). In the context of risk: Supportive adults and the school engagement of middle school students. *Family Relations 56,* 92–104.

Wright, D. B., Mayer, G. R., Cook, C. R., Crews, S. D., Kraemer, B. R., & Gale, B. (2007). A preliminary study on the effects of training using behavior support plan quality evaluation guide (BSP-QE) to improve positive behavior support plans. *Education and Treatment of Children, 30*(3), 89–106.

Yan, W., & Lin, Q. (2005). Effects of class size and length of day on kindergartners' academic achievement: Findings from the Early Childhood Longitudinal Study. *Early Education and Development, 16*(1), 49–68.

Ysseldyke, J. (2001). Reflections on a research career. *Exceptional Children, 67*(3), 295–309.

Zentall, S. S. (2005). Theory and evidence-based strategies for children with attentional problems. *Psychology in the Schools, 42*(8), 821–836.

Zhen, W., & Xue-Rong, L. (2006). A primary study of family environment characters and parental rearing patterns in the middle school students with Oppositional Defiant Disorder. [Chinese]. *Chinese Journal of Clinical Psychology, 14*(2), 175–177.

Zorn, E. (2008, February 16). NIU gunman's baffling trail reveals no motive. *Chicago Tribune*. Retrieved February 18, 2008, from http://www.chicagotribune.com/news/columnists.

INDEX

Note: Page Numbers followed by *f* refers to Figures and *t* refers to Tables.

ABC. *See* Antecedent-behavior-consequence
   recording
ACA. *See* American Counseling Association
Academic Search Premier/EBSCO Host database,
   40, 141, 210
Academic skills training, parent-directed, 73, 74
Accelerated Middle Schools, 55, 177, 199
ACCEPTS, 134, 214
ACTION program, for depressed children, 58
ADHD. *See* Attention deficit hyperactivity
   disorder
Adolescents
   delinquency/school dropout of, 76
   group interventions for, 200–201
   health-risk factors of, 7, 9
African American children, 135–36, 146, 157
Aggression prevention. *See* Violence prevention
Aggression Replacement Training (ART), 133,
   134, 180, 214
Aggressive youth, grouping, 164–65
Allen-Meares, P., 4, 202
American Counseling Association (ACA), 13
American Psychological Association (APA), 26,
   46
   Division 12 taskforce definitions of, 5–6t,
   12, 46
American School Counselor Association
   (ASCA), 13
American School Health Association (ASHA), 13
Answerable questions, in EIP, 26–27, 42, 44,
   53–54, 64
   five types of, 28f
   posing of, 169–71

Antecedent-behavior-consequence (ABC)
   recording, 91, 95, 103
Anxiety disorders, 141–47. *See* also Generalized
   anxiety disorder
   books for, 218–19
   CBT for, 143–45, 146
   clearinghouses/databases for, 218
   conceptual definition of, 141
   Coping Cat for, 54, 143–44, 199
   intervention appraisal of, 142t
   interventions for, 143–45
   SSRIs for, 143
APA. *See* American Psychological Association
ART. *See* Aggression Replacement Training
ASCA. *See* American School Counselor
   Association
ASHA. *See* American School Health Association
ASSET, 132–33, 134, 180, 214, 217
Attention deficit hyperactivity disorder (ADHD),
   43, 44, 72, 145, 148–60
   books/clearinghouses/databases for, 219
   clinical quadrants for, 182, 183t
   conceptual definition of, 149–50
   contextual adaptations for, 158
   cultural/development adaptations for, 157
   intervention appraisal for, 152t
   multimodal treatment for, 151
   outcome evaluation for, 159
   peer tutoring for, 153, 154
   proactive/reactive approaches to, 153
   process evaluation for, 158–59
   psychostimulant medication for, 151, 157
   recommended/emerging interventions for, 151

Attention deficit hyperactivity disorder (ADHD) (*Continued*)
school-based contingency management for, 153
school functioning impairments and, 148–49
self-management/organization training for, 153, 155
Tier 3 interventions for, 156

BASC. *See* Behavioral Assessment System of Children
Bear, G. G., 206, 207
Behavioral Assessment System of Children (BASC), 147, 159
Student Observation System of, 63
Behavior Education Program, 58, 177, 201
Behavior Intervention Plan (BIP), 44, 85, 90–106
books/clearinghouse/databases for, 208–9
conceptual definition of, 90–92
evidence organization/interpretation, 92
intervention appraisal for, 93–94t
Behavior problems, 4, 19, 44, 76–89
BIP. *See* Behavior Intervention Plan
Boolean operators, 32, 33t, 199–200, 205, 211, 214
Bullying prevention, 78, 118–26, 178
books/clearinghouses for, 212
clinical quadrants for, 179t
conceptual definitions of, 119–20
cyberbullying and, 120
databases for, 211
highly recommended/emerging interventions for, 122
intervention appraisal for, 121t

Campbell Collaboration clearinghouse, 32, 44, 199, 202, 203, 204–5, 208, 210, 211, 212, 213, 219
CBT. *See* Cognitive-behavioral therapy (CBT)
Center for the Social and Emotional Foundations for Early Learning, 88, 103
Check and Connect, 55, 58, 177, 199
Child Behavior Checklist, 89, 147
Children of Divorce Intervention Project (CODIP), 109, 110, 115, 116, 178
Children's Support Group (CSG), 109, 115, 116, 178
CISD. *See* Critical Incident Stress Debriefing
CISM. *See* Critical Incident Stress Management
Classroom management-based interventions, 19, 83
Clearinghouse(s), 44, 45, 46, 47
Campbell Collaboration, 32, 44, 199, 202, 203, 204–5, 208, 210, 211, 212, 213, 219

Cochrane Collaboration, 32, 44, 165, 202, 212, 219
NREPP, 32, 44, 81, 111, 115, 141, 143, 199, 205, 208, 210, 211, 212, 218, 219
WWC, 32, 139–40, 141, 199, 204, 205, 208, 212, 213–14, 218, 219
Clinical quadrant, 13–16, 13f, 19, 22, 26, 58–59, 176–78, 177t, 179–80t, 181–82, 182–83, 183t
Cochrane Collaboration clearinghouse, 32, 44, 165, 202, 212, 219
CODIP. *See* Children of Divorce Intervention Project
Cognitive-behavioral therapy (CBT), 49, 54, 143–45, 146
Comer School Development Program, 71, 74
Compliance, 76–89. *See also* Noncompliance
books for, 206–8
clearinghouses for, 204–5
clinical quadrants for, 181–82
databases for, 205–6
EIP of, 78–83
emerging interventions for, 82–83
highly recommended interventions for, 81–82
increasing student, 78
invention appraisal for, 79–80t
recommended (with caution) intervention for, 82
Consistency Management and Cooperative Discipline, 207
Contemporary education models, 9–16
data-based decision making, 13
empirically supported intervention, 12–13
multitiered systems of support and, 10–12
RTI and, 9–10
Content reflections, 72–73, 84, 102, 123, 155–56
Contextual adaptations, 40, 60–61, 145–46
for ADHD, 158
of BIP, 104
in bullying prevention, 124
for compliance, 87–88
in parent involvement, 74
for social skills, 136
Coping Cat program, 54, 143–44, 199
Coping Koala/FRIENDS program, 58, 144
Critical appraisal, 32–34, 54–58
Critical Incident Stress Debriefing (CISD), 165–66, 182
Critical Incident Stress Management (CISM), 165
CSG. *See* Children's Support Group
Cultural adaptations, 60
for ADHD, 157
for anxiety disorders, 146
of BIP, 104
in bullying interventions, 124
for compliance, 86–87

in parent involvement, 74
for social skills, 135–36
Cultural sensitivity, 34, 49–50

Dads for Life (DPL), 111–12, 116
D.A.R.E. *See* Drug Abuse Resistance Education
Database(s), 32, 45
  Academic Search Premier/EBSCO Host, 40,
    141, 210
  ERIC, 40, 44, 171, 203, 205, 208, 209, 214,
    215–16, 220
  PsycINFO, 40, 44, 63, 141, 171, 172, 200, 201,
    205, 208, 210, 211, 215, 216, 218, 219, 220
  PubMed, 30, 44, 47, 219
  Sage Education Full Text, 203
  Social Work Abstracts, 44, 171, 200
Data-based decision making, 13, 21, 26, 186
Demaray, M. K., 62, 137
Department of Education, U. S., 47, 64
  definitions of, 5–6t, 13
  Institute of Education Sciences, 32, 46
  scientifically based research definition by, 54
  studies criteria, 34
Depression, 55, 58, 145
DeRosier, M. E., 54, 131
Developmental adaptations, 49, 145–46
  for ADHD, 157
  of BIP, 103
  for bullying prevention, 124
  for compliance, 85–86
  for divorce/separation of parents, 115–16
  of parent involvement, 73–74
  for social skills, 134
Divorce/separation of parents, 107–17, 178
  books/clearinghouse/databases for, 210–11
  conceptual definition of, 107, 109
  emerging interventions for, 112
  highly recommended interventions for,
    109–10
  intervention appraisal of, 108t
  recommended (with caution) interventions
    for, 110–12
DPL. *See* Dads for Life
Drug Abuse Resistance Education (D.A.R.E.),
  166–67
DuPaul, G. J., 149, 153, 154, 158–59
Dupper, D. R., 13, 16, 24, 207

Early Risers: Skills for Success, 58, 81, 87, 89, 177,
  201, 205
Education Resources Information Center (ERIC)
  database, 40, 44, 171, 203, 205, 208, 209, 214,
  215–16, 220
Effect size (ES), of intervention, 138
EIP. *See* Evidence-informed practice

Empirical knowledge base, 22, 25–26
Empirically supported treatments (ESTs), 12–13,
  19, 53–54
Environmental risk factors, 19, 90
ERIC. *See* Education Resources Information
  Center
ES. *See* Effect size
ESTs. *See* Empirically supported treatments
Evidence
  adaption, 34–35, 42, 48–50, 175–76
  components of, 32f
  critical appraisal of, 32–34, 54–58
  efficiency/investigation and, 28, 31–32, 44–45,
    171–73, 199–202
  organization/interpretation, 46–48, 67–72,
    173–74
  school social worker utilization of, 26
  state/accessibility of, 40
Evidence-based practice (EBP), 26, 127, 204
  for divorce/separation of parents, 107
  process of, 27f
Evidence-informed practice (EIP), 23, 39, 210
  adaptation/application in, 34–35, 42, 48–50,
    175–76
  answerable questions in, 26–28, 28f, 42, 44,
    53–54, 64, 169–71
  as authority-based practice, 37–38
  collaborative effort of, 59
  on compliance, 78–83
  as cookbook practice, 38
  critical appraisal in, 32–34, 54–58
  criticisms of, 37–38
  database search sets for, 171–72
  evidence examination in, 42, 48
  evidence investigation in, 28, 31–32, 44–45,
    171–73, 199–202
  evidence organization/interpretation, 46–48,
    67–72, 173–74
  of grouping aggressive youth, 164
  issue definition in, 42, 43–44
  lessons learned from, 169–87
  outcome evaluation in, 35–36
  practitioner steps of, 42–50
  process reflection in, 42, 102, 123, 155
  school-based prevention/intervention
    research and, 42
  school need for, 3–22
  for school social workers, 42–51
  social validity of, 185–86
  for Tier 2 interventions, 52
Experimental designs, 46, 67

Families and Schools Together (FAST), 72, 73, 74,
  75, 202, 203
FAST. *See* Families and Schools Together

FastTrack, 154, 155
FBA. *See* Functional behavioral assessment
Fidelity, 92, 99, 104, 125, 159
First Step to Success, 81–82, 84, 87, 88, 89, 173, 178
Franklin, C., 90, 202, 207
Frey, A., 13, 16, 24, 207
FRIENDS intervention, 58, 144
Functional behavioral assessment (FBA), 90, 91,
    92, 101–2

GAD. *See* Generalized anxiety disorder
Generalized anxiety disorder (GAD), 141, 147
Gibbs, J., 36, 53–54, 128
Good Behavior Game, 131, 139, 207, 217
Grade retention programs, 165, 182
Gresham, F. M., 128, 159
Grief therapy, for normal grief reactions, 166, 182

Hall, C. J., 37, 39, 40
Harris, M. B., 90, 202, 207
Hispanic children, 135
    ADHD and, 157
    anxiety disorder interventions for, 146
    compliance and, 87

Iatrogenic school-based interventions, 48, 161–68
    aggression/violence prevention program, 165
    authority based practice and, 162
    books/databases for, 220
    CISD, 165–66
    clinical quadrants for, 182
    conceptual definition of, 161–63
    grade retention programs, 165, 182
    grouping aggressive youth, 164–65
    individual grief therapy, for normal grief
        reactions, 166, 182
    "zero tolerance" discipline policy, 167
IDEA. *See* Individuals with Disabilities Education
    Improvement Act
IEPs. *See* Individualized education plans
Incredible Years program, 58, 70, 71, 73, 74,
    75, 81, 87, 88, 89, 131, 134, 181, 199,
    205, 213
Individualized education plans (IEPs), 24, 40, 91,
    170
Individual risk factors, 4, 19, 21
Individuals with Disabilities Education
    Improvement Act (IDEA) (2004), 10, 90,
    127, 164
Intervention, 7–9, 12–13, 19, 27, 33, 34, 36, 44, 53,
    138, 144, 146. *See also* Classroom
    management-based interventions;
    Response to intervention; Social skills
    intervention
    adapting/applying of, 59–61

emerging category of, 48, 58, 72, 82–83, 112, 122,
    134, 151
highly recommended category of, 47, 54–55,
    69–71, 81–82, 109–10, 122, 131–32
iatrogenic category of, 48, 161–68,
    182, 220
for individuals, with chronic conditions, 10
manualized, 38, 39, 47, 54
for parent involvement, 68t
proactive/targeted, 10
recommend category of, 47–48, 55, 58, 71–72,
    82, 110–12, 132, 151
Tier 1 levels of, 6–7, 18, 40, 85, 123,
    126, 136
Tier 2 levels of, 18, 40, 52, 54–55, 56–57t, 58,
    60–61, 73, 85, 115, 134, 145, 176–77, 178,
    199–202
Tier 3 levels of, 18, 85, 105, 106, 115, 145, 156,
    183, 201
Iowa Strengthening Families Program (ISFP), 71,
    73, 74
ISFP. *See* Iowa Strengthening Families Program

Kavale, K. A., 138, 149, 214
Knowledge-practice gap, 4–5, 16–22, 23–41

Manualized intervention, 38, 39, 47, 54
Math and Parent Partnership (MAPPS), 203
Mental health services, 4, 16, 25, 52
Meta-analyses, 46, 67, 72, 78, 92, 120, 164, 171,
    174, 200

NASP. *See* National Association of School
    Psychologists
NASW. *See* National Association of Social
    Workers
National Association of School Psychologists
    (NASP), 13, 187
National Association of Social Workers (NASW),
    3, 13, 17
National Network of Partnership Schools,
    75, 202
National Registry of Evidence-Based Programs
    and Practices (NREPP) clearinghouse, 32,
    44, 81, 111, 115, 141, 143, 199, 205, 208, 210, 211,
    212, 218, 219
National School Social Work Survey Project
    (2008), 17–18, 189–98
New Beginnings, 111, 116
No Child Left Behind, 40, 60, 66, 118
Noncompliance, 44, 78, 87, 181, 204
Normal grief reactions, individual grief therapy
    for, 166, 182
NREPP. *See* National Registry of Evidence-Based
    Programs and Practices

ODR. *See* Office Discipline Referral data
Office Discipline Referral (ODR) data, 88–89
Olweus, D., 120
Olweus Bullying Program: Steps to Respect, 122, 123, 124, 178
Oppositional defiant disorder, 76, 83
Outcome evaluation, 35–36, 184
  for ADHD, 159
  for anxiety disorder, 147
  for BIP, 105
  for bullying, 125–26
  of compliance, 88–89
  of divorce/separation of parents intervention, 116–17
  of parent involvement, 73–75
  for social skills, 137–38

Parent involvement, 66–75
  books for, 204
  clearinghouses for, 202–3
  clinical quadrants for, 177*t*
  databases for, 203–4
  emerging interventions for, 72
  evidence organization/interpretation of, 67–72
  highly recommended interventions for, 69–71
  interventions for, 68*t*
  outcome evaluation of, 73–75
  parent training/tutoring, 69
  recommended interventions for, 71–72
  reflections on, 72–73
PATHS. *See* Promoting Alternative Thinking Strategies
Peer Interactions in Primary School (PIPS), 185
Peer reviewed studies, 67, 81, 92, 141
Person-in-environment focus, 19, 90
PHT. *See* Potentially harmful treatments (PHT)
PIPS. *See* Peer Interactions in Primary School
Posttraumatic stress disorder (PTSD), 145, 165
Potentially harmful treatments (PHT), 163–64*t*
  substance abuse prevention programs as, 166
Prepare, 134, 214, 217
Primary Project, 133, 213
Problem
  analysis, 53
  identification, 52–53
  operationalization of, 39
Process, 44, 72, 83–84
  of EBP, 27*f*
  reflections, 42, 102, 123, 155
Process evaluation, 60–61, 104, 116–17, 184
  for ADHD, 158–59
  on bullying, 125
  on compliance interventions, 88
  in parent involvement, 74
  for social skills, 136–37

Professional books, 31, 44, 45, 47, 201–2, 206–12, 216–19
Promoting Alternative Thinking Strategies (PATHS), 154, 155, 202, 212
PsycINFO database, 40, 44, 63, 141, 171, 172, 200, 201, 205, 208, 210, 211, 215, 216, 218, 219, 220
PTSD. *See* Posttraumatic stress disorder
PubMed database, 30, 44, 47, 219

QED. *See* Quasi-experimental design
Quasi-experimental design (QED), 34, 47, 72, 164, 174

Rainbows for All Gods' Children, 112–15, 116, 173
Raines, J. C., 36, 48, 63, 199, 205, 210, 212
Randomized controlled trial (RCT), 34, 38, 47, 78, 92, 164, 174
Rathvon, N., 131, 139, 217
RCT. *See* Randomized controlled trial
Reliability, 27, 34, 113
Research. *See also* School-based prevention/intervention research
  barriers to implementing, 24–26
  method section of, 34–35
Response to intervention (RTI), 9–13, 12*f*, 16, 19, 22, 48, 168, 176–78
  data-based decision making in, 13, 21
  empirically supported interventions in, 12–13
  locating content within, 85
  multitiered systems of support in, 10, 12
  problem-solving steps in, 52–53, 53*f*
  support service personnel in, 14–15*t*
  Tier 2 interventions amd, 52
Risk factors, 8*t*, 15
  adolescent health, 7, 9
  environmental, 19, 90
  individual, 4, 19, 21
RTI. *See* Response to intervention

Safe and Drug-Free Schools, 118
Sage Education Full Text database, 203
SAMHSA. *See* Substance Abuse and Mental Health Services Administration
School-based prevention/intervention research, 13, 16, 42, 176
  comprehensive approaches to, 9
  primary prevention and, 6–7
  screening/early intervention, 7–9
School Situations Scale-Revised (SSQ-R), 159
School social work
  complex nature of, 39–40
  history of, 3–9
  individual risk factors addressed by, 4, 19, 21
  legislators/policy makers and, 23

School Social Work Association of America (SSWAA), 3, 13, 17–18, 187
School social workers
  caseloads of, 25
  consultation and, 90
  EIP for, 42–51
  evidence utilization by, 26
  workshops/peer supervision for, 24
School Social Work Survey (2008) findings summary, 20–21t
School-wide Information System (SWIS), 88–89
School-wide positive behavior support (SWPBS), 10, 82, 176
  characteristics of, 11t
  support service personnel role in, 14–15
Scientific evidence, hierarchy of, 35f
Scott, T. M., 92, 101
Screening, 7–9, 13
Second Step, 132, 202, 212, 213
Selective serotonin reuptake inhibitors (SSRIs), 143
Single subject design studies, 84, 105, 174, 175
Skillstreaming, 133–34, 214, 217
Social Information Processing, 55, 199
Social skills, 19, 44, 86, 122
  acquisition/performance deficits, 128, 137
  groups for, 52
  instruction, 18
  strengths/weakness of programs for, 139–40
  teaching of, 83
Social Skills Improvement System (SSIS), 137–38, 185
Social skills intervention, 127–40, 178, 202
  books for, 216–17
  clearinghouses for, 212–14
  clinical quadrants for, 179–80t
  conceptual definition of, 127–28
  databases for, 214–16
  emerging interventions for, 134
  highly recommended interventions for, 131–32
  intervention appraisal of, 129–30t
  recommended interventions for, 132
Social Skills Rating System (SSRS), 89, 105, 137
Social validity, 136, 147, 175, 185–86
Social Work Abstracts database, 44, 171, 200
"Social Work Shooter," 29–31
Special education services, 4, 66, 149
SSIS. See Social Skills Improvement System
SSQ-R. See School Situations Scale-Revised
SSRIs. See Selective serotonin reuptake inhibitors
SSRS. See Social Skills Rating System
SSWAA. See School Social Work Association of America
Stoner, G., 149, 158–59

Substance Abuse and Mental Health Services Administration (SAMHSA), 32, 114, 131, 132, 133, 199, 204, 208, 212
Substance abuse prevention programs, 78, 166–67, 182
Support person personnel, 14–15t
SWIS. See School-wide Information System
SWPBS. See Schoolwide positive behavior support
Systematic reviews, 34, 46, 164, 175
Systematic Screening for Behavior Disorders, 89

Technical Assistance Center on Positive Behavioral Interventions and Supports, 87, 88
Tier 1 (primary) prevention, 6–7, 18, 40, 85
  for bullying prevention, 123, 126
  for social skills, 136
Tier 2 (secondary) prevention, 18, 40, 52, 56–57t, 73, 85, 115, 176–77
  for anxiety disorder, 145
  books for, 201–2
  clearinghouses for, 199
  databases for, 199–201
  for divorce/separation of parents, 178
  emerging interventions for, 58
  evidence investigation of, 199–202
  highly recommended interventions for, 54–55
  recommended (with caution) interventions for, 55, 58
  for social skills, 134
  time/location of, 60–61
Tier 3 (tertiary) prevention, 18, 85, 105, 106, 115, 183, 201
  for ADHD, 156
  for anxiety disorder, 145

Validity, 27, 32, 34, 45, 75, 113, 187. See also Social validity
Violence prevention, 4, 78, 120, 165, 182, 204

Walker. H. M., 6, 64, 83, 92, 206, 207
What Works Clearinghouse (WWC), 32, 139–40, 141, 199, 204, 205, 208, 212, 213–14, 218, 219
Whole-school approaches, to bullying, 120, 125
WWC. See What Works Clearinghouse

Youth Matters, 122, 178

"Zero Tolerance" discipline policy, 167, 182

CPSIA information can be obtained at www.ICGtesting.com
Printed in the USA
BVOW03s0335040314

346602BV00001B/2/P